Volume 3...

...and I have no idea what to write here.

The. Author.

Naoshi Komi

NAOSHI KOMI was born in Kochi Prefecture, Japan, on March 28, 1986. His first serialized work in *Weekly Shonen Jump* was the series *Double Arts*. His current series, *Nisekoi*, is serialized in *Weekly Shonen Jump*.

NISEKOI:
False Love
VOLUME 3
SHONEN JUMP Manga Edition

Story and Art by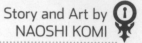
NAOSHI KOMI

Translation ✒ Camellia Nieh
Touch-Up Art & Lettering ✒ Stephen Dutro
Design ✒ Fawn Lau
Shonen Jump Series Editor ✒ John Bae
Graphic Novel Editor ✒ Amy Yu

NISEKOI © 2011 by Naoshi Komi
All rights reserved.
First published in Japan in 2011
by SHUEISHA Inc., Tokyo.
English translation rights arranged
by SHUEISHA Inc.

The stories, characters and incidents mentioned
in this publication are entirely fictional.

Printed in the U.S.A.

Published by VIZ Media, LLC
P.O. Box 77010
San Francisco, CA 94107

10 9 8 7 6 5 3 4 2 1
First printing, May 2014

www.shonenjump.com   www.viz.com

NISEKOI

False Love

vol. 3: What's in a Name?

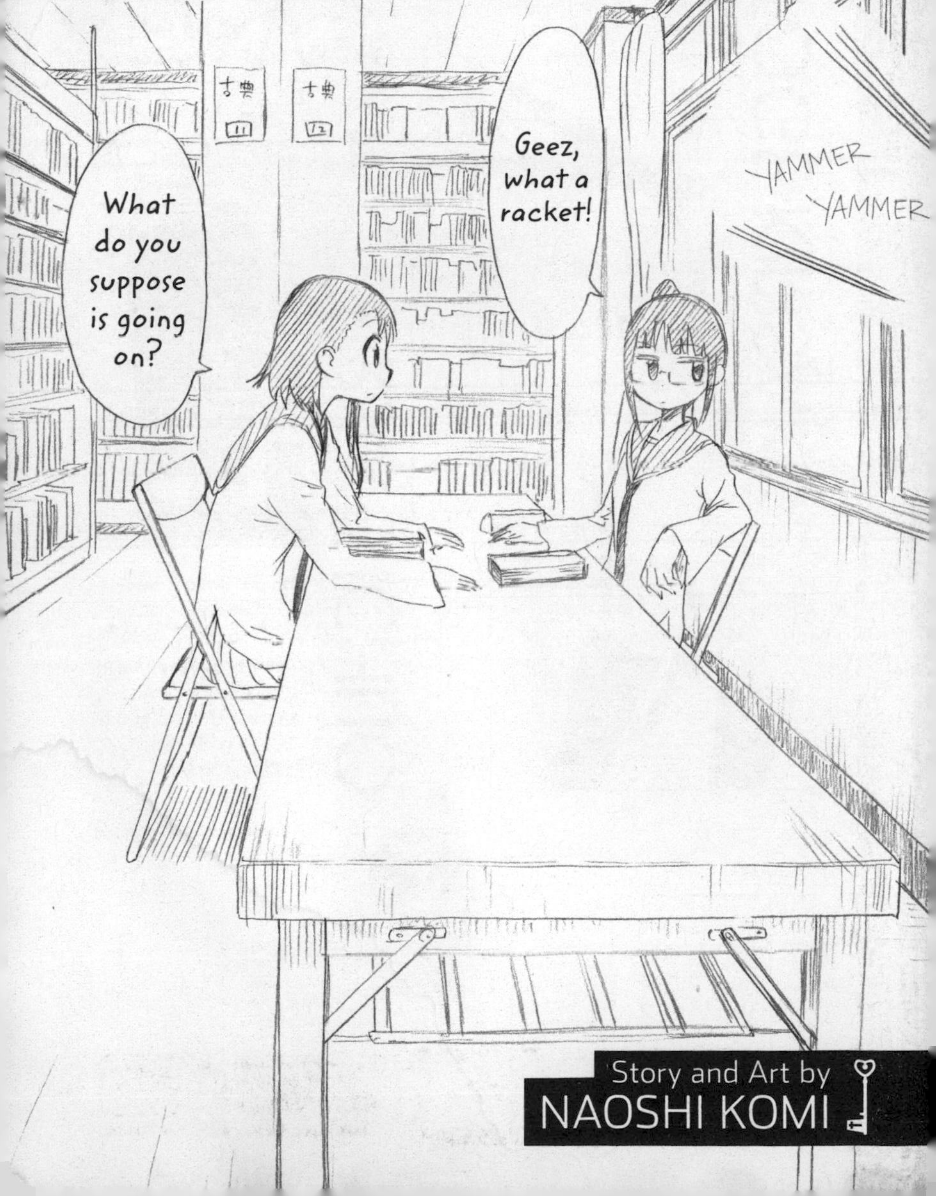
YAMMER
YAMMER
Geez, what a racket!
What do you suppose is going on?

Story and Art by
NAOSHI KOMI

CHITOGE KIRISAKI

A half-Japanese bombshell with stellar athletic abilities. Short-tempered and violent. Comes from a family of gangsters.

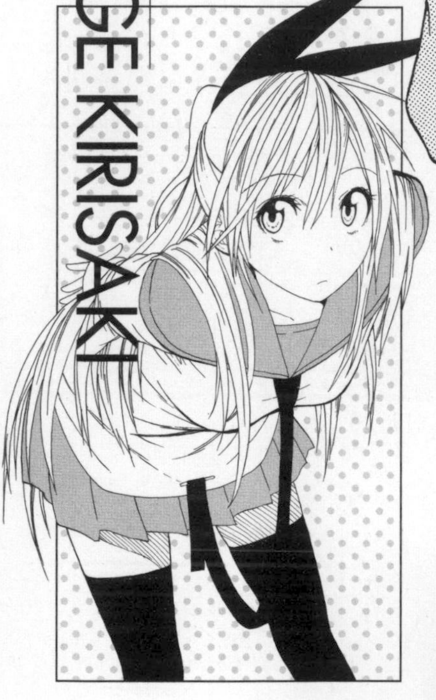

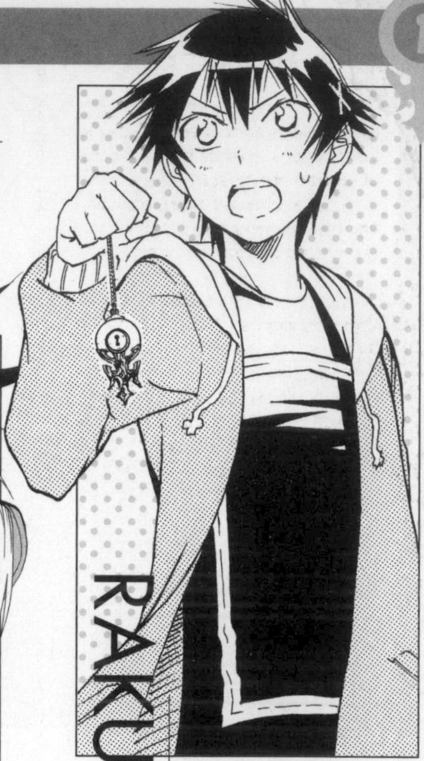

RAKU ICHIJO

A normal teen whose family happens to be yakuza. Cherishes a pendant given to him by a girl he met ten years ago. Has a crush on Kosaki.

SHU MAIKO

Raku's best friend. Outgoing and girl-crazy. Always tuned in to the latest gossip at school.

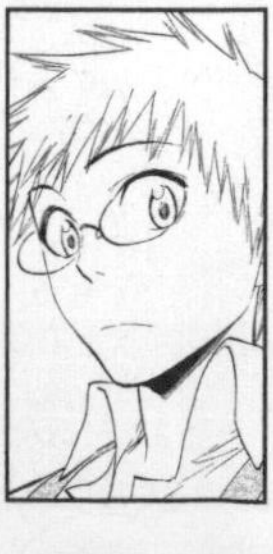

SEISHIRO TSUGUMI

Adopted by Claude as a young child and raised as a top-notch assassin, Seishiro is 100% devoted to Chitoge. But is there more to Chitoge's new body-guard than meets the eye?

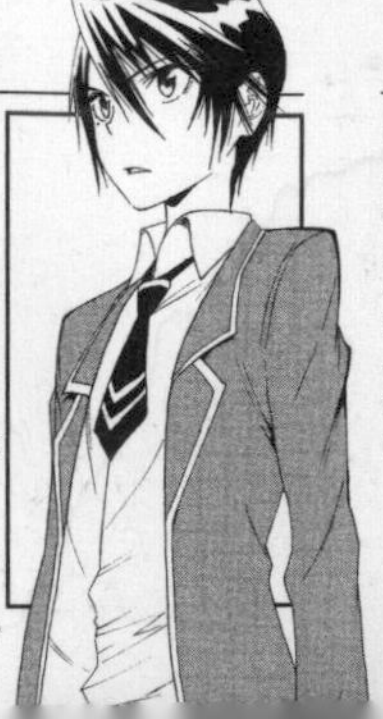

CLAUDE

Executive member of the Beehive and protector of Chitoge. Suspicious of Raku and Chitoge's relationship.

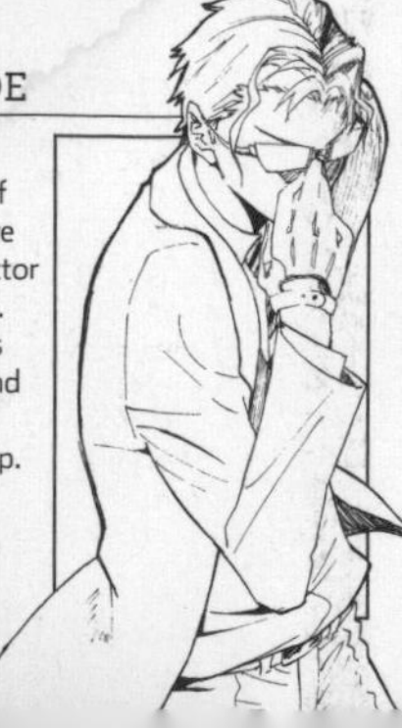

THE STORY THUS FAR

Raku Ichijo is an ordinary teen...who just happens to come from a family of yakuza! His most treasured item is a pendant he was given ten years ago by a girl whom he promised to meet again one day and marry.

When super-babe Chitoge Kirisaki transfers into Raku's class, it's clear from the get-go that they don't get along. Unfortunately, thanks to family circumstances, Raku and Chitoge are forced to pretend to be a couple—even at school! Raku wants his crush, Kosaki Onodera, to know the truth about his relationship with Chitoge, but he can't seem to find a way to tell her. Meanwhile, Chitoge has already told Kosaki and Ruri that she and Raku are a false couple. Kosaki has a secret crush on Raku and resolves to tell him how she feels, but somehow the right moment never seems to come.

Slowly, Raku and Chitoge realize they don't hate each other as they did at first. Meanwhile, Claude sends his protégé, Seishiro Tsugumi, to rescue Chitoge from Raku's evil clutches. Utterly devoted to Chitoge, Seishiro challenges Raku to battle for the right to be her protector. But what chance does Raku stand against a highly trained assassin?!

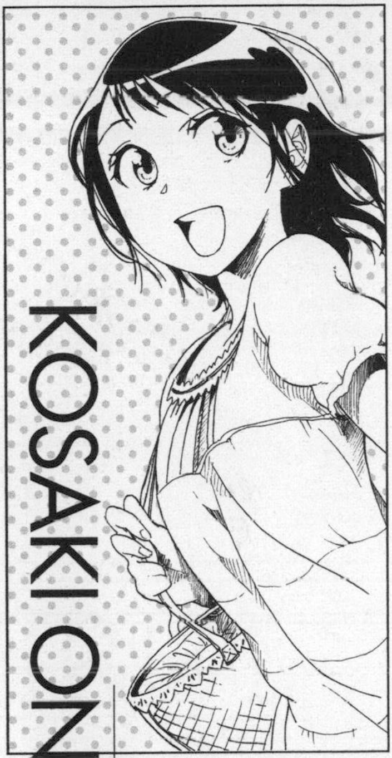

KOSAKI ONODERA

A girl Raku has a crush on. Beautiful and sweet, Kosaki has no shortage of admirers. She's a terrible cook but makes food that *looks* amazing.

CHITOGE'S FATHER

Leader of the Beehive, a gang with designs on the Shuei-Gumi's turf.

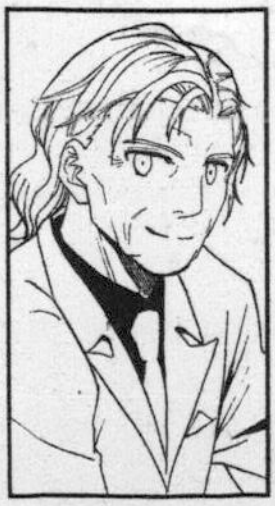

RAKU'S FATHER

Leader of the Shuei-Gumi, the yakuza syn-dicate at war with the Beehive.

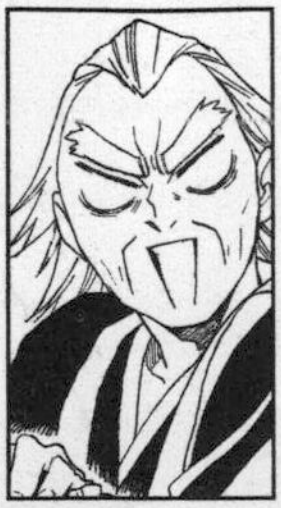

RURI MIYAMOTO

Kosaki's best gal pal. Comes off as aloof, but is actually a devoted and highly intuitive friend.

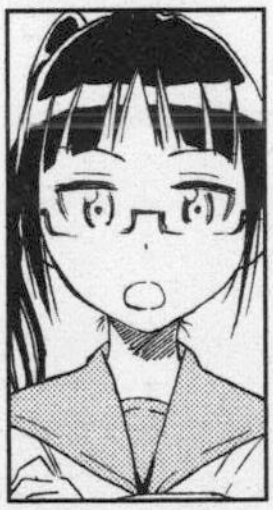

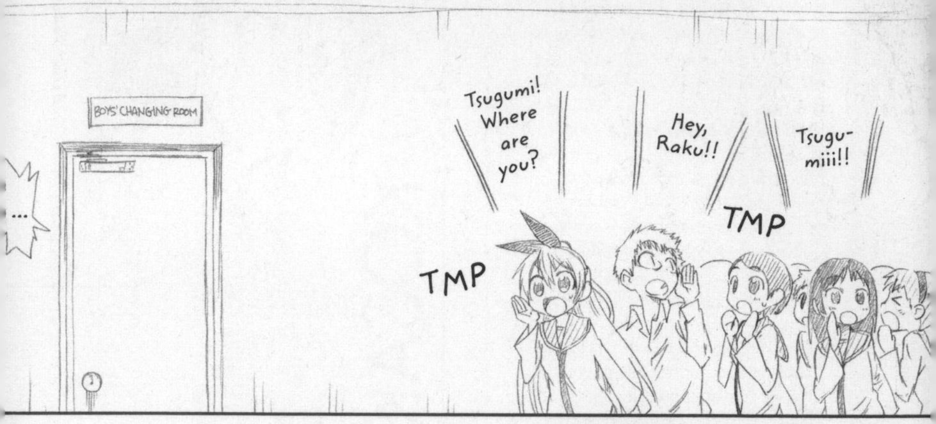
Tsugu-
miii!!
TMP
Hey,
Raku!!
Tsugumi!
Where
are
you?
TMP
...
BOYS' CHANGING ROOM

NISEKOI

False Love

vol. 3: What's in a Name?

TABLE OF CONTENTS

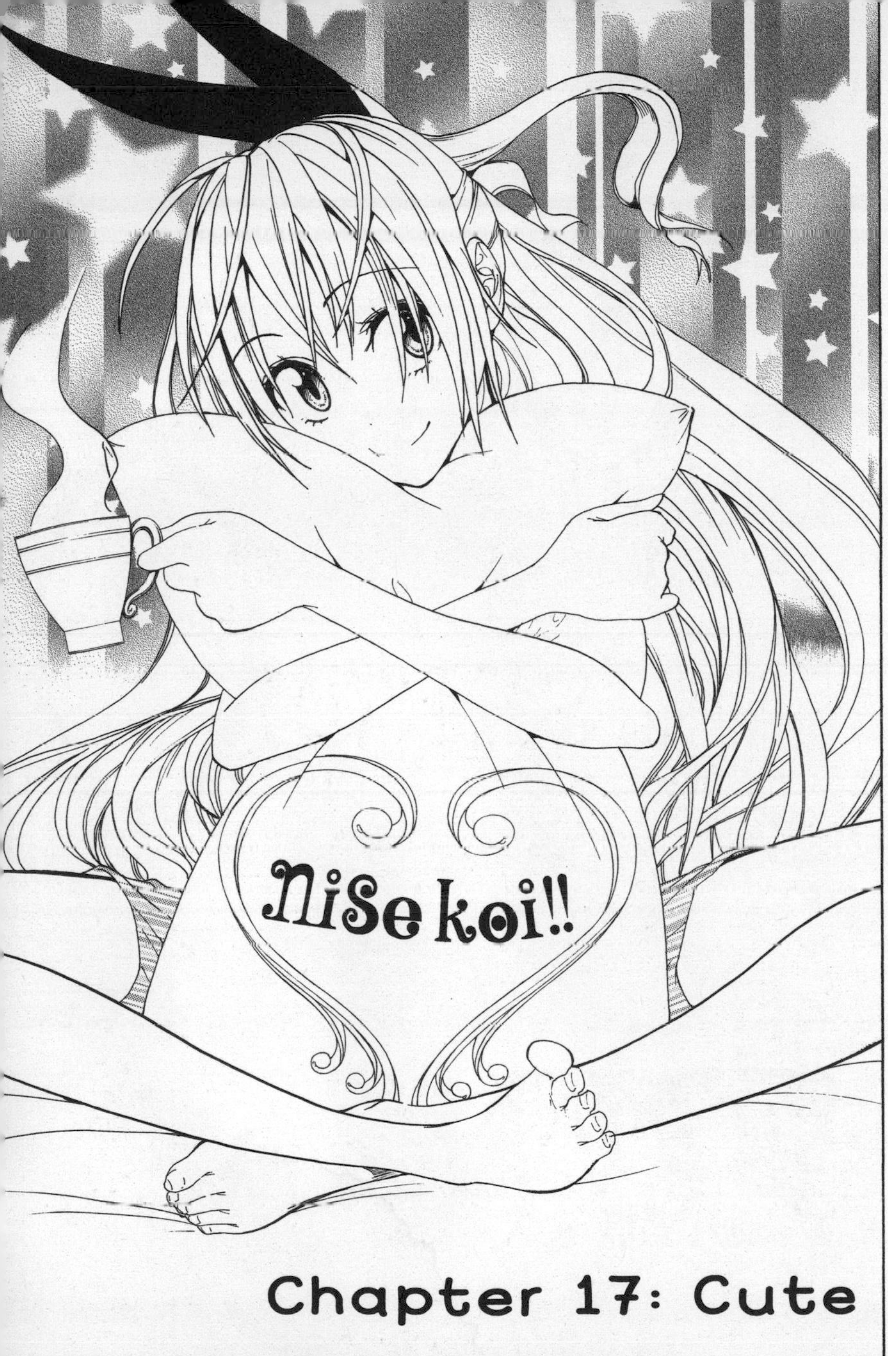
Nisekoi!!

Chapter 17: Cute

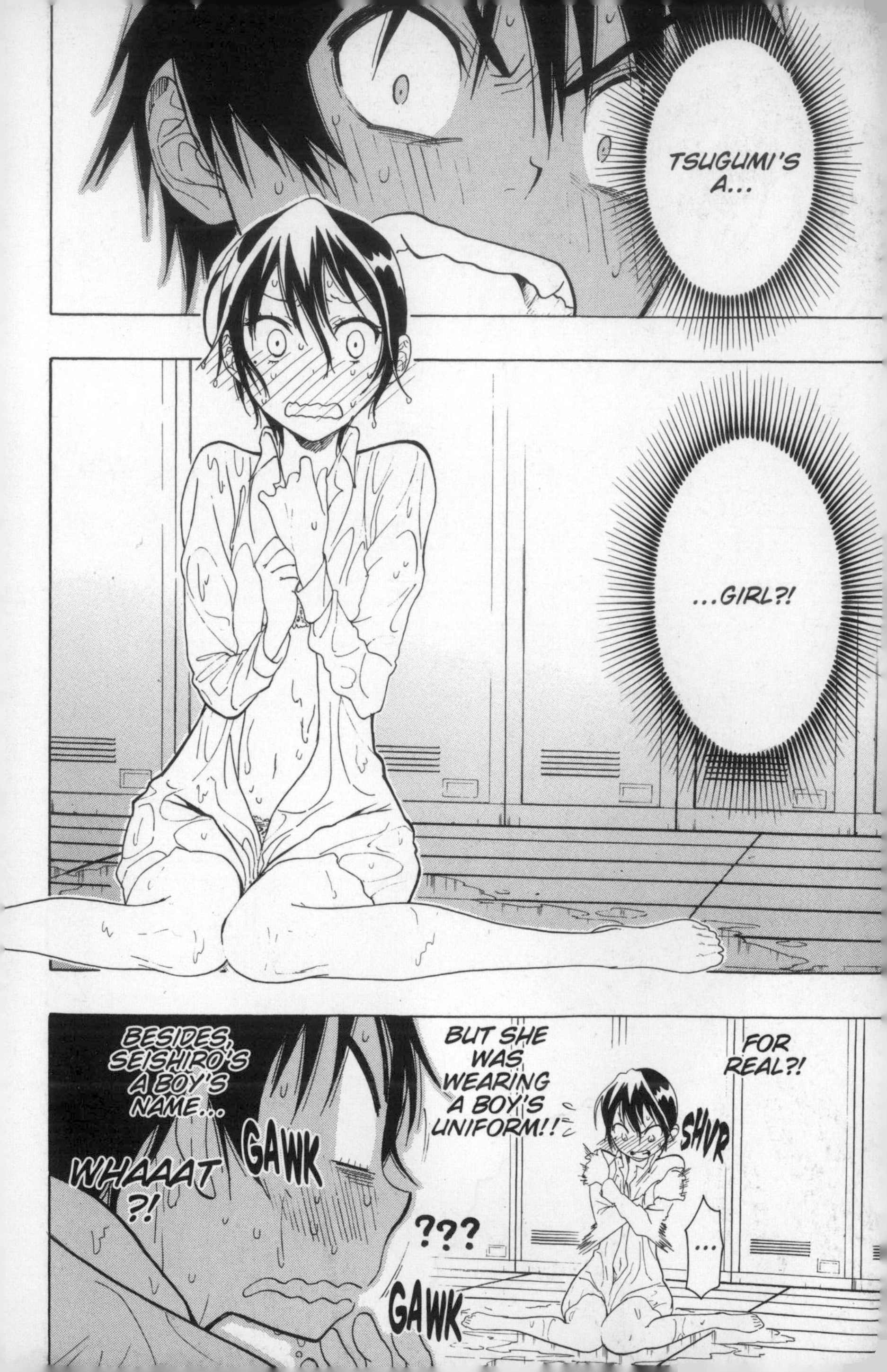
TSUGUMI'S A...
...GIRL?!
FOR REAL?!
SHVR
...
BUT SHE WAS WEARING A BOY'S UNIFORM!!
BESIDES, SEISHIRO'S A BOY'S NAME...
GAWK
WHAAAT ?!
???
GAWK

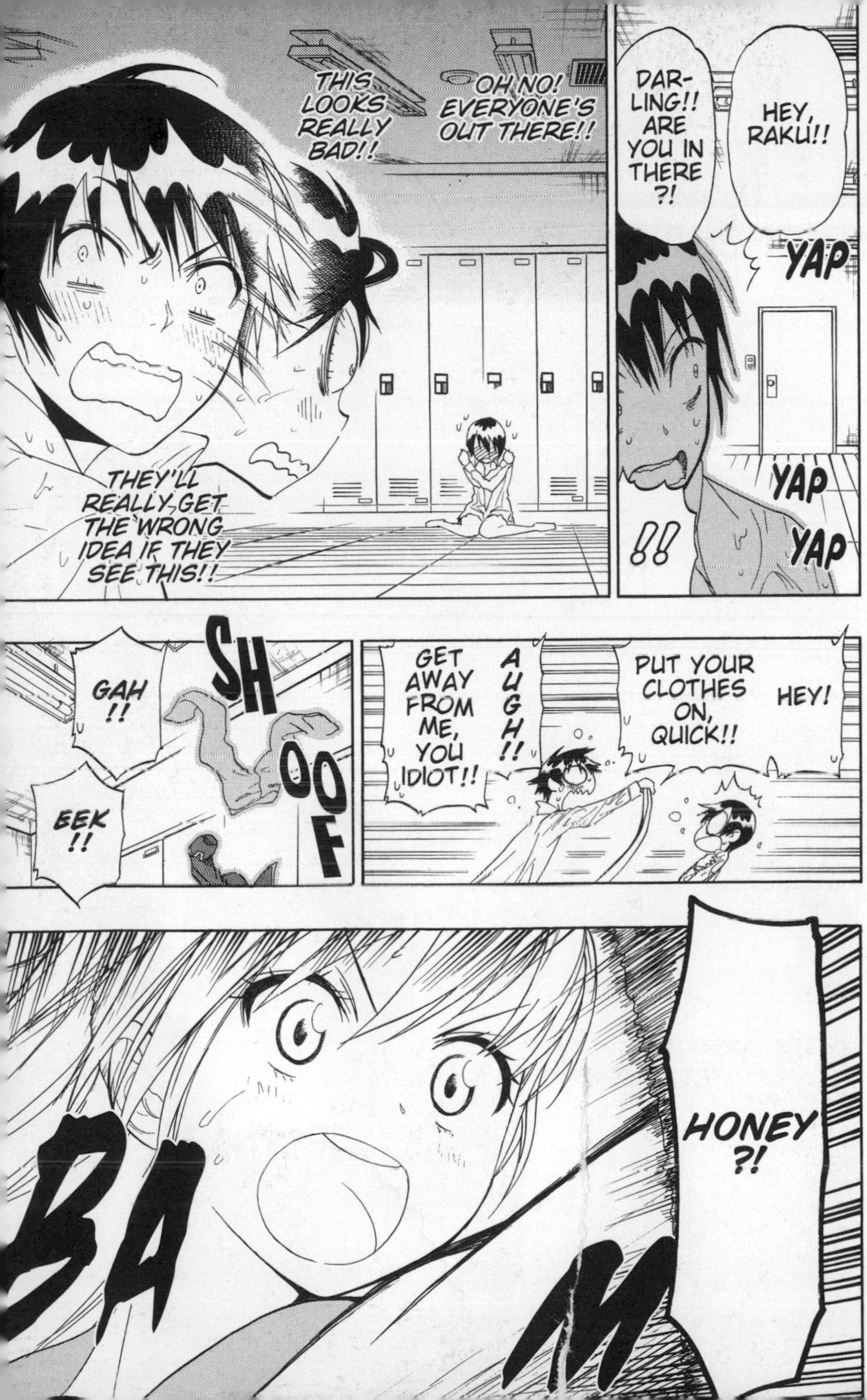
HEY, RAKU!!
DARLING!! ARE YOU IN THERE?!
YAP
YAP
YAP
!!
OH NO! EVERYONE'S OUT THERE!!
THIS LOOKS REALLY BAD!!
THEY'LL REALLY GET THE WRONG IDEA IF THEY SEE THIS!!
HEY!
PUT YOUR CLOTHES ON, QUICK!!
AUGH!!
GET AWAY FROM ME, YOU IDIOT!!
SHOOOF
GAH!!
EEK!!
HONEY?!
BAM

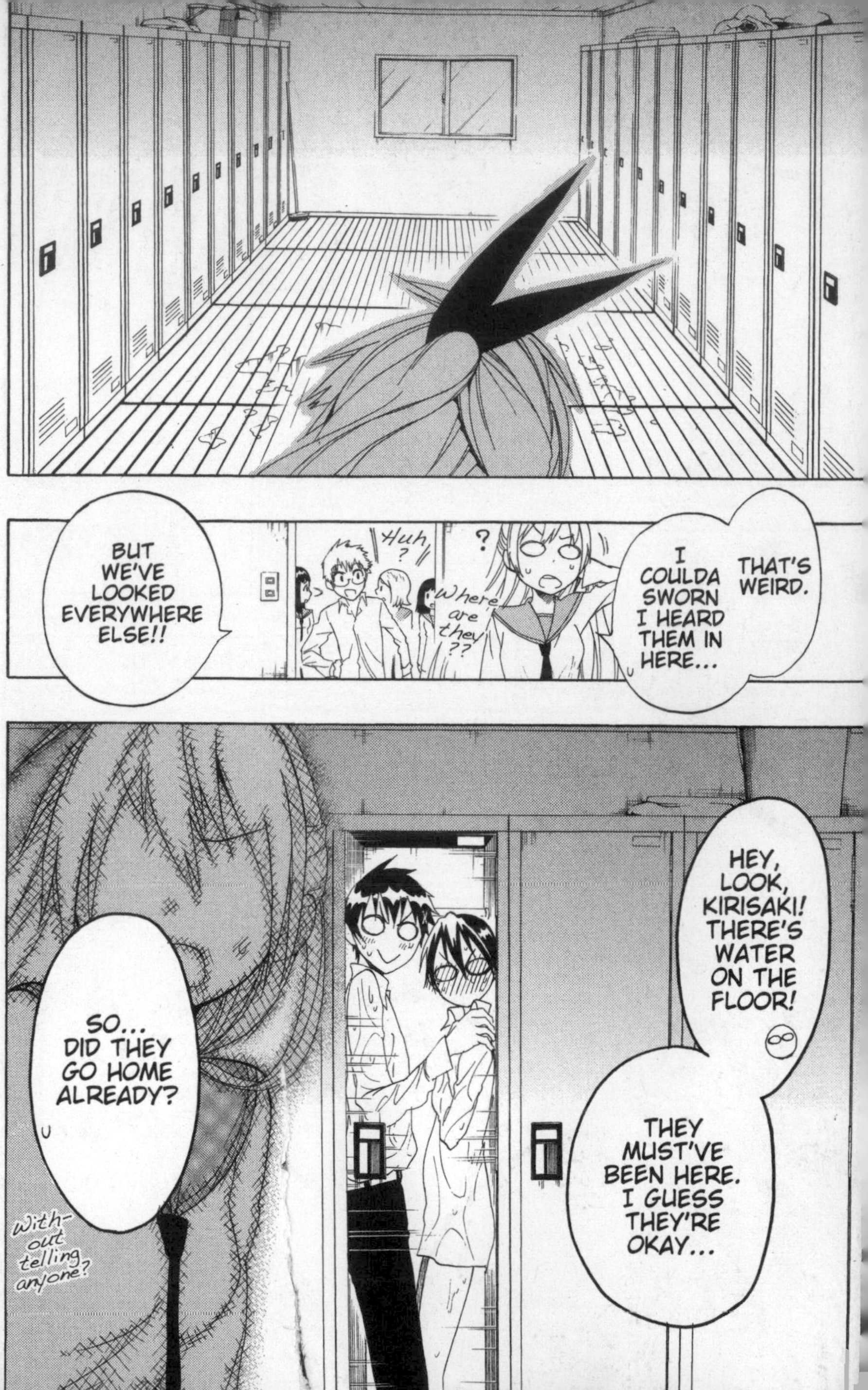
THAT'S WEIRD.
I COULDA SWORN I HEARD THEM IN HERE...
?
Where are they??
Huh??
BUT WE'VE LOOKED EVERYWHERE ELSE!!
HEY, LOOK, KIRISAKI! THERE'S WATER ON THE FLOOR!
THEY MUST'VE BEEN HERE. I GUESS THEY'RE OKAY...
SO... DID THEY GO HOME ALREADY?
With-out telling anyone?

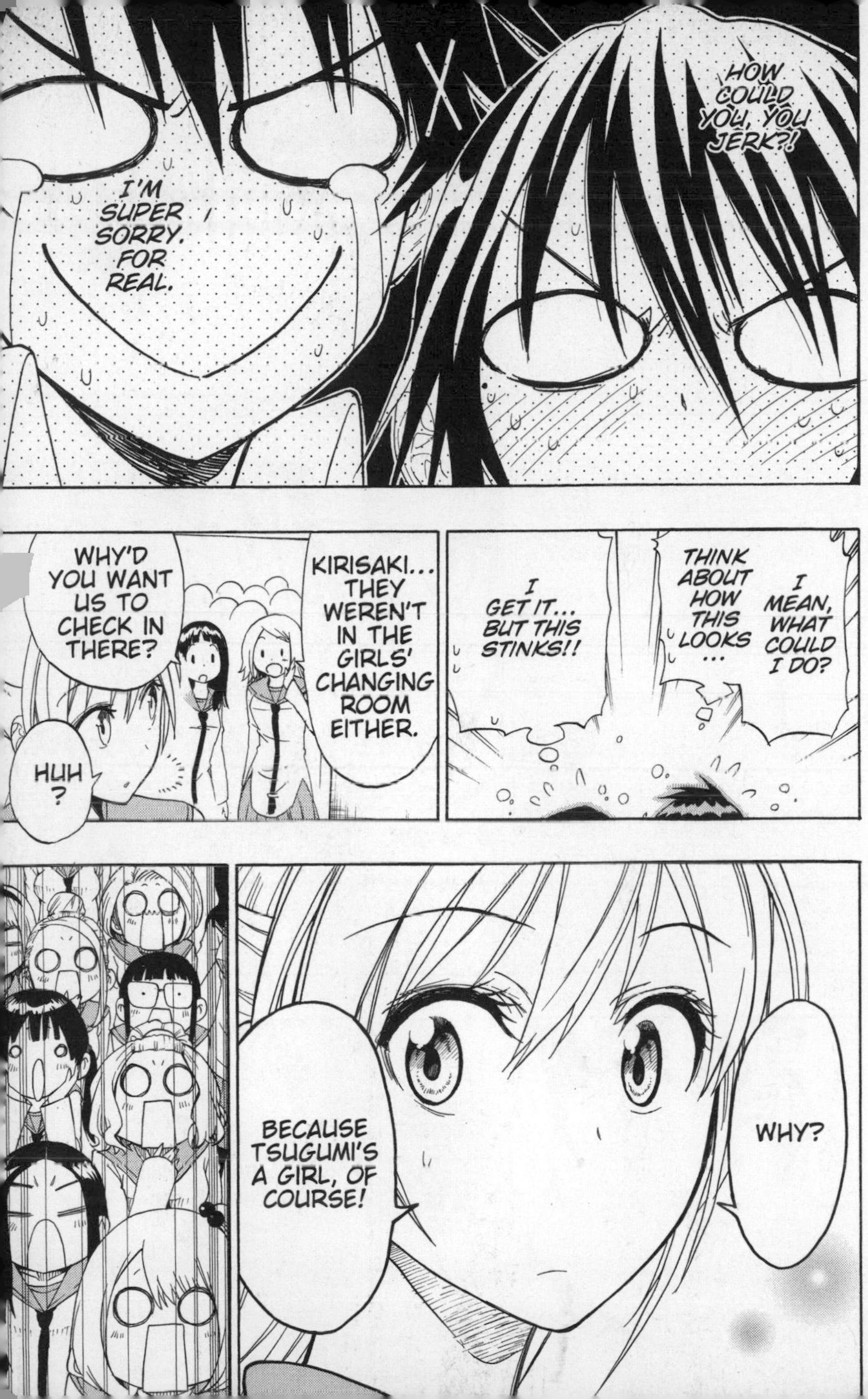
HOW COULD YOU, YOU JERK?!
I'M SUPER SORRY. FOR REAL.
I MEAN, WHAT COULD I DO?
THINK ABOUT HOW THIS LOOKS...
I GET IT... BUT THIS STINKS!!
KIRISAKI... THEY WEREN'T IN THE GIRLS' CHANGING ROOM EITHER.
WHY'D YOU WANT US TO CHECK IN THERE?
HUH?
WHY?
BECAUSE TSUGUMI'S A GIRL, OF COURSE!

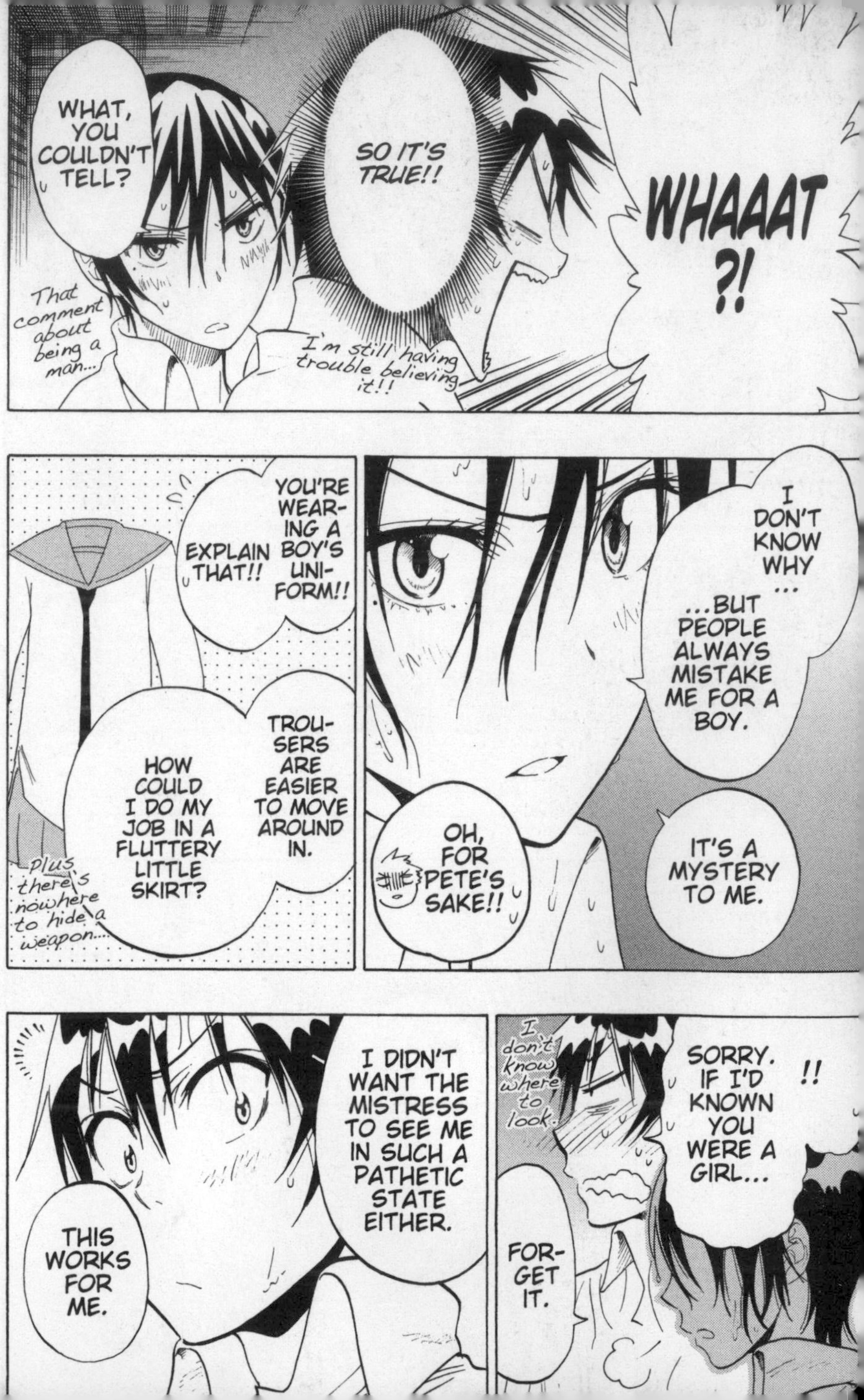
WHAAAT?!
SO IT'S TRUE!!
I'm still having trouble believing it!!
WHAT, YOU COULDN'T TELL?
That comment about being a man...
I DON'T KNOW WHY...
...BUT PEOPLE ALWAYS MISTAKE ME FOR A BOY.
IT'S A MYSTERY TO ME.
OH, FOR PETE'S SAKE!!
YOU'RE WEARING A BOY'S UNIFORM!!
EXPLAIN THAT!!
TROUSERS ARE EASIER TO MOVE AROUND IN.
HOW COULD I DO MY JOB IN A FLUTTERY LITTLE SKIRT?
plus there's nowhere to hide a weapon....
SORRY. IF I'D KNOWN YOU WERE A GIRL...
!!
I don't know where to look.
FORGET IT.
I DIDN'T WANT THE MISTRESS TO SEE ME IN SUCH A PATHETIC STATE EITHER.
THIS WORKS FOR ME.

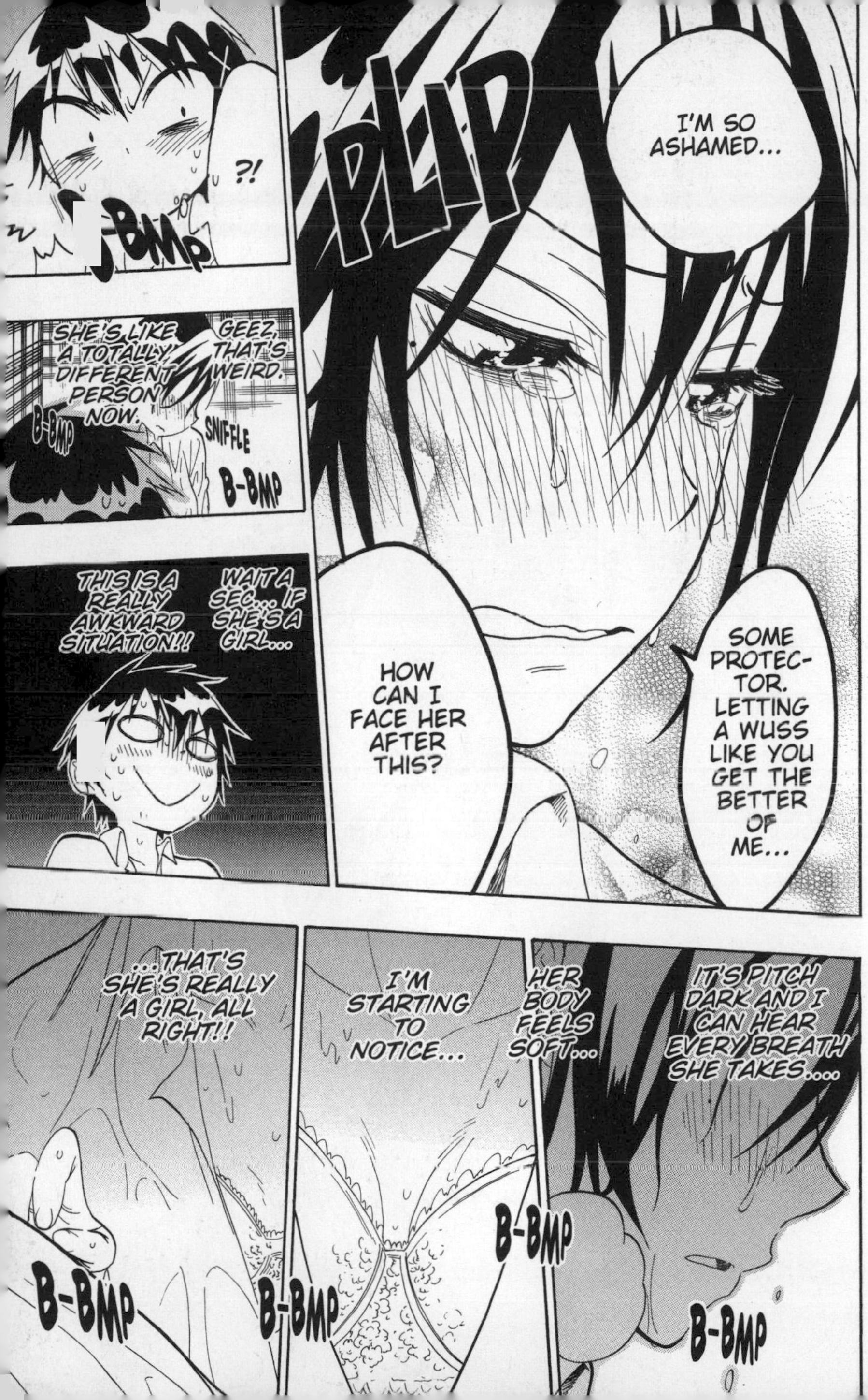
PLIP
I'M SO ASHAMED...
SOME PROTECTOR. LETTING A WUSS LIKE YOU GET THE BETTER OF ME...
HOW CAN I FACE HER AFTER THIS?
?!
BMP
GEEZ, THAT'S WEIRD.
SHE'S LIKE A TOTALLY DIFFERENT PERSON NOW.
B-BMP
SNIFFLE
B-BMP
WAIT A SEC... IF SHE'S A GIRL...
THIS IS A REALLY AWKWARD SITUATION!!
IT'S PITCH DARK AND I CAN HEAR EVERY BREATH SHE TAKES....
HER BODY FEELS SOFT...
B-BMP
B-BMP
I'M STARTING TO NOTICE...
B-BMP
...THAT'S SHE'S REALLY A GIRL, ALL RIGHT!!
B-BMP

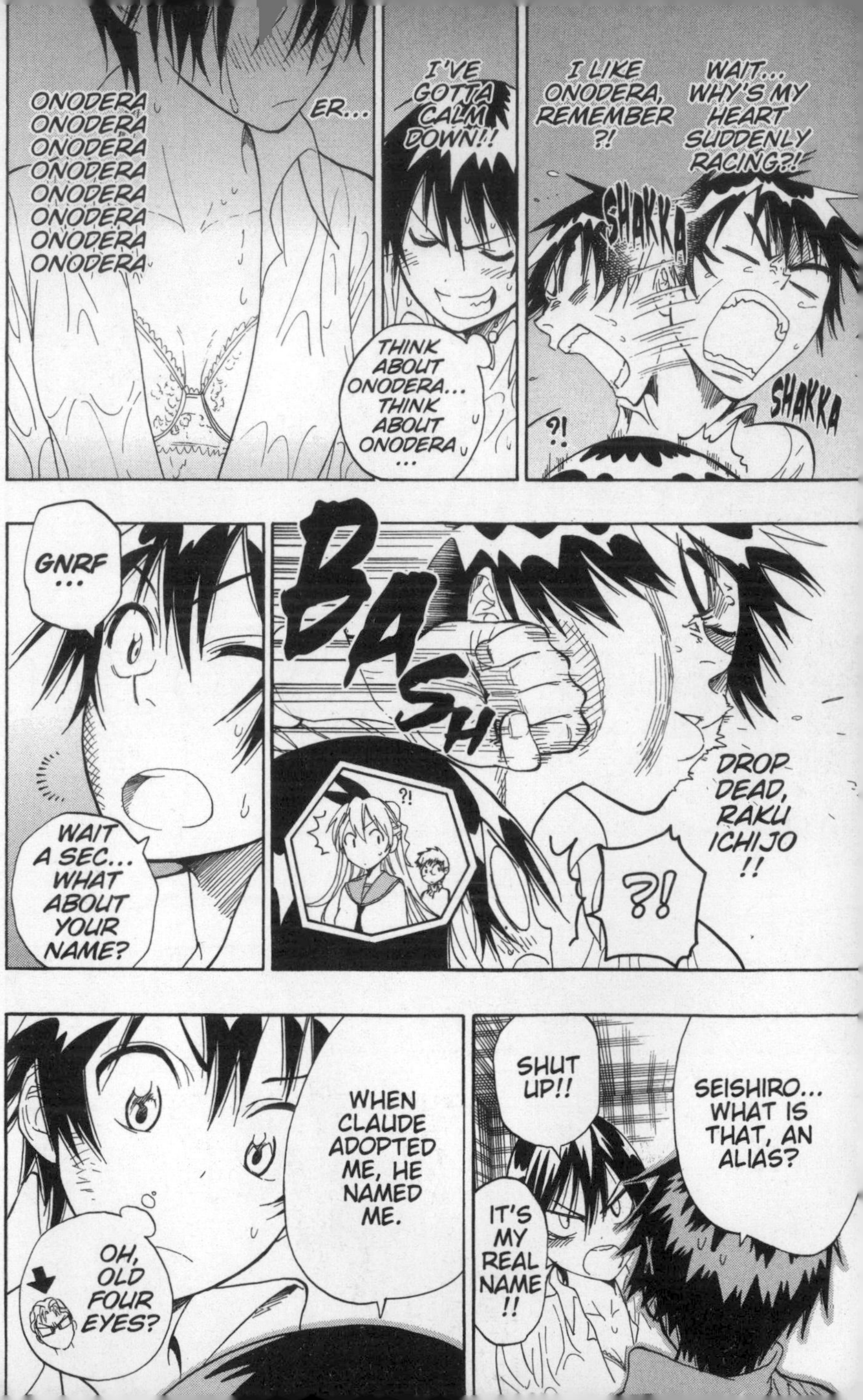
WAIT... WHY'S MY HEART SUDDENLY RACING?!
I LIKE ONODERA, REMEMBER?!
SHAKKA
SHAKKA
?!
I'VE GOTTA CALM DOWN!!
THINK ABOUT ONODERA... THINK ABOUT ONODERA...
ER...
ONODERA ONODERA ONODERA ONODERA ONODERA ONODERA ONODERA ONODERA
BASH
DROP DEAD, RAKU ICHIJO!!
?!
?!
GNRF...
WAIT A SEC... WHAT ABOUT YOUR NAME?
SEISHIRO... WHAT IS THAT, AN ALIAS?
SHUT UP!!
IT'S MY REAL NAME!!
WHEN CLAUDE ADOPTED ME, HE NAMED ME.
OH, OLD FOUR EYES?

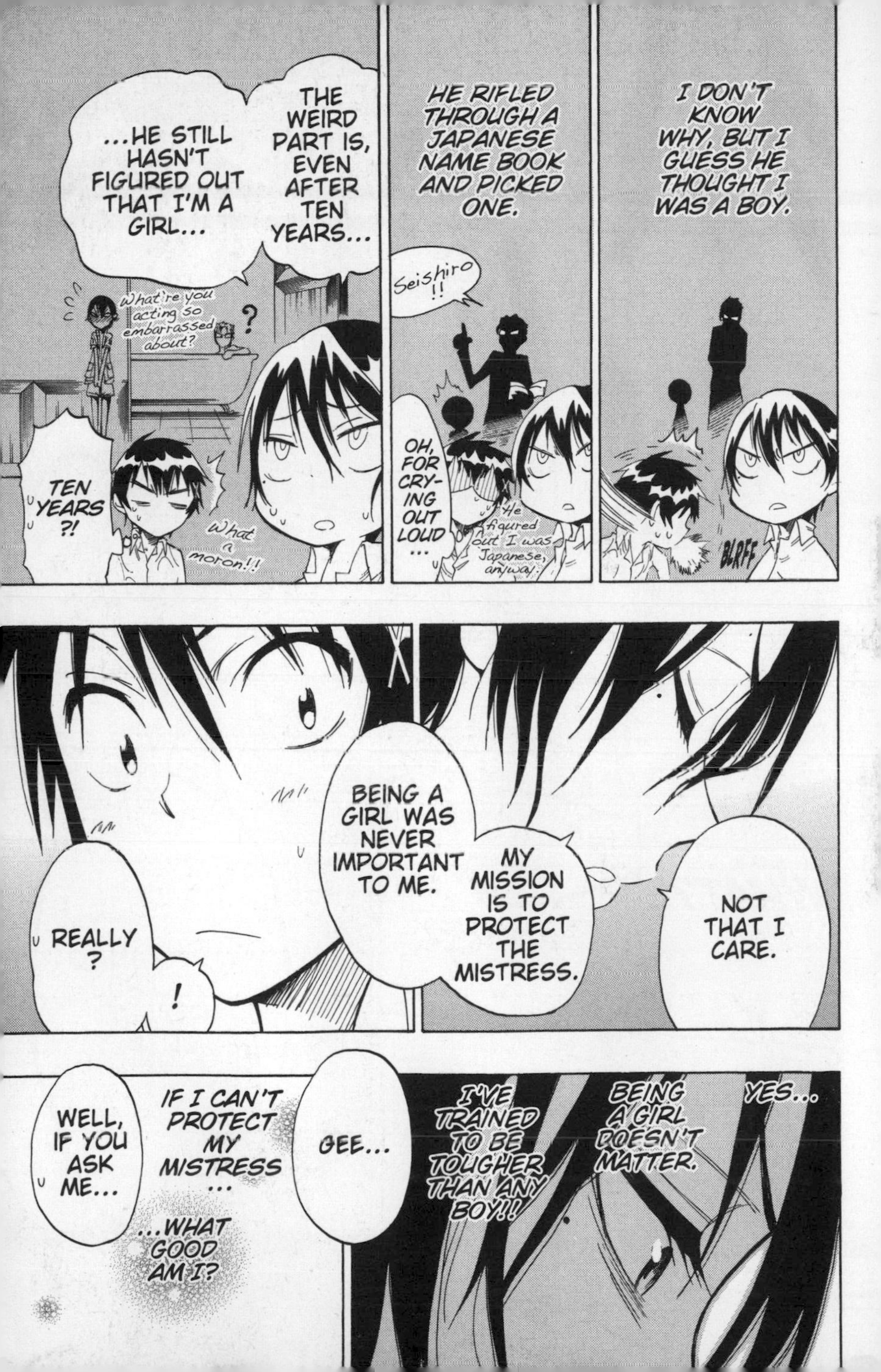
I DON'T KNOW WHY, BUT I GUESS HE THOUGHT I WAS A BOY.
BLRFF
HE RIFLED THROUGH A JAPANESE NAME BOOK AND PICKED ONE.
Seishiro!!
OH, FOR CRYING OUT LOUD...
He figured out I was Japanese, anyway.
THE WEIRD PART IS, EVEN AFTER TEN YEARS...
...HE STILL HASN'T FIGURED OUT THAT I'M A GIRL...
What're you acting so embarrassed about?
?
TEN YEARS?!
What a moron!!
NOT THAT I CARE.
MY MISSION IS TO PROTECT THE MISTRESS.
BEING A GIRL WAS NEVER IMPORTANT TO ME.
REALLY?
!
YES...
BEING A GIRL DOESN'T MATTER.
I'VE TRAINED TO BE TOUGHER THAN ANY BOY!!
GEE...
IF I CAN'T PROTECT MY MISTRESS...
...WHAT GOOD AM I?
WELL, IF YOU ASK ME...

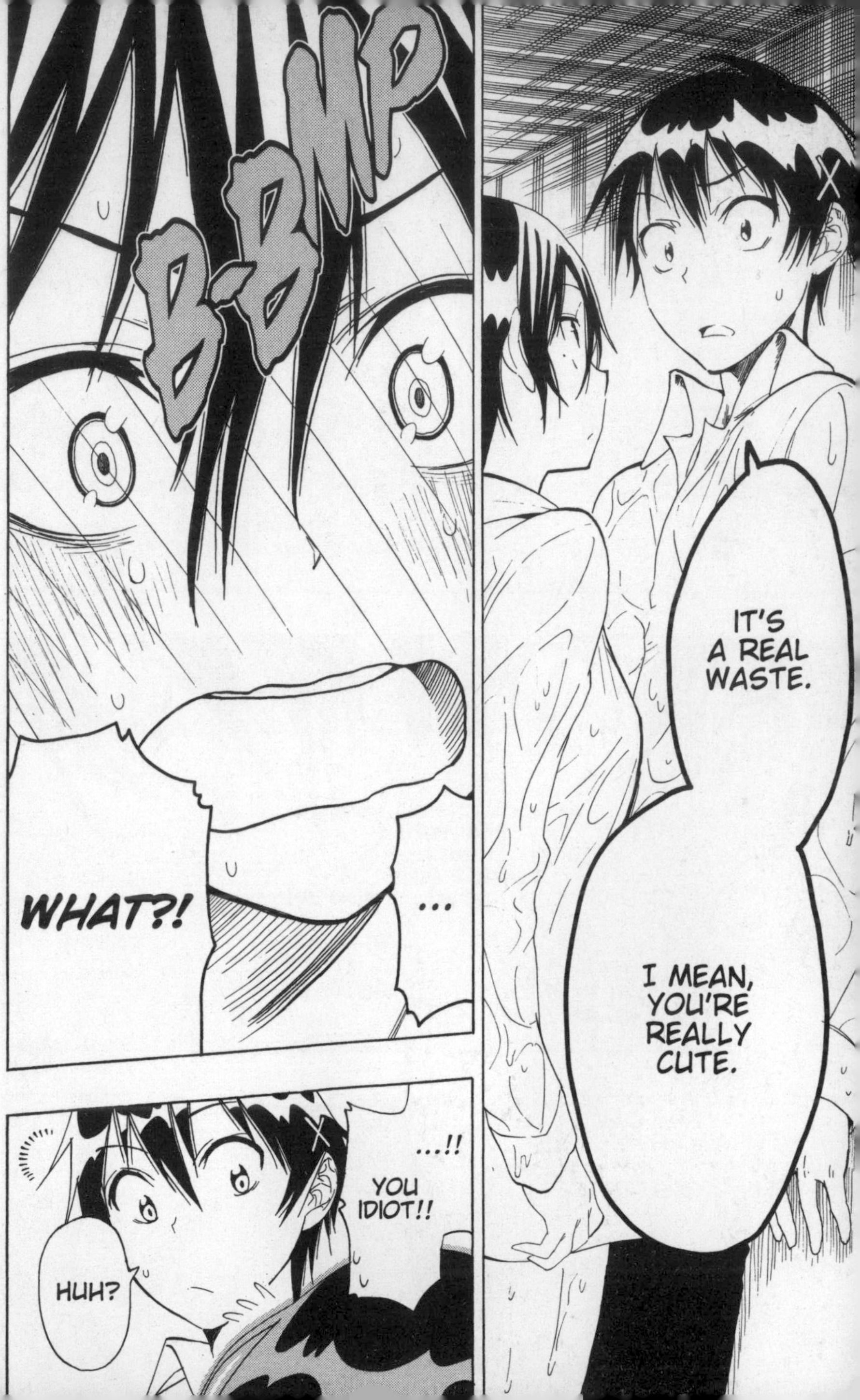
IT'S A REAL WASTE.
I MEAN, YOU'RE REALLY CUTE.
B-BMP
...
WHAT?!
...!!
YOU IDIOT!!
HUH?

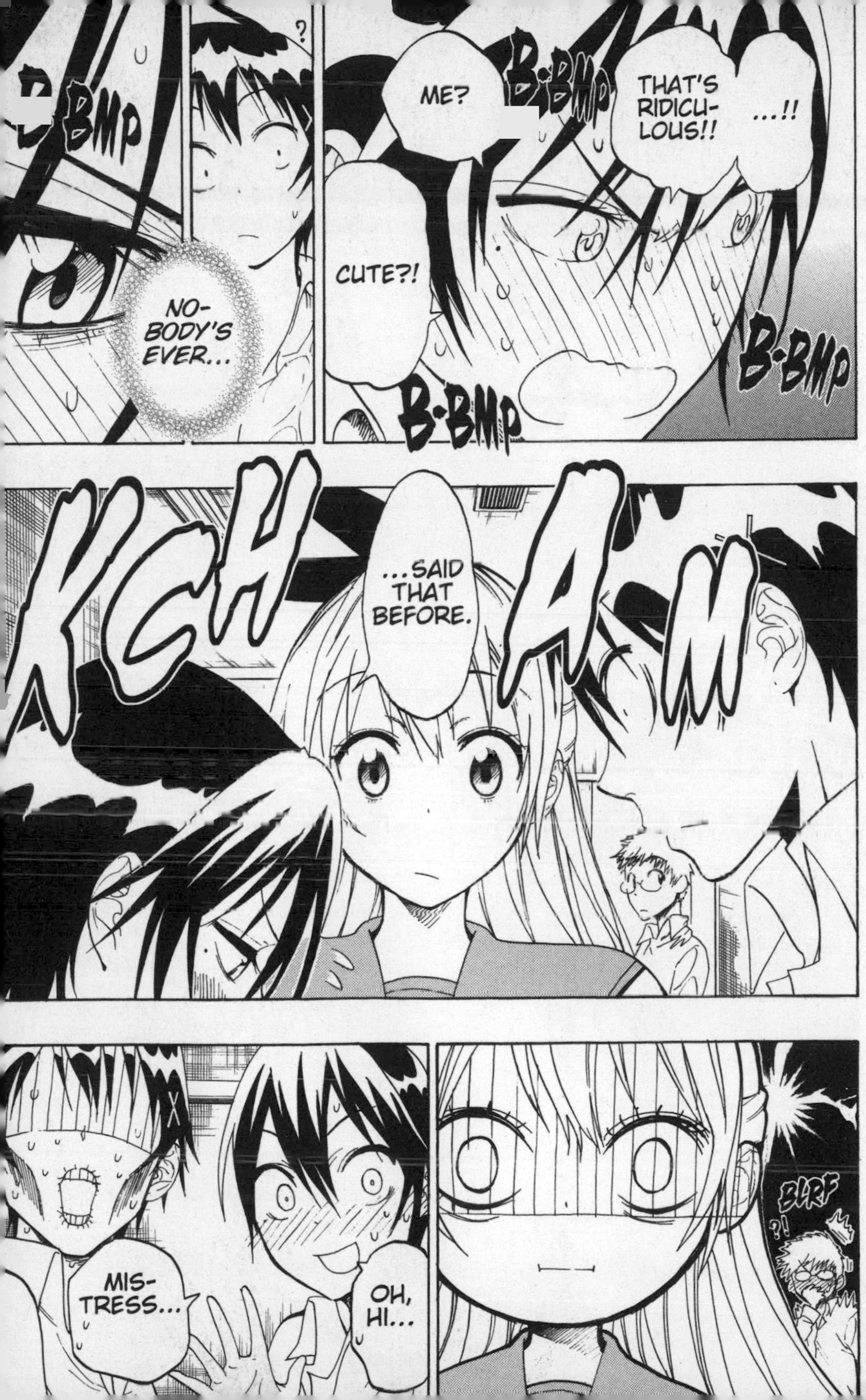
...!!
THAT'S RIDICULOUS!!
B-BMP
ME?
B-BMP
CUTE?!
B-BMP
B-BMP
?
BMP
NO-BODY'S EVER...
KCH-A-M
...SAID THAT BEFORE.
BLRF
?!
OH, HI...
MIS-TRESS...

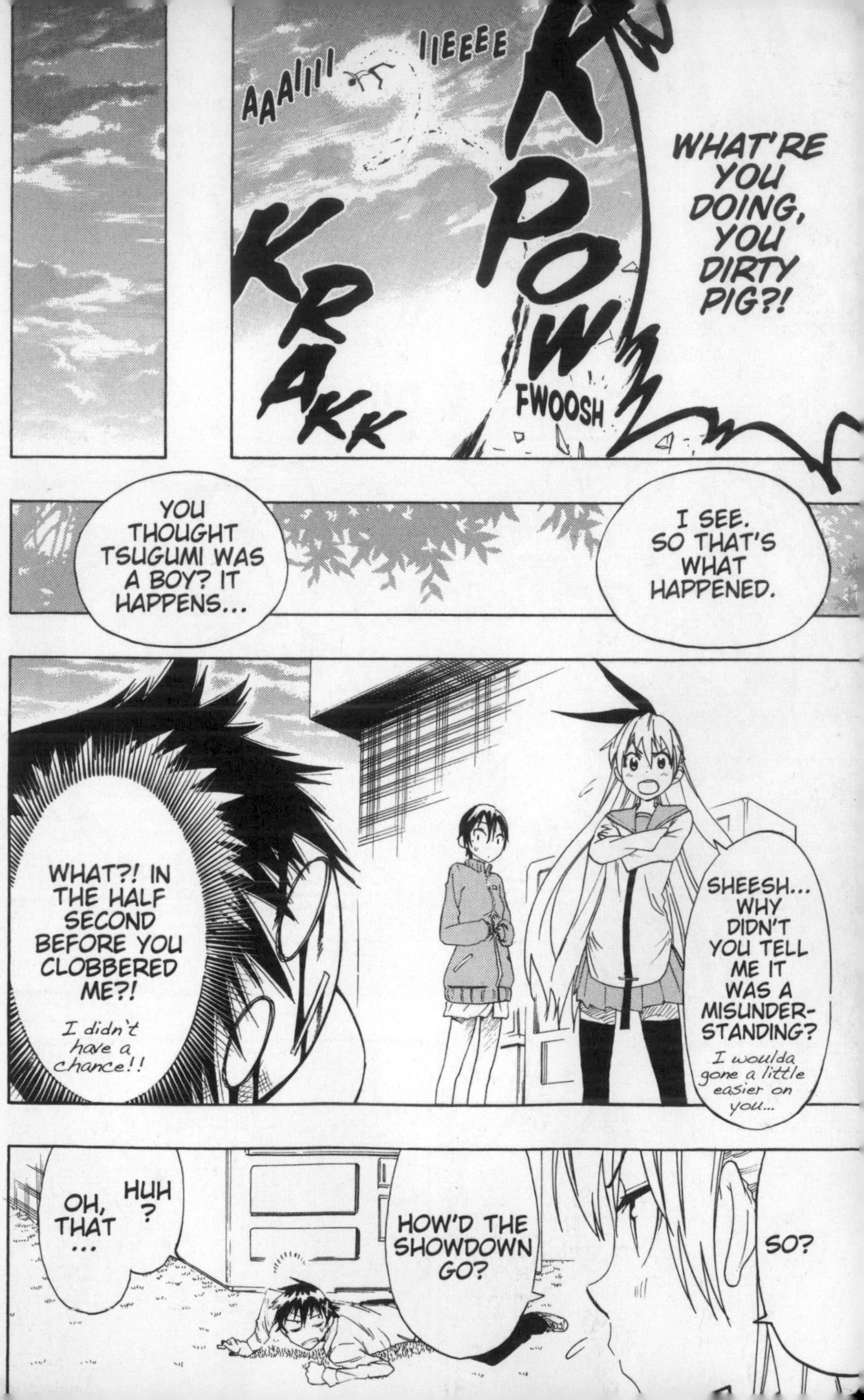
KPOW
WHAT'RE YOU DOING, YOU DIRTY PIG?!
IIEEEE
AAAIIII
KRAKK
FWOOSH
I SEE. SO THAT'S WHAT HAPPENED.
YOU THOUGHT TSUGUMI WAS A BOY? IT HAPPENS...
SHEESH... WHY DIDN'T YOU TELL ME IT WAS A MISUNDER-STANDING?
I woulda gone a little easier on you...
WHAT?! IN THE HALF SECOND BEFORE YOU CLOBBERED ME?!
I didn't have a chance!!
SO?
HOW'D THE SHOWDOWN GO?
HUH?
OH, THAT...

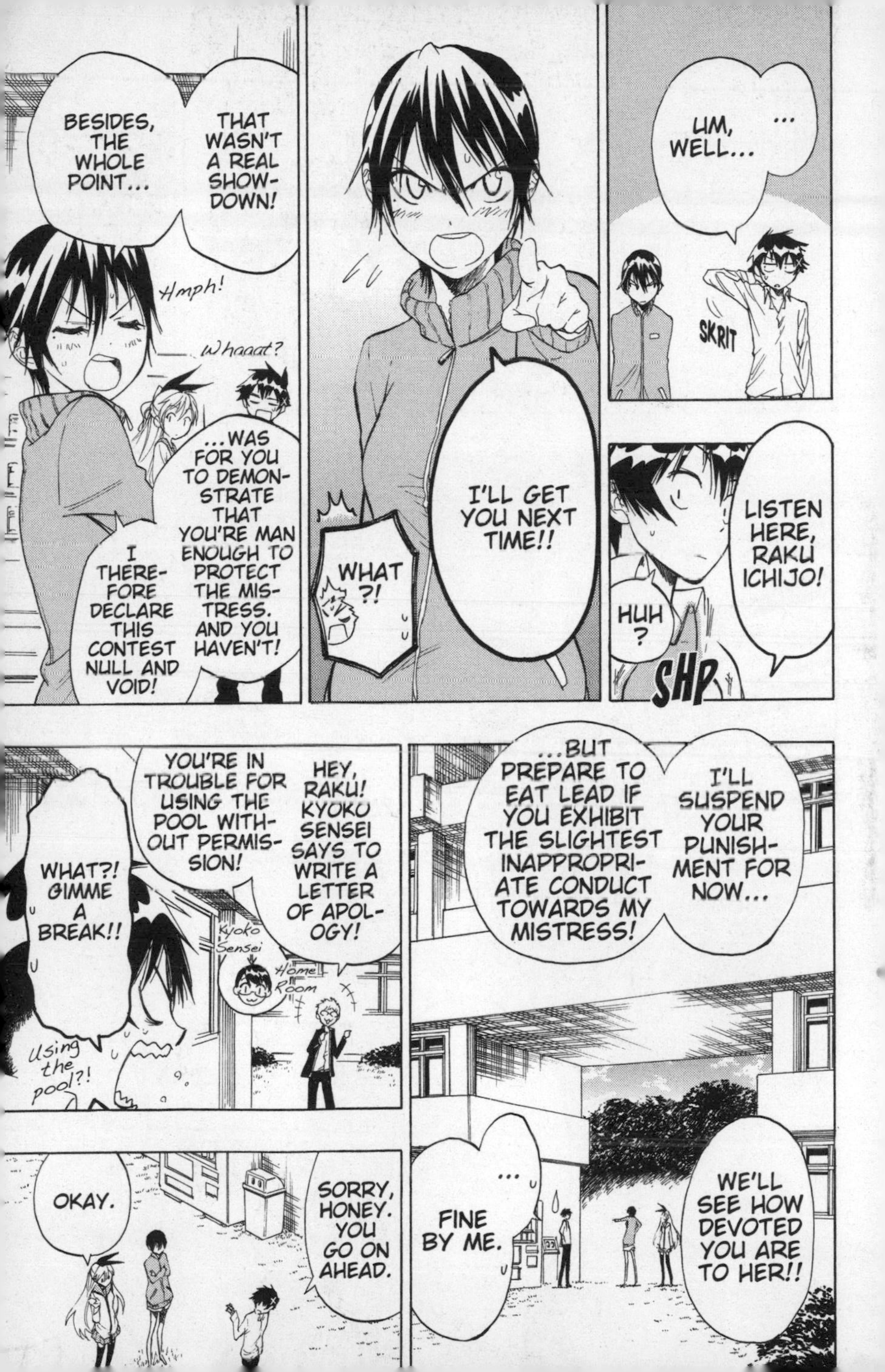
...
UM, WELL...
SKRIT
LISTEN HERE, RAKU ICHIJO!
HUH?
SHP
I'LL GET YOU NEXT TIME!!
WHAT?!
THAT WASN'T A REAL SHOW-DOWN!
BESIDES, THE WHOLE POINT...
Hmph!
...WAS FOR YOU TO DEMON-STRATE THAT YOU'RE MAN ENOUGH TO PROTECT THE MIS-TRESS. AND YOU HAVEN'T!
Whaaat?
I THERE-FORE DECLARE THIS CONTEST NULL AND VOID!
I'LL SUSPEND YOUR PUNISH-MENT FOR NOW...
...BUT PREPARE TO EAT LEAD IF YOU EXHIBIT THE SLIGHTEST INAPPROPRI-ATE CONDUCT TOWARDS MY MISTRESS!
WE'LL SEE HOW DEVOTED YOU ARE TO HER!!
...
FINE BY ME.
HEY, RAKU! KYOKO SENSEI SAYS TO WRITE A LETTER OF APOL-OGY!
YOU'RE IN TROUBLE FOR USING THE POOL WITH-OUT PERMIS-SION!
Kyoko Sensei
Home Room
WHAT?! GIMME A BREAK!!
Using the pool?!
SORRY, HONEY. YOU GO ON AHEAD.
OKAY.

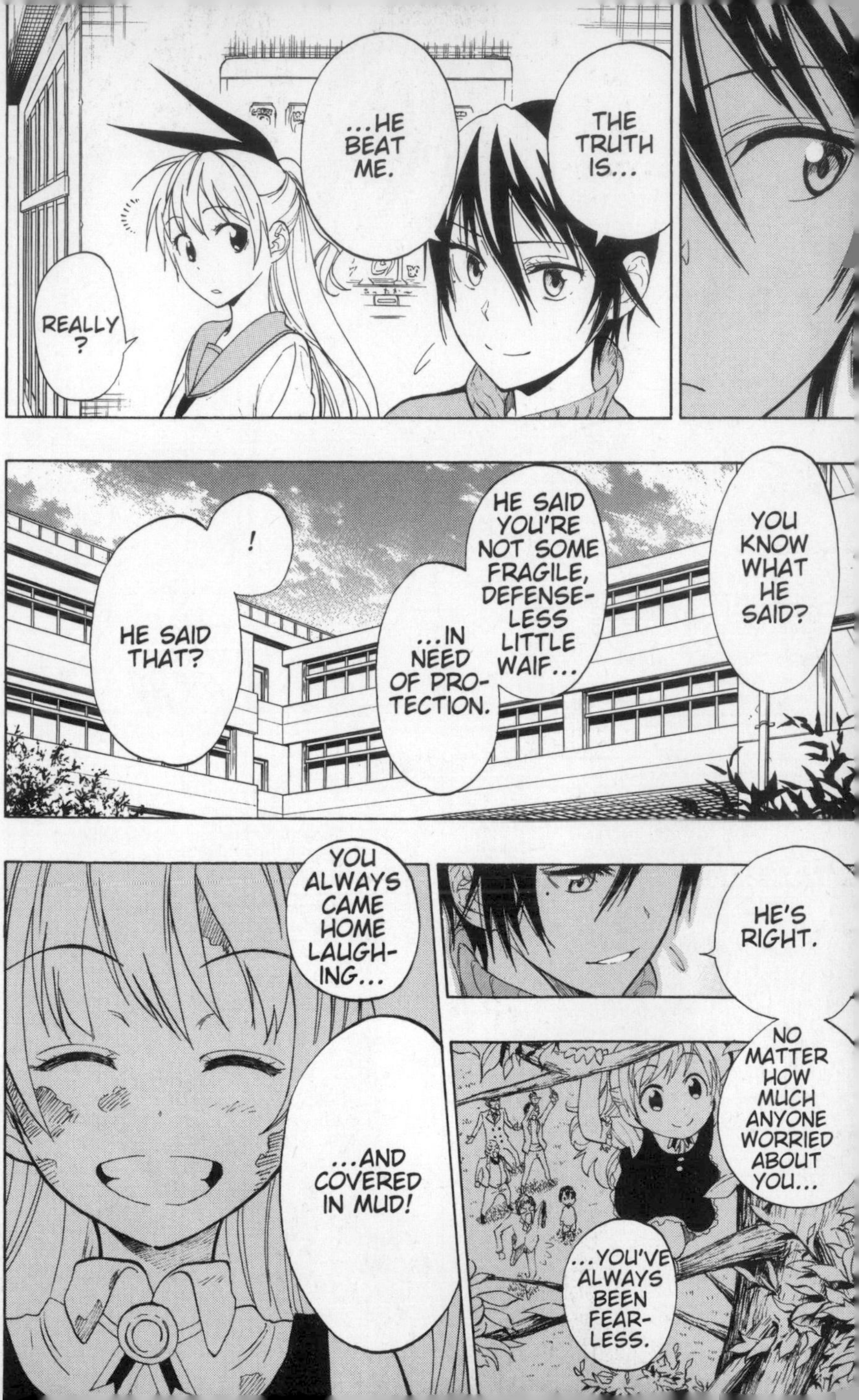
THE TRUTH IS...
...HE BEAT ME.
REALLY?
YOU KNOW WHAT HE SAID?
HE SAID YOU'RE NOT SOME FRAGILE, DEFENSELESS LITTLE WAIF...
...IN NEED OF PROTECTION.
!
HE SAID THAT?
HE'S RIGHT.
NO MATTER HOW MUCH ANYONE WORRIED ABOUT YOU...
...YOU'VE ALWAYS BEEN FEARLESS.
YOU ALWAYS CAME HOME LAUGHING...
...AND COVERED IN MUD!

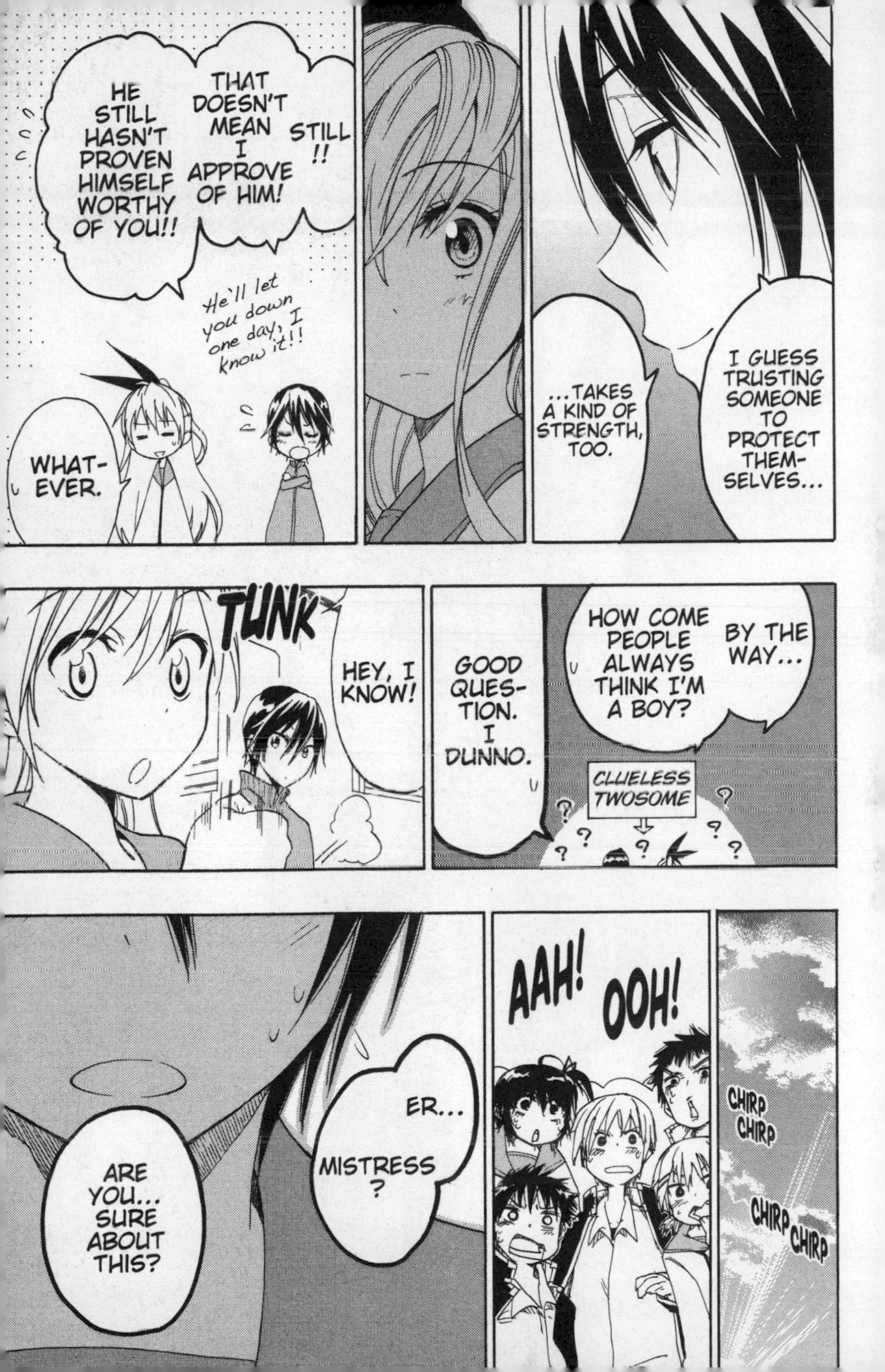
I GUESS TRUSTING SOMEONE TO PROTECT THEMSELVES...
...TAKES A KIND OF STRENGTH, TOO.
STILL!!
THAT DOESN'T MEAN I APPROVE OF HIM!
HE STILL HASN'T PROVEN HIMSELF WORTHY OF YOU!!
He'll let you down one day, I know it!!
WHATEVER.
BY THE WAY...
HOW COME PEOPLE ALWAYS THINK I'M A BOY?
GOOD QUESTION. I DUNNO.
CLUELESS TWOSOME
HEY, I KNOW!
TUNK
CHIRP CHIRP
CHIRP CHIRP
OOH!
AAH!
ER...
MISTRESS?
ARE YOU... SURE ABOUT THIS?

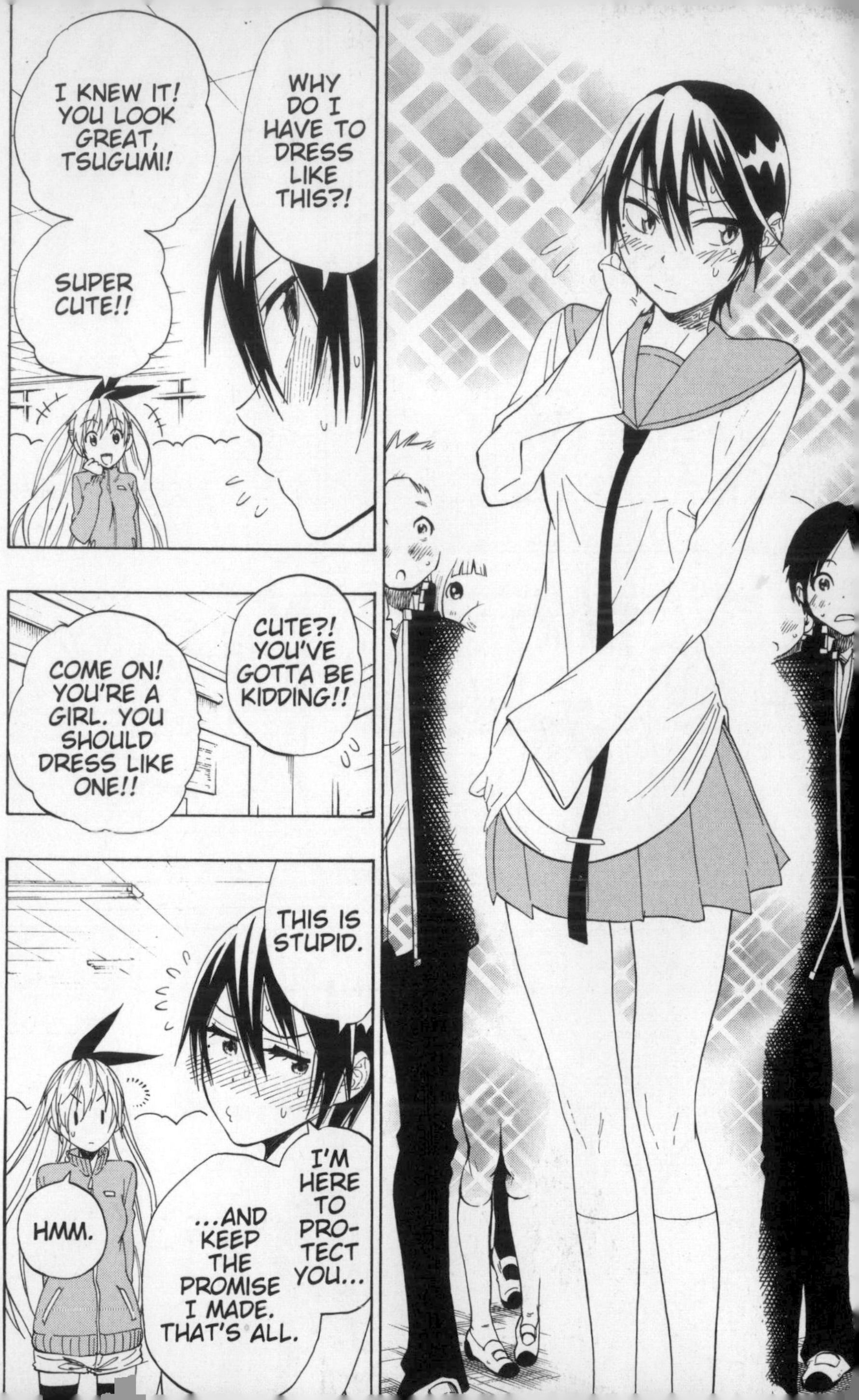
WHY DO I HAVE TO DRESS LIKE THIS?!
I KNEW IT! YOU LOOK GREAT, TSUGUMI!
SUPER CUTE!!
CUTE?! YOU'VE GOTTA BE KIDDING!!
COME ON! YOU'RE A GIRL. YOU SHOULD DRESS LIKE ONE!!
THIS IS STUPID.
I'M HERE TO PRO-TECT YOU...
...AND KEEP THE PROMISE I MADE. THAT'S ALL.
HMM.

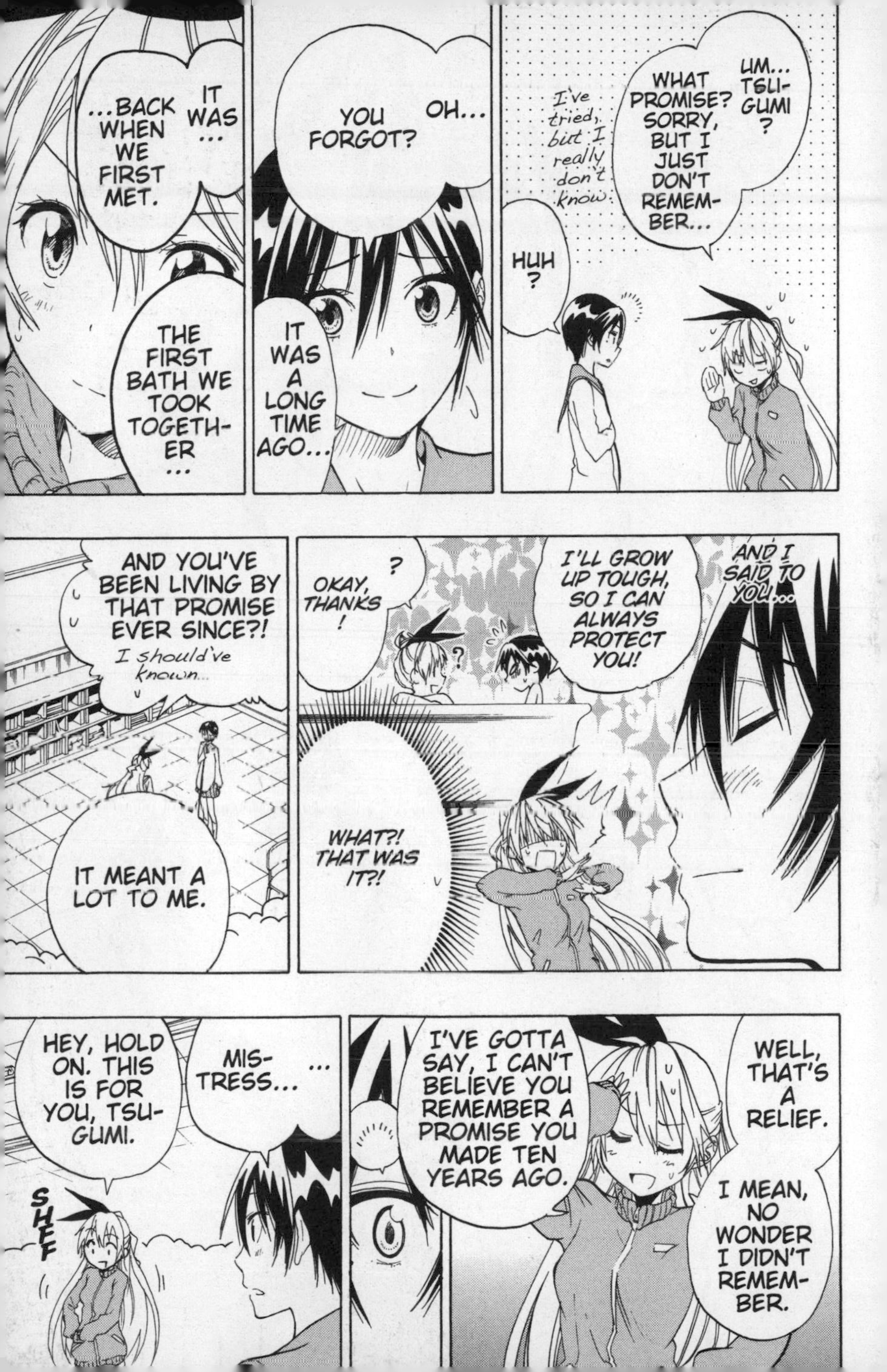
UM... TSUGUMI?
WHAT PROMISE? SORRY, BUT I JUST DON'T REMEMBER...
I've tried, but I really don't know.
HUH?
OH...
YOU FORGOT?
IT WAS A LONG TIME AGO...
IT WAS...
...BACK WHEN WE FIRST MET.
THE FIRST BATH WE TOOK TOGETHER...
AND I SAID TO YOU...
I'LL GROW UP TOUGH, SO I CAN ALWAYS PROTECT YOU!
OKAY, THANKS!
?
WHAT?! THAT WAS IT?!
AND YOU'VE BEEN LIVING BY THAT PROMISE EVER SINCE?!
I should've known...
IT MEANT A LOT TO ME.
WELL, THAT'S A RELIEF.
I MEAN, NO WONDER I DIDN'T REMEMBER.
I'VE GOTTA SAY, I CAN'T BELIEVE YOU REMEMBER A PROMISE YOU MADE TEN YEARS AGO.
...
MISTRESS...
HEY, HOLD ON. THIS IS FOR YOU, TSUGUMI.
SHFF

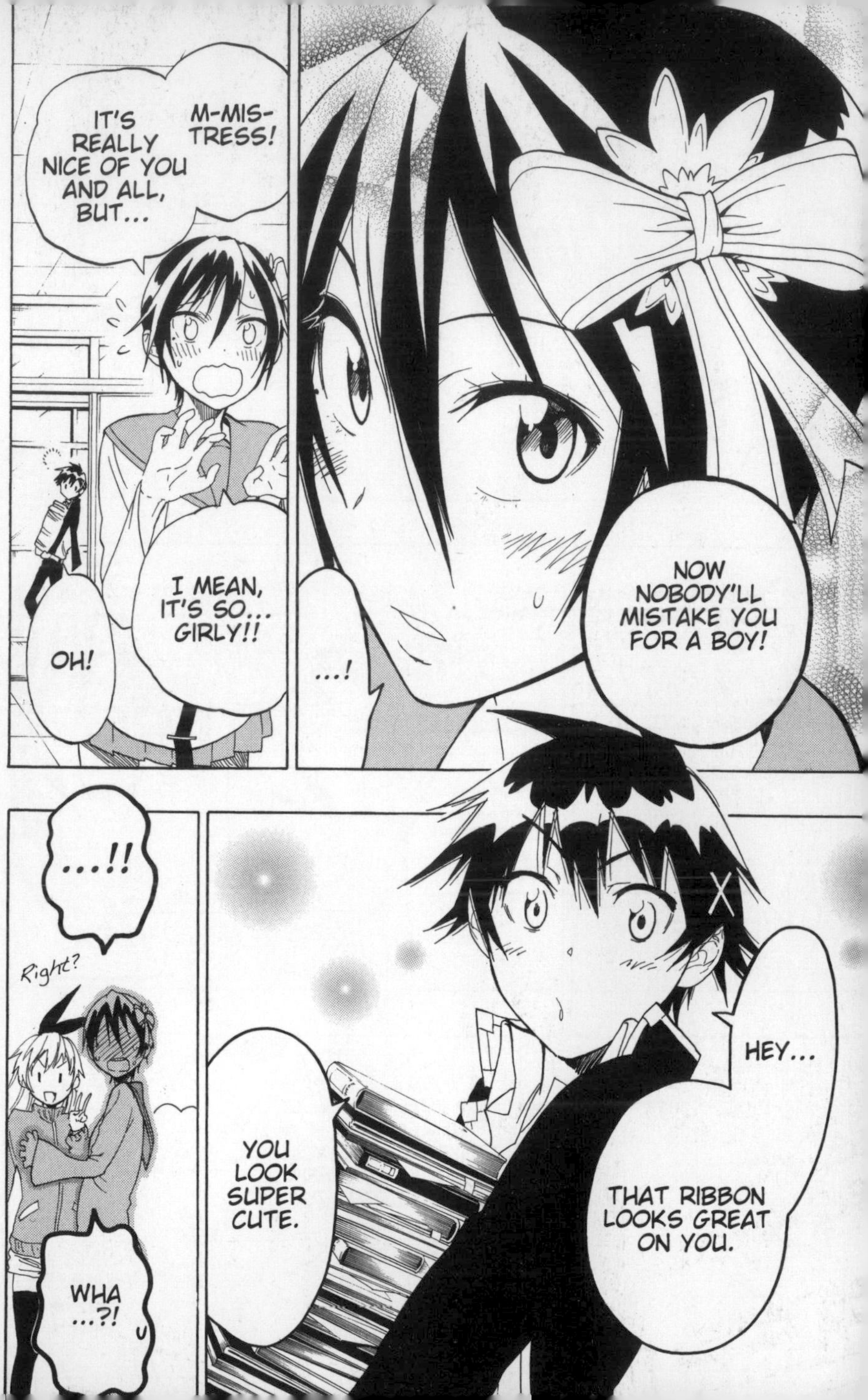
NOW NOBODY'LL MISTAKE YOU FOR A BOY!
...!
M-MIS-TRESS!
IT'S REALLY NICE OF YOU AND ALL, BUT...
I MEAN, IT'S SO... GIRLY!!
OH!
HEY...
THAT RIBBON LOOKS GREAT ON YOU.
YOU LOOK SUPER CUTE.
...!!
Right?
WHA ...?!

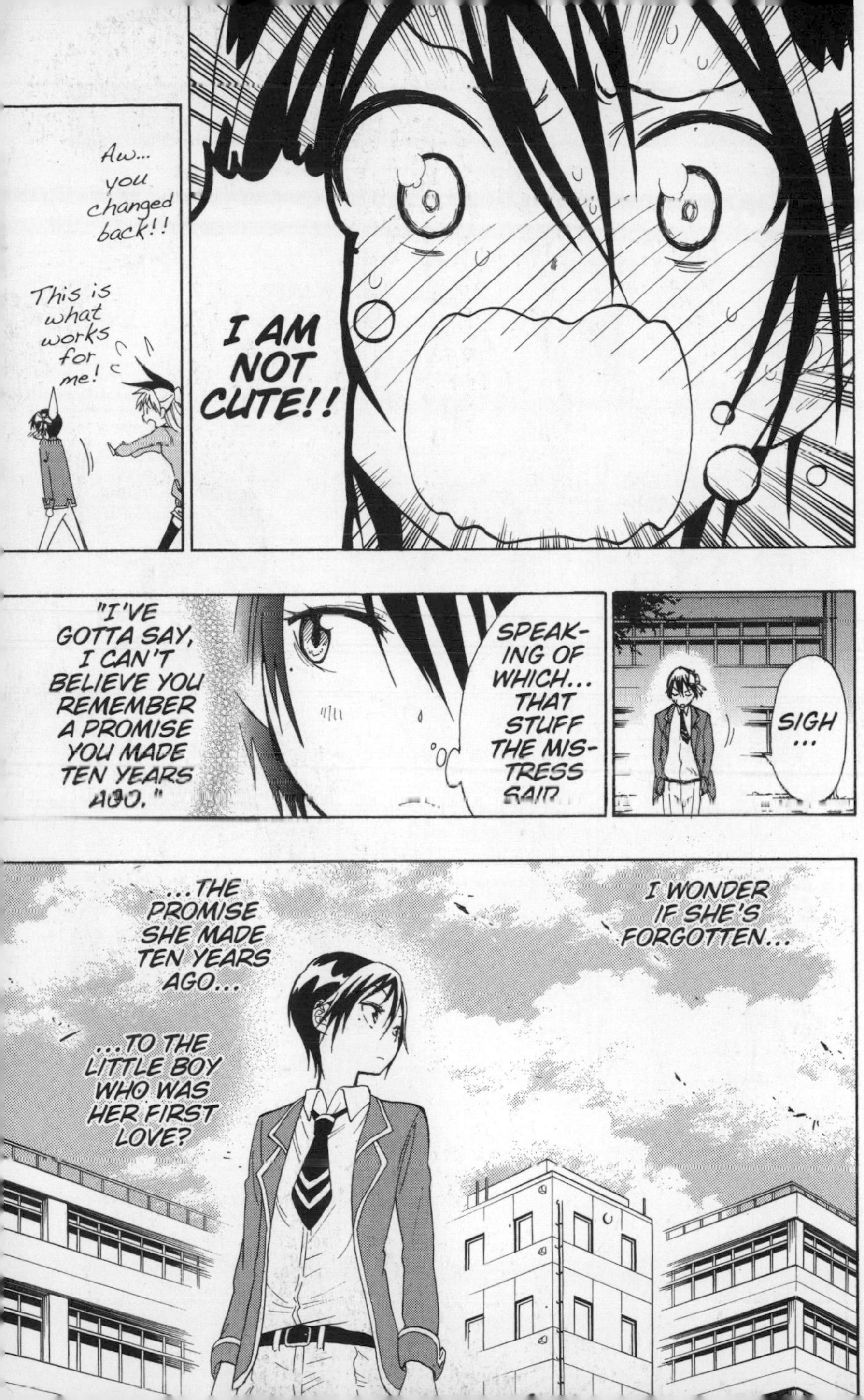
I AM NOT CUTE!!
Aw... you changed back!!
This is what works for me!
SIGH...
SPEAK-ING OF WHICH... THAT STUFF THE MIS-TRESS SAID
"I'VE GOTTA SAY, I CAN'T BELIEVE YOU REMEMBER A PROMISE YOU MADE TEN YEARS AGO."
I WONDER IF SHE'S FORGOTTEN...
...THE PROMISE SHE MADE TEN YEARS AGO...
...TO THE LITTLE BOY WHO WAS HER FIRST LOVE?

Chapter 17: Intermission

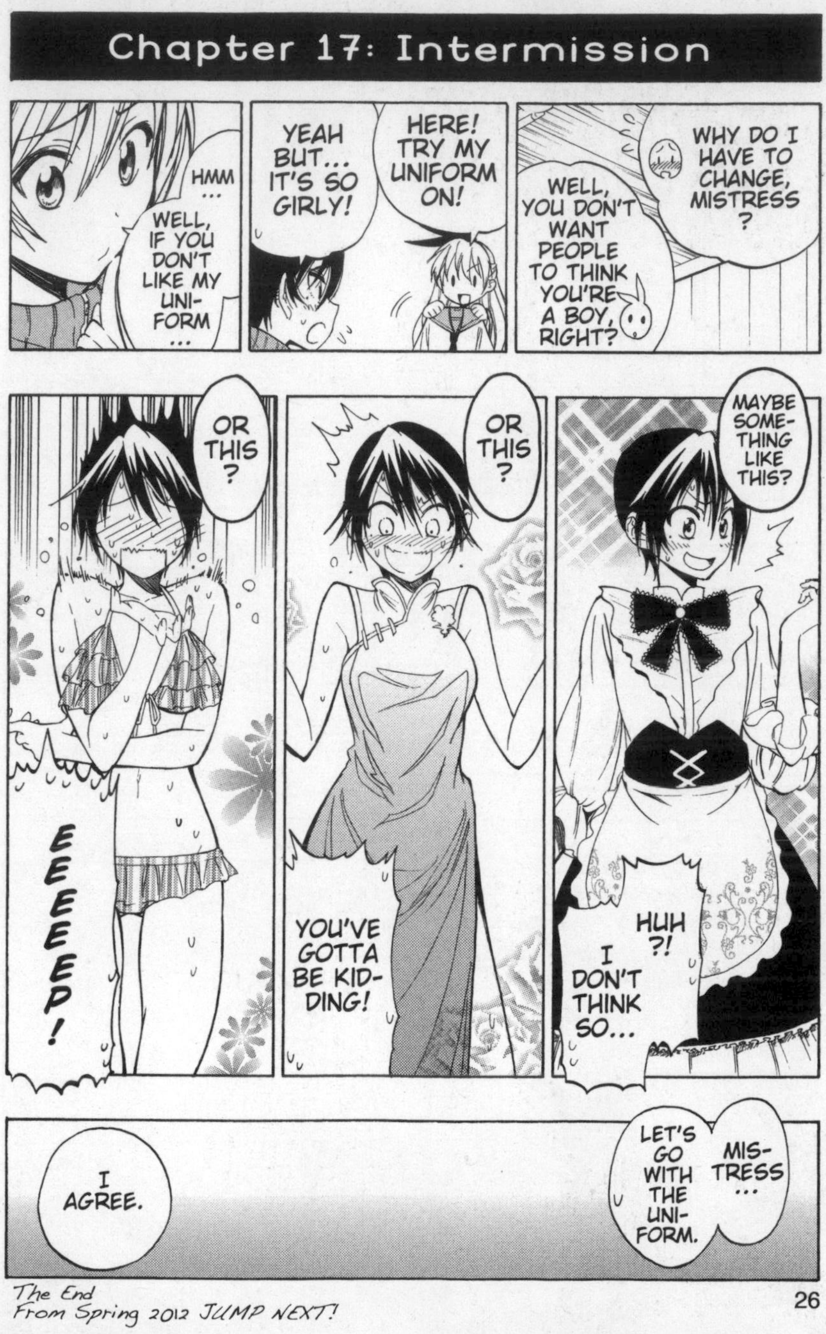
WHY DO I HAVE TO CHANGE, MISTRESS?
WELL, YOU DON'T WANT PEOPLE TO THINK YOU'RE A BOY, RIGHT?
HERE! TRY MY UNIFORM ON!
YEAH BUT... IT'S SO GIRLY!
HMM...
WELL, IF YOU DON'T LIKE MY UNI-FORM...
MAYBE SOME-THING LIKE THIS?
HUH?!
I DON'T THINK SO...
OR THIS?
YOU'VE GOTTA BE KID-DING!
OR THIS?
EEEEEP!
MIS-TRESS...
LET'S GO WITH THE UNI-FORM.
I AGREE.

The End
From Spring 2012 JUMP NEXT!

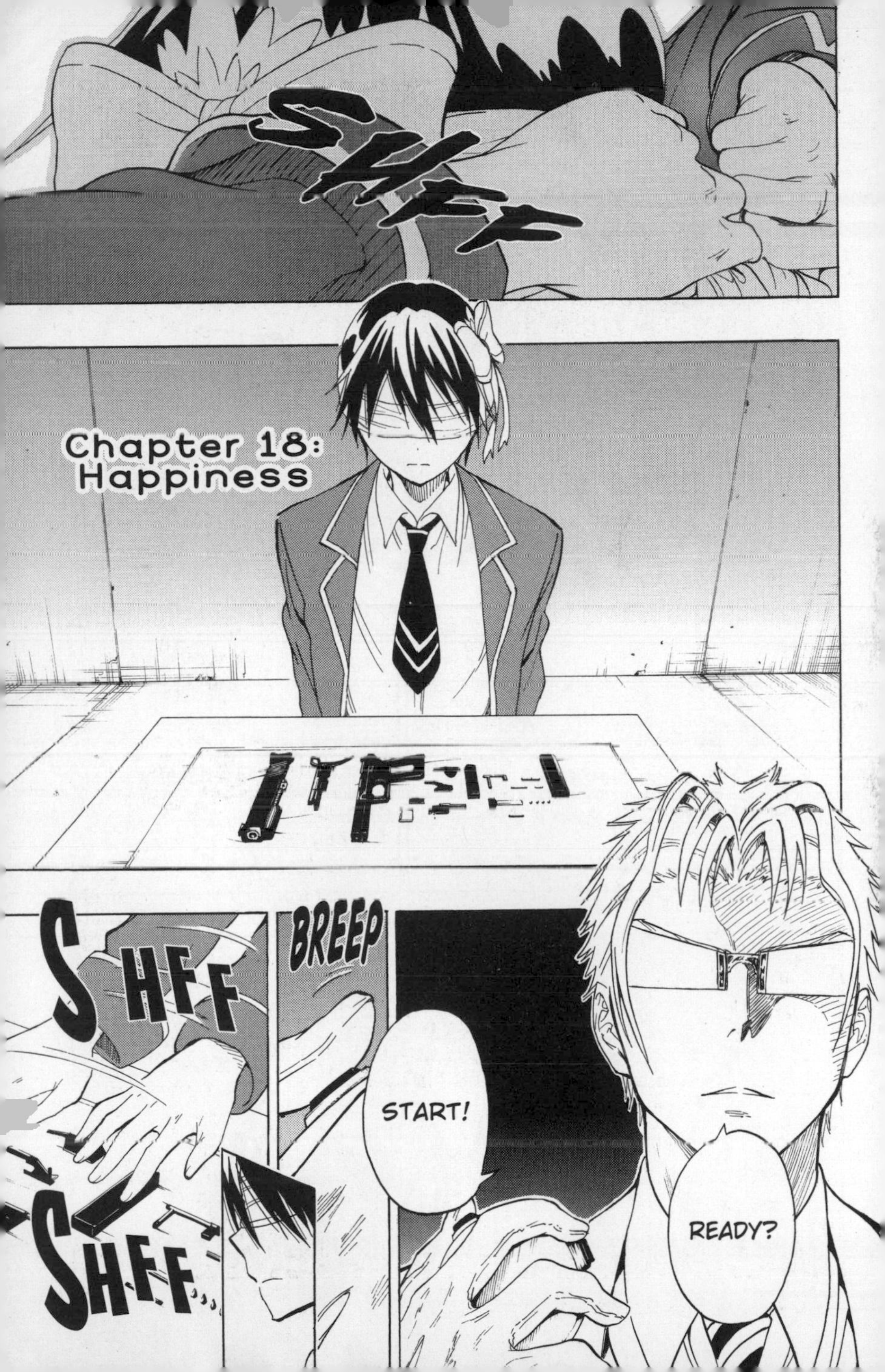
SHFF
Chapter 18:
Happiness
READY?
START!
BREEP
SHFF
SHFF...

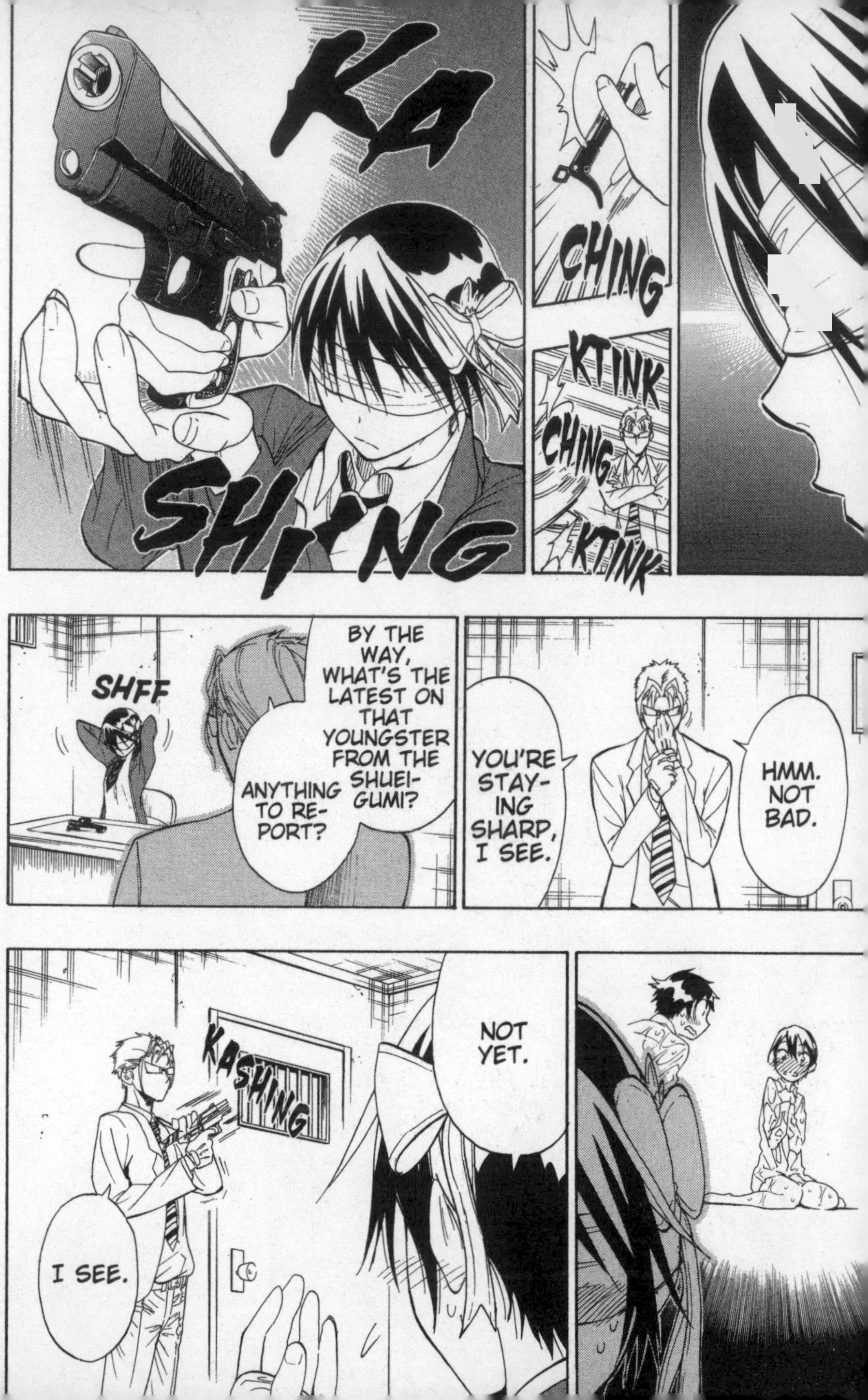
CHING
KTINK
CHING
KTINK
KA
SHING
HMM. NOT BAD.
YOU'RE STAYING SHARP, I SEE.
BY THE WAY, WHAT'S THE LATEST ON THAT YOUNGSTER FROM THE SHUEI-GUMI?
ANYTHING TO REPORT?
SHFF
NOT YET.
KASHING
I SEE.

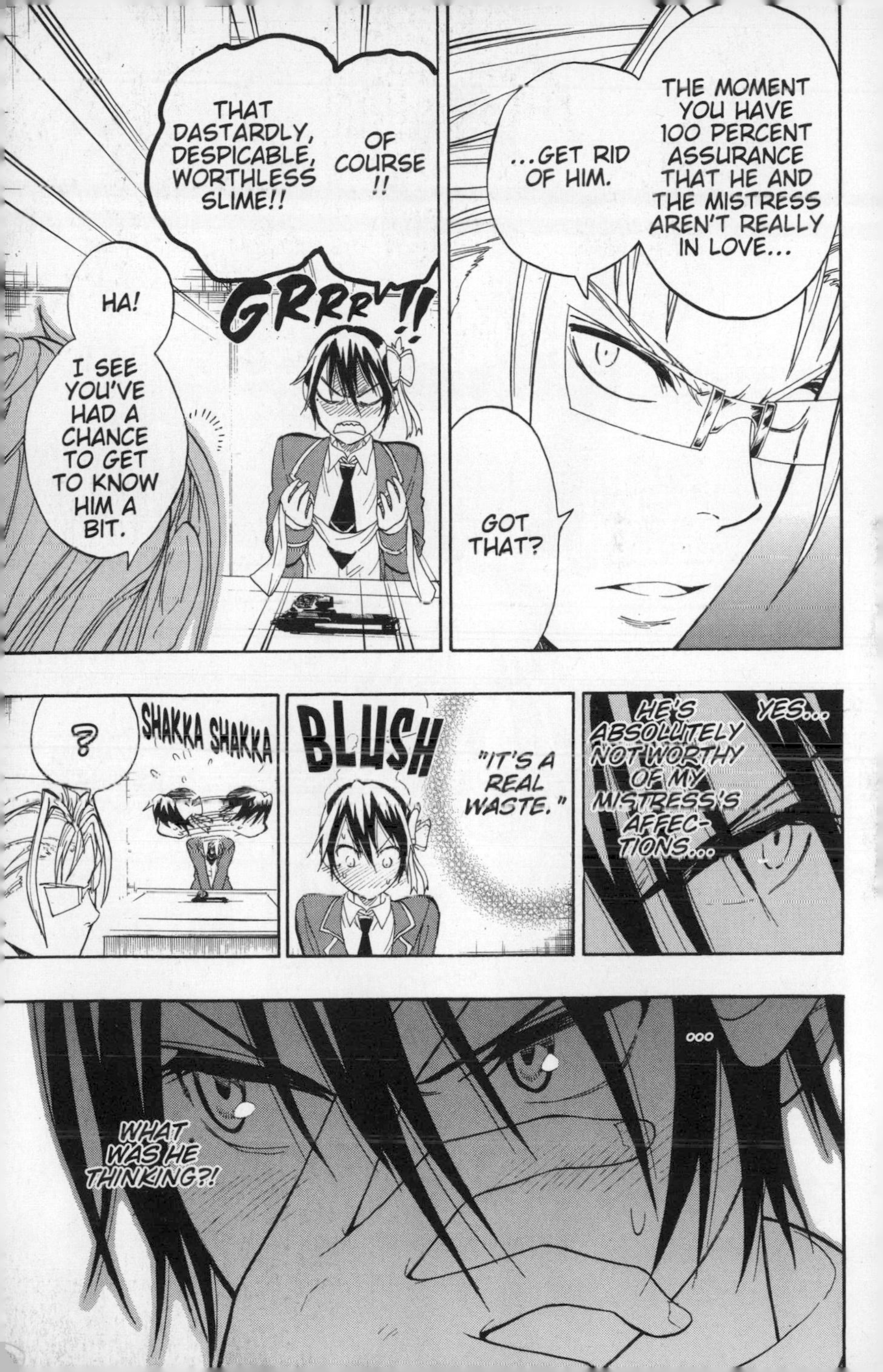
THE MOMENT YOU HAVE 100 PERCENT ASSURANCE THAT HE AND THE MISTRESS AREN'T REALLY IN LOVE...
...GET RID OF HIM.
GOT THAT?
OF COURSE!!
THAT DASTARDLY, DESPICABLE, WORTHLESS SLIME!!
GRRRT!!
HA!
I SEE YOU'VE HAD A CHANCE TO GET TO KNOW HIM A BIT.
YES...
HE'S ABSOLUTELY NOT WORTHY OF MY MISTRESS'S AFFEC-TIONS...
BLUSH
"IT'S A REAL WASTE."
SHAKKA SHAKKA
?
...
WHAT WAS HE THINKING?!

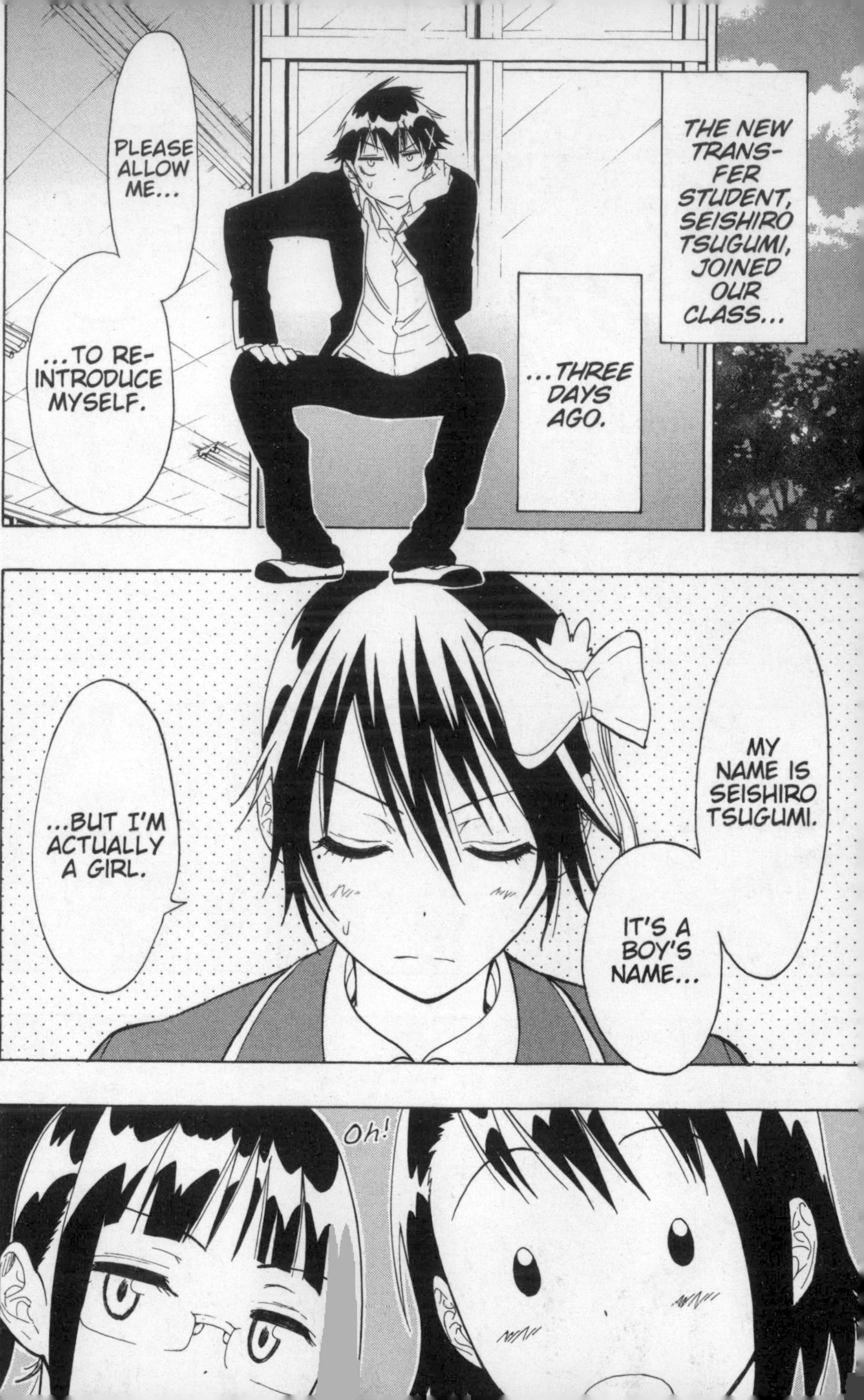
THE NEW TRANS-FER STUDENT, SEISHIRO TSUGUMI, JOINED OUR CLASS...
...THREE DAYS AGO.
PLEASE ALLOW ME...
...TO RE-INTRODUCE MYSELF.
MY NAME IS SEISHIRO TSUGUMI.
IT'S A BOY'S NAME...
...BUT I'M ACTUALLY A GIRL.
Oh!

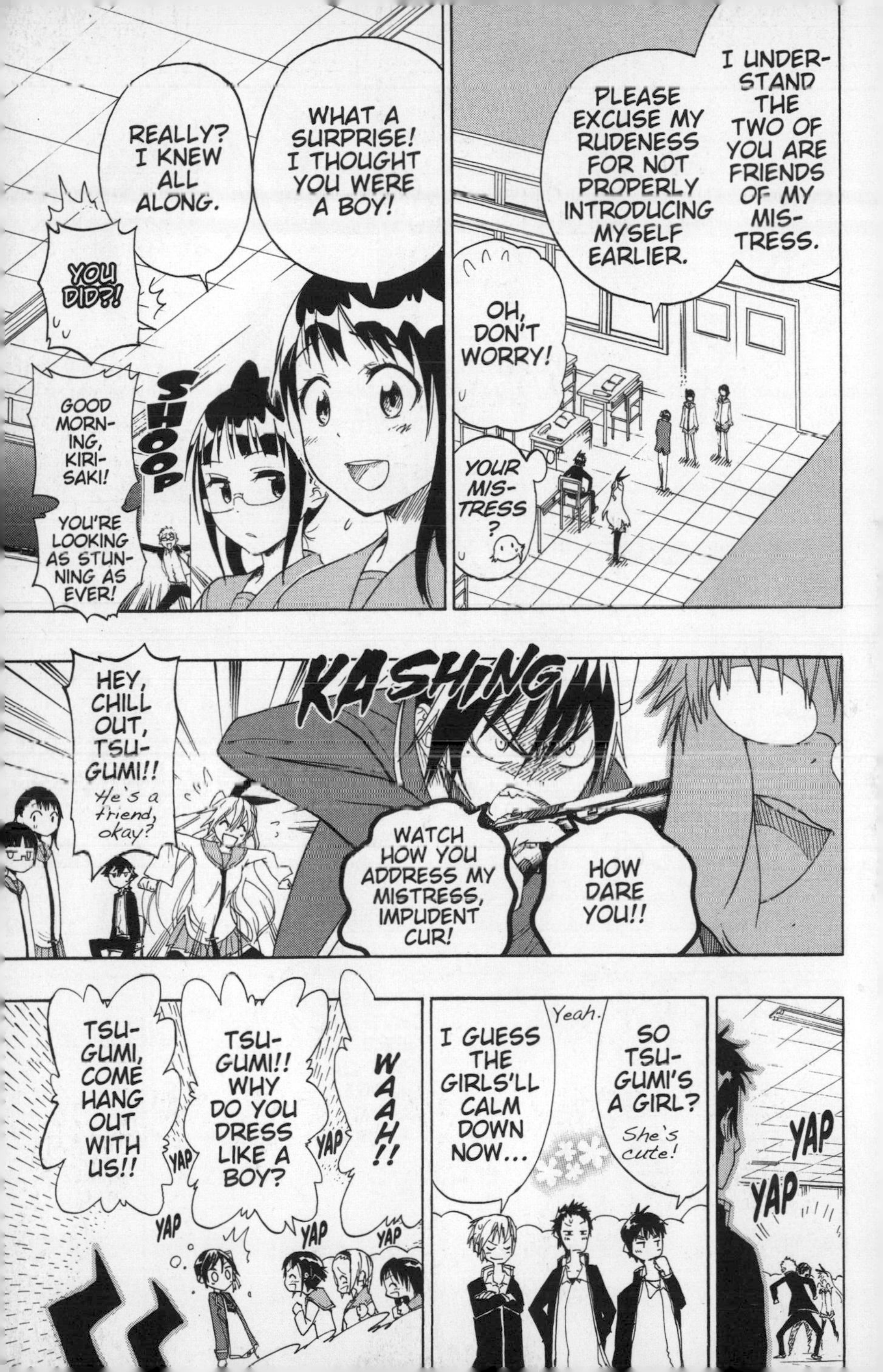

I UNDERSTAND THE TWO OF YOU ARE FRIENDS OF MY MISTRESS.
PLEASE EXCUSE MY RUDENESS FOR NOT PROPERLY INTRODUCING MYSELF EARLIER.
OH, DON'T WORRY!
YOUR MISTRESS?
WHAT A SURPRISE! I THOUGHT YOU WERE A BOY!
REALLY? I KNEW ALL ALONG.
YOU DID?!
SHOOP
GOOD MORNING, KIRISAKI!
YOU'RE LOOKING AS STUNNING AS EVER!
KASHING
HOW DARE YOU!!
WATCH HOW YOU ADDRESS MY MISTRESS, IMPUDENT CUR!
HEY, CHILL OUT, TSUGUMI!!
He's a friend, okay?
YAP
YAP
SO TSUGUMI'S A GIRL?
She's cute!
Yeah.
I GUESS THE GIRLS'LL CALM DOWN NOW...
WAAAH!!
YAP
TSUGUMI!! WHY DO YOU DRESS LIKE A BOY?
YAP
TSUGUMI, COME HANG OUT WITH US!!
YAP
YAP
YAP

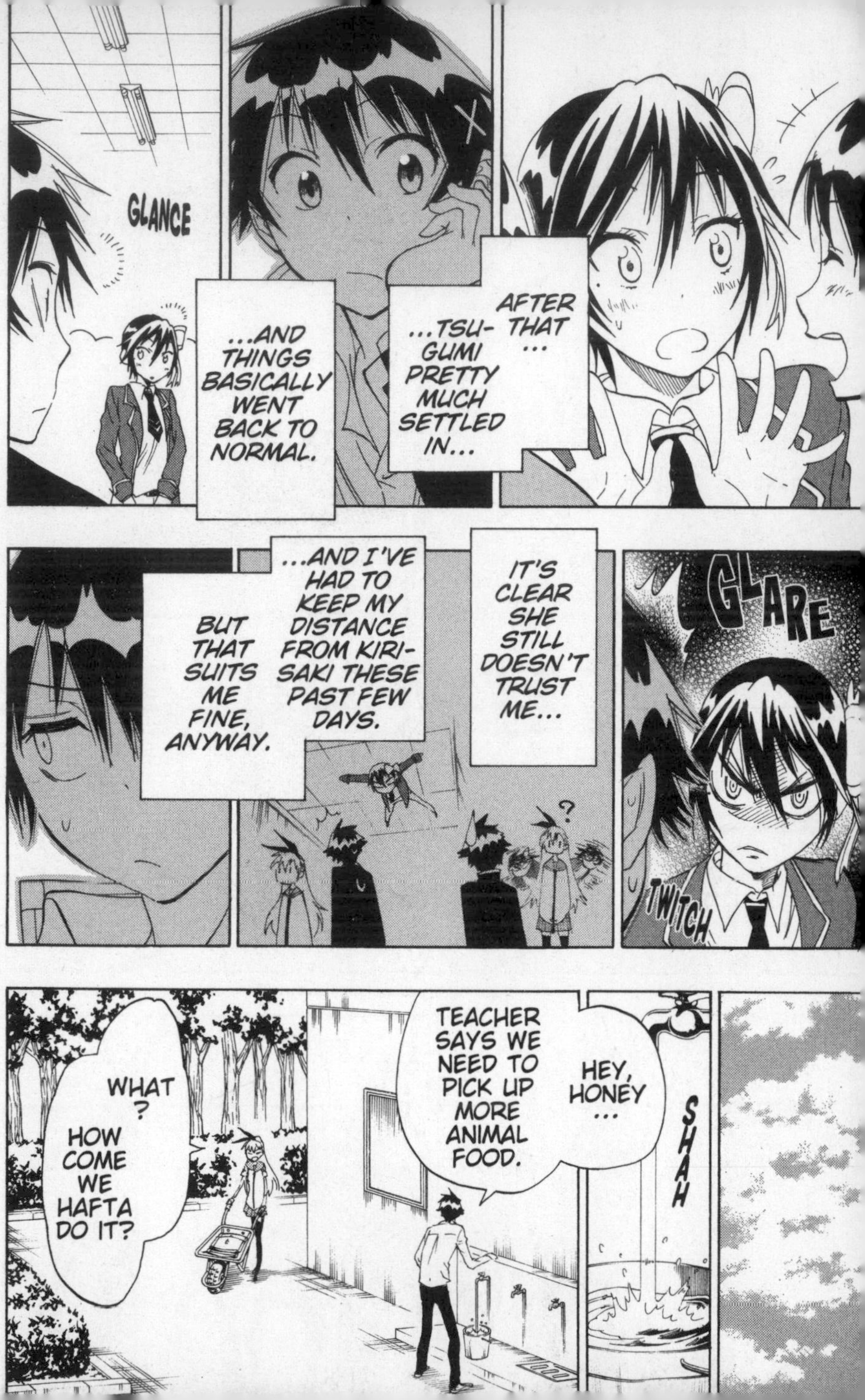
AFTER THAT...
...TSU-GUMI PRETTY MUCH SETTLED IN...
...AND THINGS BASICALLY WENT BACK TO NORMAL.
GLANCE
GLARE
TWITCH
IT'S CLEAR SHE STILL DOESN'T TRUST ME...
...AND I'VE HAD TO KEEP MY DISTANCE FROM KIRI-SAKI THESE PAST FEW DAYS.
BUT THAT SUITS ME FINE, ANYWAY.
SHAH
HEY, HONEY...
TEACHER SAYS WE NEED TO PICK UP MORE ANIMAL FOOD.
WHAT? HOW COME WE HAFTA DO IT?

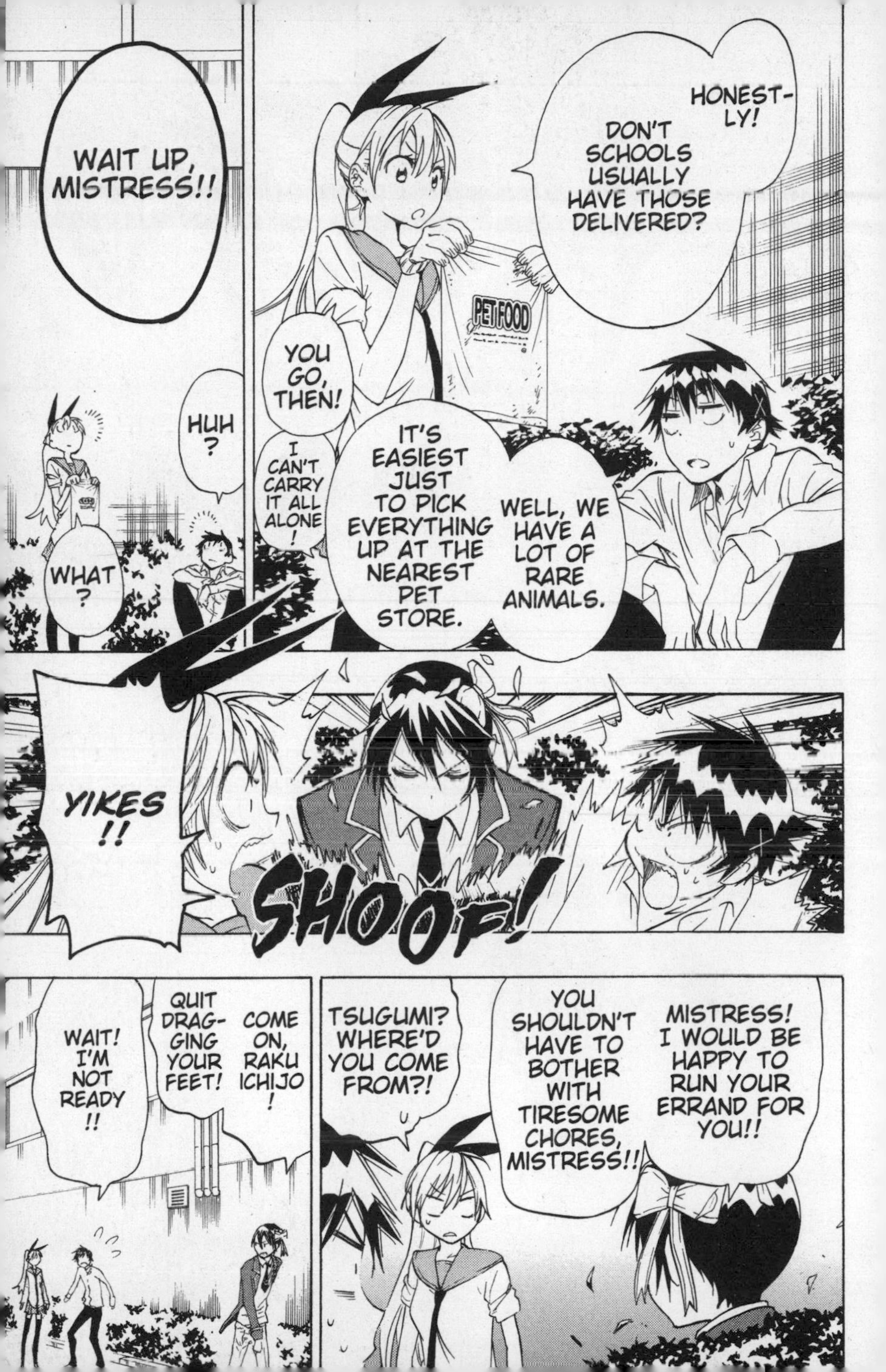
HONESTLY! DON'T SCHOOLS USUALLY HAVE THOSE DELIVERED?
WELL, WE HAVE A LOT OF RARE ANIMALS.
IT'S EASIEST JUST TO PICK EVERYTHING UP AT THE NEAREST PET STORE.
YOU GO, THEN!
I CAN'T CARRY IT ALL ALONE!
PET FOOD
WAIT UP, MISTRESS!!
HUH?
WHAT?
YIKES!!
SHOOF!
MISTRESS! I WOULD BE HAPPY TO RUN YOUR ERRAND FOR YOU!!
YOU SHOULDN'T HAVE TO BOTHER WITH TIRESOME CHORES, MISTRESS!!
TSUGUMI? WHERE'D YOU COME FROM?!
COME ON, RAKU ICHIJO!
QUIT DRAGGING YOUR FEET!
WAIT! I'M NOT READY!!

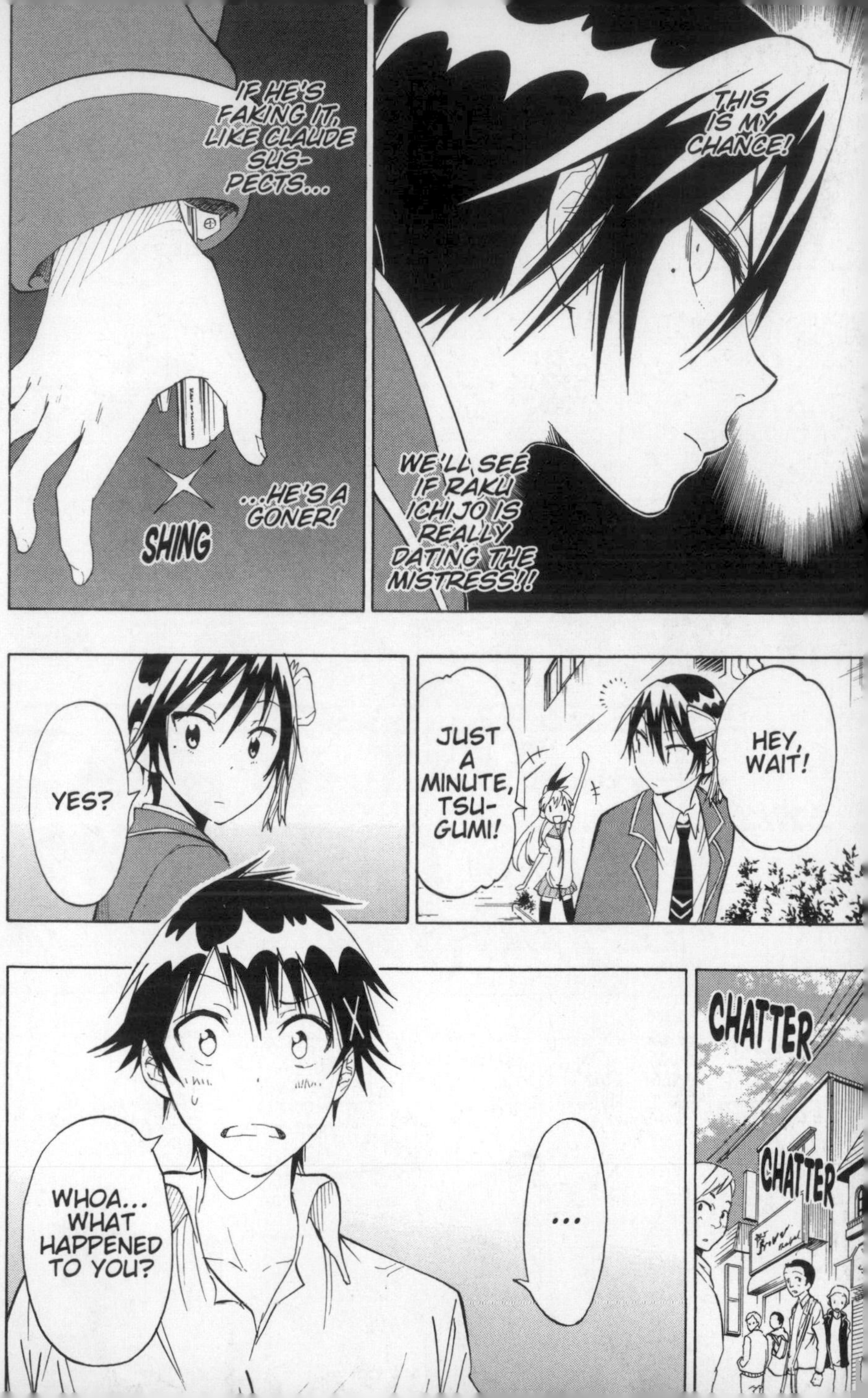
THIS IS MY CHANCE!
WE'LL SEE IF RAKU ICHIJO IS REALLY DATING THE MISTRESS!!
IF HE'S FAKING IT, LIKE CLAUDE SUS-PECTS...
...HE'S A GONER!
SHING
HEY, WAIT!
JUST A MINUTE, TSU-GUMI!
YES?
CHATTER
CHATTER
...
WHOA... WHAT HAPPENED TO YOU?

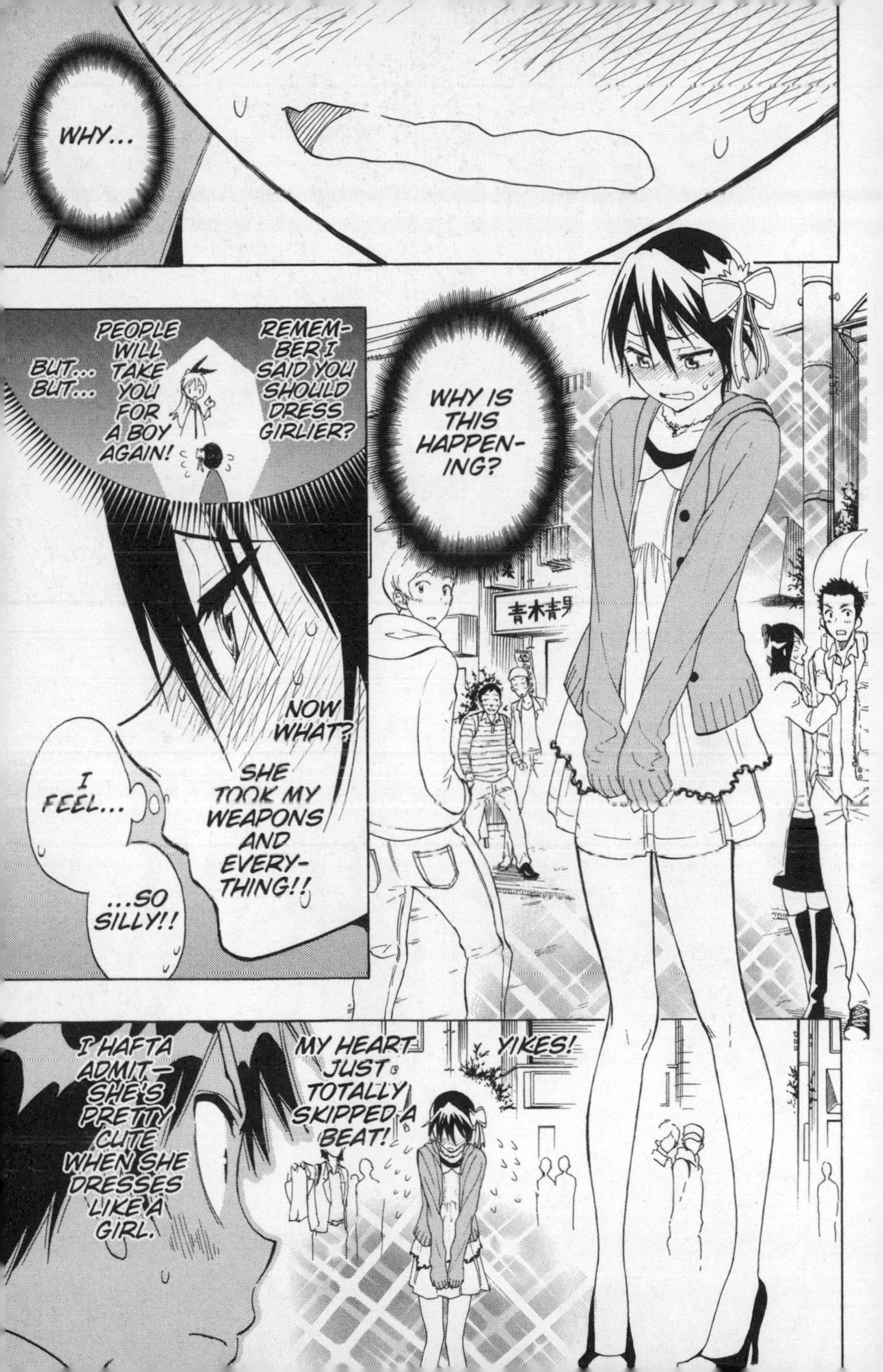
WHY...
WHY IS THIS HAPPENING?
REMEMBER I SAID YOU SHOULD DRESS GIRLIER?
PEOPLE WILL TAKE YOU FOR A BOY AGAIN!
BUT... BUT...
NOW WHAT?
SHE TOOK MY WEAPONS AND EVERYTHING!!
I FEEL...
...SO SILLY!!
YIKES!
MY HEART JUST TOTALLY SKIPPED A BEAT!
I HAFTA ADMIT— SHE'S PRETTY CUTE WHEN SHE DRESSES LIKE A GIRL.

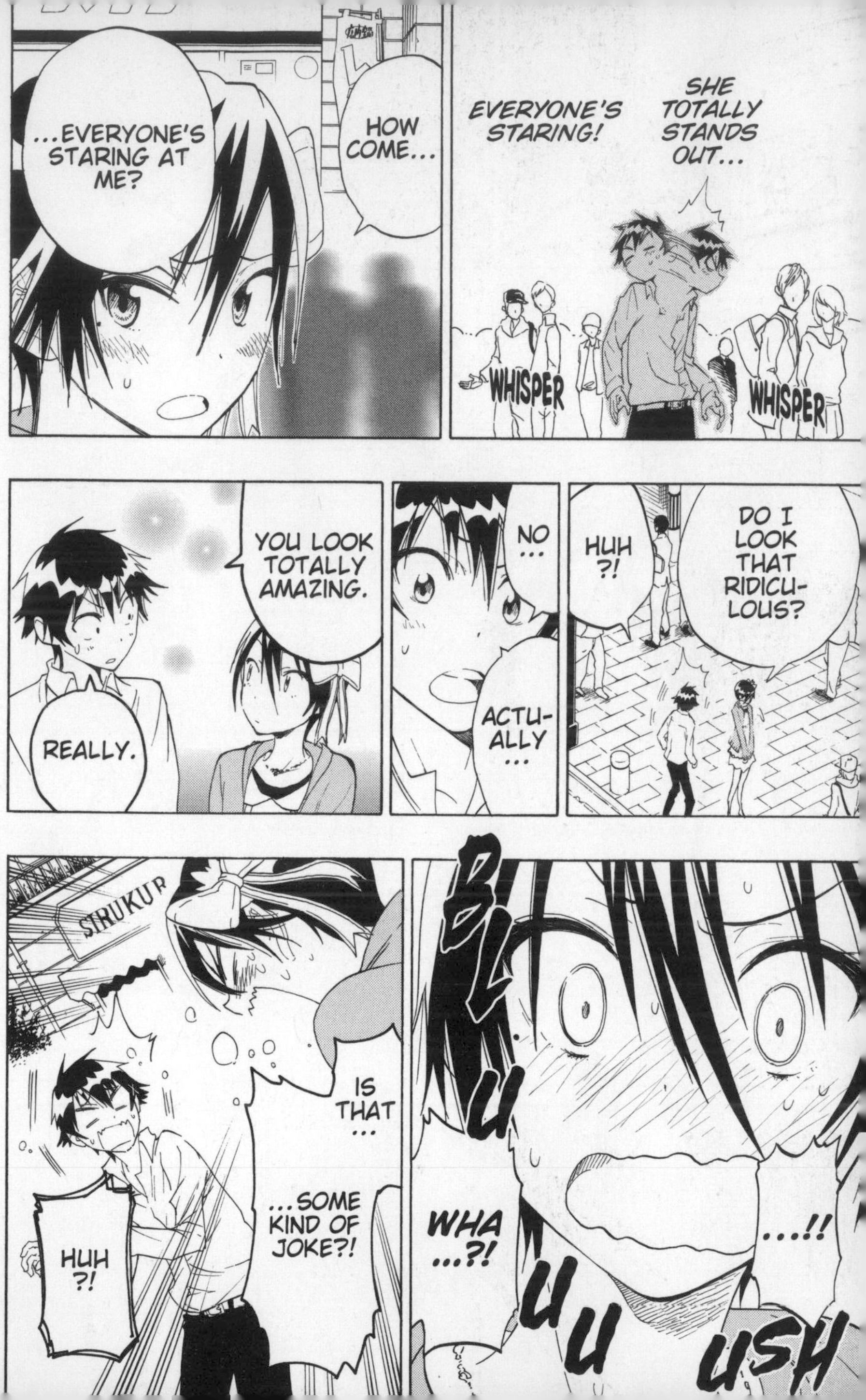
SHE TOTALLY STANDS OUT...
EVERYONE'S STARING!
WHISPER
WHISPER
HOW COME...
...EVERYONE'S STARING AT ME?
DO I LOOK THAT RIDICULOUS?
HUH?!
NO...
ACTU-ALLY...
YOU LOOK TOTALLY AMAZING.
REALLY.
BLUUUUUSH
...!!
WHA...?!
SIRUKUR
IS THAT...
...SOME KIND OF JOKE?!
HUH?!

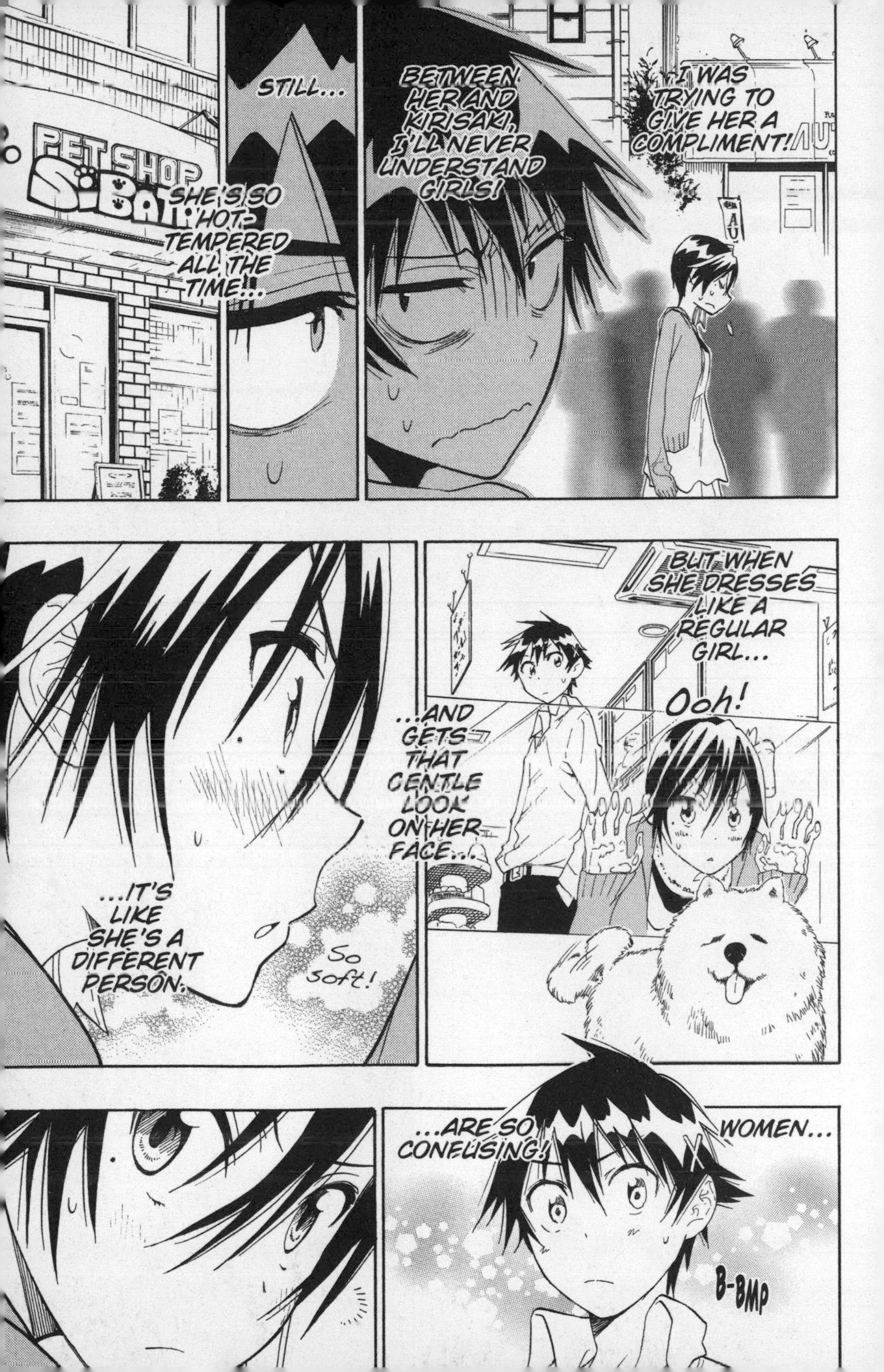
I WAS TRYING TO GIVE HER A COMPLIMENT!
BETWEEN HER AND KIRISAKI, I'LL NEVER UNDERSTAND GIRLS!
STILL...
SHE'S SO HOT-TEMPERED ALL THE TIME...
PET SHOP
BUT WHEN SHE DRESSES LIKE A REGULAR GIRL...
Ooh!
...AND GETS THAT GENTLE LOOK ON HER FACE...
...IT'S LIKE SHE'S A DIFFERENT PERSON.
So soft!
WOMEN...
...ARE SO CONFUSING!
B-BMP

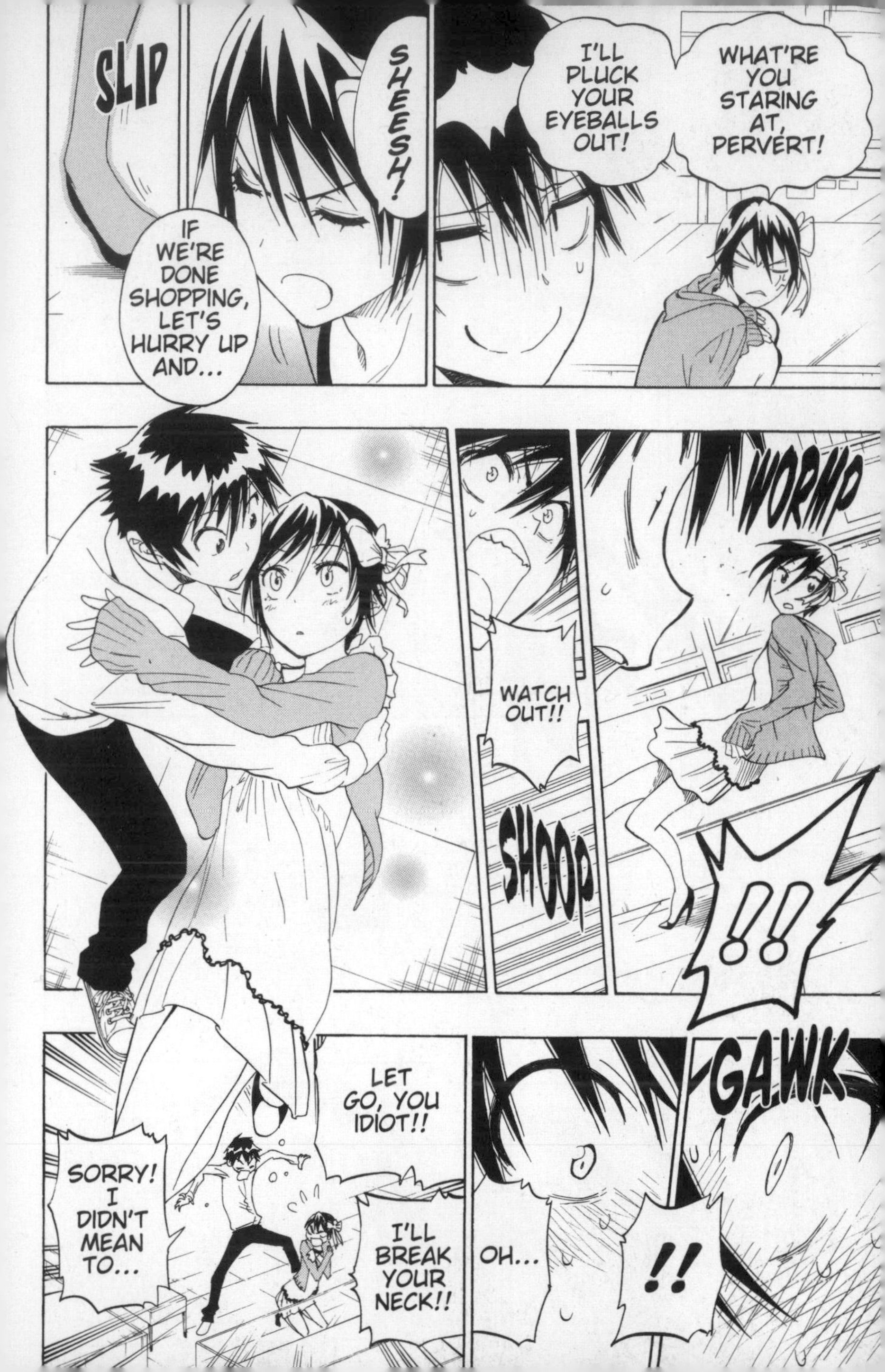
WHAT'RE YOU STARING AT, PERVERT!
I'LL PLUCK YOUR EYEBALLS OUT!
SHEESH!
SLIP
IF WE'RE DONE SHOPPING, LET'S HURRY UP AND...
WORMP
!!
WATCH OUT!!
SHOOP
GAWK
!!
OH...
LET GO, YOU IDIOT!!
I'LL BREAK YOUR NECK!!
SORRY! I DIDN'T MEAN TO...

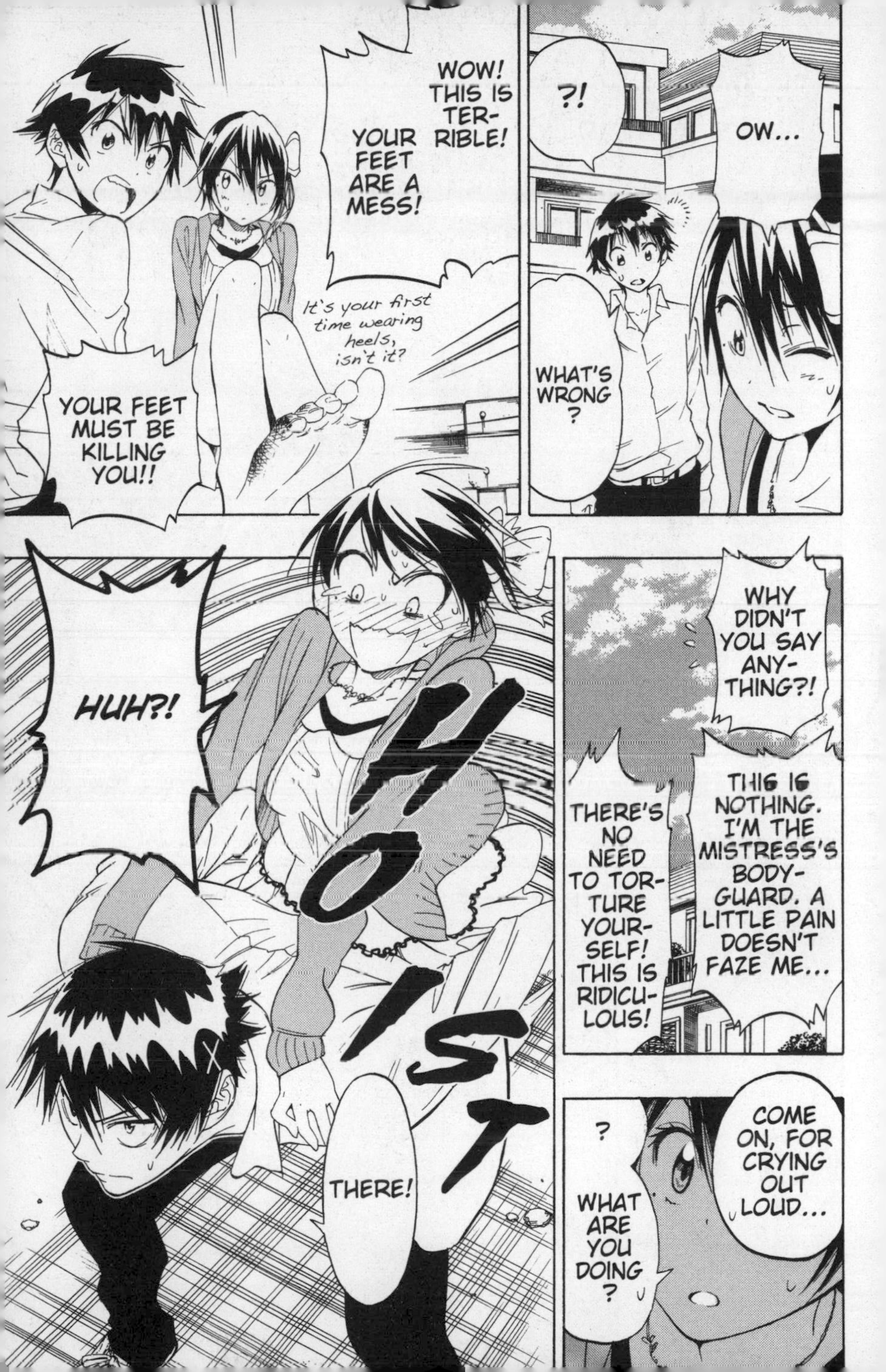
OW...
?!
WHAT'S WRONG?
WOW! THIS IS TERRIBLE!
YOUR FEET ARE A MESS!
It's your first time wearing heels, isn't it?
YOUR FEET MUST BE KILLING YOU!!
WHY DIDN'T YOU SAY ANYTHING?!
THIS IS NOTHING. I'M THE MISTRESS'S BODYGUARD. A LITTLE PAIN DOESN'T FAZE ME...
THERE'S NO NEED TO TORTURE YOURSELF! THIS IS RIDICULOUS!
COME ON, FOR CRYING OUT LOUD...
?
WHAT ARE YOU DOING?
HUH?!
HOIST
THERE!

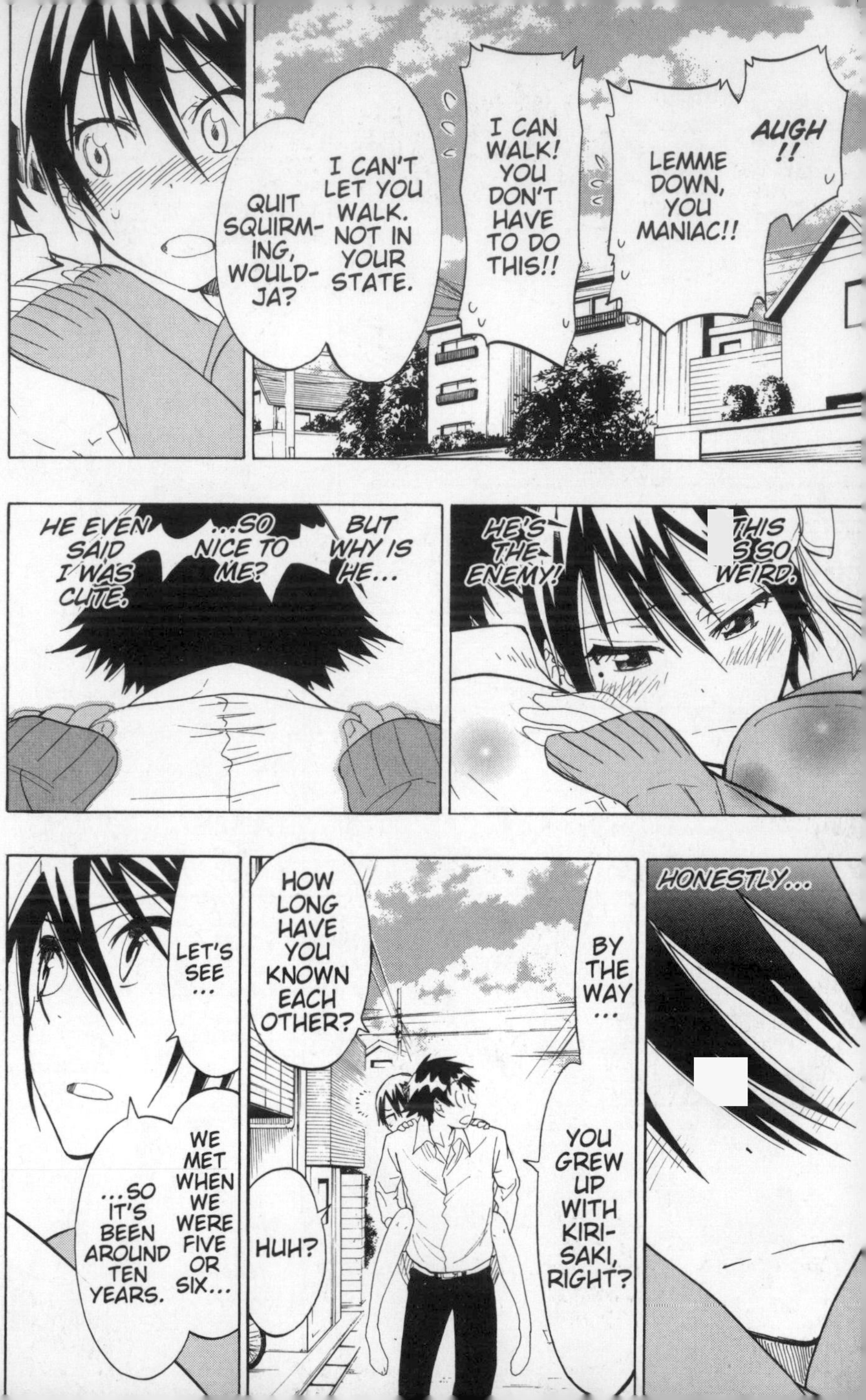
AUGH!!
LEMME DOWN, YOU MANIAC!!
I CAN WALK! YOU DON'T HAVE TO DO THIS!!
I CAN'T LET YOU WALK. NOT IN YOUR STATE.
QUIT SQUIRMING, WOULDJA?
THIS S SO WEIRD.
HE'S THE ENEMY!
BUT WHY IS HE...
...SO NICE TO ME?
HE EVEN SAID I WAS CUTE.
HONESTLY...
BY THE WAY...
YOU GREW UP WITH KIRISAKI, RIGHT?
HUH?
HOW LONG HAVE YOU KNOWN EACH OTHER?
LET'S SEE...
WE MET WHEN WE WERE FIVE OR SIX...
...SO IT'S BEEN AROUND TEN YEARS.

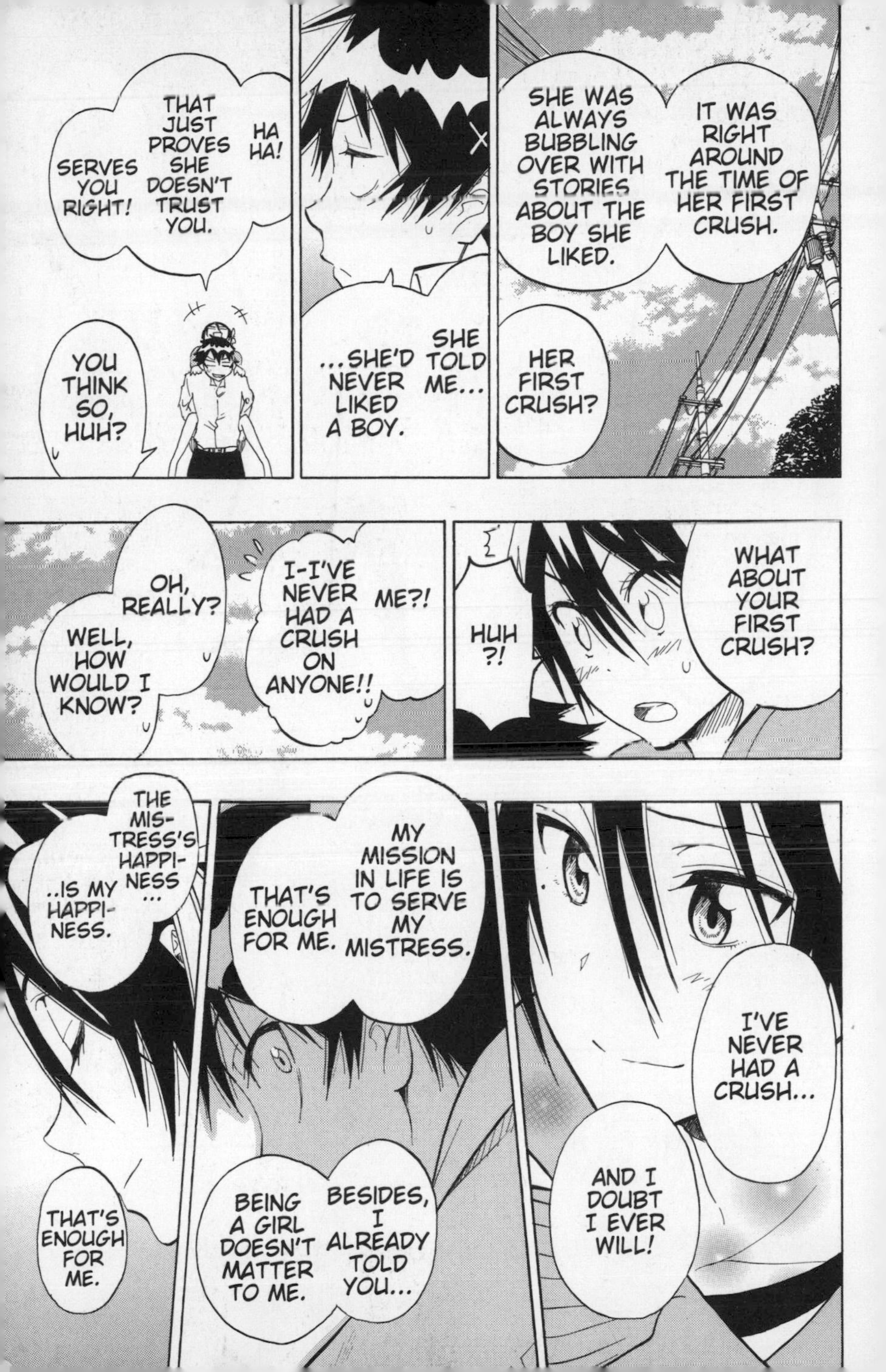
IT WAS RIGHT AROUND THE TIME OF HER FIRST CRUSH.
SHE WAS ALWAYS BUBBLING OVER WITH STORIES ABOUT THE BOY SHE LIKED.
HER FIRST CRUSH?
SHE TOLD ME...
...SHE'D NEVER LIKED A BOY.
HA HA!
THAT JUST PROVES SHE DOESN'T TRUST YOU.
SERVES YOU RIGHT!
YOU THINK SO, HUH?
WHAT ABOUT YOUR FIRST CRUSH?
HUH ?!
ME?!
I-I'VE NEVER HAD A CRUSH ON ANYONE!!
OH, REALLY?
WELL, HOW WOULD I KNOW?
I'VE NEVER HAD A CRUSH...
AND I DOUBT I EVER WILL!
MY MISSION IN LIFE IS TO SERVE MY MISTRESS.
THAT'S ENOUGH FOR ME.
BESIDES, I ALREADY TOLD YOU...
BEING A GIRL DOESN'T MATTER TO ME.
THE MIS-TRESS'S HAPPI-NESS...
..IS MY HAPPI-NESS.
THAT'S ENOUGH FOR ME.

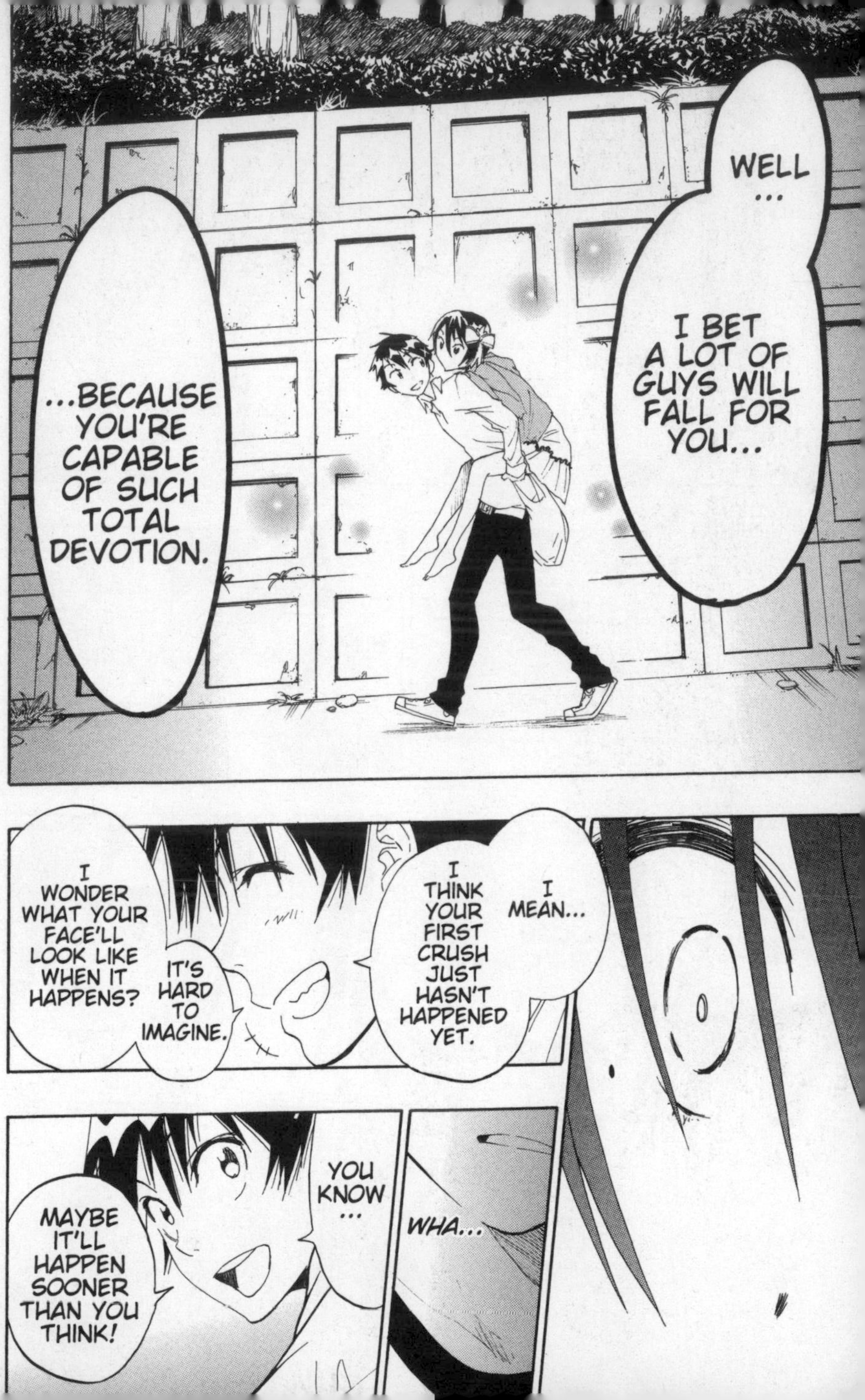
WELL ...
I BET A LOT OF GUYS WILL FALL FOR YOU...
...BECAUSE YOU'RE CAPABLE OF SUCH TOTAL DEVOTION.
I MEAN...
I THINK YOUR FIRST CRUSH JUST HASN'T HAPPENED YET.
IT'S HARD TO IMAGINE.
I WONDER WHAT YOUR FACE'LL LOOK LIKE WHEN IT HAPPENS?
WHA...
YOU KNOW ...
MAYBE IT'LL HAPPEN SOONER THAN YOU THINK!

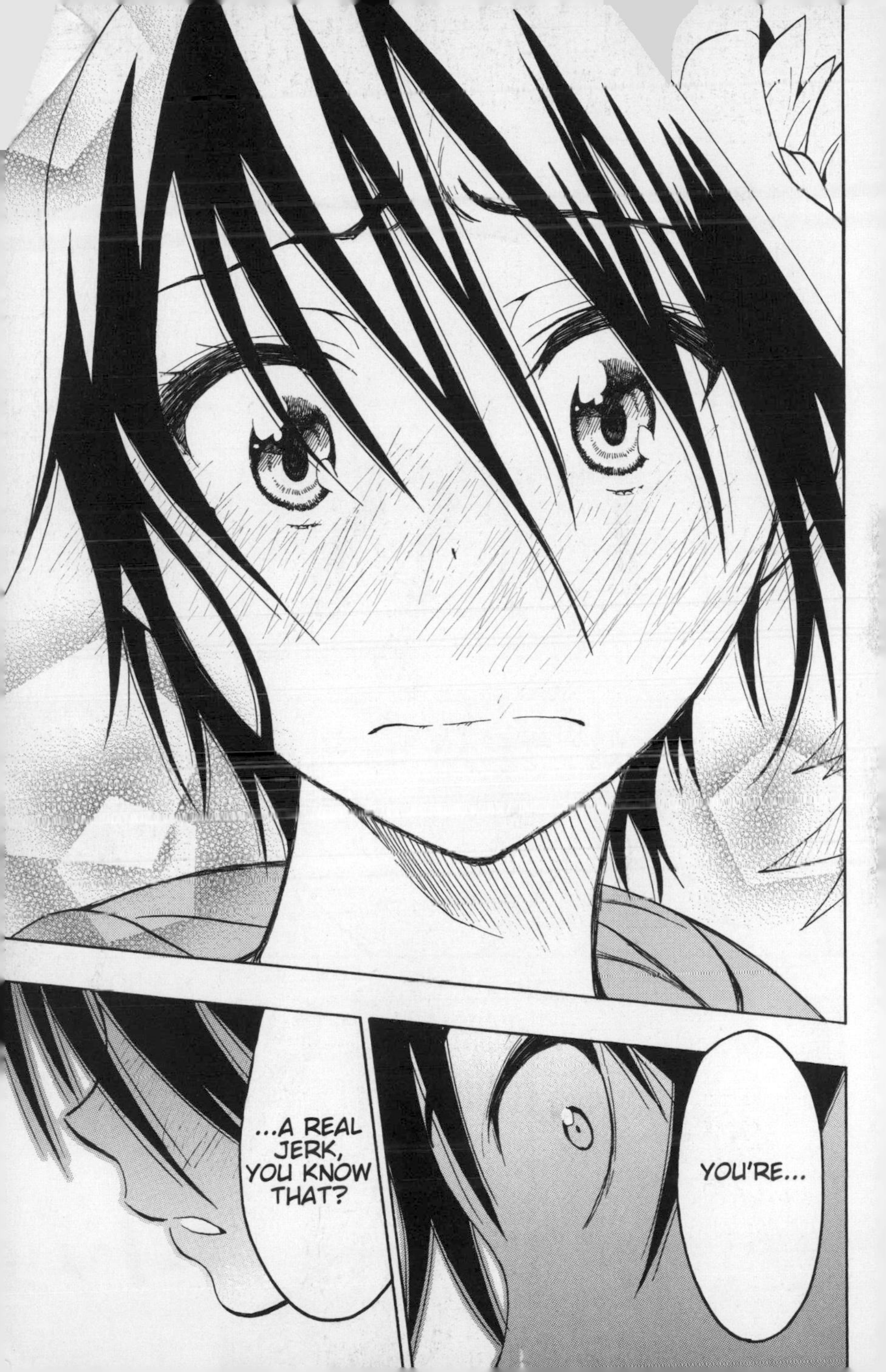
YOU'RE...
...A REAL JERK, YOU KNOW THAT?

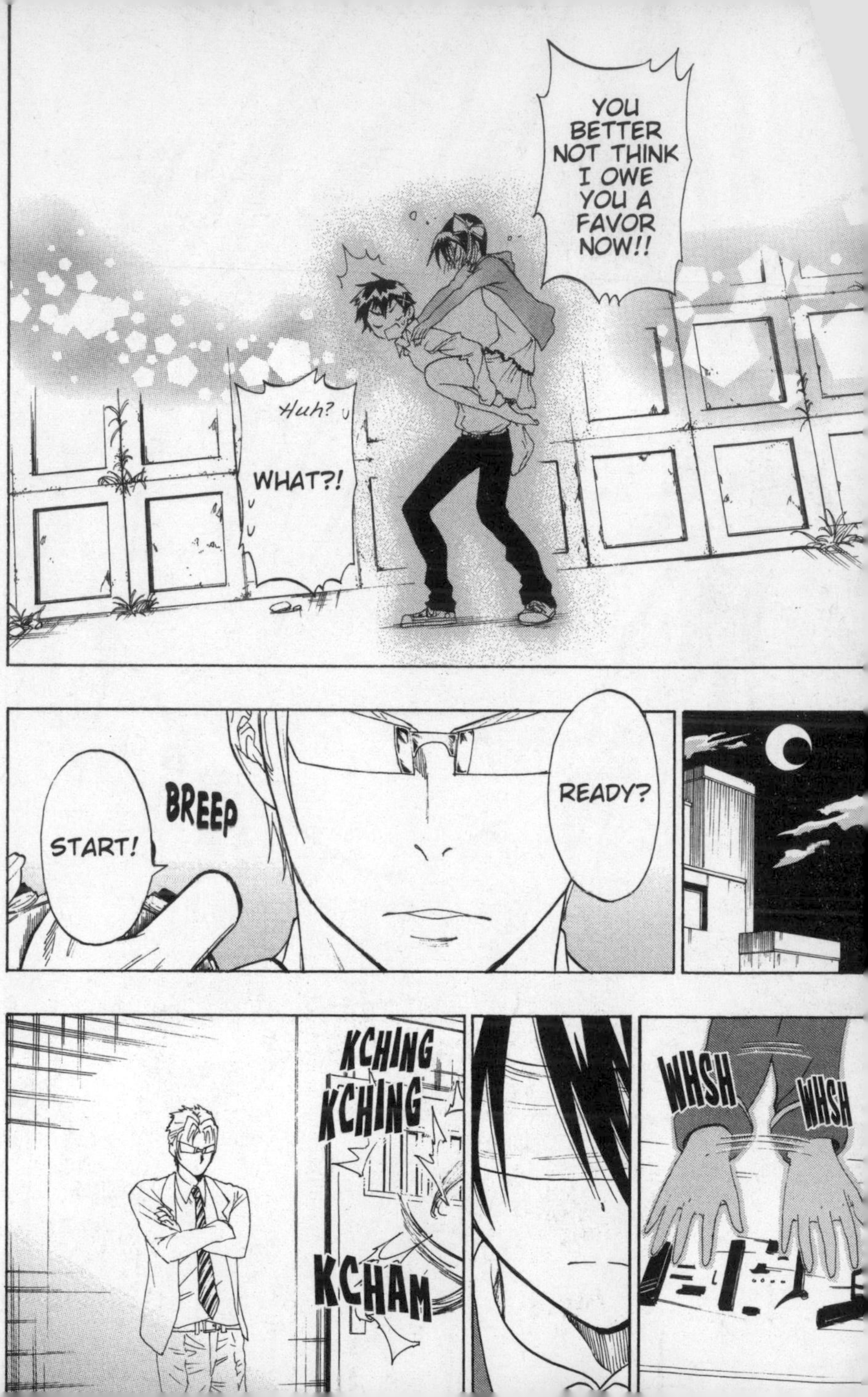
YOU BETTER NOT THINK I OWE YOU A FAVOR NOW!!
Huh?
WHAT?!
READY?
BREEP
START!
WHSH
WHSH
KCHING
KCHING
KCHAM

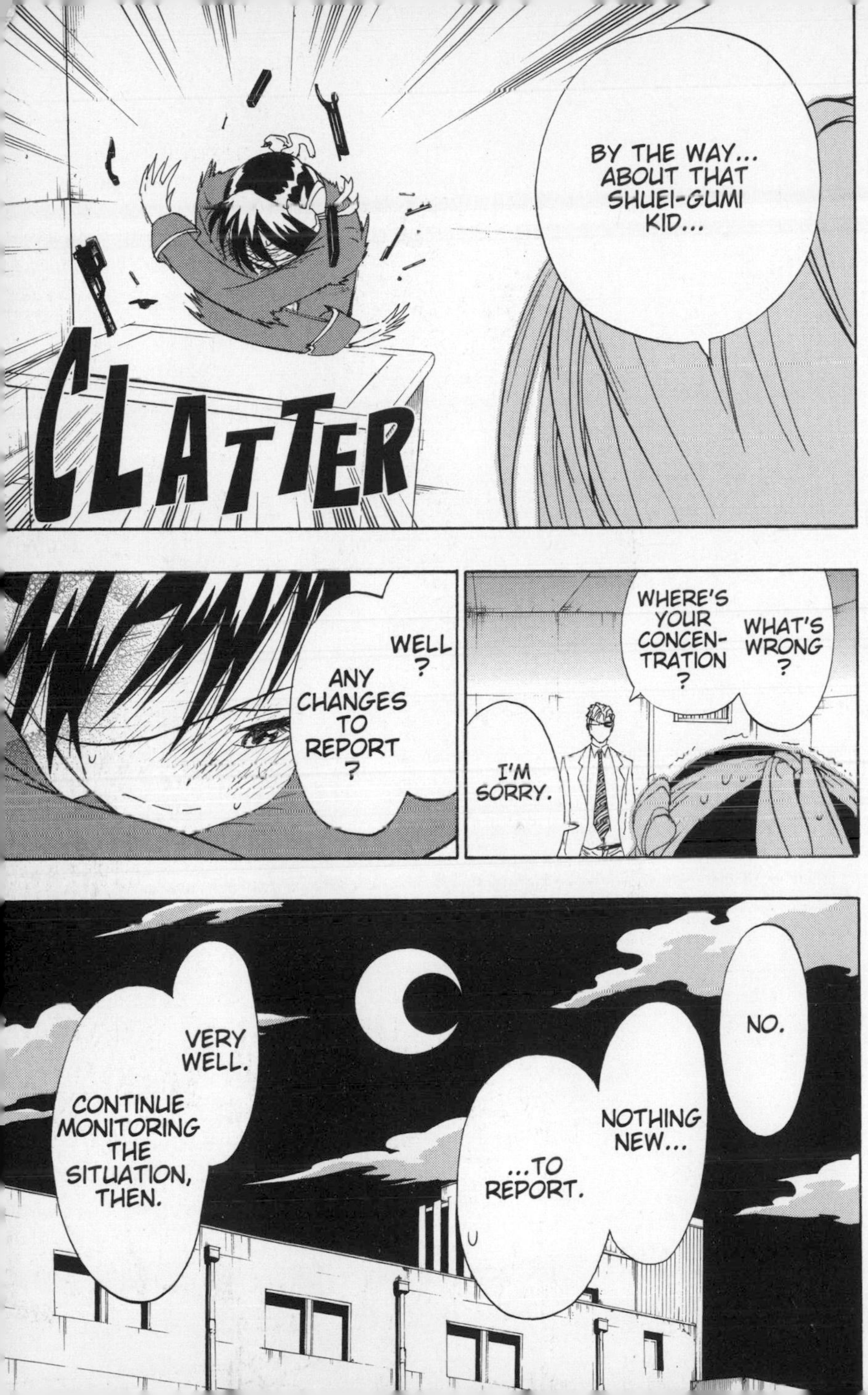
BY THE WAY... ABOUT THAT SHUEI-GUMI KID...
CLATTER
WHAT'S WRONG?
WHERE'S YOUR CONCENTRATION?
I'M SORRY.
WELL?
ANY CHANGES TO REPORT?
NO.
NOTHING NEW...
...TO REPORT.
VERY WELL.
CONTINUE MONITORING THE SITUATION, THEN.

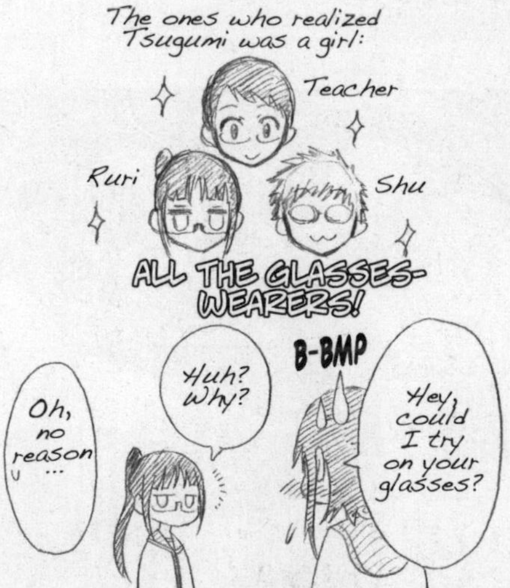
The ones who realized Tsugumi was a girl:
Teacher
Ruri
Shu
ALL THE GLASSES-WEARERS!
Hey, could I try on your glasses?
B-BMP
Huh? Why?
Oh, no reason...

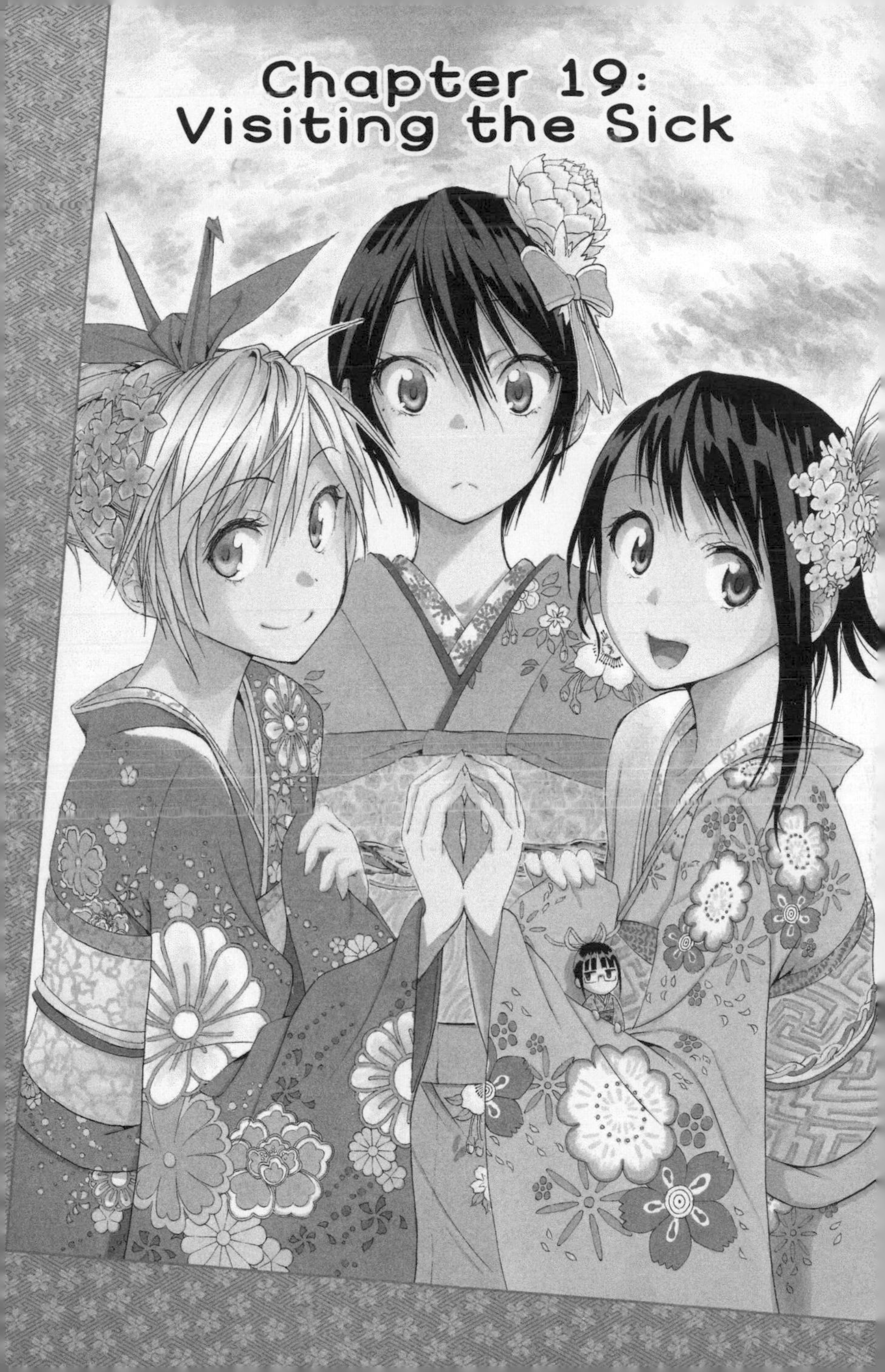
Chapter 19:
Visiting the Sick

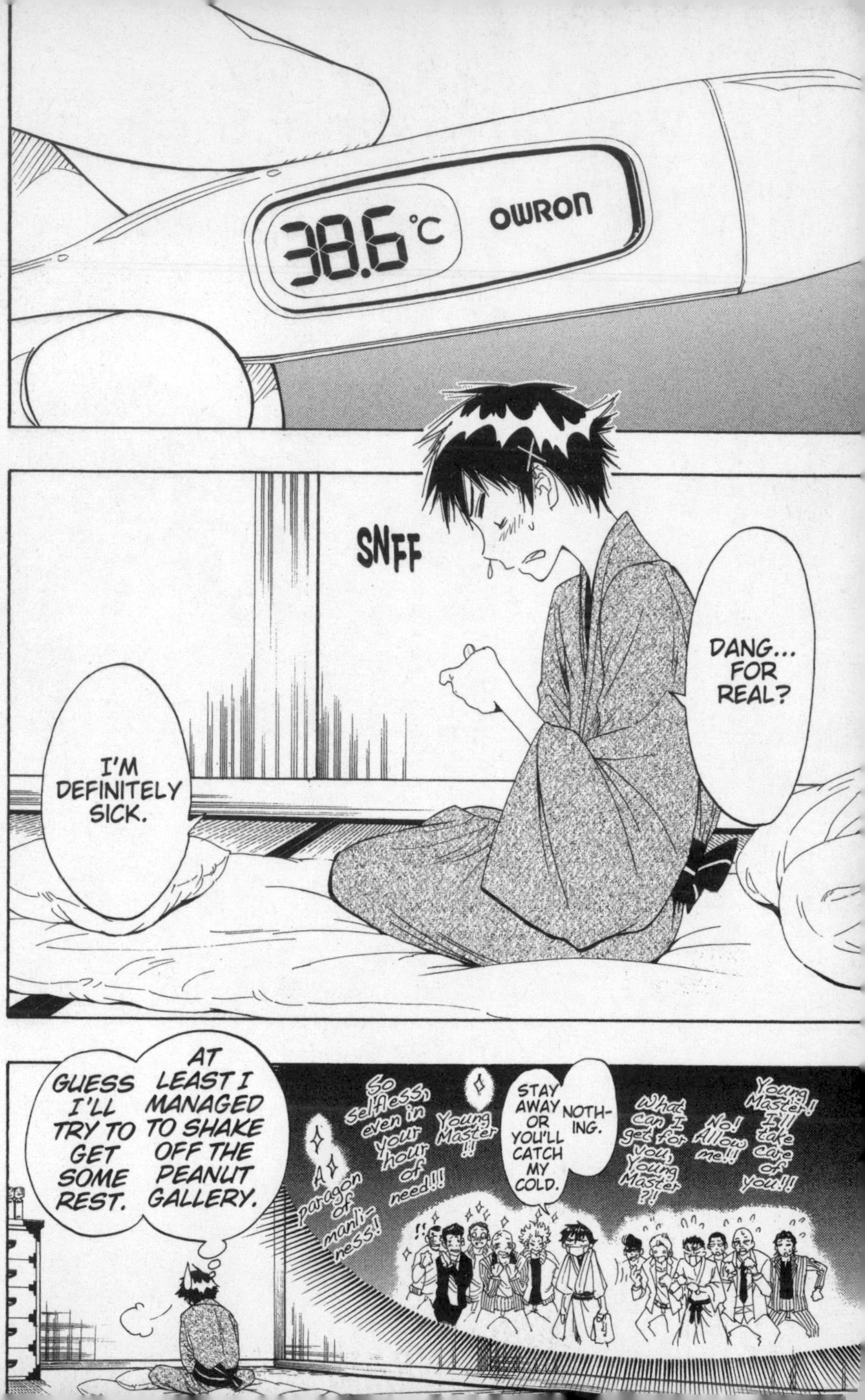
38.6 °C
OWRON
DANG... FOR REAL?
SNFF
I'M DEFINITELY SICK.
Young Master! I'll take care of you!!
No! Allow me!!
What can I get for you, Young Master?!
NOTHING.
STAY AWAY OR YOU'LL CATCH MY COLD.
Young Master!!
So selfless, even in your hour of need!!!
A paragon of manliness!
AT LEAST I MANAGED TO SHAKE OFF THE PEANUT GALLERY.
GUESS I'LL TRY TO GET SOME REST.

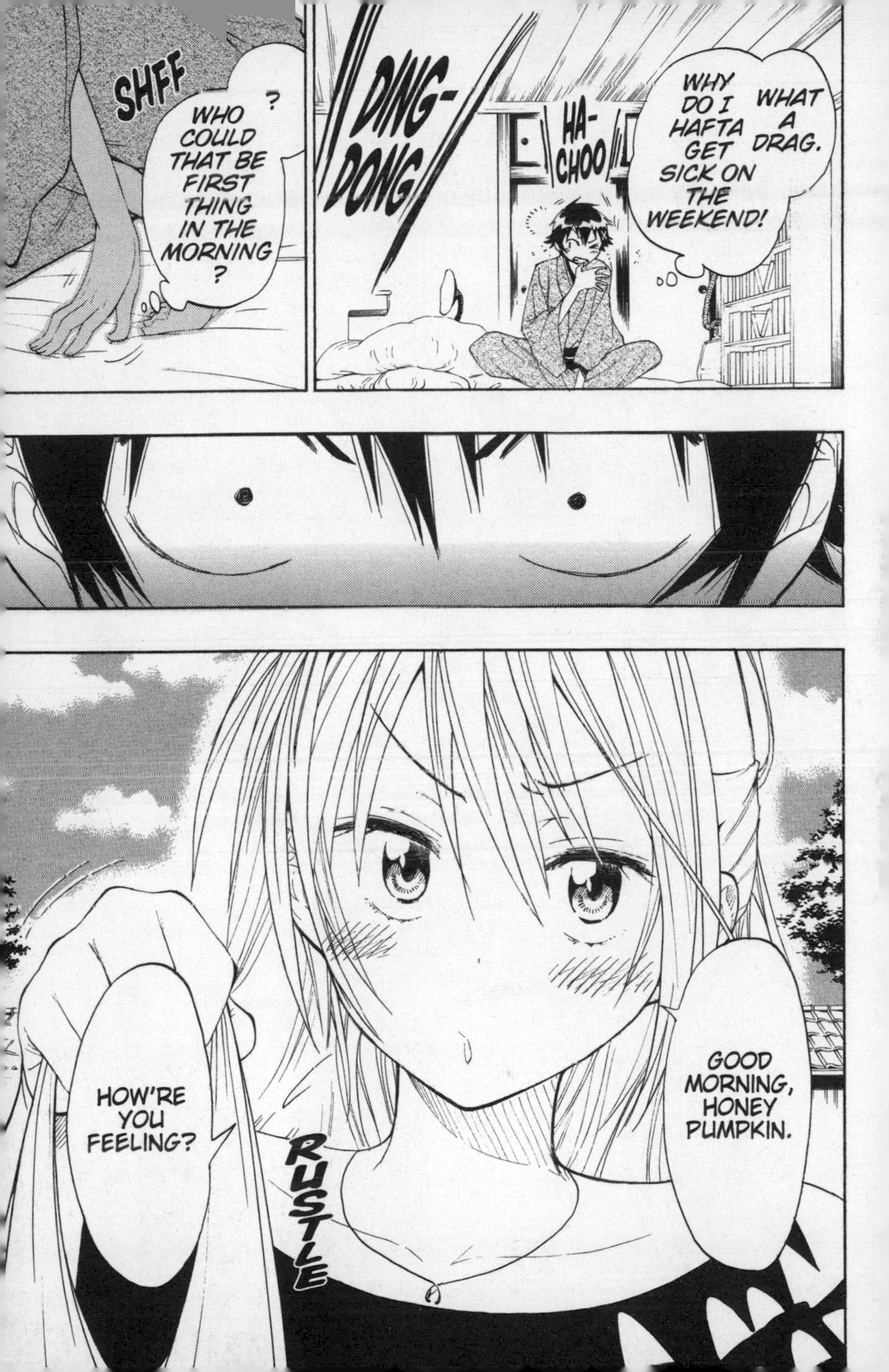
WHAT A DRAG.
WHY DO I HAFTA GET SICK ON THE WEEKEND!
HA-CHOO
DING-DONG
SHFF
? WHO COULD THAT BE FIRST THING IN THE MORNING?
GOOD MORNING, HONEY PUMPKIN.
RUSTLE
HOW'RE YOU FEELING?

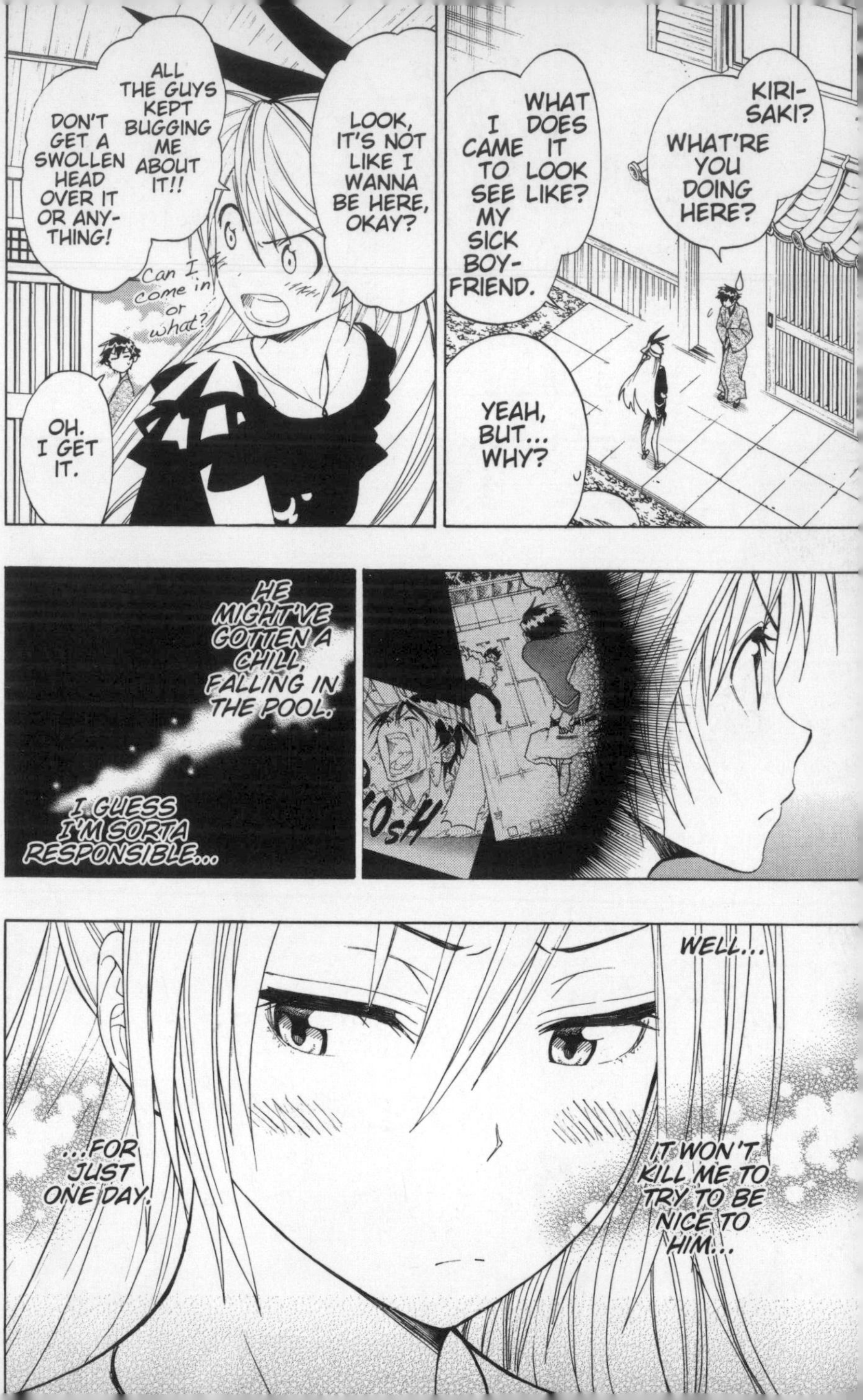
KIRI-SAKI? WHAT'RE YOU DOING HERE?
WHAT DOES IT LOOK LIKE? I CAME TO SEE MY SICK BOY-FRIEND.
YEAH, BUT... WHY?
LOOK, IT'S NOT LIKE I WANNA BE HERE, OKAY?
ALL THE GUYS KEPT BUGGING ME ABOUT IT!!
DON'T GET A SWOLLEN HEAD OVER IT OR ANY-THING!
Can I come in or what?
OH. I GET IT.
HE MIGHT'VE GOTTEN A CHILL, FALLING IN THE POOL.
I GUESS I'M SORTA RESPONSIBLE...
WELL...
IT WON'T KILL ME TO TRY TO BE NICE TO HIM...
...FOR JUST ONE DAY.

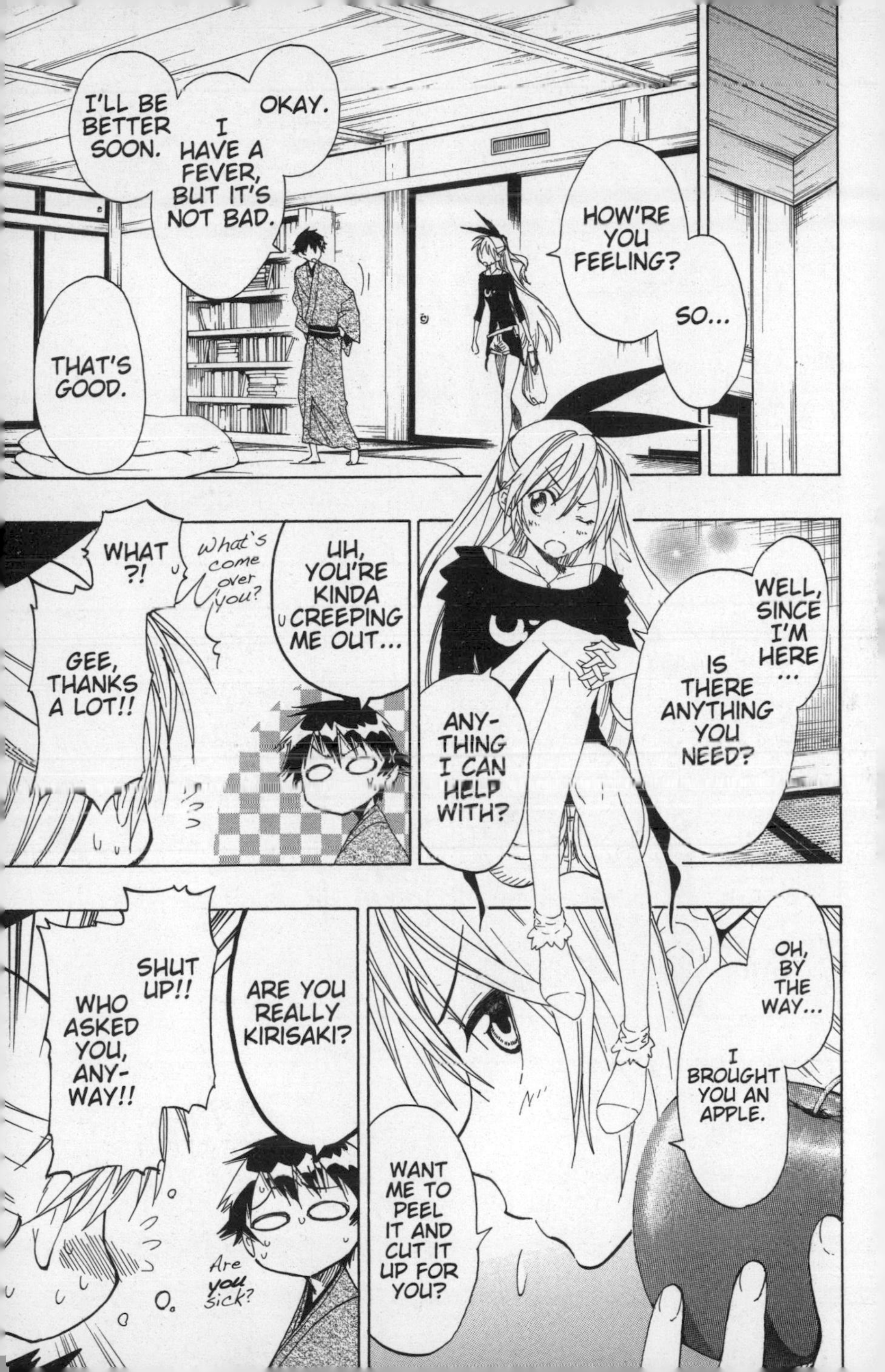
HOW'RE YOU FEELING?
SO...
OKAY. I HAVE A FEVER, BUT IT'S NOT BAD.
I'LL BE BETTER SOON.
THAT'S GOOD.
WELL, SINCE I'M HERE...
IS THERE ANYTHING YOU NEED?
ANYTHING I CAN HELP WITH?
UH, YOU'RE KINDA CREEPING ME OUT...
What's come over you?
WHAT?!
GEE, THANKS A LOT!!
OH, BY THE WAY...
I BROUGHT YOU AN APPLE.
WANT ME TO PEEL IT AND CUT IT UP FOR YOU?
ARE YOU REALLY KIRISAKI?
Are you sick?
SHUT UP!!
WHO ASKED YOU, ANYWAY!!

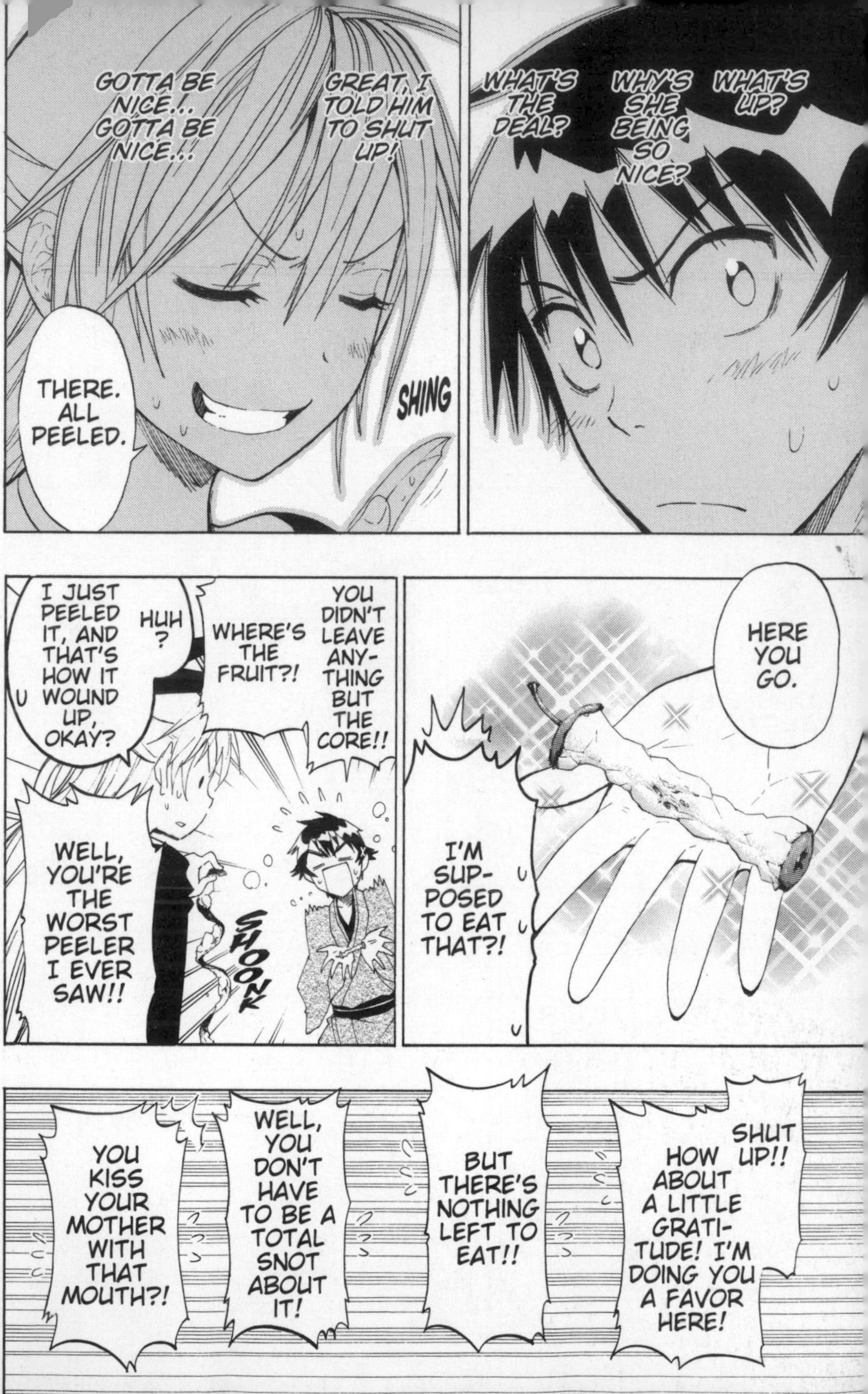

WHAT'S UP?
WHY'S SHE BEING SO NICE?
WHAT'S THE DEAL?
GREAT, I TOLD HIM TO SHUT UP!
GOTTA BE NICE... GOTTA BE NICE...
SHING
THERE. ALL PEELED.
HERE YOU GO.
I'M SUP-POSED TO EAT THAT?!
YOU DIDN'T LEAVE ANY-THING BUT THE CORE!!
WHERE'S THE FRUIT?!
HUH?
I JUST PEELED IT, AND THAT'S HOW IT WOUND UP, OKAY?
SHOONK
WELL, YOU'RE THE WORST PEELER I EVER SAW!!
SHUT UP!!
HOW ABOUT A LITTLE GRATI-TUDE! I'M DOING YOU A FAVOR HERE!
BUT THERE'S NOTHING LEFT TO EAT!!
WELL, YOU DON'T HAVE TO BE A TOTAL SNOT ABOUT IT!
YOU KISS YOUR MOTHER WITH THAT MOUTH?!

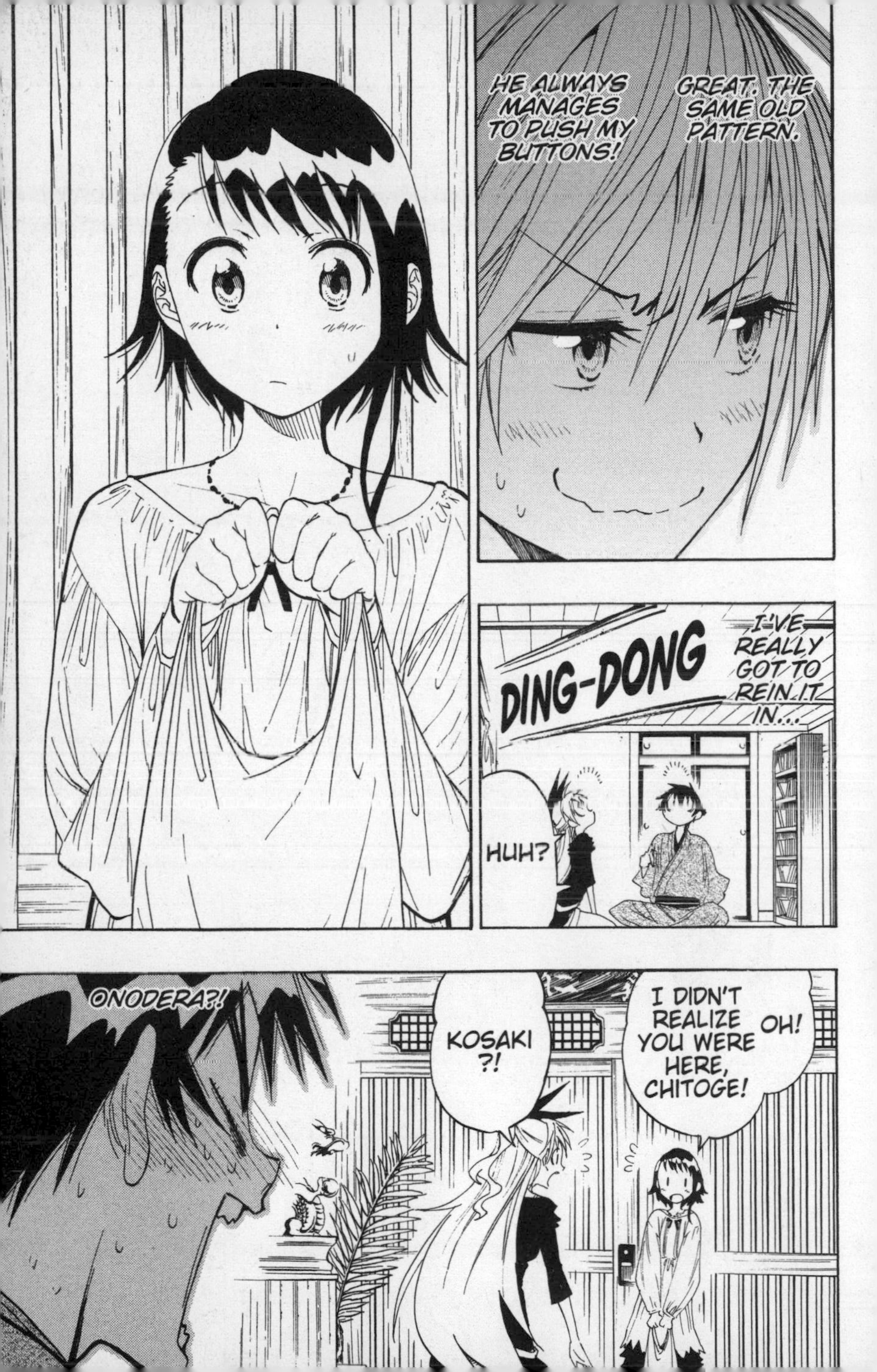
GREAT. THE SAME OLD PATTERN.
HE ALWAYS MANAGES TO PUSH MY BUTTONS!
I'VE REALLY GOT TO REIN IT IN...
DING-DONG
HUH?
OH! I DIDN'T REALIZE YOU WERE HERE, CHITOGE!
KOSAKI ?!
ONODERA?!

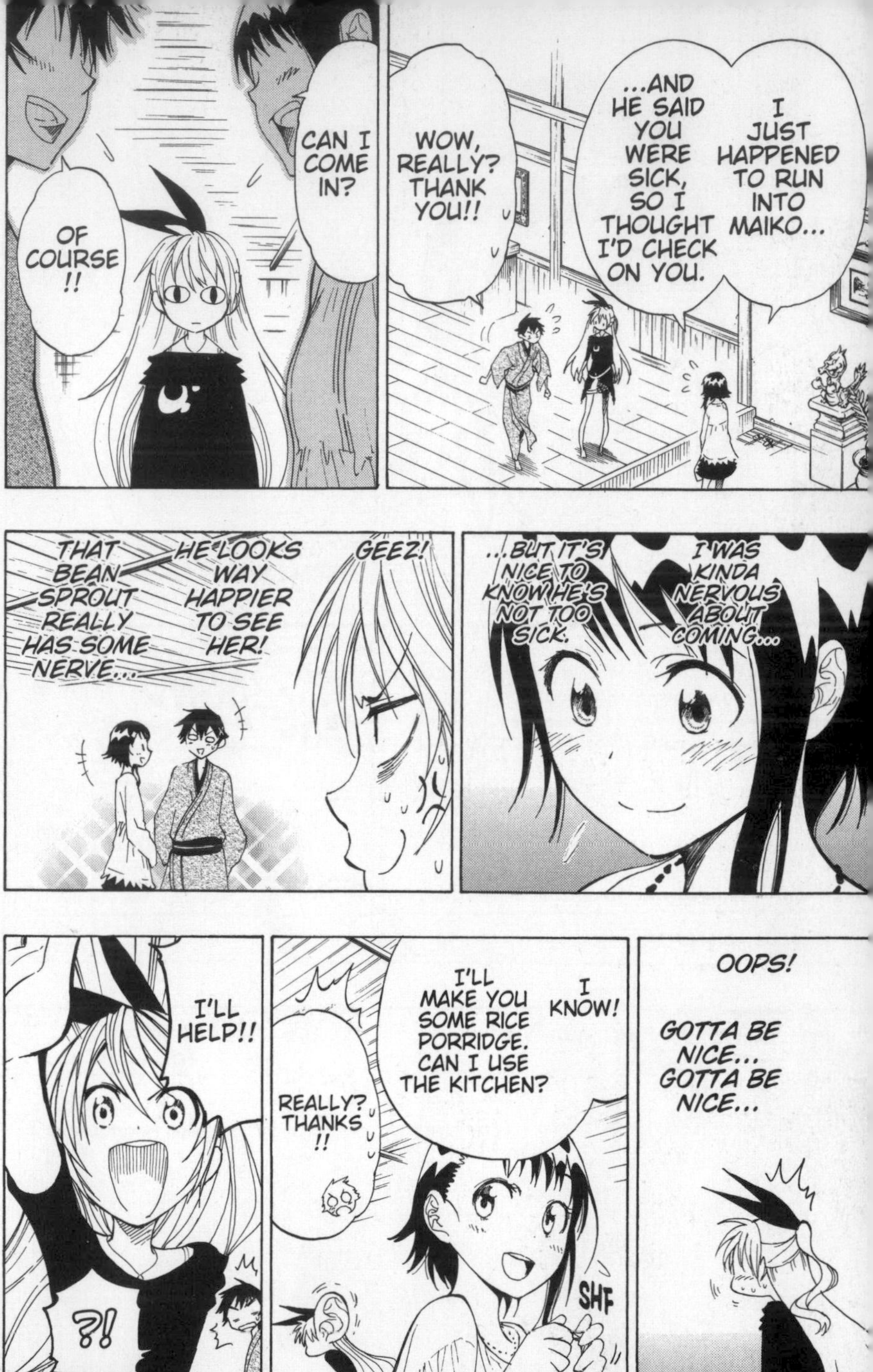
I JUST HAPPENED TO RUN INTO MAIKO...
...AND HE SAID YOU WERE SICK, SO I THOUGHT I'D CHECK ON YOU.
WOW, REALLY? THANK YOU!!
CAN I COME IN?
OF COURSE!!
I WAS KINDA NERVOUS ABOUT COMING...
...BUT IT'S NICE TO KNOW HE'S NOT TOO SICK.
GEEZ!
HE LOOKS WAY HAPPIER TO SEE HER!
THAT BEAN SPROUT REALLY HAS SOME NERVE...
OOPS!
GOTTA BE NICE... GOTTA BE NICE...
I KNOW!
I'LL MAKE YOU SOME RICE PORRIDGE. CAN I USE THE KITCHEN?
REALLY? THANKS!!
SHF
I'LL HELP!!
?!

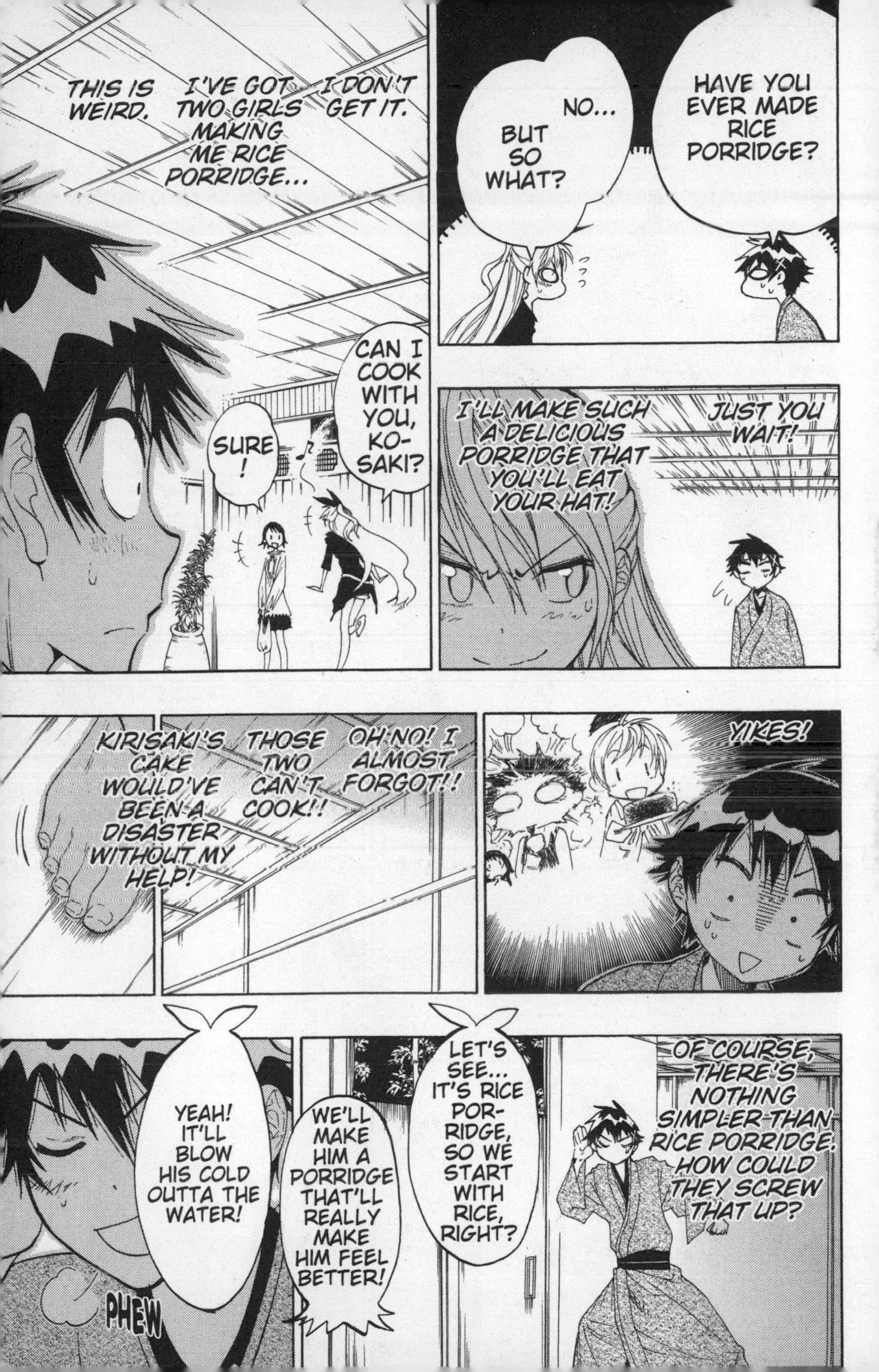
HAVE YOU EVER MADE RICE PORRIDGE?
NO... BUT SO WHAT?
JUST YOU WAIT!
I'LL MAKE SUCH A DELICIOUS PORRIDGE THAT YOU'LL EAT YOUR HAT!
I DON'T GET IT.
I'VE GOT TWO GIRLS MAKING ME RICE PORRIDGE...
THIS IS WEIRD.
CAN I COOK WITH YOU, KO-SAKI?
SURE!
YIKES!
OH NO! I ALMOST FORGOT!!
THOSE TWO CAN'T COOK!!
KIRISAKI'S CAKE WOULD'VE BEEN A DISASTER WITHOUT MY HELP!
OF COURSE, THERE'S NOTHING SIMPLER THAN RICE PORRIDGE. HOW COULD THEY SCREW THAT UP?
LET'S SEE... IT'S RICE POR-RIDGE, SO WE START WITH RICE, RIGHT?
WE'LL MAKE HIM A PORRIDGE THAT'LL REALLY MAKE HIM FEEL BETTER!
YEAH! IT'LL BLOW HIS COLD OUTTA THE WATER!
PHEW

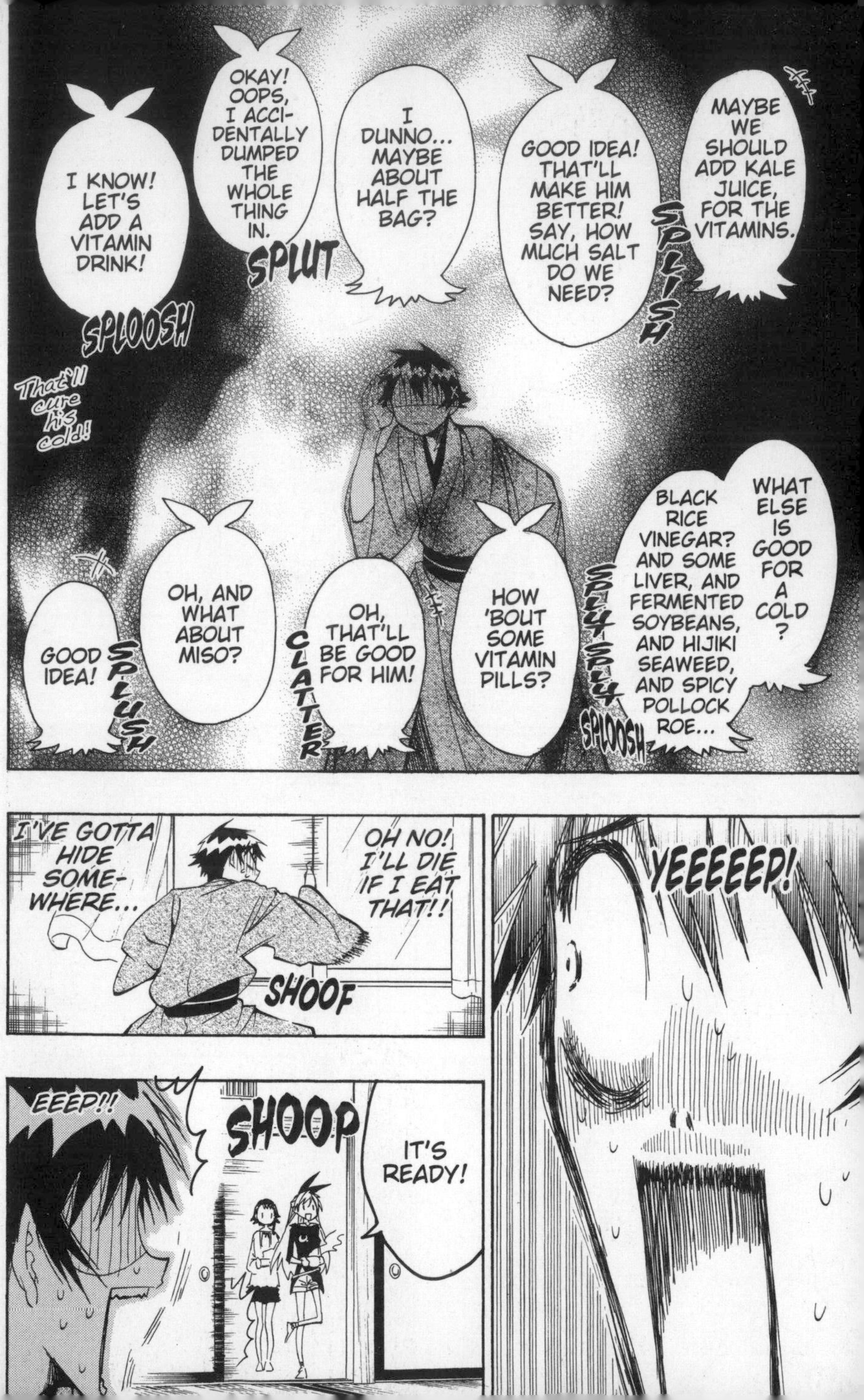
MAYBE WE SHOULD ADD KALE JUICE, FOR THE VITAMINS.
GOOD IDEA! THAT'LL MAKE HIM BETTER! SAY, HOW MUCH SALT DO WE NEED?
SPLISH
I DUNNO... MAYBE ABOUT HALF THE BAG?
OKAY! OOPS, I ACCIDENTALLY DUMPED THE WHOLE THING IN.
SPLUT
I KNOW! LET'S ADD A VITAMIN DRINK!
SPLOOSH
That'll cure his cold!
WHAT ELSE IS GOOD FOR A COLD?
BLACK RICE VINEGAR? AND SOME LIVER, AND FERMENTED SOYBEANS, AND HIJIKI SEAWEED, AND SPICY POLLOCK ROE...
SPLOOSH
SPLUT SPLUT
HOW 'BOUT SOME VITAMIN PILLS?
OH, THAT'LL BE GOOD FOR HIM!
CLATTER
OH, AND WHAT ABOUT MISO?
GOOD IDEA!
SPLUSH
YEEEEEP!
OH NO! I'LL DIE IF I EAT THAT!!
I'VE GOTTA HIDE SOMEWHERE...
SHOOF
IT'S READY!
SHOOP
EEEP!!

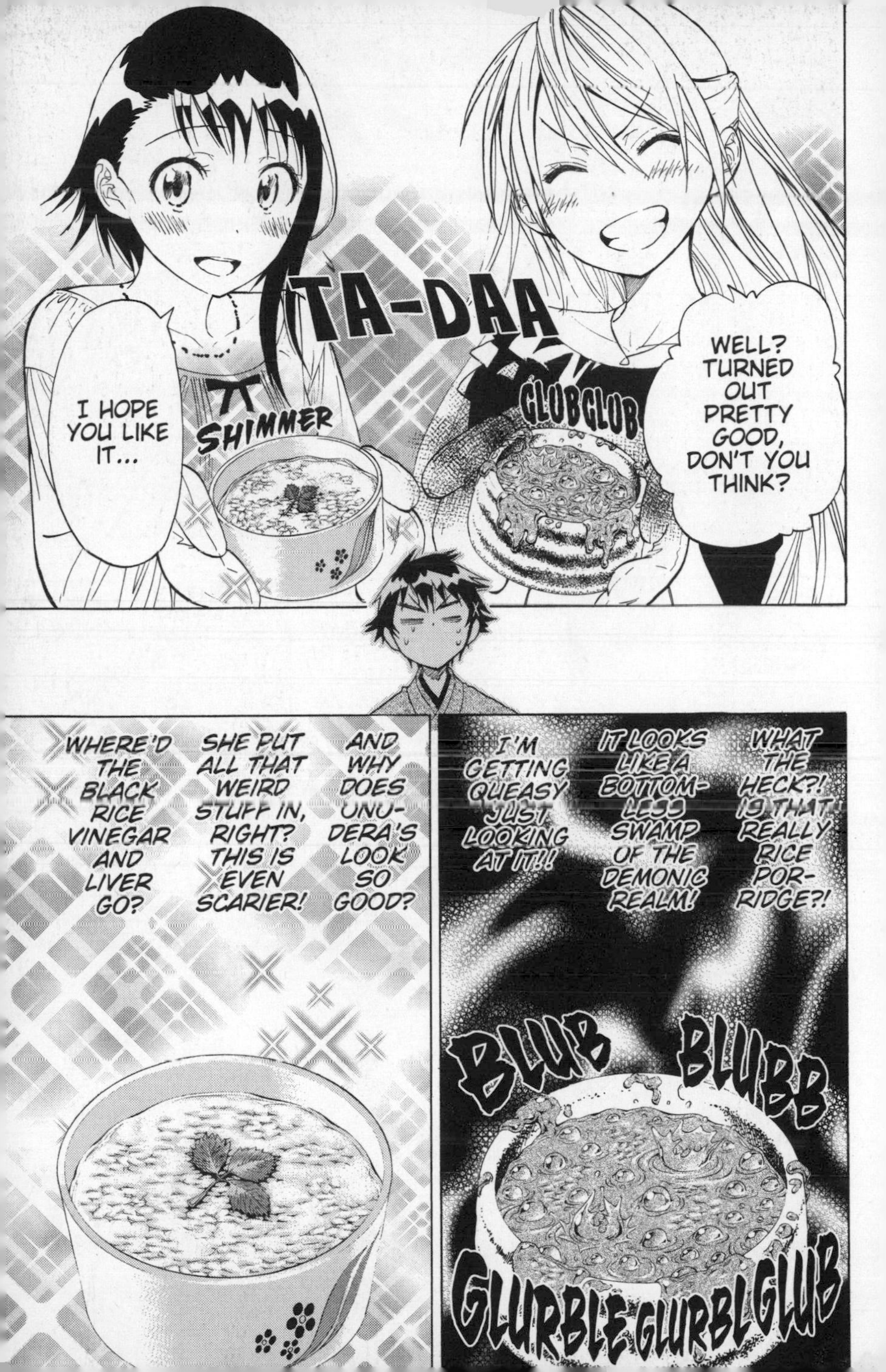
WELL? TURNED OUT PRETTY GOOD, DON'T YOU THINK?
CLUBGLUB
TA-DAA
SHIMMER
I HOPE YOU LIKE IT...
WHAT THE HECK?! IS THAT REALLY RICE PORRIDGE?!
IT LOOKS LIKE A BOTTOMLESS SWAMP OF THE DEMONIC REALM!
I'M GETTING QUEASY JUST LOOKING AT IT!!
BLUBB
BLUB
GLURBLE GLURBL GLUB
AND WHY DOES ONODERA'S LOOK SO GOOD?
SHE PUT ALL THAT WEIRD STUFF IN, RIGHT? THIS IS EVEN SCARIER!
WHERE'D THE BLACK RICE VINEGAR AND LIVER GO?

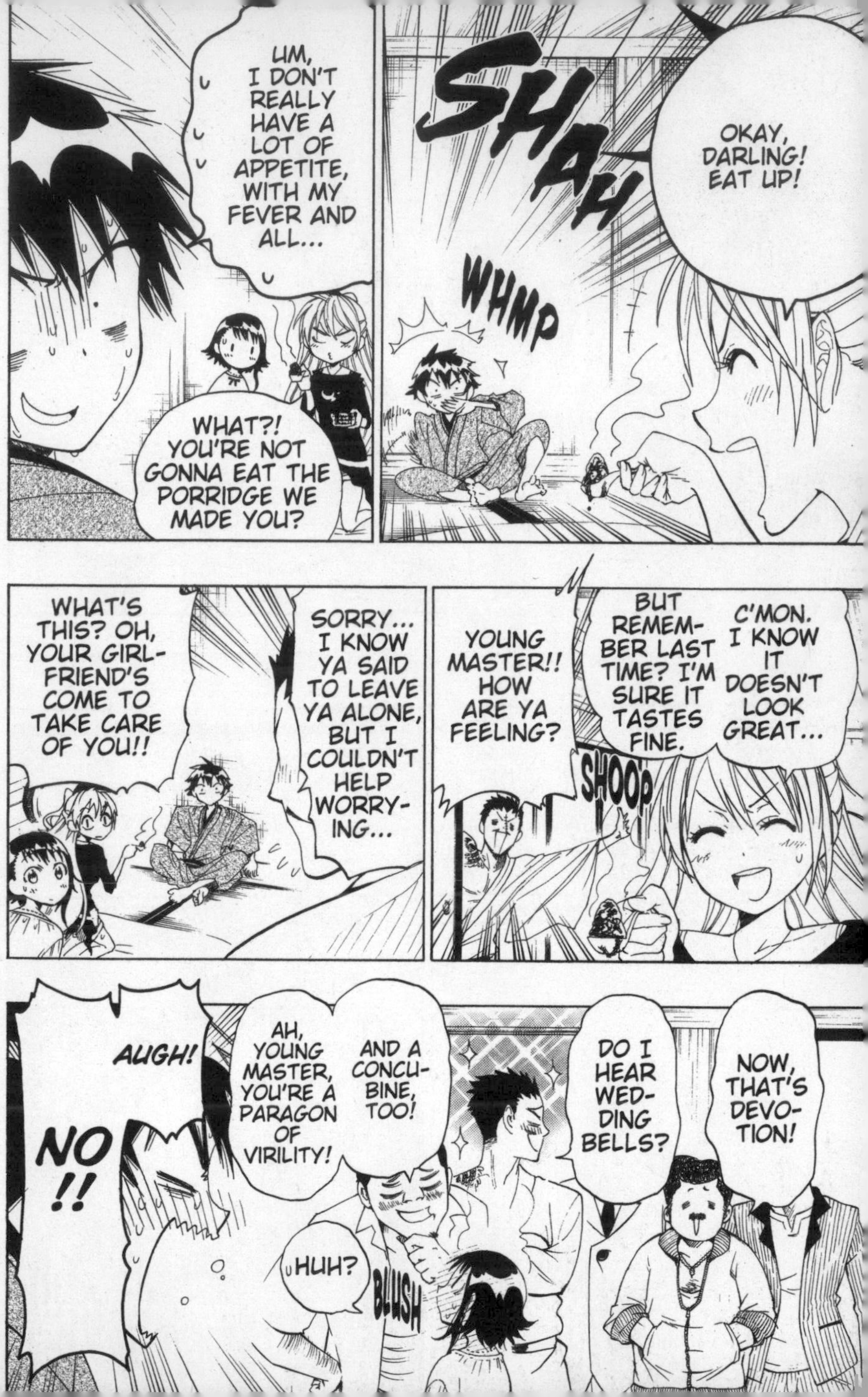
OKAY, DARLING! EAT UP!
SHAH
WHMP
UM, I DON'T REALLY HAVE A LOT OF APPETITE, WITH MY FEVER AND ALL...
WHAT?! YOU'RE NOT GONNA EAT THE PORRIDGE WE MADE YOU?
C'MON. I KNOW IT DOESN'T LOOK GREAT...
BUT REMEMBER LAST TIME? I'M SURE IT TASTES FINE.
SHOOP
YOUNG MASTER!! HOW ARE YA FEELING?
SORRY... I KNOW YA SAID TO LEAVE YA ALONE, BUT I COULDN'T HELP WORRYING...
WHAT'S THIS? OH, YOUR GIRLFRIEND'S COME TO TAKE CARE OF YOU!!
NOW, THAT'S DEVOTION!
DO I HEAR WEDDING BELLS?
AND A CONCUBINE, TOO!
AH, YOUNG MASTER, YOU'RE A PARAGON OF VIRILITY!
BLUSH
HUH?
AUGH!
NO!!

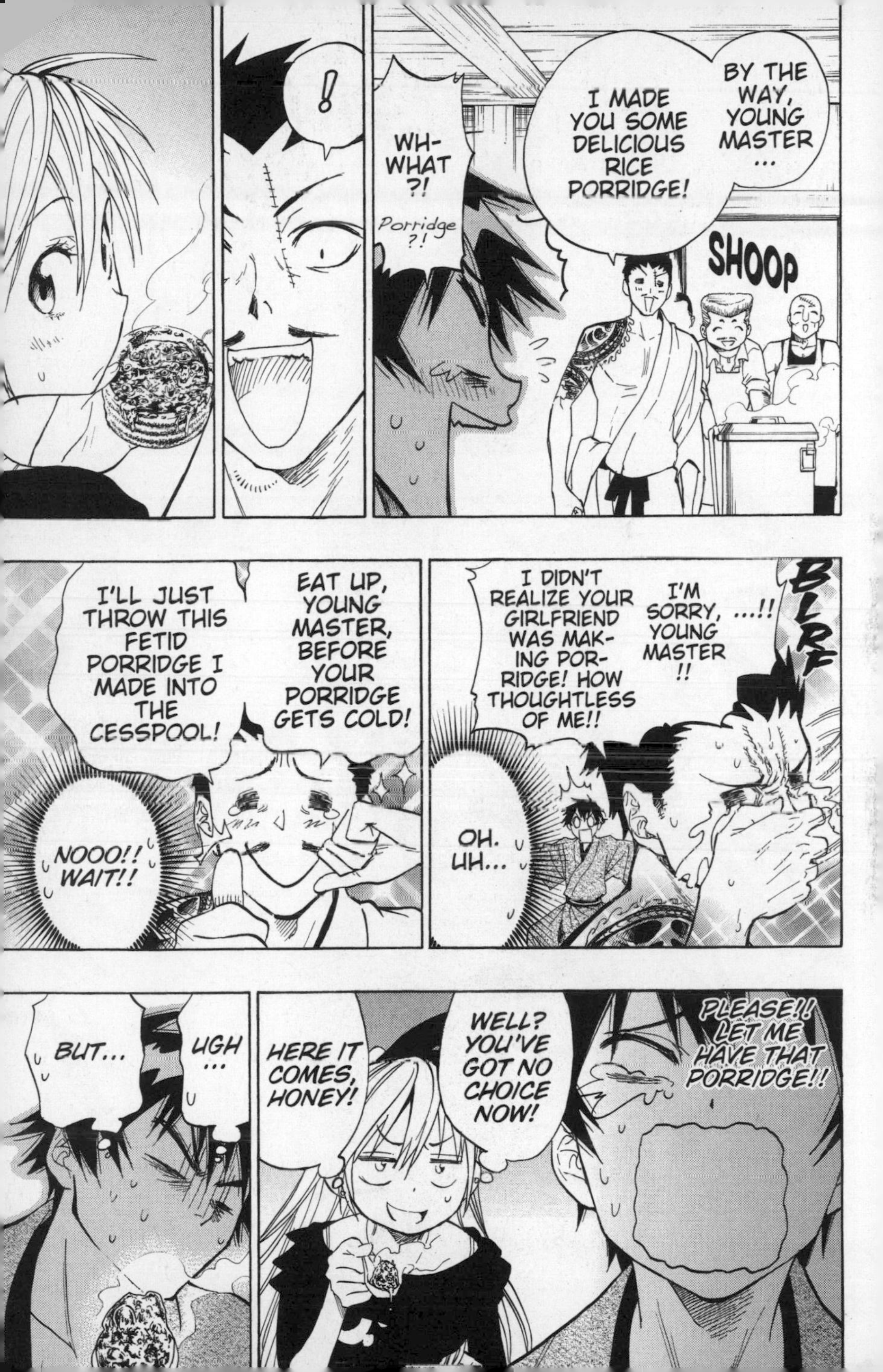
BY THE WAY, YOUNG MASTER ...
I MADE YOU SOME DELICIOUS RICE PORRIDGE!
SHOOP
WH- WHAT ?!
Porridge ?!
!
BLRF
I'M SORRY, YOUNG MASTER !!
...!!
I DIDN'T REALIZE YOUR GIRLFRIEND WAS MAK- ING POR- RIDGE! HOW THOUGHTLESS OF ME!!
OH. UH...
EAT UP, YOUNG MASTER, BEFORE YOUR PORRIDGE GETS COLD!
I'LL JUST THROW THIS FETID PORRIDGE I MADE INTO THE CESSPOOL!
NOOO!! WAIT!!
PLEASE!! LET ME HAVE THAT PORRIDGE!!
WELL? YOU'VE GOT NO CHOICE NOW!
HERE IT COMES, HONEY!
UGH ...
BUT...

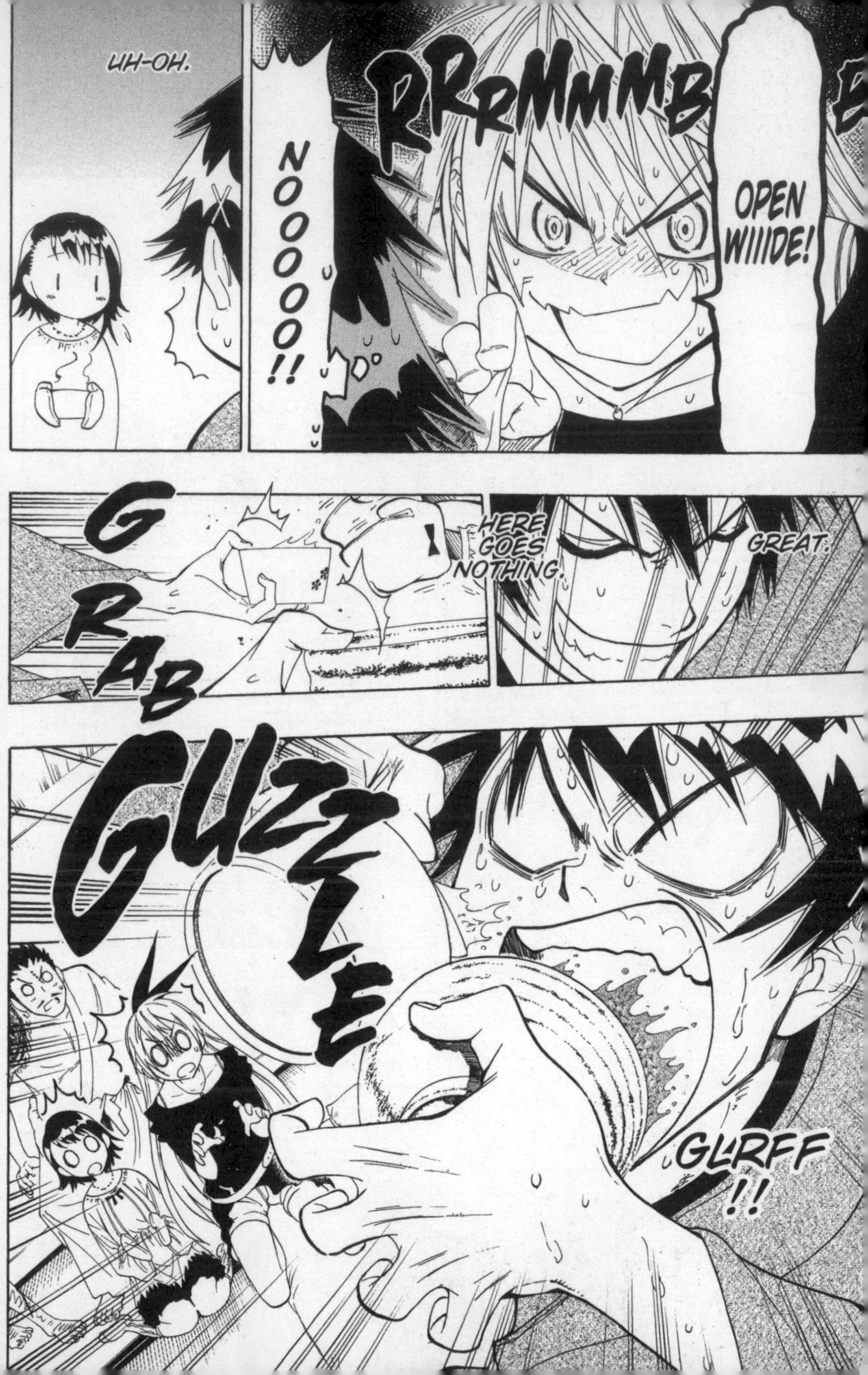
OPEN WIIIDE!
RRRMMMB
NOOOOOO!!
UH-OH.
GREAT.
HERE GOES NOTHING.
GRAB
GUZZLE
GLRFF!!

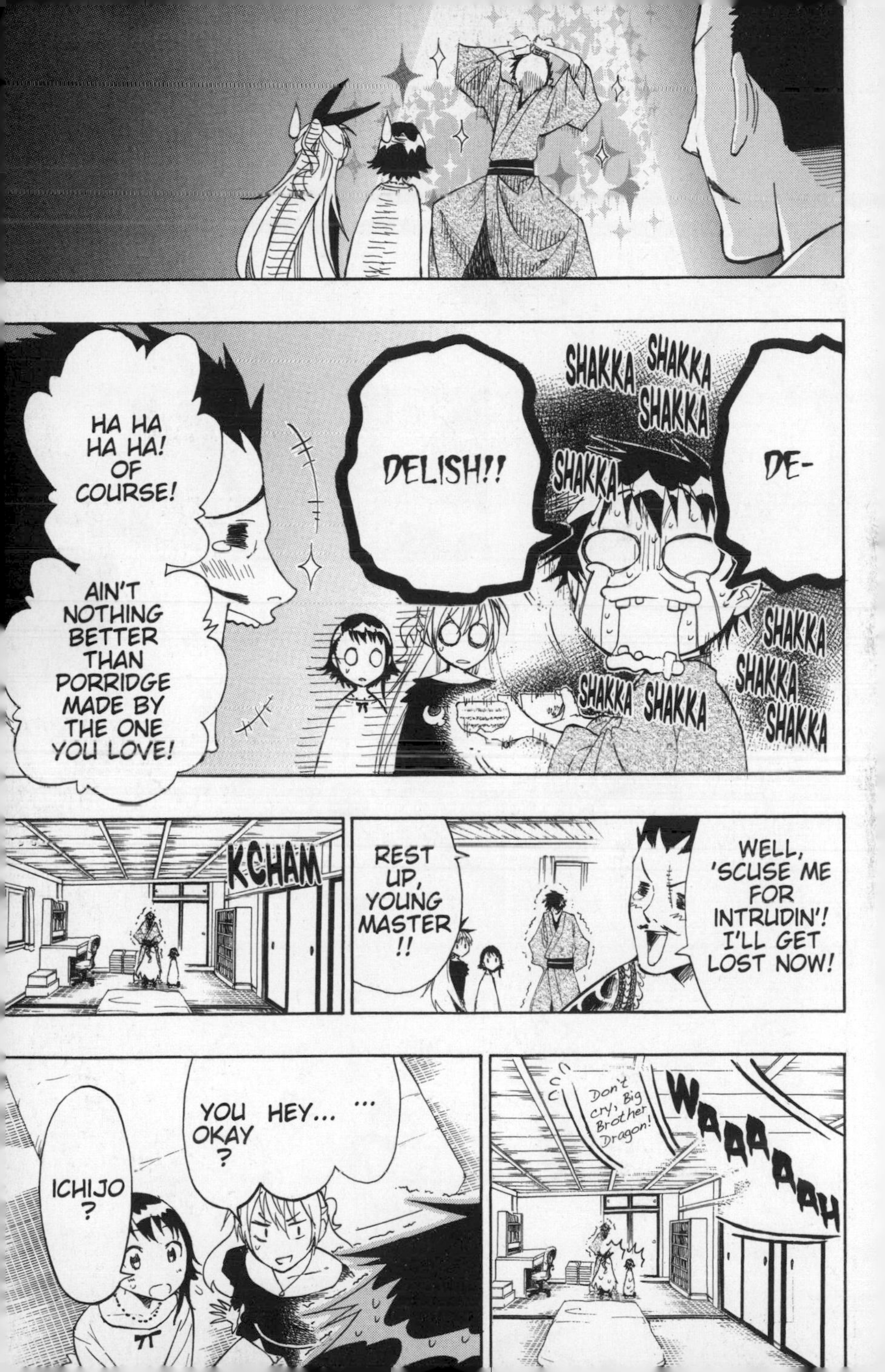

DE-
SHAKKA SHAKKA SHAKKA SHAKKA
SHAKKA SHAKKA SHAKKA
SHAKKA SHAKKA
DELISH!!
HA HA HA HA! OF COURSE!
AIN'T NOTHING BETTER THAN PORRIDGE MADE BY THE ONE YOU LOVE!
WELL, 'SCUSE ME FOR INTRUDIN'! I'LL GET LOST NOW!
REST UP, YOUNG MASTER!!
KCHAM
WAAAAAAH
Don't cry, Big Brother Dragon!
... HEY... YOU OKAY?
ICHIJO?

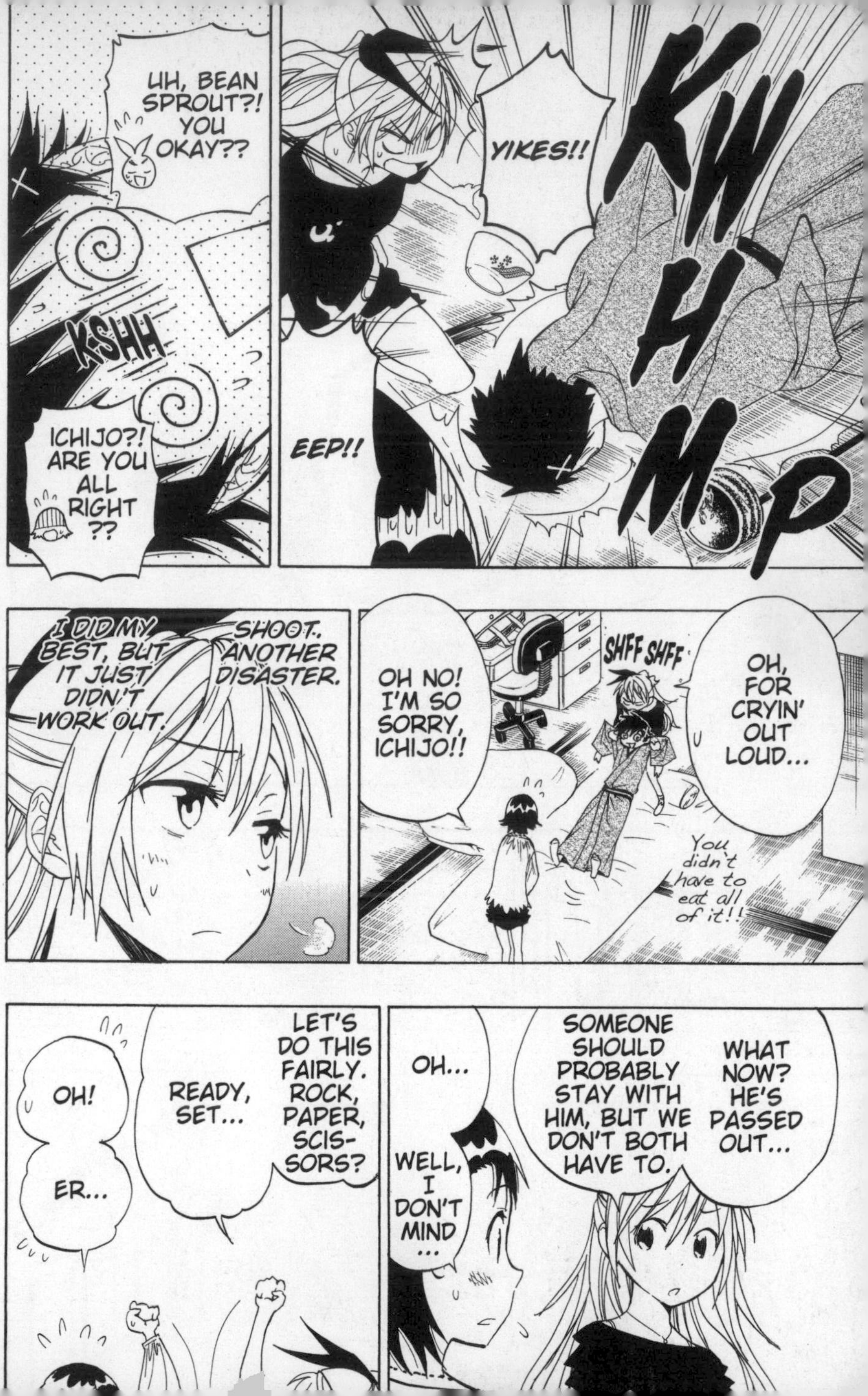
KWHHMMP
YIKES!!
EEP!!
UH, BEAN SPROUT?! YOU OKAY??
KSHH
ICHIJO?! ARE YOU ALL RIGHT ??
OH, FOR CRYIN' OUT LOUD...
You didn't have to eat all of it!!
SHFF SHFF
OH NO! I'M SO SORRY, ICHIJO!!
SHOOT. ANOTHER DISASTER.
I DID MY BEST, BUT IT JUST DIDN'T WORK OUT.
WHAT NOW? HE'S PASSED OUT...
SOMEONE SHOULD PROBABLY STAY WITH HIM, BUT WE DON'T BOTH HAVE TO.
OH...
WELL, I DON'T MIND ...
LET'S DO THIS FAIRLY. ROCK, PAPER, SCIS-SORS?
READY, SET...
OH!
ER...

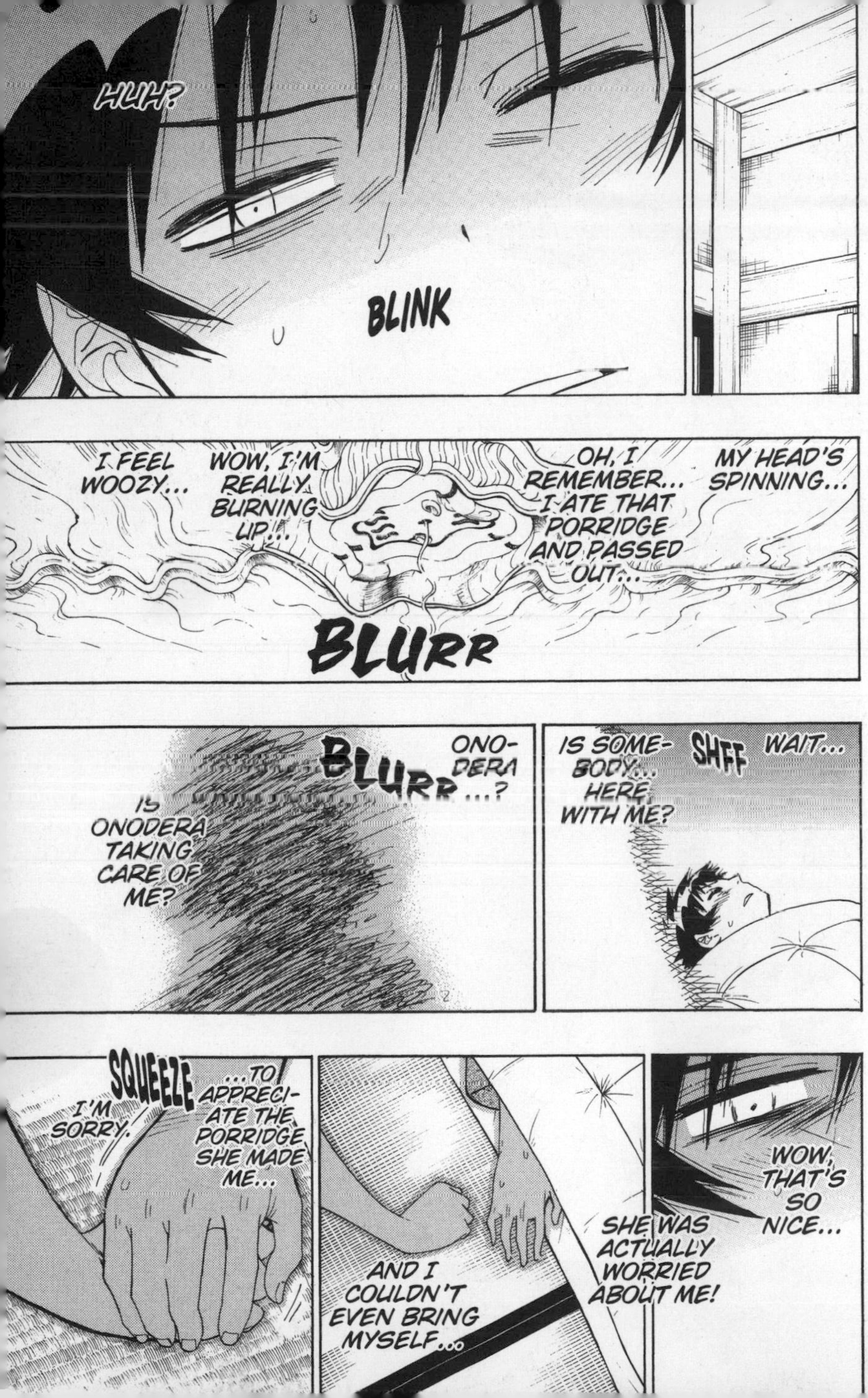
HUH?
BLINK
MY HEAD'S SPINNING...
OH, I REMEMBER... I ATE THAT PORRIDGE AND PASSED OUT...
WOW, I'M REALLY BURNING UP...
I FEEL WOOZY...
BLURR
WAIT...
SHFF
IS SOMEBODY... HERE, WITH ME?
ONODERA...?
BLURR
IS ONODERA TAKING CARE OF ME?
WOW, THAT'S SO NICE...
SHE WAS ACTUALLY WORRIED ABOUT ME!
AND I COULDN'T EVEN BRING MYSELF...
...TO APPRECIATE THE PORRIDGE SHE MADE ME...
SQUEEZE
I'M SORRY.

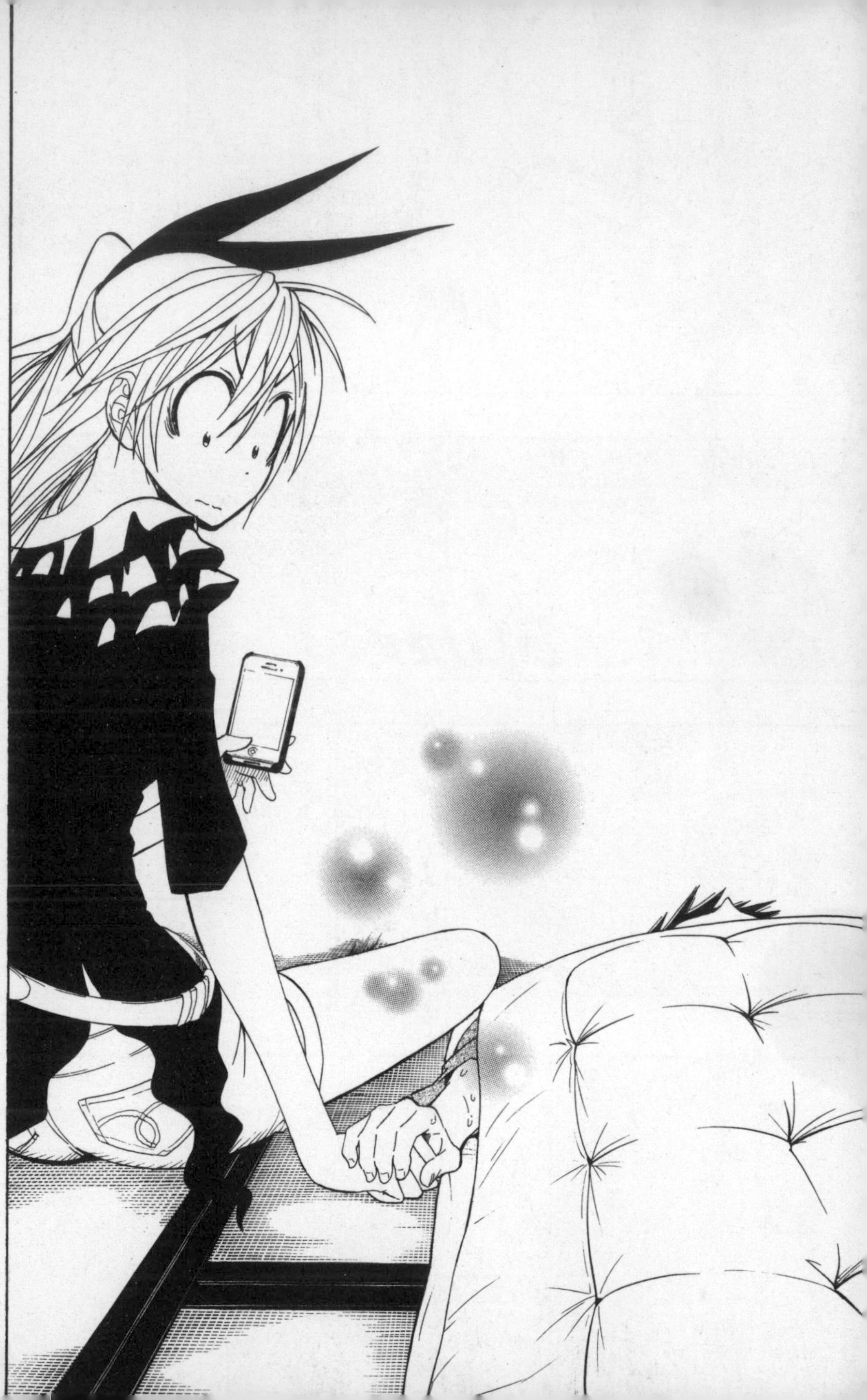

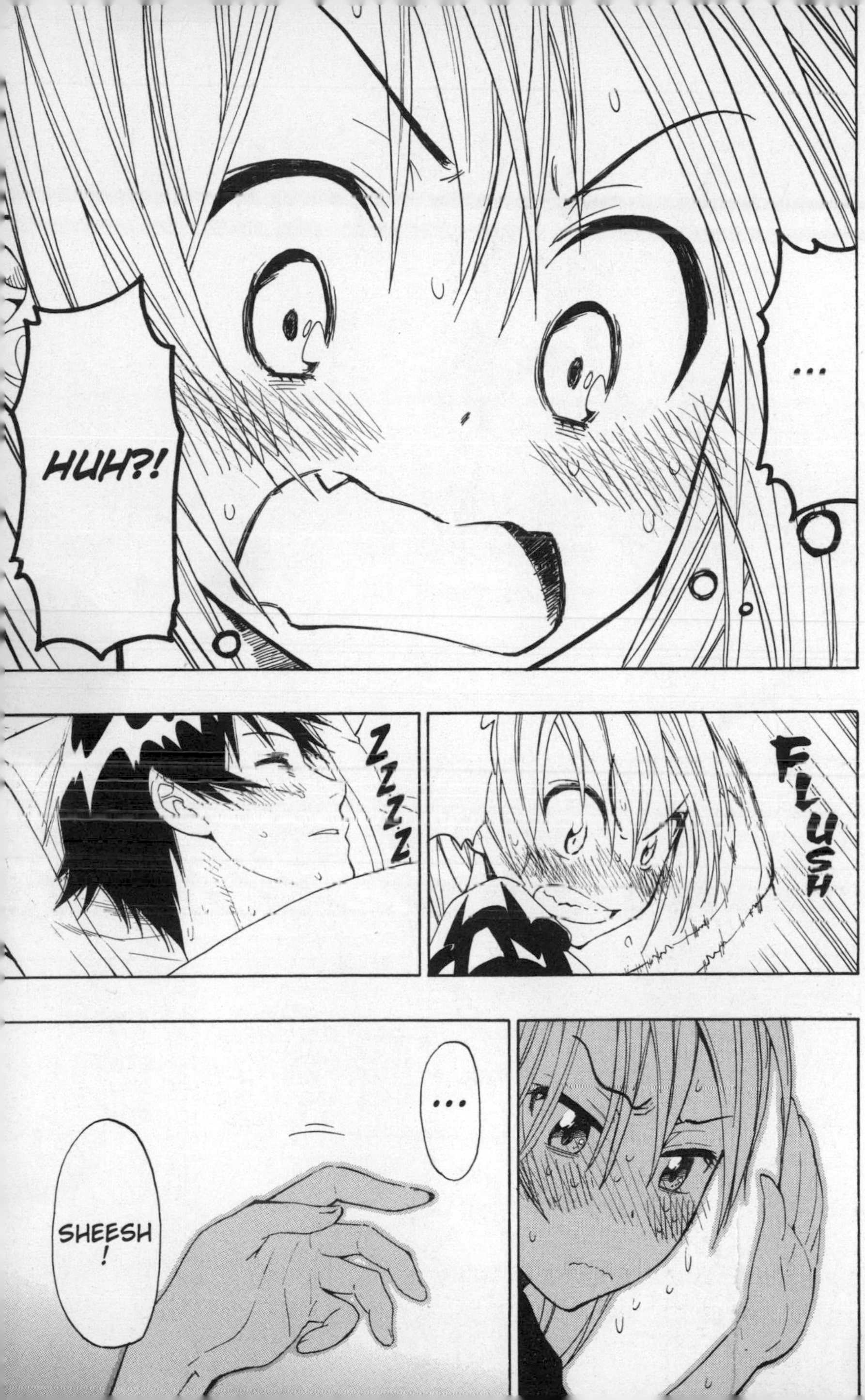
...
HUH?!
FLUSH
ZZZZ
...
SHEESH!

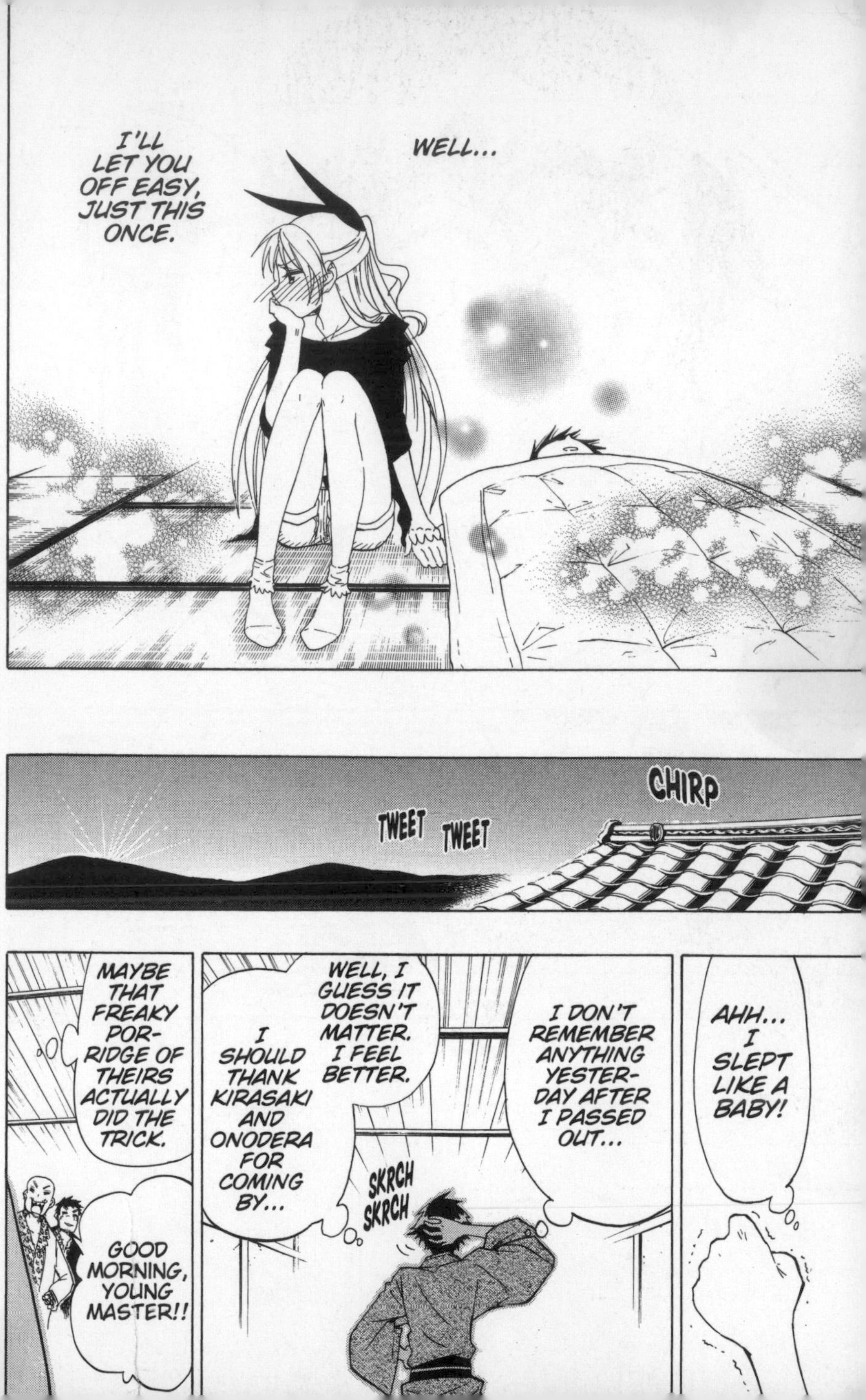
WELL...
I'LL LET YOU OFF EASY, JUST THIS ONCE.
CHIRP
TWEET TWEET
AHH... I SLEPT LIKE A BABY!
I DON'T REMEMBER ANYTHING YESTER-DAY AFTER I PASSED OUT...
WELL, I GUESS IT DOESN'T MATTER. I FEEL BETTER.
I SHOULD THANK KIRASAKI AND ONODERA FOR COMING BY...
SKRCH SKRCH
MAYBE THAT FREAKY POR-RIDGE OF THEIRS ACTUALLY DID THE TRICK.
GOOD MORNING, YOUNG MASTER!!

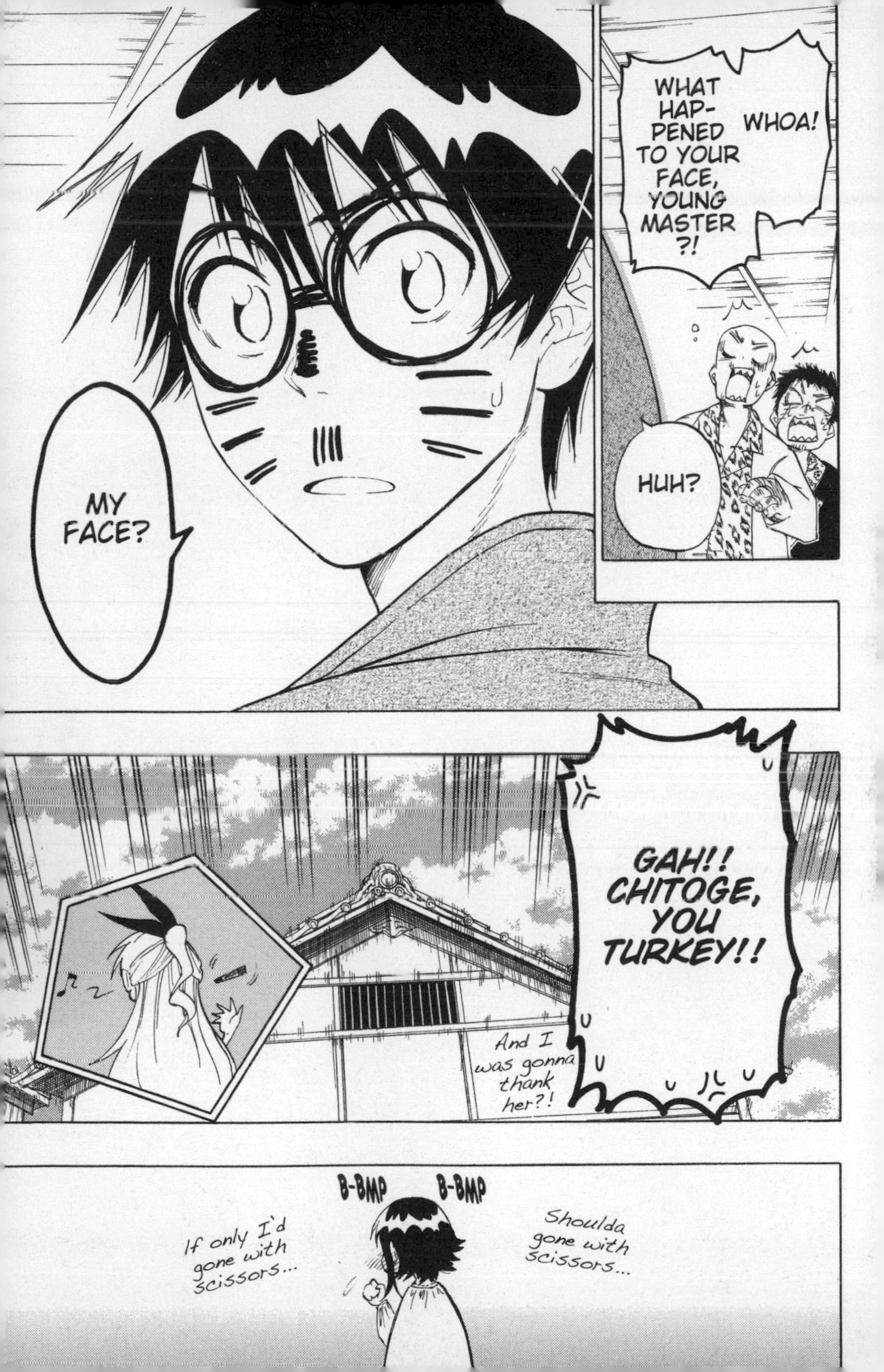
WHOA!
WHAT HAPPENED TO YOUR FACE, YOUNG MASTER ?!
HUH?
MY FACE?
GAH!! CHITOGE, YOU TURKEY!!
And I was gonna thank her?!
B-BMP B-BMP
Shoulda gone with scissors...
If only I'd gone with scissors...

Delish!!
GOBBLE
GOBBLE
We're not worthy!
Man, Big Brother, your porridge is da best!!
Too good!
I toldja to throw that away!!
sniffle

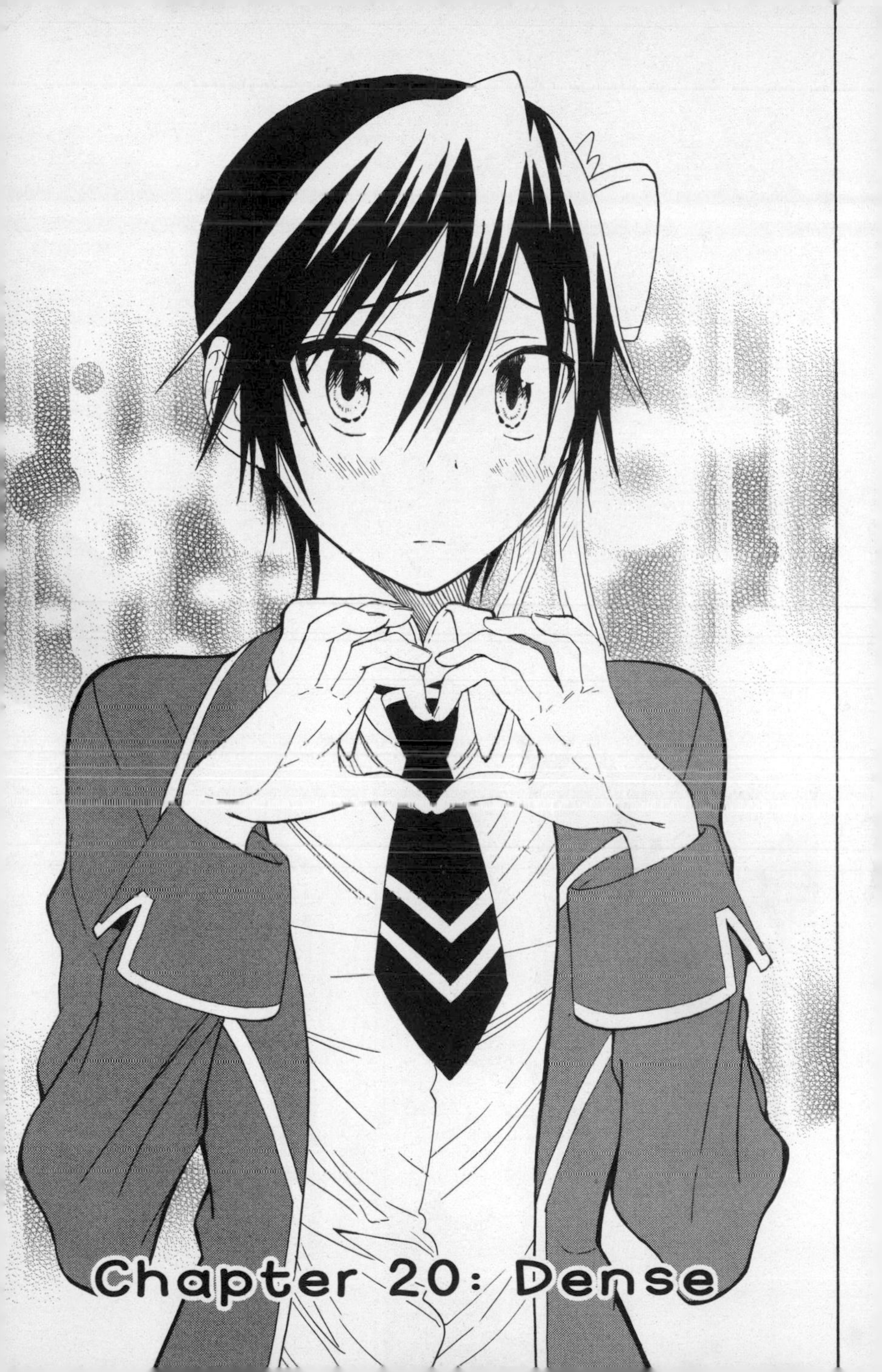
Chapter 20: Dense

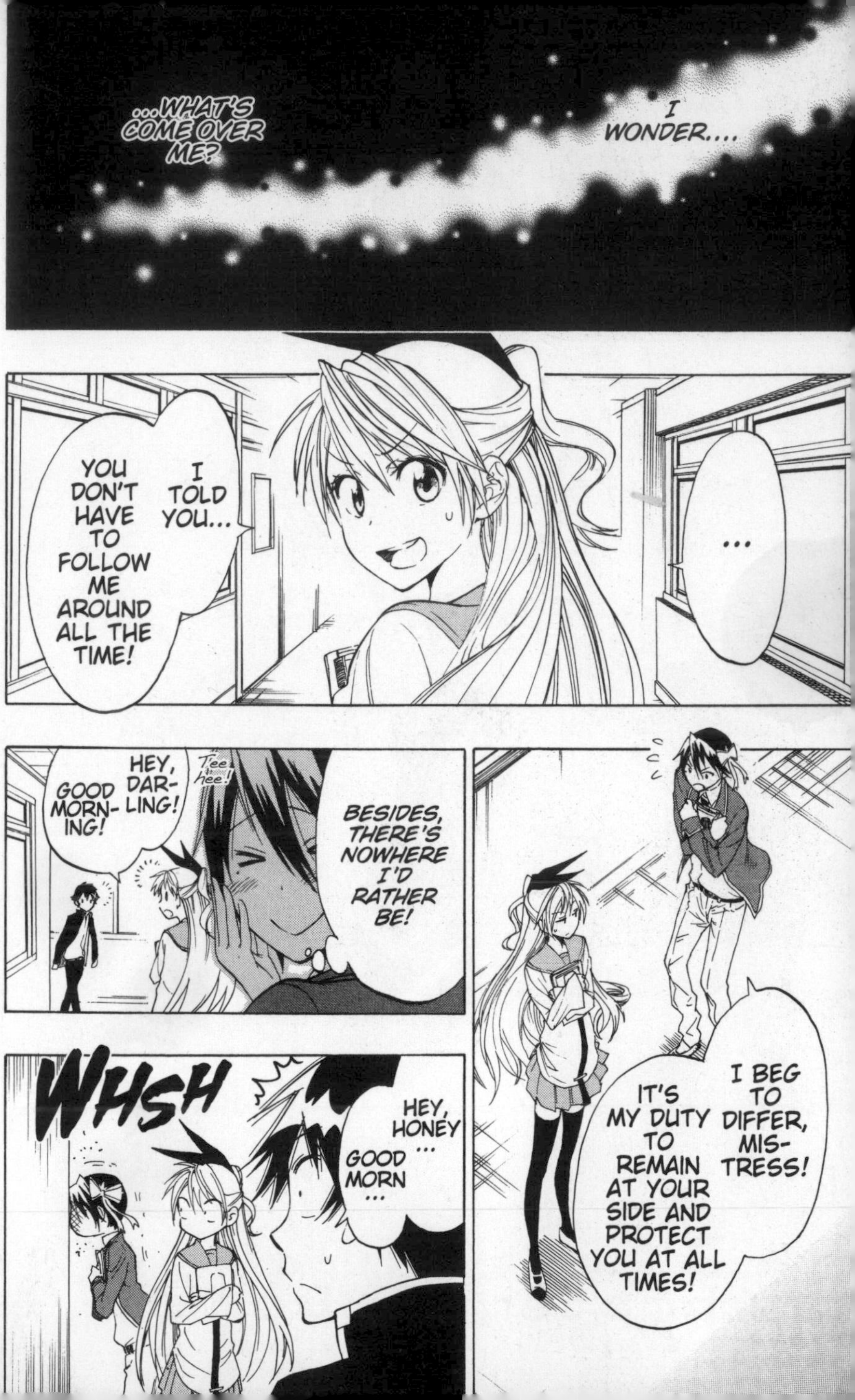
I WONDER....
...WHAT'S COME OVER ME?
...
I TOLD YOU...
YOU DON'T HAVE TO FOLLOW ME AROUND ALL THE TIME!
I BEG TO DIFFER, MIS-TRESS!
IT'S MY DUTY TO REMAIN AT YOUR SIDE AND PROTECT YOU AT ALL TIMES!
BESIDES, THERE'S NOWHERE I'D RATHER BE!
Tee hee!
HEY, DAR-LING!
GOOD MORN-ING!
HEY, HONEY...
GOOD MORN...
WHSH

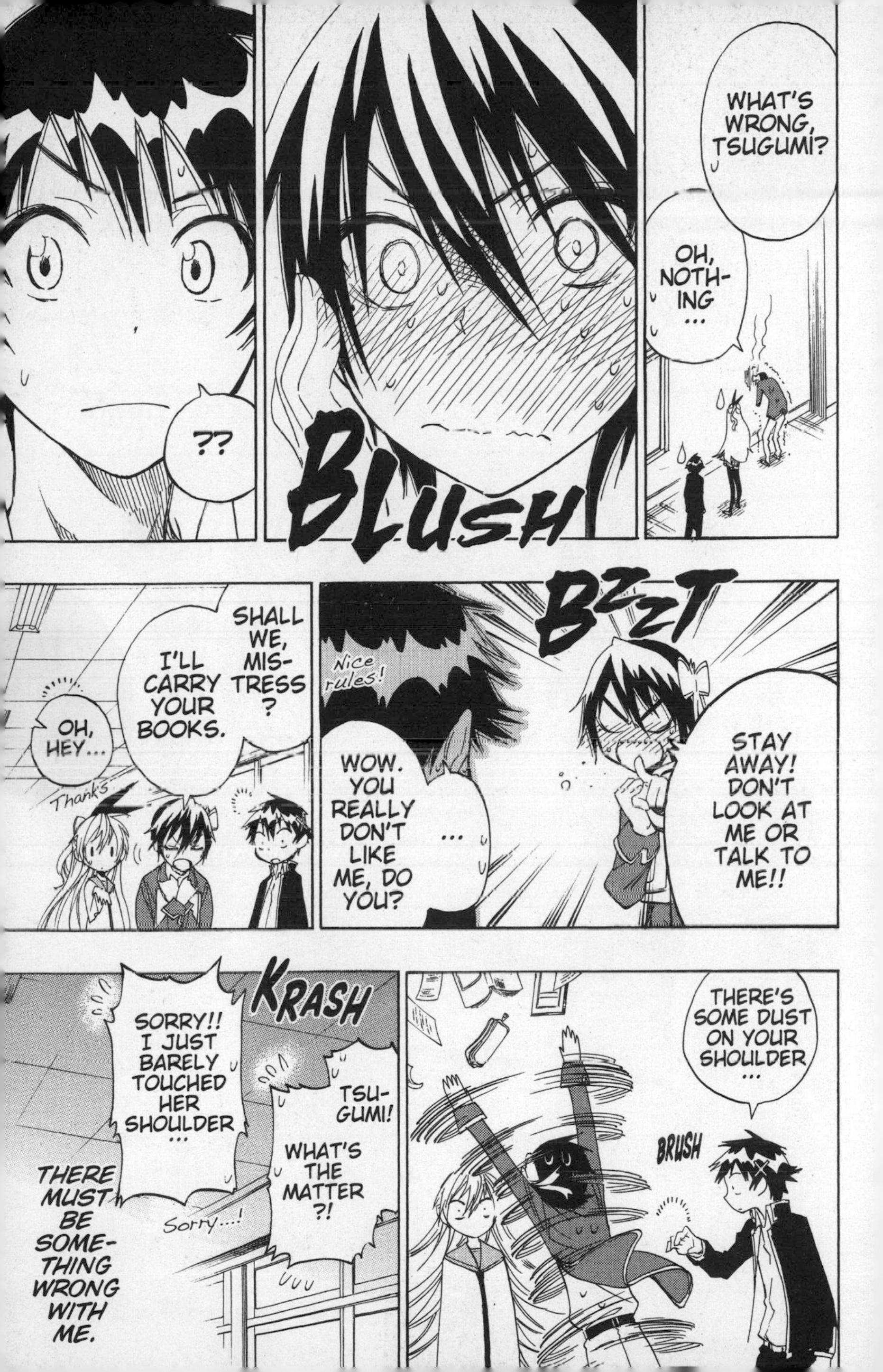
WHAT'S WRONG, TSUGUMI?
OH, NOTHING...
BLUSH
??
BZZT
STAY AWAY! DON'T LOOK AT ME OR TALK TO ME!!
Nice rules!
WOW. YOU REALLY DON'T LIKE ME, DO YOU?
...
SHALL WE, MISTRESS?
I'LL CARRY YOUR BOOKS.
OH, HEY...
Thanks
THERE'S SOME DUST ON YOUR SHOULDER...
BRUSH
KRASH
TSUGUMI!
WHAT'S THE MATTER?!
SORRY!! I JUST BARELY TOUCHED HER SHOULDER...
Sorry...!
THERE MUST BE SOMETHING WRONG WITH ME.

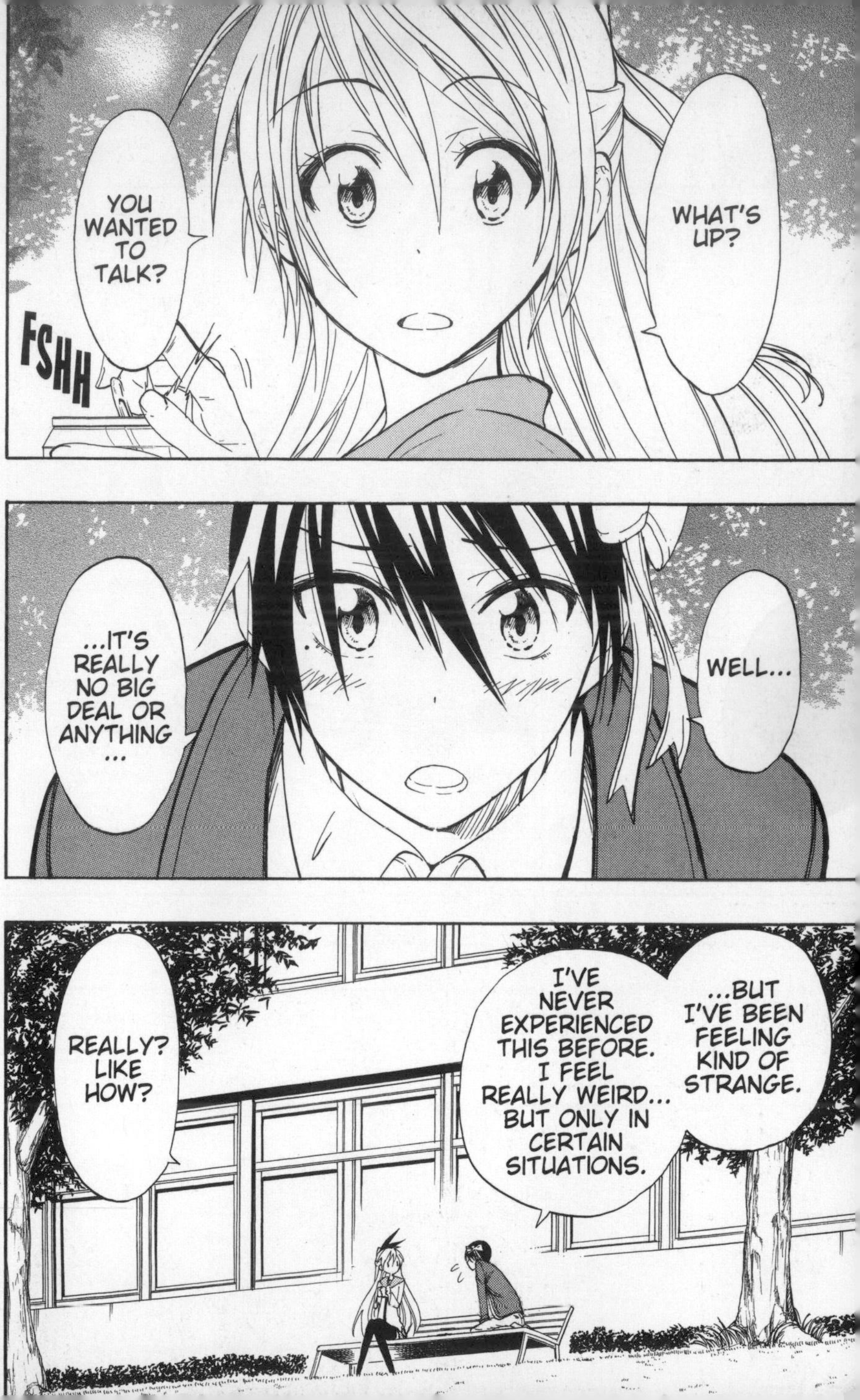
WHAT'S UP?
YOU WANTED TO TALK?
FSHH
WELL...
...IT'S REALLY NO BIG DEAL OR ANYTHING...
...BUT I'VE BEEN FEELING KIND OF STRANGE.
I'VE NEVER EXPERIENCED THIS BEFORE. I FEEL REALLY WEIRD... BUT ONLY IN CERTAIN SITUATIONS.
REALLY? LIKE HOW?

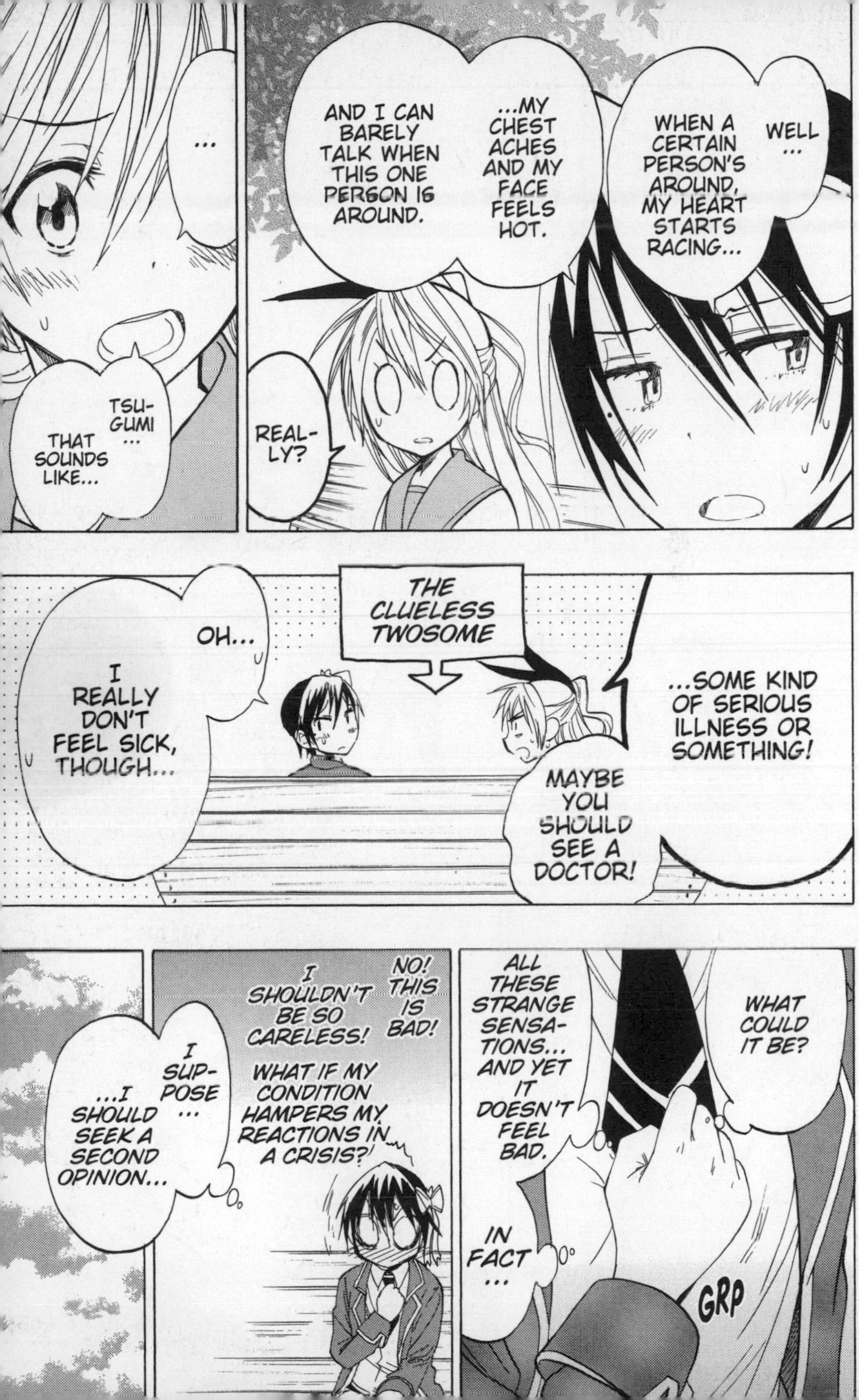
WELL...
WHEN A CERTAIN PERSON'S AROUND, MY HEART STARTS RACING...
...MY CHEST ACHES AND MY FACE FEELS HOT.
AND I CAN BARELY TALK WHEN THIS ONE PERSON IS AROUND.
REAL-LY?
...
TSU-GUMI... THAT SOUNDS LIKE...
...SOME KIND OF SERIOUS ILLNESS OR SOMETHING!
MAYBE YOU SHOULD SEE A DOCTOR!
THE CLUELESS TWOSOME
OH...
I REALLY DON'T FEEL SICK, THOUGH...
WHAT COULD IT BE?
ALL THESE STRANGE SENSA-TIONS... AND YET IT DOESN'T FEEL BAD.
IN FACT...
GRP
NO! THIS IS BAD!
I SHOULDN'T BE SO CARELESS!
WHAT IF MY CONDITION HAMPERS MY REACTIONS IN A CRISIS?
I SUP-POSE...
...I SHOULD SEEK A SECOND OPINION...

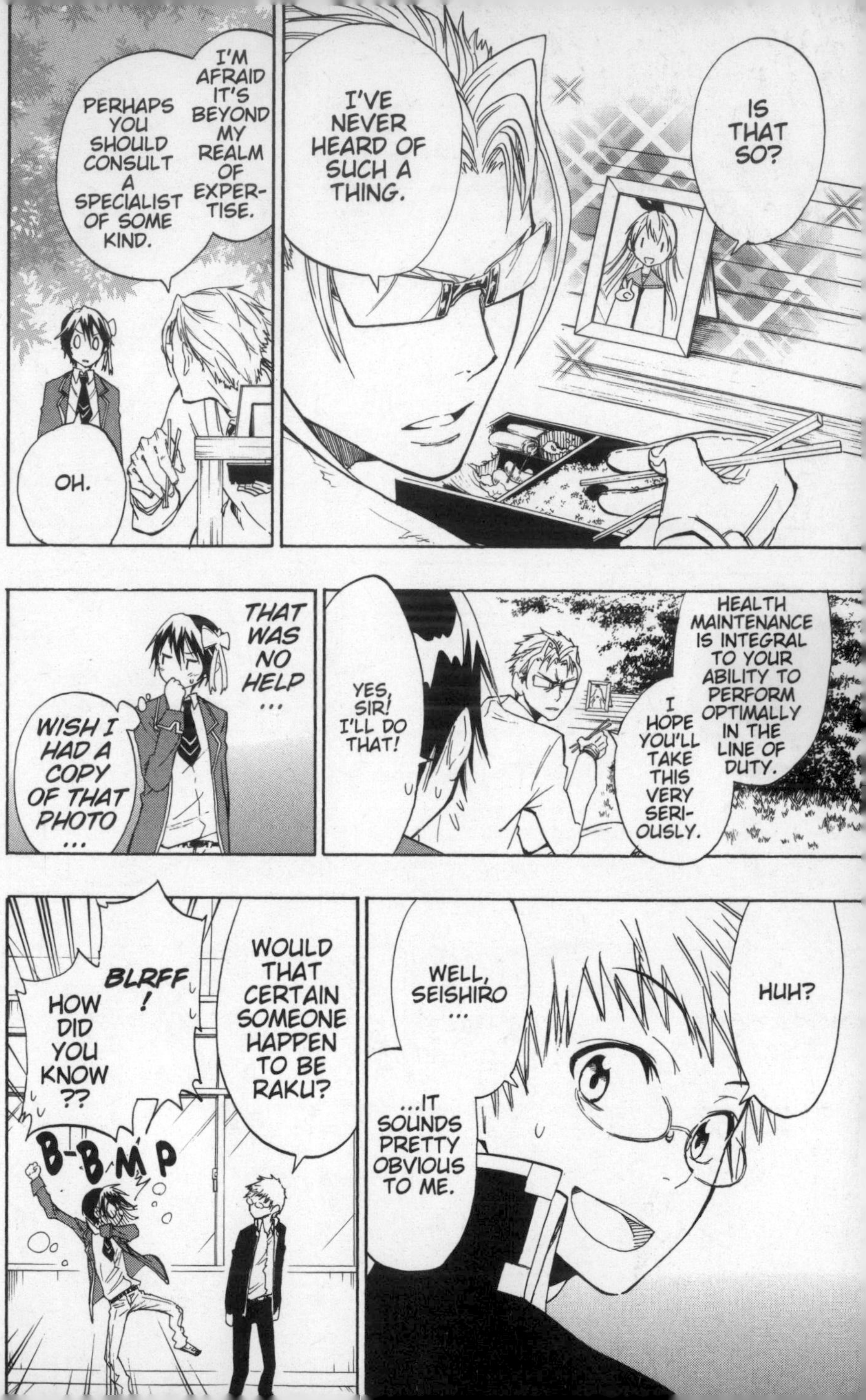
IS THAT SO?
I'VE NEVER HEARD OF SUCH A THING.
I'M AFRAID IT'S BEYOND MY REALM OF EXPERTISE.
PERHAPS YOU SHOULD CONSULT A SPECIALIST OF SOME KIND.
OH.
HEALTH MAINTENANCE IS INTEGRAL TO YOUR ABILITY TO PERFORM OPTIMALLY IN THE LINE OF DUTY.
I HOPE YOU'LL TAKE THIS VERY SERI-OUSLY.
YES, SIR! I'LL DO THAT!
THAT WAS NO HELP...
WISH I HAD A COPY OF THAT PHOTO...
HUH?
WELL, SEISHIRO...
...IT SOUNDS PRETTY OBVIOUS TO ME.
WOULD THAT CERTAIN SOMEONE HAPPEN TO BE RAKU?
BLRFF!
HOW DID YOU KNOW??
B-BMP

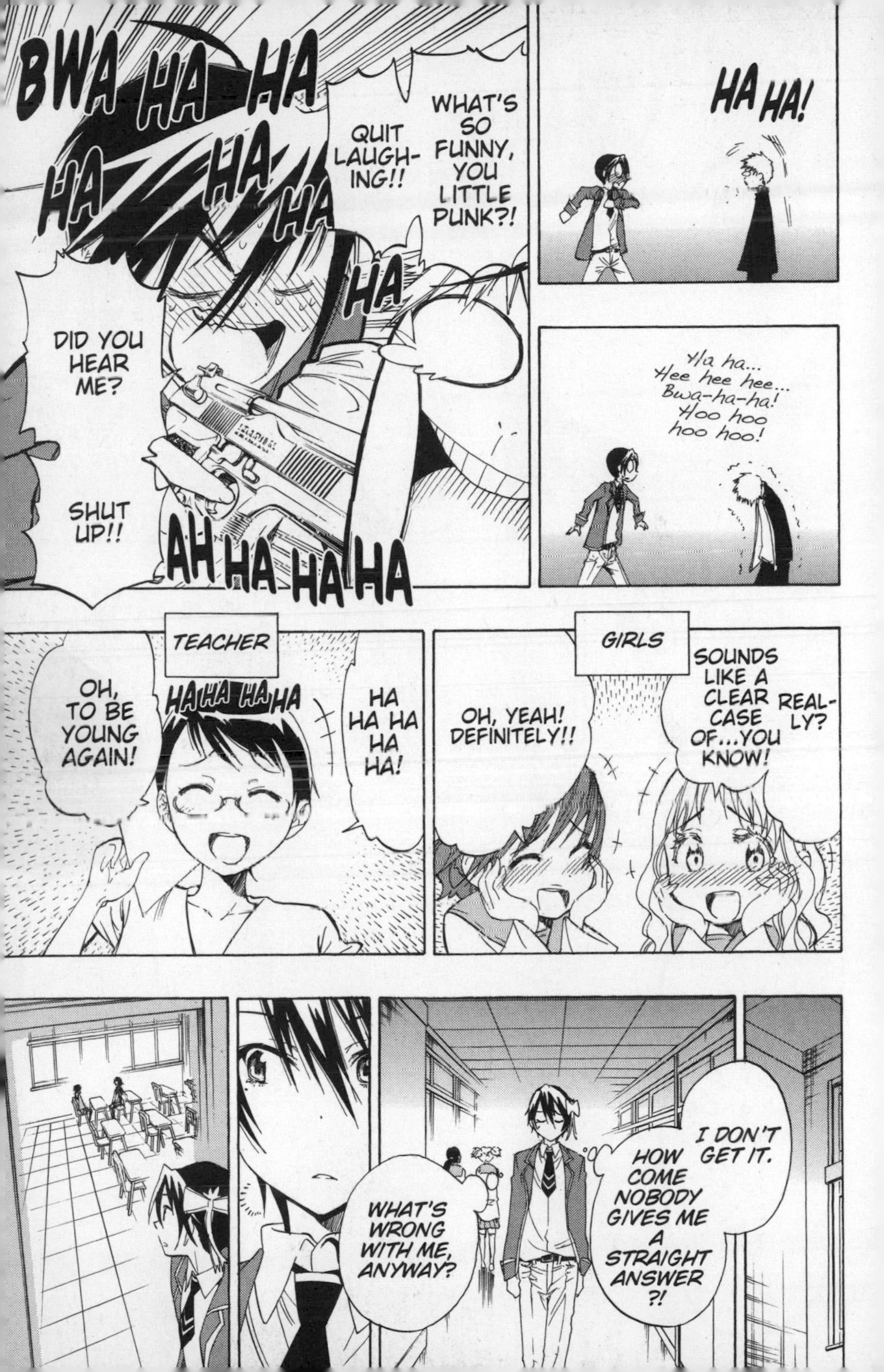
HA HA!
Ha ha... Hee hee hee... Bwa-ha-ha! Hoo hoo hoo hoo!
WHAT'S SO FUNNY, YOU LITTLE PUNK?!
QUIT LAUGHING!!
BWA HA HA HA HA HA HA HA
DID YOU HEAR ME?
SHUT UP!!
AH HA HA HA
GIRLS
REALLY?
SOUNDS LIKE A CLEAR CASE OF...YOU KNOW!
OH, YEAH! DEFINITELY!!
TEACHER
HA HA HA HA HA!
HA HA HA HA HA
OH, TO BE YOUNG AGAIN!
I DON'T GET IT.
HOW COME NOBODY GIVES ME A STRAIGHT ANSWER?!
WHAT'S WRONG WITH ME, ANYWAY?

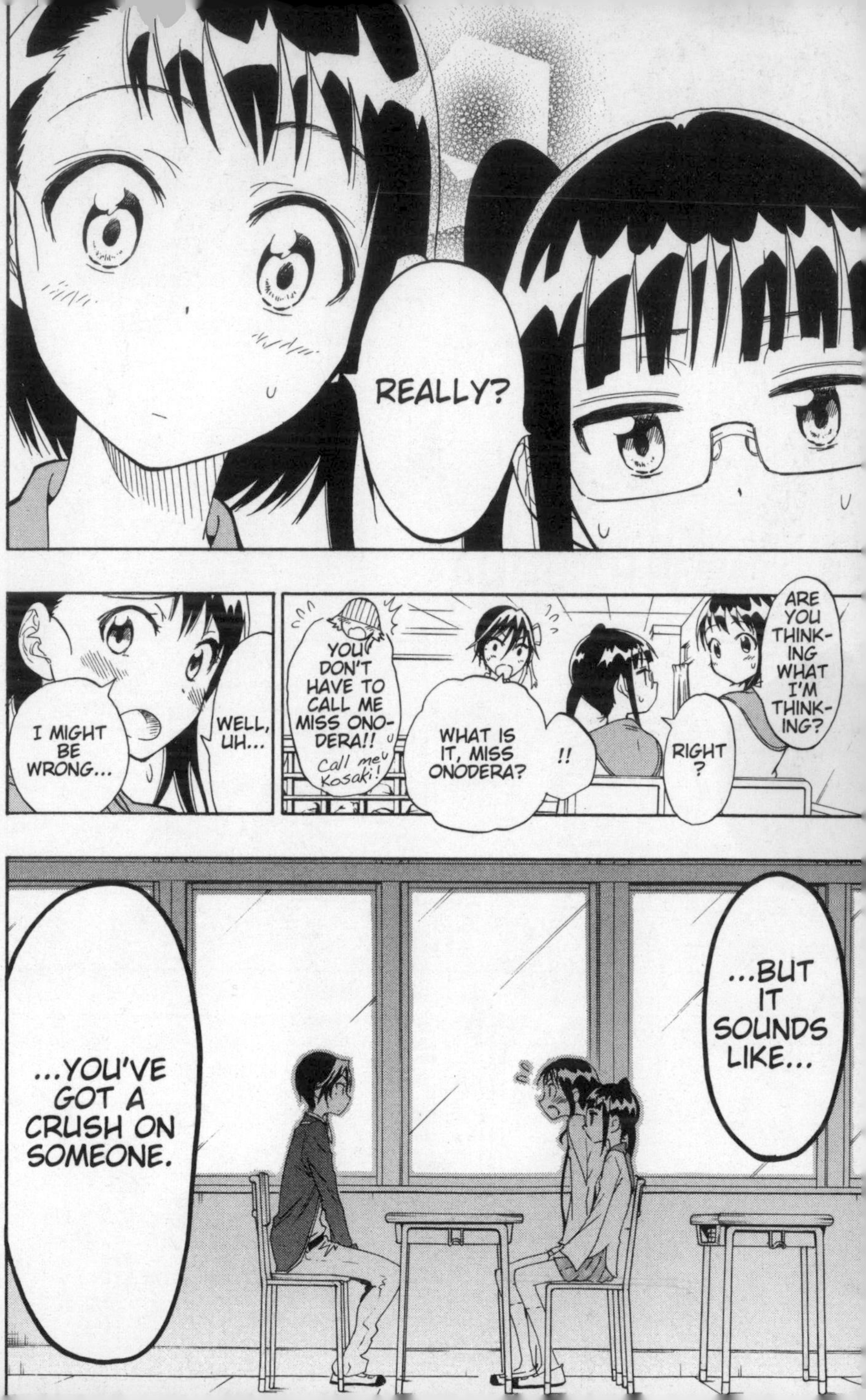
REALLY?
ARE YOU THINKING WHAT I'M THINKING?
RIGHT?
!!
WHAT IS IT, MISS ONODERA?
YOU DON'T HAVE TO CALL ME MISS ONODERA!!
Call me Kosaki!
WELL, UH...
I MIGHT BE WRONG...
...BUT IT SOUNDS LIKE...
...YOU'VE GOT A CRUSH ON SOMEONE.

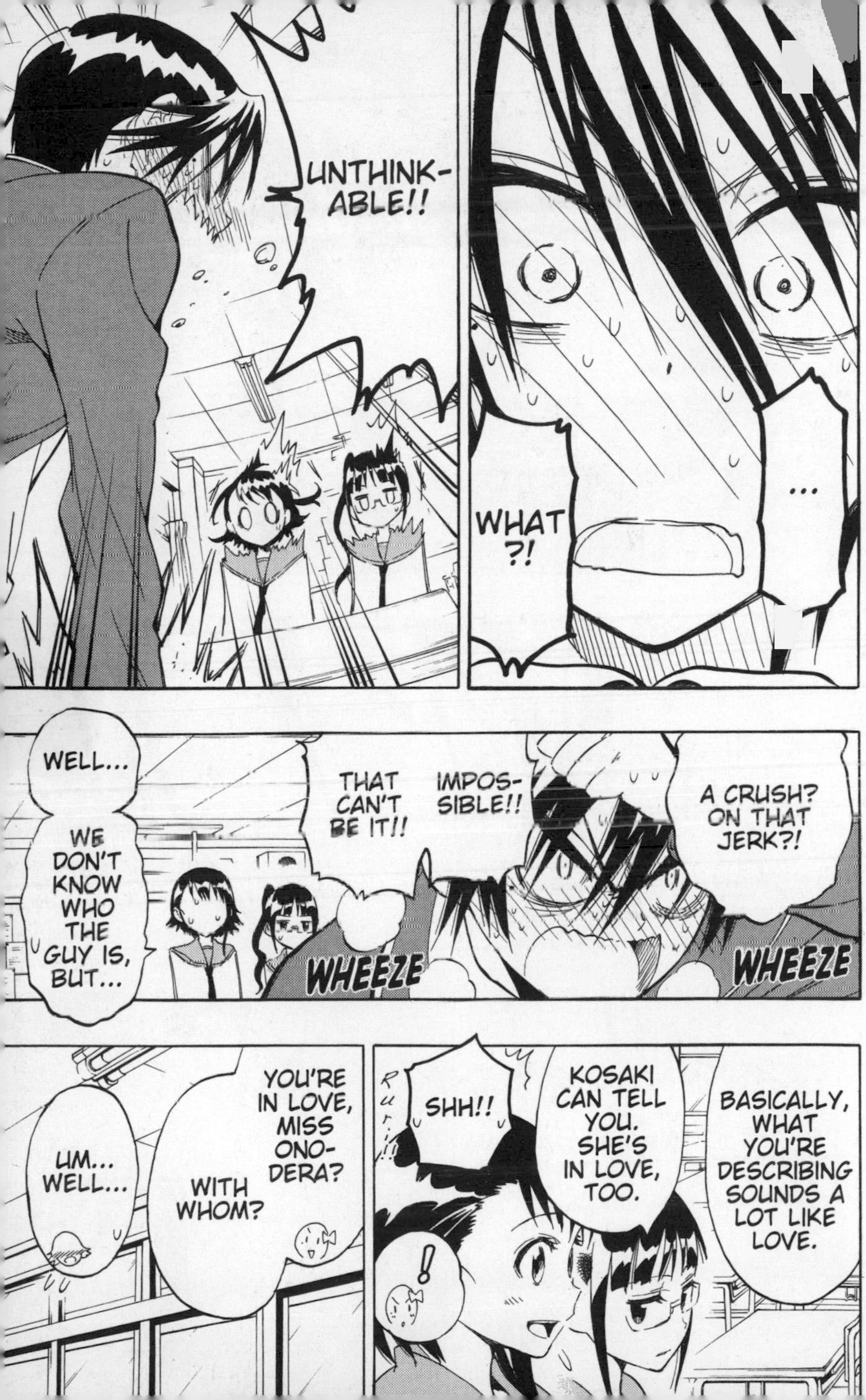
...
WHAT?!
UNTHINKABLE!!
A CRUSH? ON THAT JERK?!
WHEEZE
IMPOSSIBLE!!
THAT CAN'T BE IT!!
WHEEZE
WELL...
WE DON'T KNOW WHO THE GUY IS, BUT...
BASICALLY, WHAT YOU'RE DESCRIBING SOUNDS A LOT LIKE LOVE.
KOSAKI CAN TELL YOU. SHE'S IN LOVE, TOO.
SHH!!
Ruri!!
!
YOU'RE IN LOVE, MISS ONODERA?
WITH WHOM?
UM... WELL...

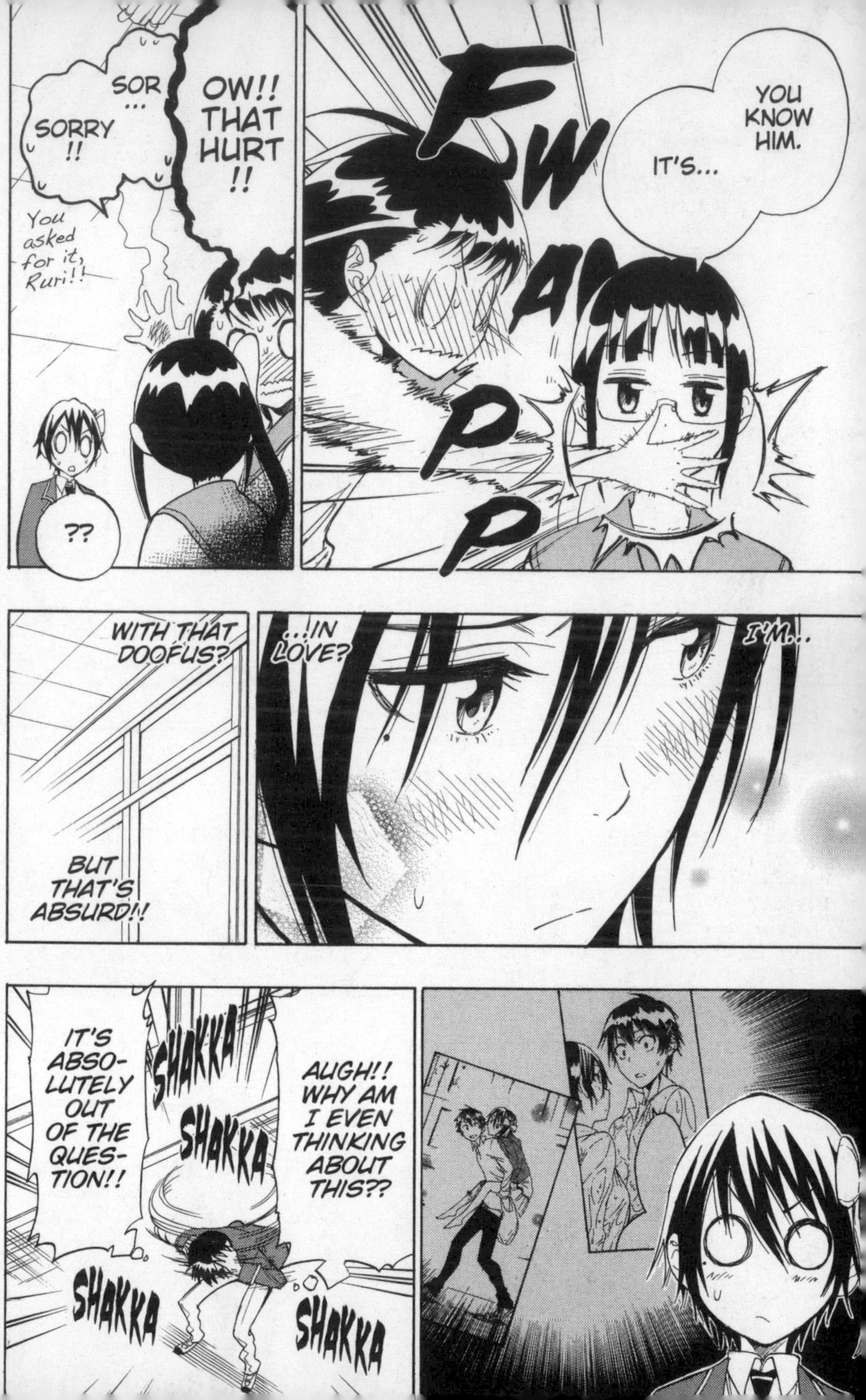
YOU KNOW HIM.
IT'S...
FWAPP
OW!! THAT HURT!!
SOR... SORRY!!
You asked for it, Ruri!!
??
I'M...
...IN LOVE?
WITH THAT DOOFUS?
BUT THAT'S ABSURD!!
AUGH!! WHY AM I EVEN THINKING ABOUT THIS??
IT'S ABSO-LUTELY OUT OF THE QUES-TION!!
SHAKKA
SHAKKA
SHAKKA
SHAKKA

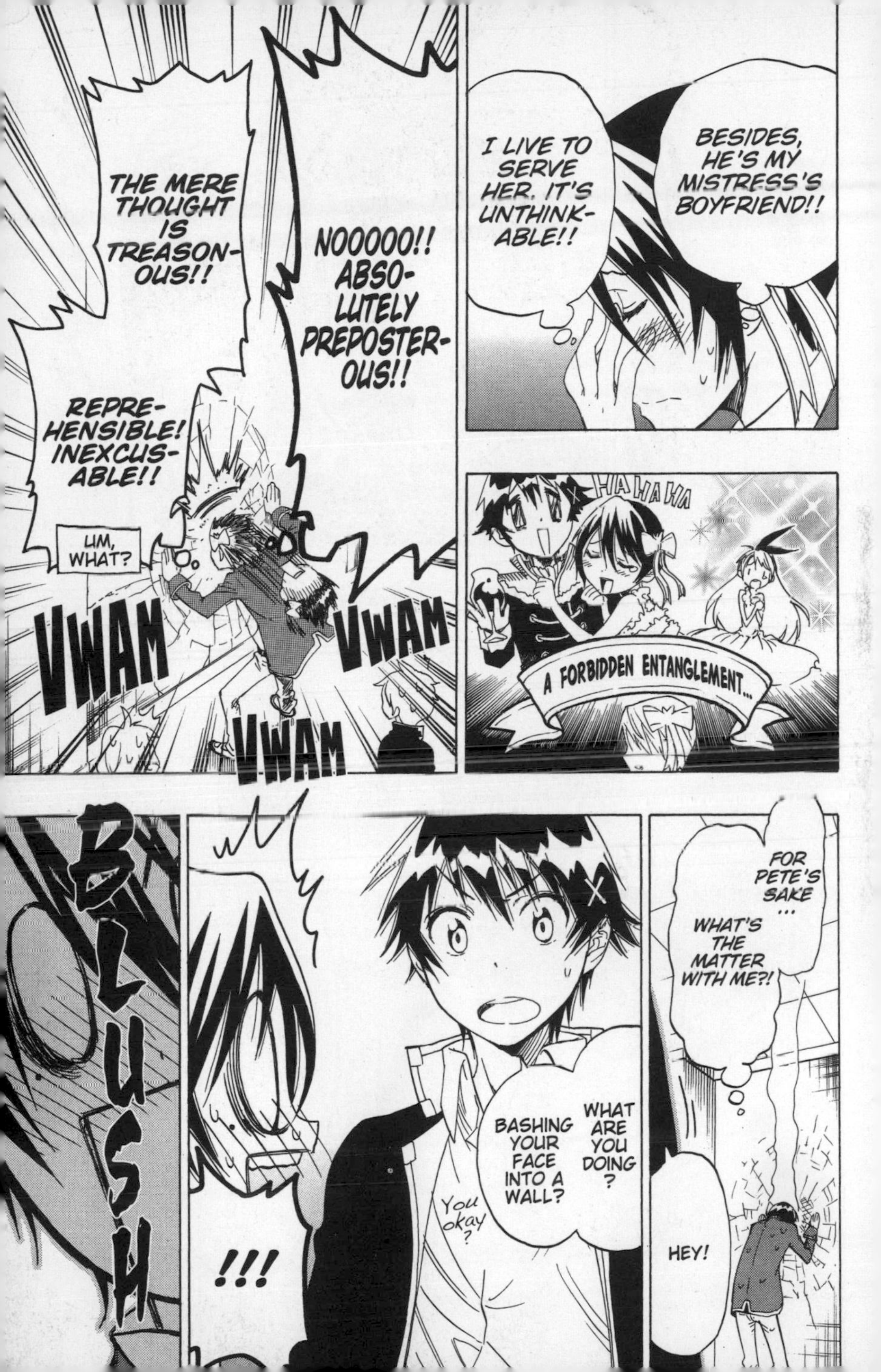
BESIDES, HE'S MY MISTRESS'S BOYFRIEND!!
I LIVE TO SERVE HER. IT'S UNTHINK-ABLE!!
HA HA HA
A FORBIDDEN ENTANGLEMENT...
NOOOOO!! ABSO-LUTELY PREPOSTER-OUS!!
THE MERE THOUGHT IS TREASON-OUS!!
REPRE-HENSIBLE! INEXCUS-ABLE!!
UM, WHAT?
VWAM
VWAM
VWAM
FOR PETE'S SAKE ... WHAT'S THE MATTER WITH ME?!
HEY!
WHAT ARE YOU DOING?
BASHING YOUR FACE INTO A WALL?
You okay?
!!!
BLUSH

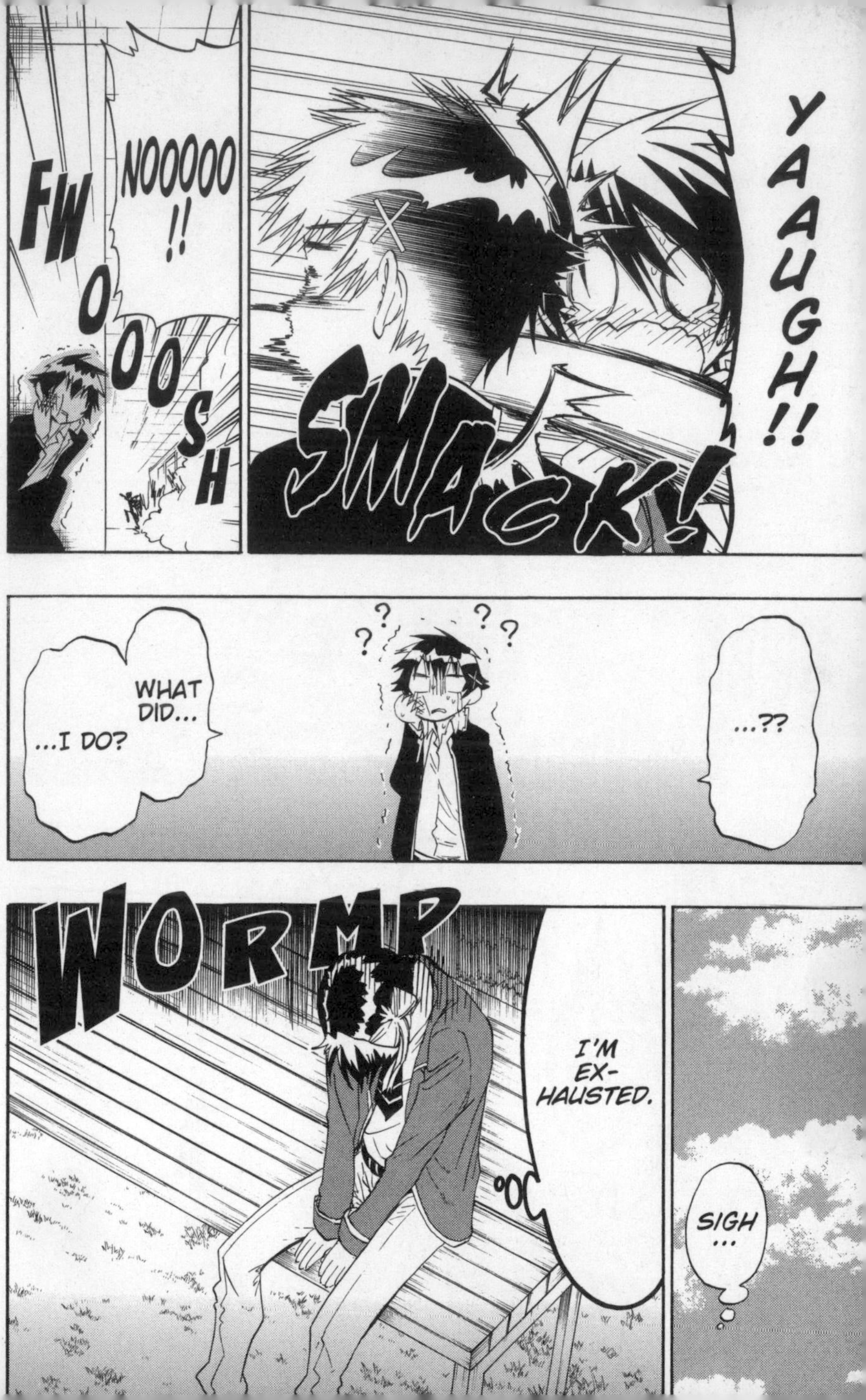
YAAUGH!!
SMACK!
NOOOOO!!
FWOOOSH
...??
WHAT DID...
...I DO?
SIGH...
I'M EX-HAUSTED.
WORMP

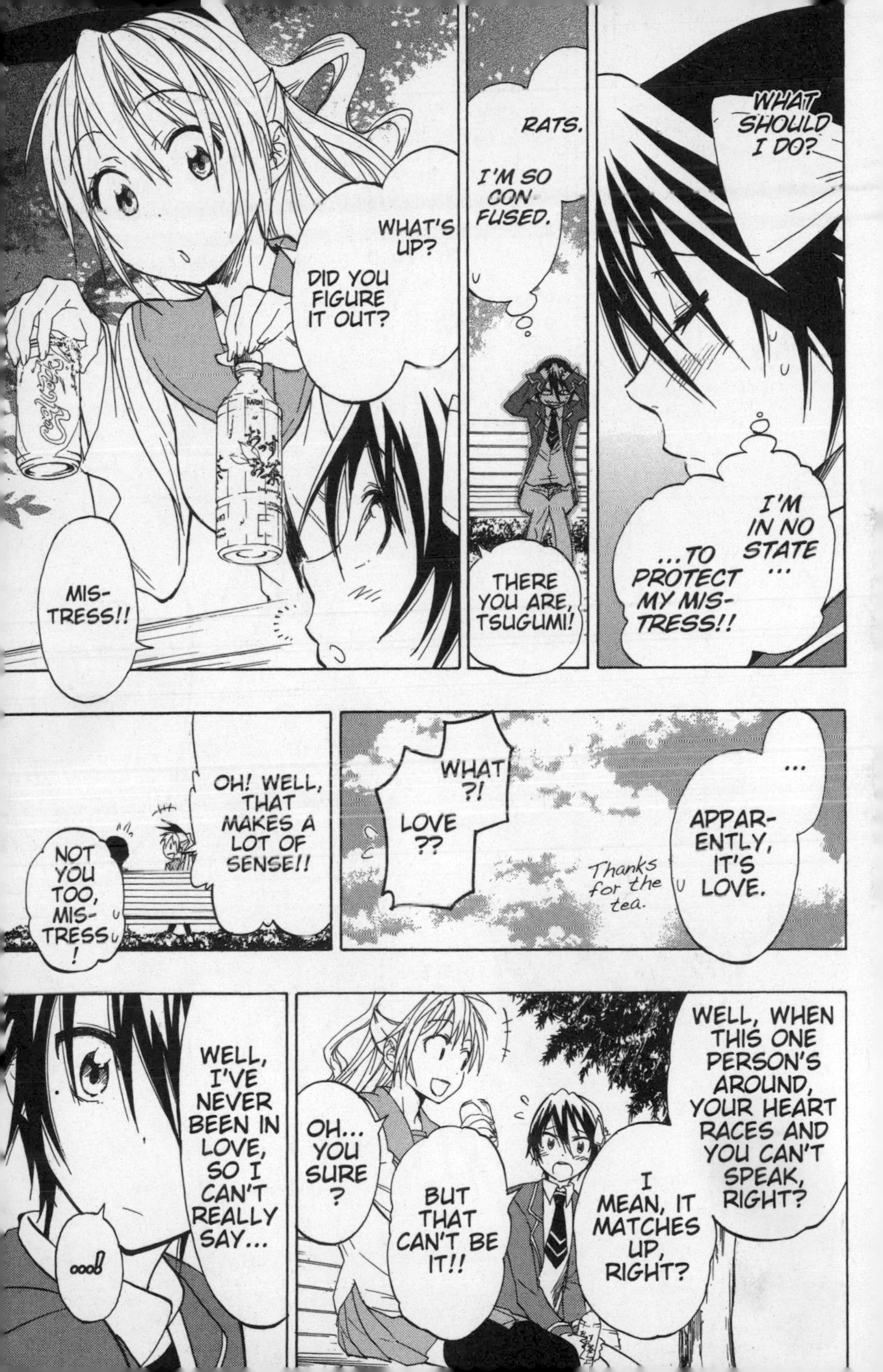
WHAT SHOULD I DO?
I'M IN NO STATE...
...TO PROTECT MY MISTRESS!!
RATS.
I'M SO CONFUSED.
THERE YOU ARE, TSUGUMI!
WHAT'S UP?
DID YOU FIGURE IT OUT?
MISTRESS!!
...
APPARENTLY, IT'S LOVE.
Thanks for the tea.
WHAT?!
LOVE??
OH! WELL, THAT MAKES A LOT OF SENSE!!
NOT YOU TOO, MISTRESS!
WELL, WHEN THIS ONE PERSON'S AROUND, YOUR HEART RACES AND YOU CAN'T SPEAK, RIGHT?
I MEAN, IT MATCHES UP, RIGHT?
BUT THAT CAN'T BE IT!!
OH... YOU SURE?
WELL, I'VE NEVER BEEN IN LOVE, SO I CAN'T REALLY SAY...
ooo!

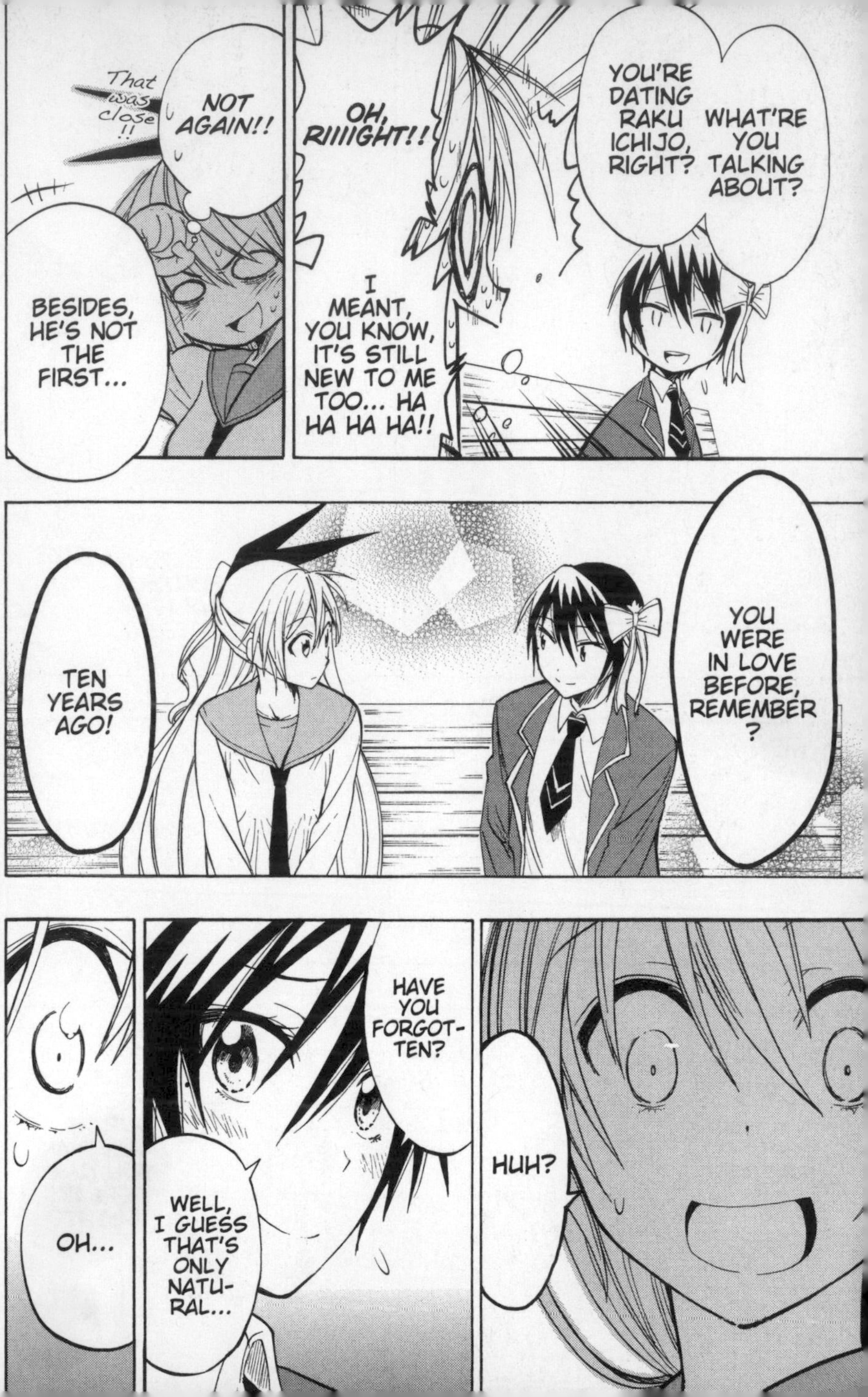
WHAT'RE YOU TALKING ABOUT?
YOU'RE DATING RAKU ICHIJO, RIGHT?
OH, RIIIGHT!!
I MEANT, YOU KNOW, IT'S STILL NEW TO ME TOO... HA HA HA HA!!
NOT AGAIN!!
That was close!!
BESIDES, HE'S NOT THE FIRST...
YOU WERE IN LOVE BEFORE, REMEMBER?
TEN YEARS AGO!
HUH?
HAVE YOU FORGOT-TEN?
WELL, I GUESS THAT'S ONLY NATU-RAL...
OH...

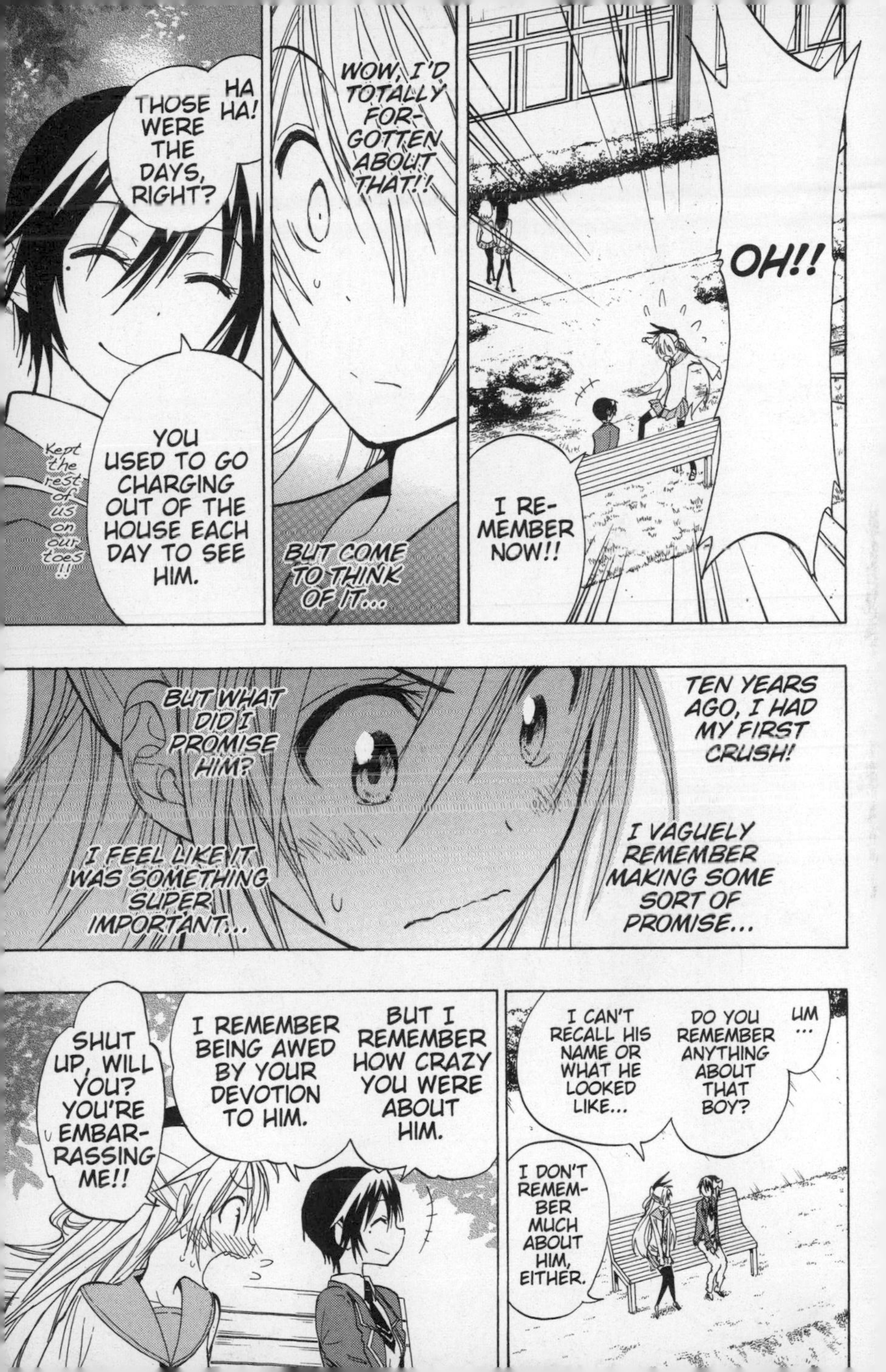
OH!!
I RE-MEMBER NOW!!
WOW, I'D TOTALLY FOR-GOTTEN ABOUT THAT!!
BUT COME TO THINK OF IT...
HA HA! THOSE WERE THE DAYS, RIGHT?
YOU USED TO GO CHARGING OUT OF THE HOUSE EACH DAY TO SEE HIM.
Kept the rest of us on our toes!!
TEN YEARS AGO, I HAD MY FIRST CRUSH!
I VAGUELY REMEMBER MAKING SOME SORT OF PROMISE...
BUT WHAT DID I PROMISE HIM?
I FEEL LIKE IT WAS SOMETHING SUPER IMPORTANT...
UM...
DO YOU REMEMBER ANYTHING ABOUT THAT BOY?
I CAN'T RECALL HIS NAME OR WHAT HE LOOKED LIKE...
I DON'T REMEMBER MUCH ABOUT HIM, EITHER.
BUT I REMEMBER HOW CRAZY YOU WERE ABOUT HIM.
I REMEMBER BEING AWED BY YOUR DEVOTION TO HIM.
SHUT UP, WILL YOU? YOU'RE EMBARRASSING ME!!

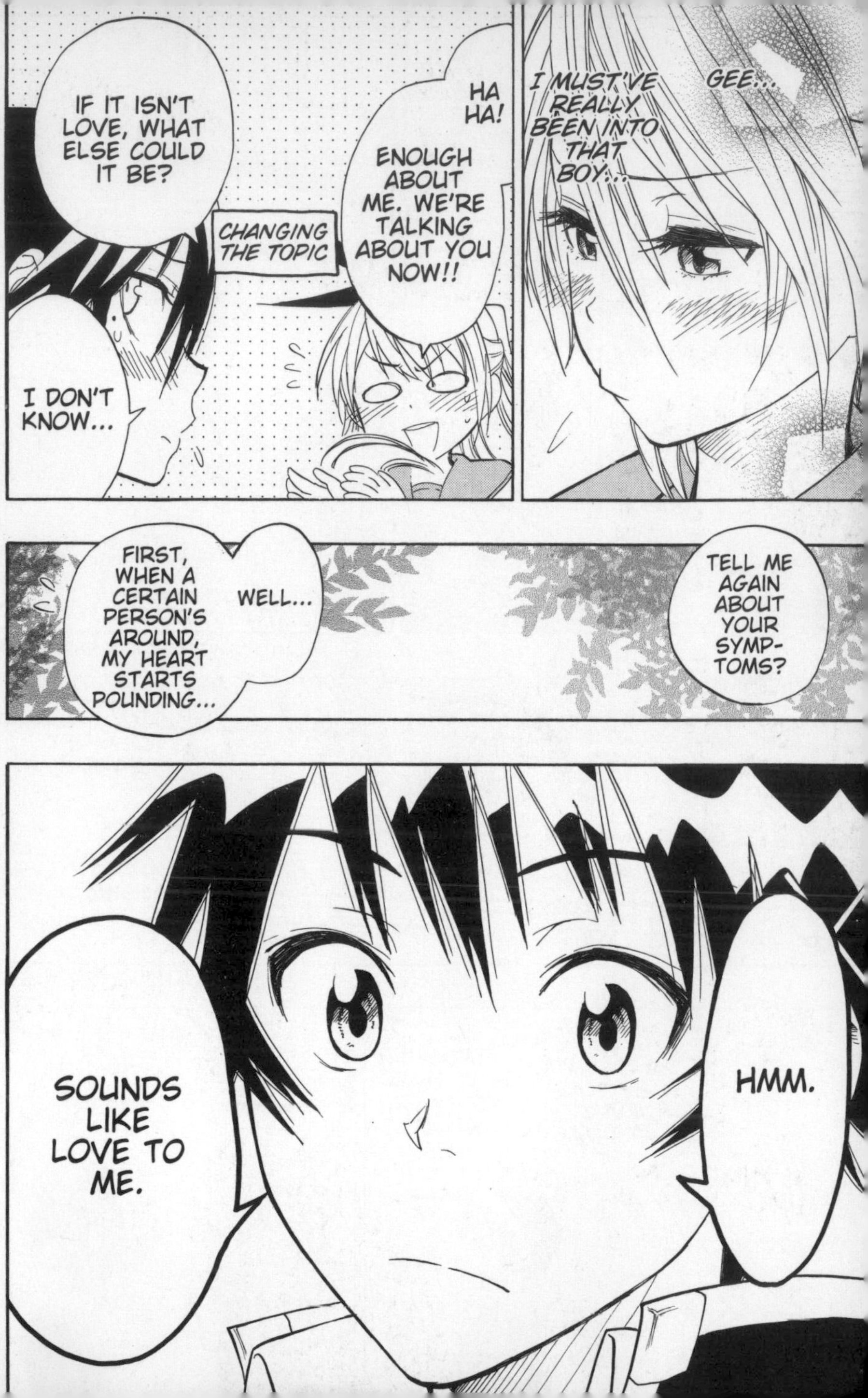
GEE...
I MUST'VE REALLY BEEN INTO THAT BOY...
HA HA!
ENOUGH ABOUT ME. WE'RE TALKING ABOUT YOU NOW!!
CHANGING THE TOPIC
IF IT ISN'T LOVE, WHAT ELSE COULD IT BE?
I DON'T KNOW...
TELL ME AGAIN ABOUT YOUR SYMPTOMS?
WELL...
FIRST, WHEN A CERTAIN PERSON'S AROUND, MY HEART STARTS POUNDING...
HMM.
SOUNDS LIKE LOVE TO ME.

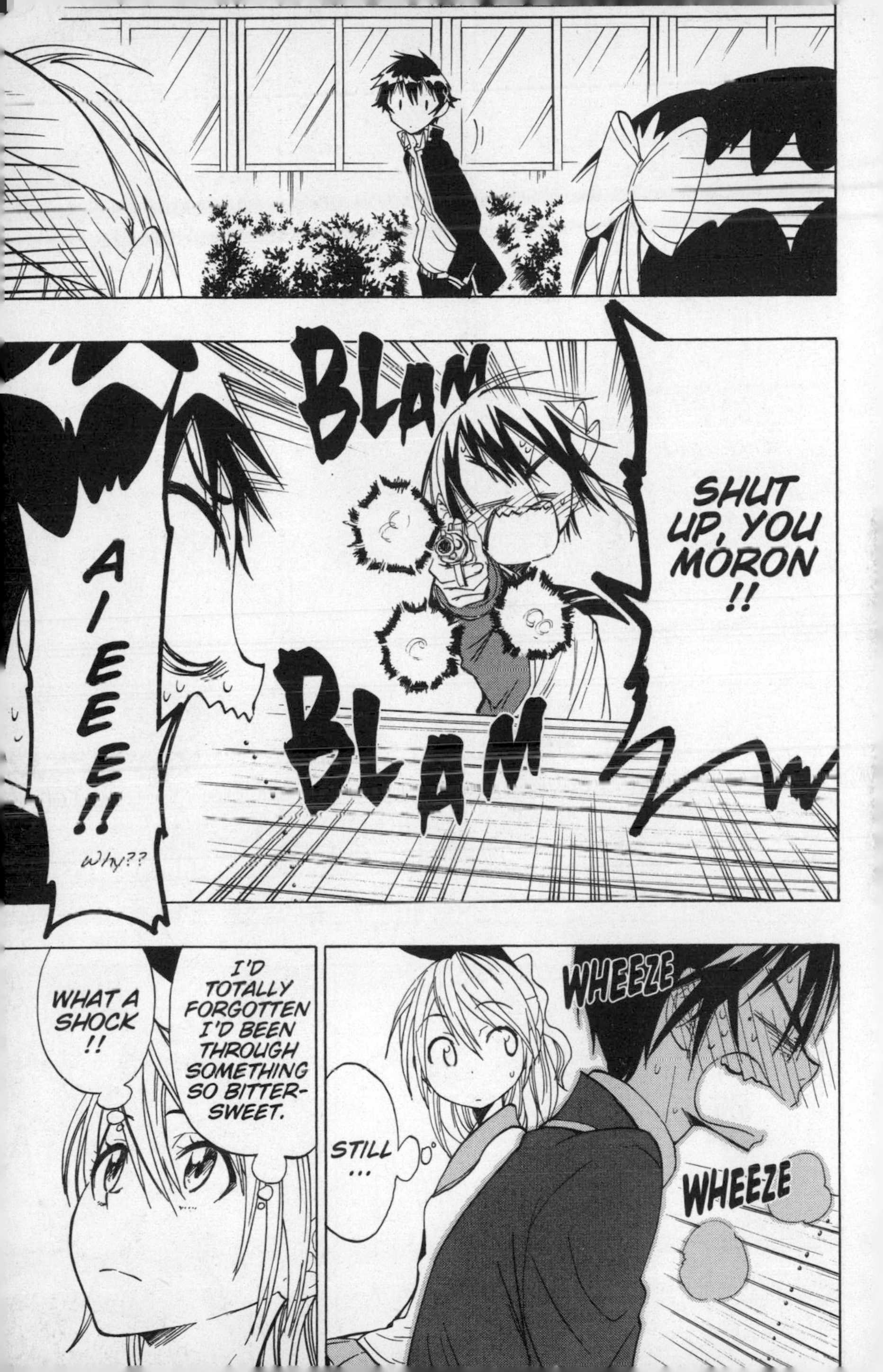
BLAM
SHUT UP, YOU MORON !!
BLAM
AIEEE!!
why??
WHEEZE
WHEEZE
STILL ...
I'D TOTALLY FORGOTTEN I'D BEEN THROUGH SOMETHING SO BITTER-SWEET.
WHAT A SHOCK !!

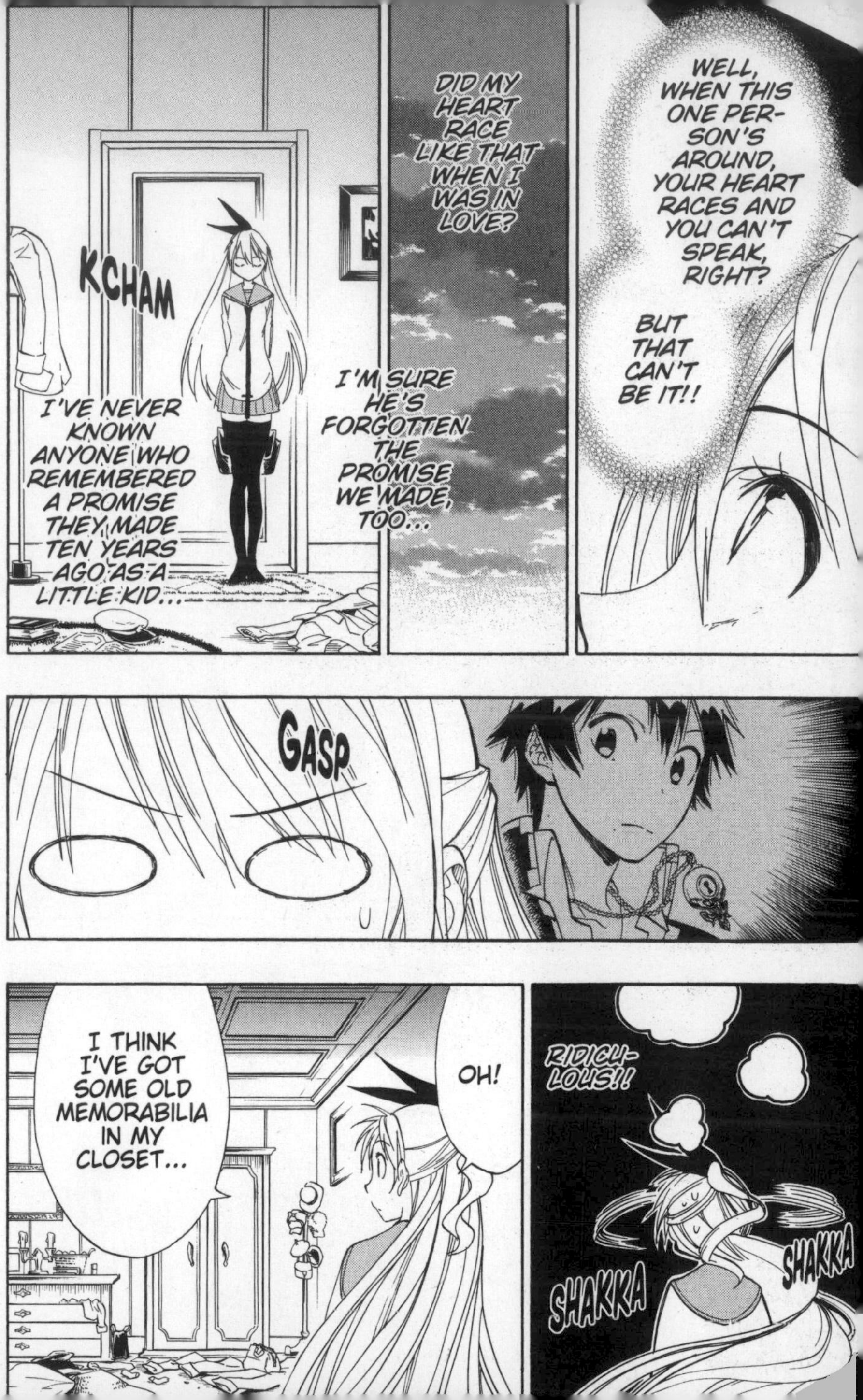
WELL, WHEN THIS ONE PERSON'S AROUND, YOUR HEART RACES AND YOU CAN'T SPEAK, RIGHT?
BUT THAT CAN'T BE IT!!
DID MY HEART RACE LIKE THAT WHEN I WAS IN LOVE?
I'M SURE HE'S FORGOTTEN THE PROMISE WE MADE, TOO...
KCHAM
I'VE NEVER KNOWN ANYONE WHO REMEMBERED A PROMISE THEY MADE TEN YEARS AGO AS A LITTLE KID...
GASP
RIDICU-LOUS!!
SHAKKA
SHAKKA
OH!
I THINK I'VE GOT SOME OLD MEMORABILIA IN MY CLOSET...

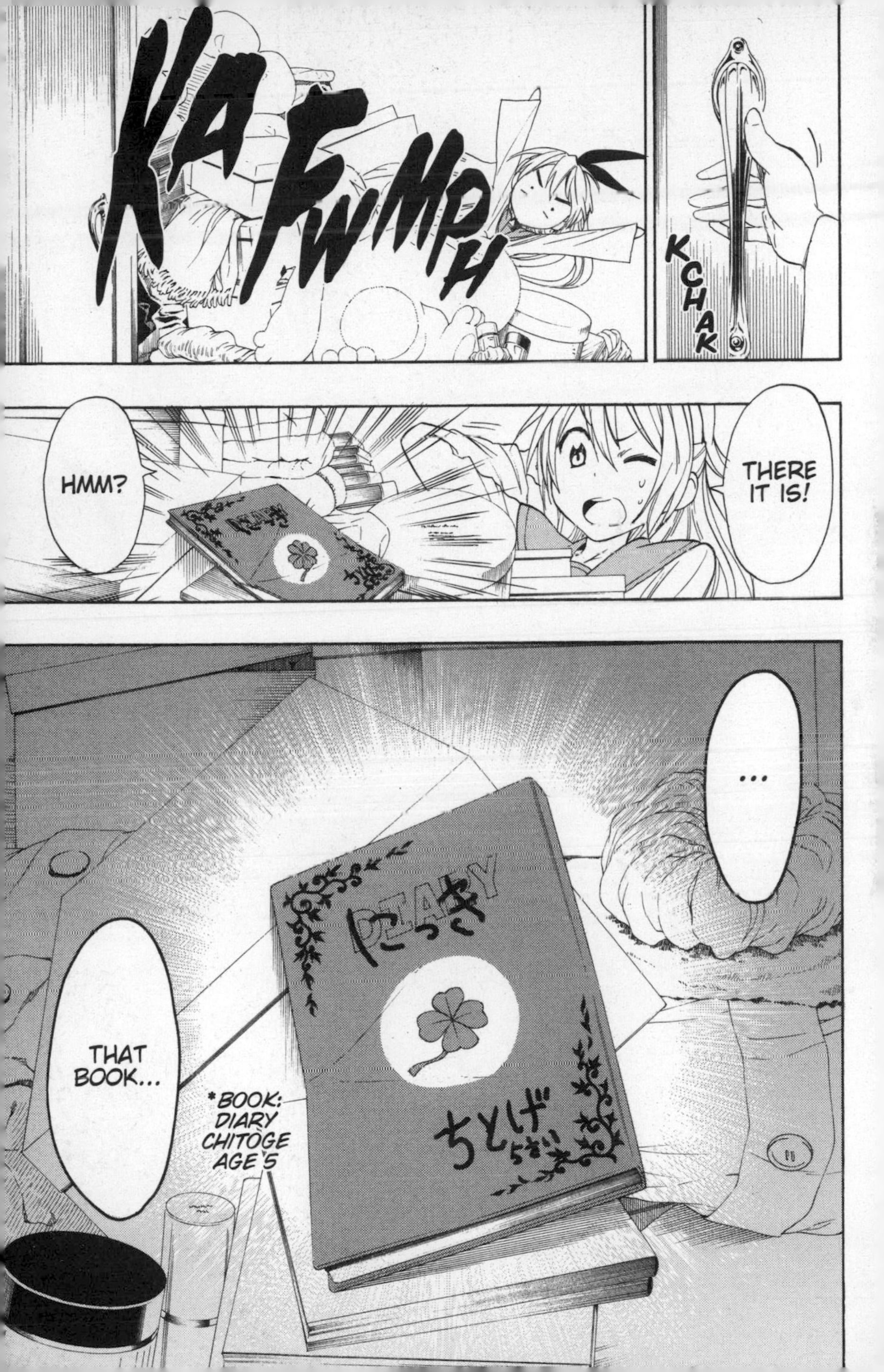
KCHAK
KA-FWUMPH
THERE IT IS!
HMM?
...
THAT BOOK...
DIARY
にっき
ちとげ 5さい
*BOOK: DIARY CHITOGE AGE 5

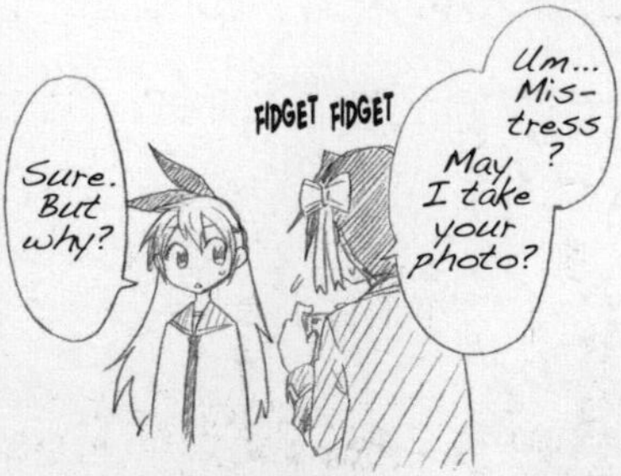
Um... Mis-tress? May I take your photo?
FIDGET FIDGET
Sure. But why?

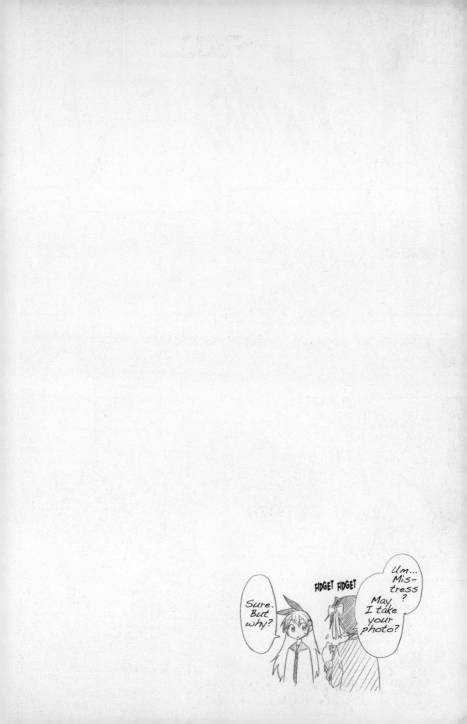

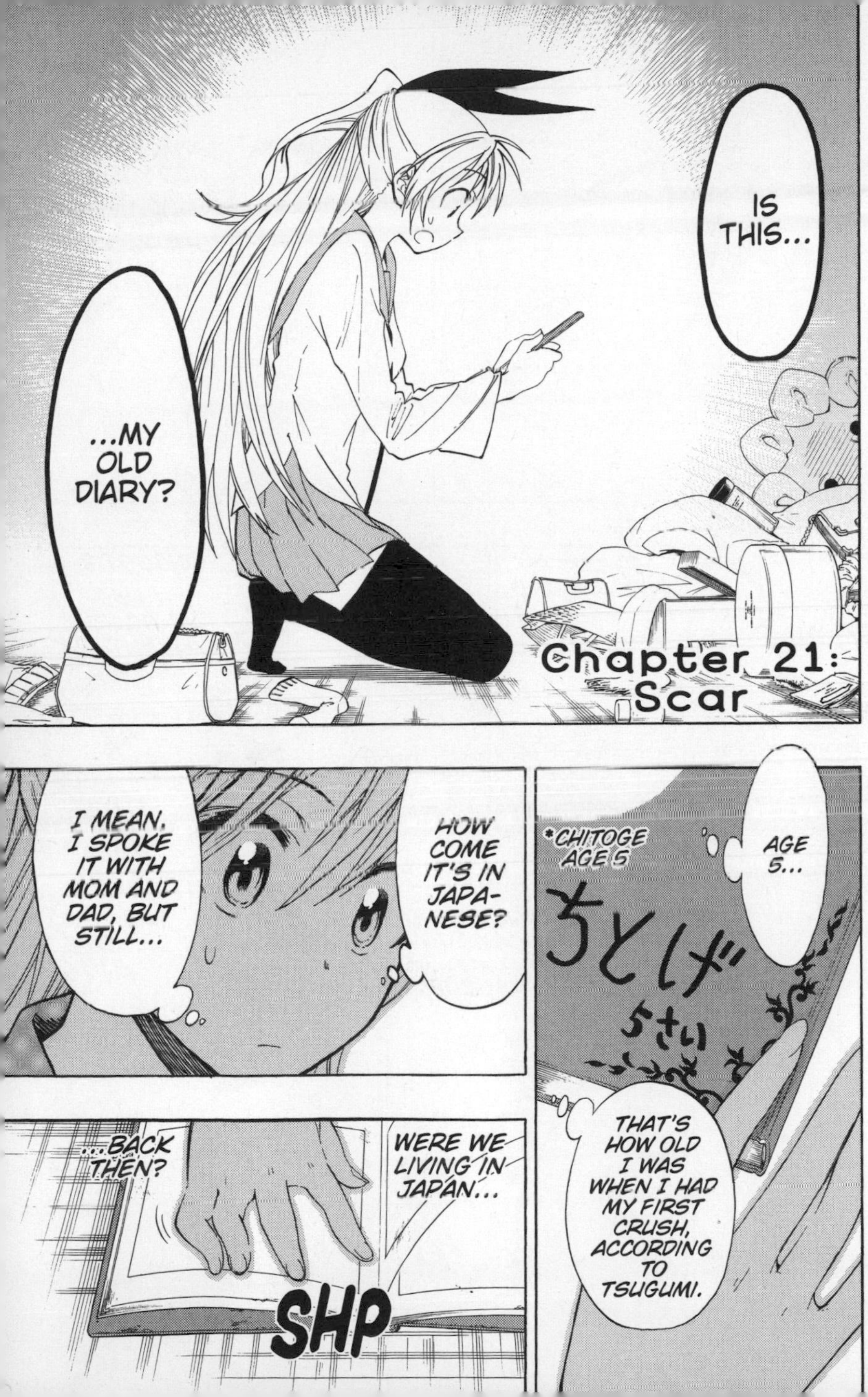
IS THIS...
...MY OLD DIARY?
Chapter 21: Scar
AGE 5...
*CHITOGE AGE 5
ちとげ
5さい
THAT'S HOW OLD I WAS WHEN I HAD MY FIRST CRUSH, ACCORDING TO TSUGUMI.
HOW COME IT'S IN JAPANESE?
I MEAN, I SPOKE IT WITH MOM AND DAD, BUT STILL...
WERE WE LIVING IN JAPAN...
...BACK THEN?
SHP

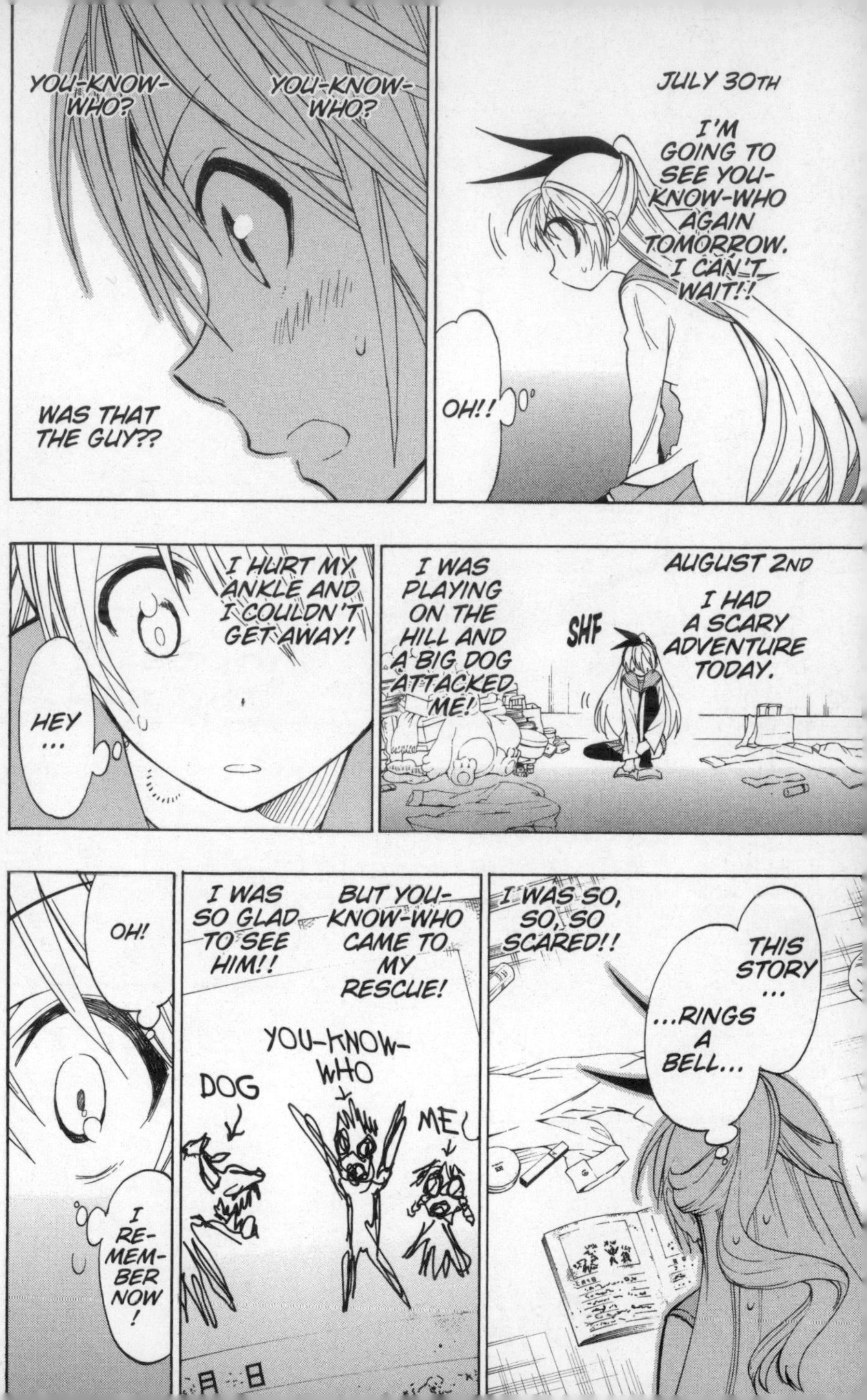
JULY 30TH
I'M GOING TO SEE YOU-KNOW-WHO AGAIN TOMORROW. I CAN'T WAIT!!
OH!!
YOU-KNOW-WHO?
YOU-KNOW-WHO?
WAS THAT THE GUY??
AUGUST 2ND
I HAD A SCARY ADVENTURE TODAY.
SHF
I WAS PLAYING ON THE HILL AND A BIG DOG ATTACKED ME!
I HURT MY ANKLE AND I COULDN'T GET AWAY!
HEY ...
THIS STORY ...
...RINGS A BELL...
I WAS SO, SO, SO SCARED!!
BUT YOU-KNOW-WHO CAME TO MY RESCUE!
I WAS SO GLAD TO SEE HIM!!
YOU-KNOW-WHO
DOG
ME
OH!
I REMEMBER NOW!

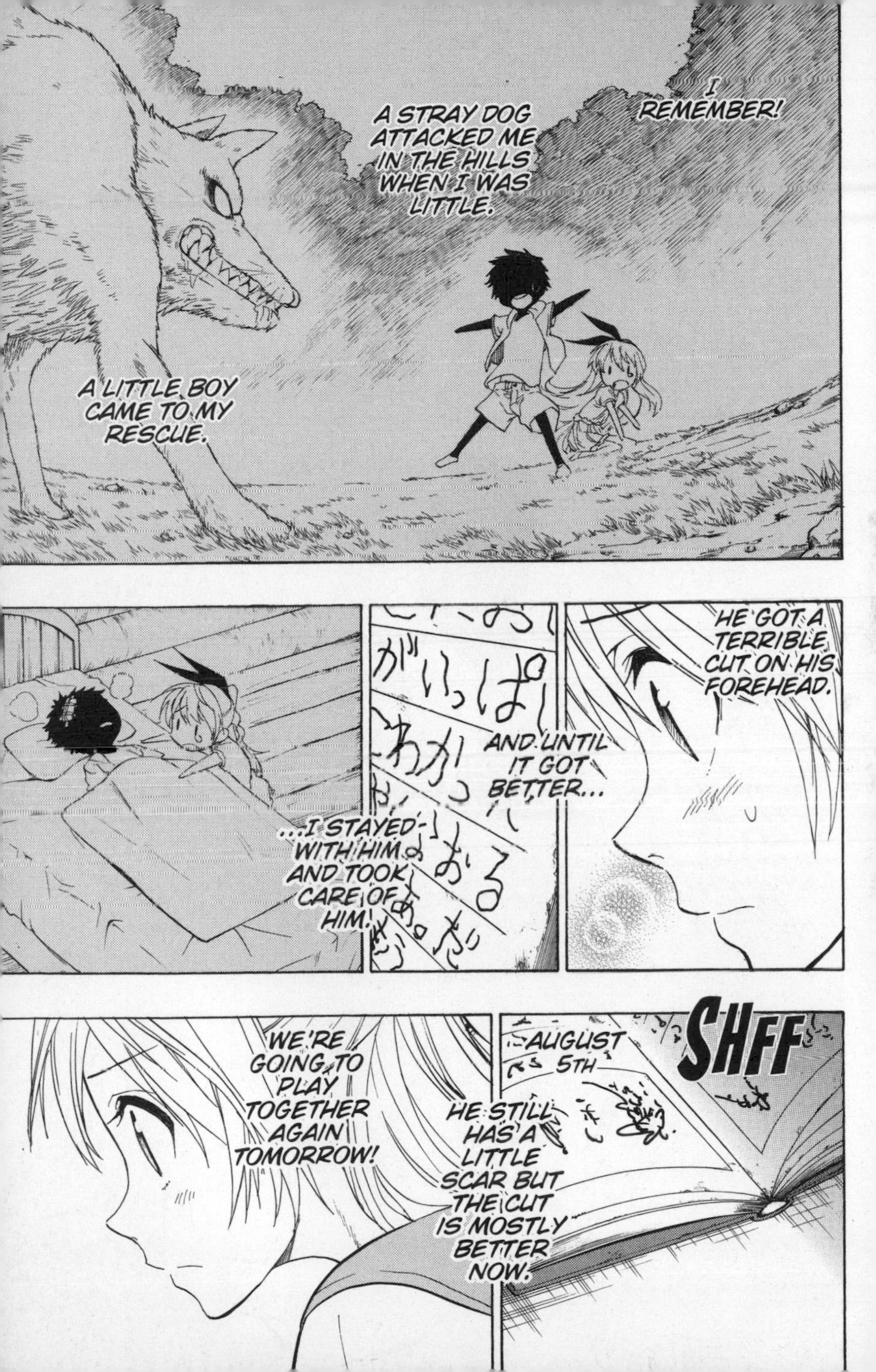
I REMEMBER!
A STRAY DOG ATTACKED ME IN THE HILLS WHEN I WAS LITTLE.
A LITTLE BOY CAME TO MY RESCUE.
HE GOT A TERRIBLE CUT ON HIS FOREHEAD.
AND UNTIL IT GOT BETTER...
...I STAYED WITH HIM AND TOOK CARE OF HIM!
SHFF
AUGUST 5TH
HE STILL HAS A LITTLE SCAR BUT THE CUT IS MOSTLY BETTER NOW.
WE'RE GOING TO PLAY TOGETHER AGAIN TOMORROW!

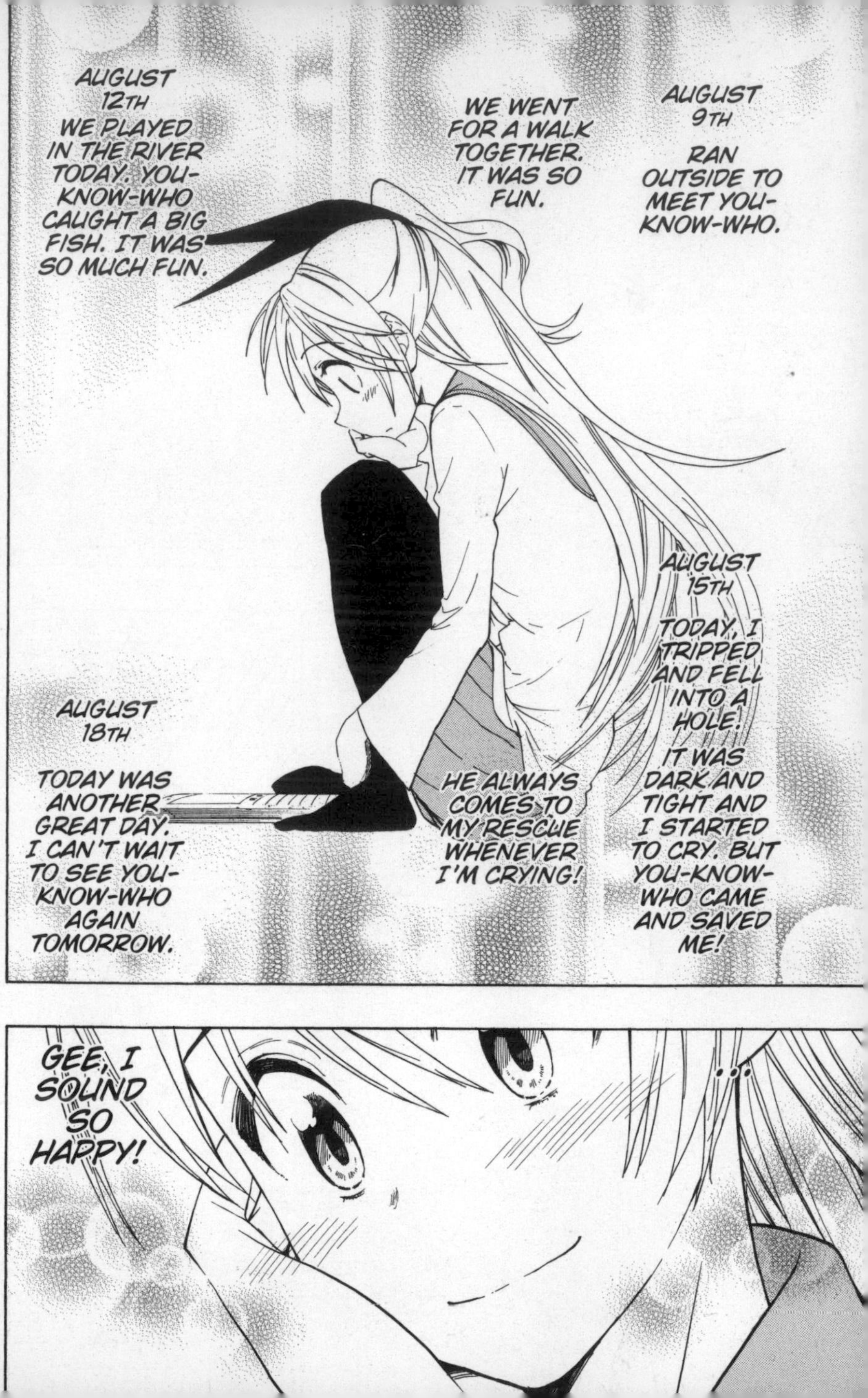
AUGUST 9TH
RAN OUTSIDE TO MEET YOU-KNOW-WHO.
WE WENT FOR A WALK TOGETHER. IT WAS SO FUN.
AUGUST 12TH
WE PLAYED IN THE RIVER TODAY. YOU-KNOW-WHO CAUGHT A BIG FISH. IT WAS SO MUCH FUN.
AUGUST 15TH
TODAY, I TRIPPED AND FELL INTO A HOLE!
IT WAS DARK AND TIGHT AND I STARTED TO CRY. BUT YOU-KNOW-WHO CAME AND SAVED ME!
HE ALWAYS COMES TO MY RESCUE WHENEVER I'M CRYING!
AUGUST 18TH
TODAY WAS ANOTHER GREAT DAY. I CAN'T WAIT TO SEE YOU-KNOW-WHO AGAIN TOMORROW.
...
GEE, I SOUND SO HAPPY!

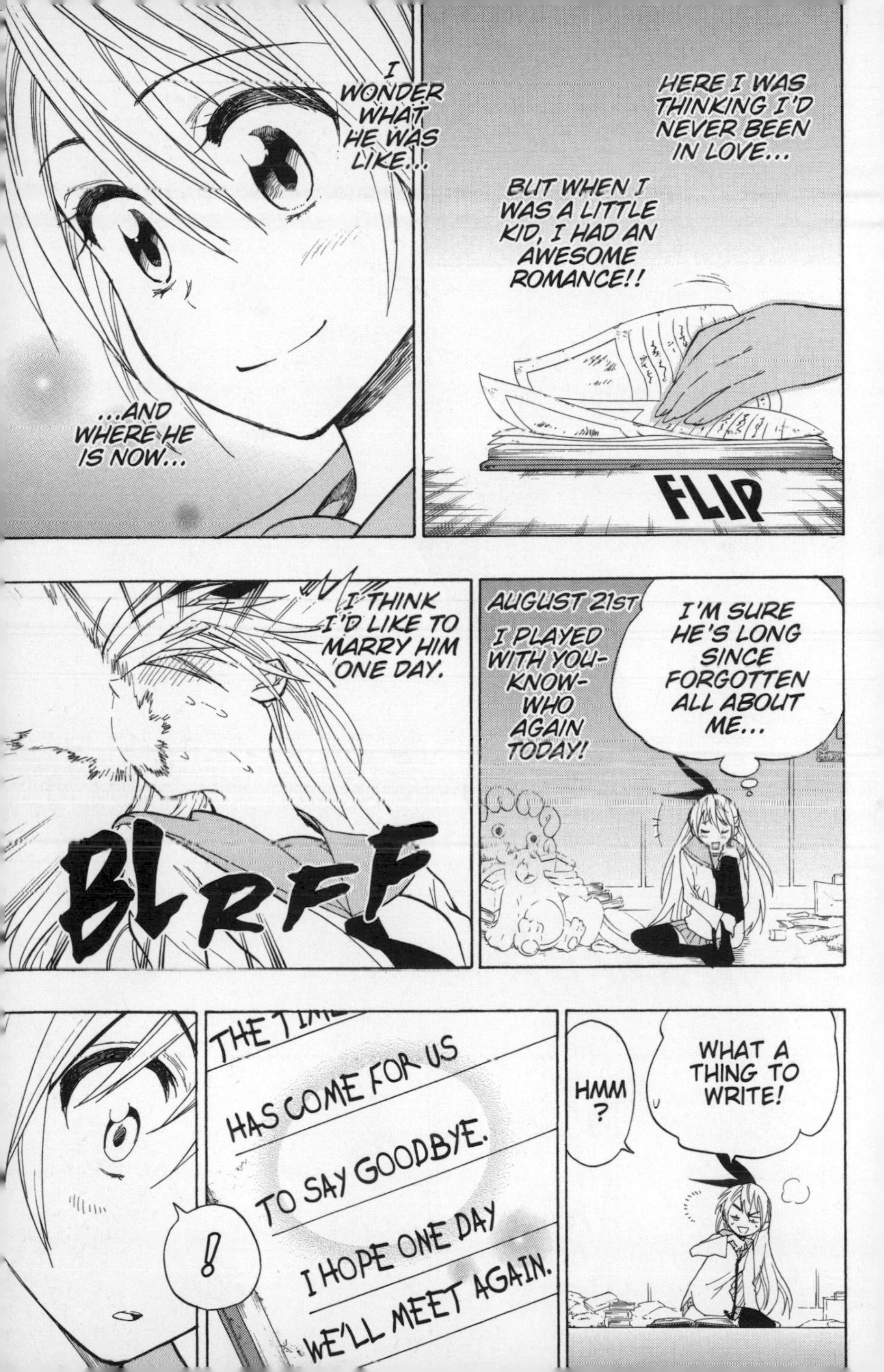
HERE I WAS THINKING I'D NEVER BEEN IN LOVE...
BUT WHEN I WAS A LITTLE KID, I HAD AN AWESOME ROMANCE!!
FLIP
I WONDER WHAT HE WAS LIKE...
...AND WHERE HE IS NOW...
AUGUST 21ST
I PLAYED WITH YOU-KNOW-WHO AGAIN TODAY!
I'M SURE HE'S LONG SINCE FORGOTTEN ALL ABOUT ME...
I THINK I'D LIKE TO MARRY HIM ONE DAY.
BLRFF
WHAT A THING TO WRITE!
HMM?
THE
HAS COME FOR US
TO SAY GOODBYE.
I HOPE ONE DAY
WE'LL MEET AGAIN.
!

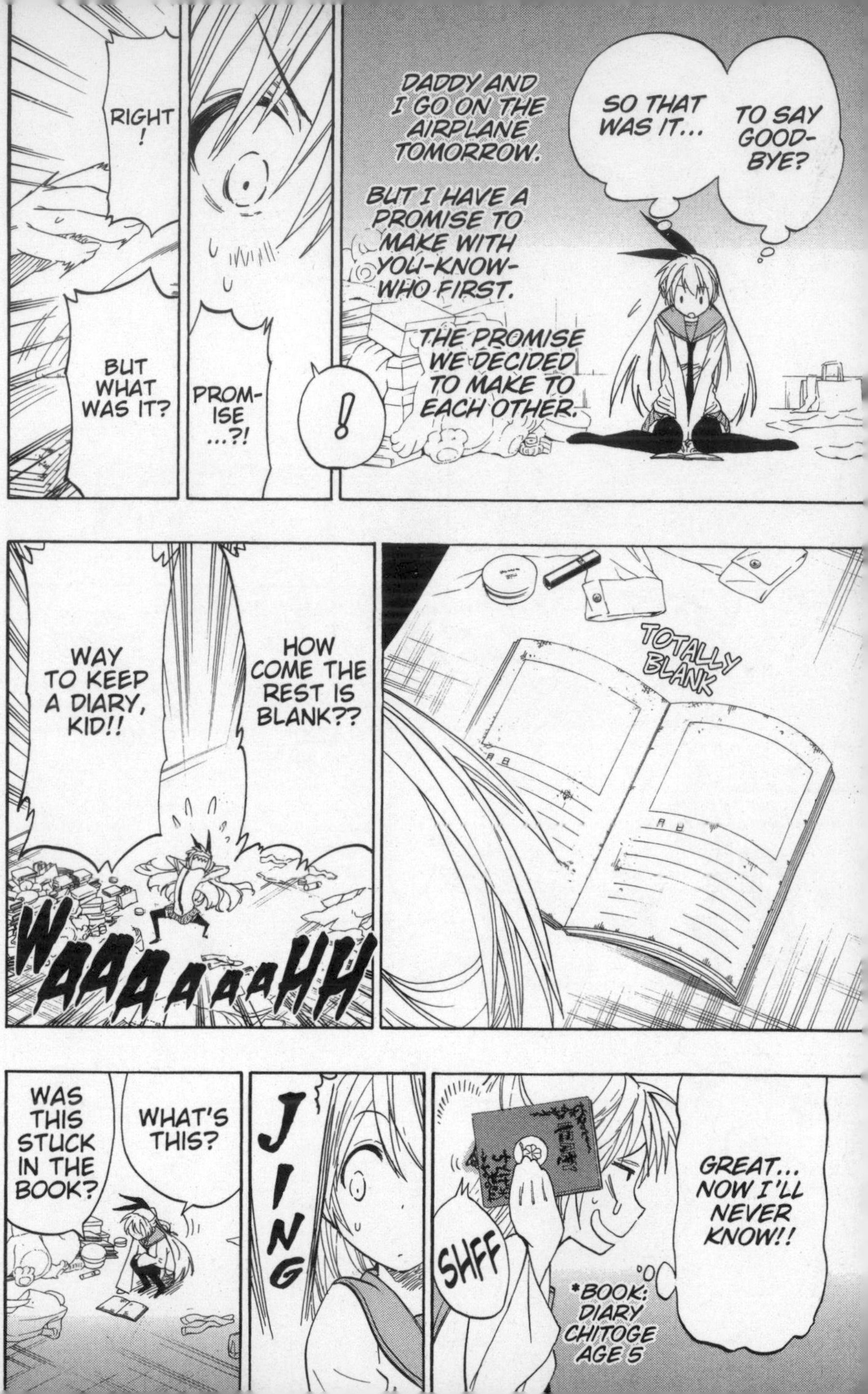
SO THAT WAS IT... TO SAY GOOD-BYE?
DADDY AND I GO ON THE AIRPLANE TOMORROW.
BUT I HAVE A PROMISE TO MAKE WITH YOU-KNOW-WHO FIRST.
THE PROMISE WE DECIDED TO MAKE TO EACH OTHER.
!
PROMISE...?!
RIGHT!
BUT WHAT WAS IT?
TOTALLY BLANK
HOW COME THE REST IS BLANK??
WAY TO KEEP A DIARY, KID!!
WAAAAAAAHH
GREAT... NOW I'LL NEVER KNOW!!
SHFF
*BOOK: DIARY CHITOGE AGE 5
JING
WHAT'S THIS?
WAS THIS STUCK IN THE BOOK?

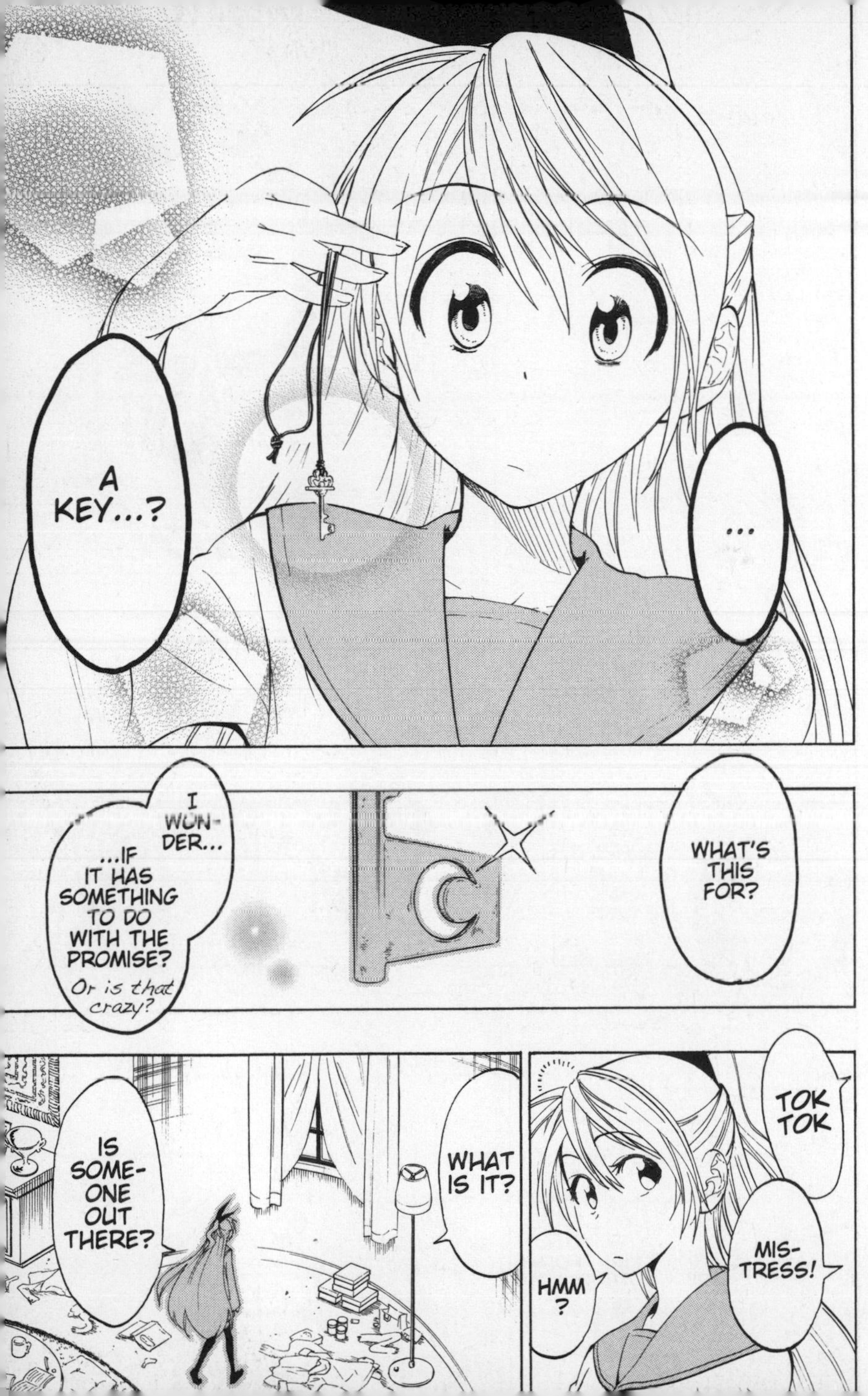
...
A KEY...?
WHAT'S THIS FOR?
I WONDER...
...IF IT HAS SOMETHING TO DO WITH THE PROMISE? Or is that crazy?
TOK TOK
MISTRESS!
HMM?
WHAT IS IT?
IS SOMEONE OUT THERE?

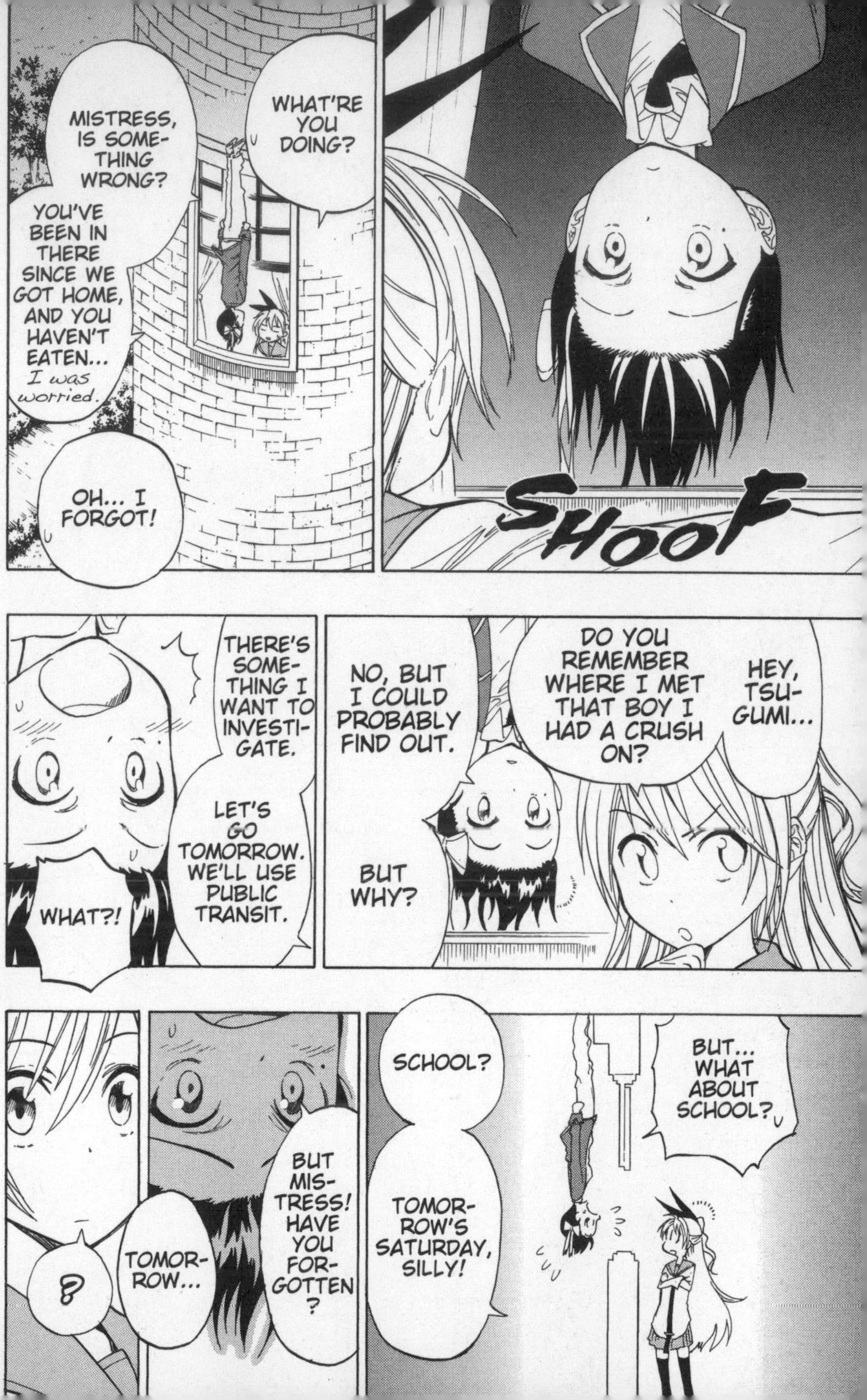
SHOOF
WHAT'RE YOU DOING?
MISTRESS, IS SOMETHING WRONG?
YOU'VE BEEN IN THERE SINCE WE GOT HOME, AND YOU HAVEN'T EATEN... I was worried.
OH... I FORGOT!
HEY, TSUGUMI...
DO YOU REMEMBER WHERE I MET THAT BOY I HAD A CRUSH ON?
NO, BUT I COULD PROBABLY FIND OUT.
BUT WHY?
THERE'S SOMETHING I WANT TO INVESTIGATE.
LET'S GO TOMORROW. WE'LL USE PUBLIC TRANSIT.
WHAT?!
BUT... WHAT ABOUT SCHOOL?
SCHOOL?
TOMORROW'S SATURDAY, SILLY!
BUT MISTRESS! HAVE YOU FORGOTTEN?
TOMORROW...
?

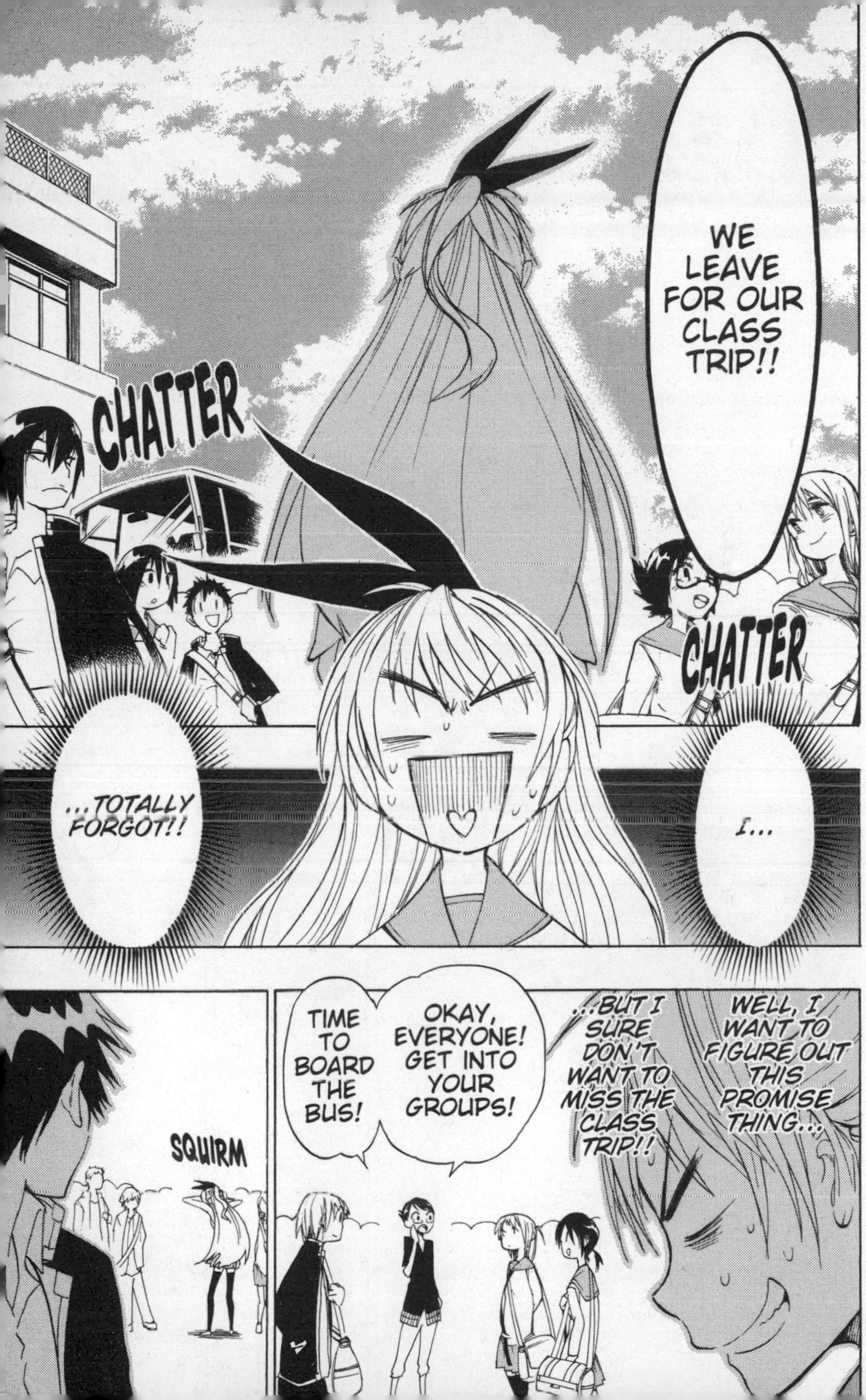
WE LEAVE FOR OUR CLASS TRIP!!
CHATTER
CHATTER
I...
...TOTALLY FORGOT!!
WELL, I WANT TO FIGURE OUT THIS PROMISE THING...
...BUT I SURE DON'T WANT TO MISS THE CLASS TRIP!!
OKAY, EVERYONE! GET INTO YOUR GROUPS!
TIME TO BOARD THE BUS!
SQUIRM

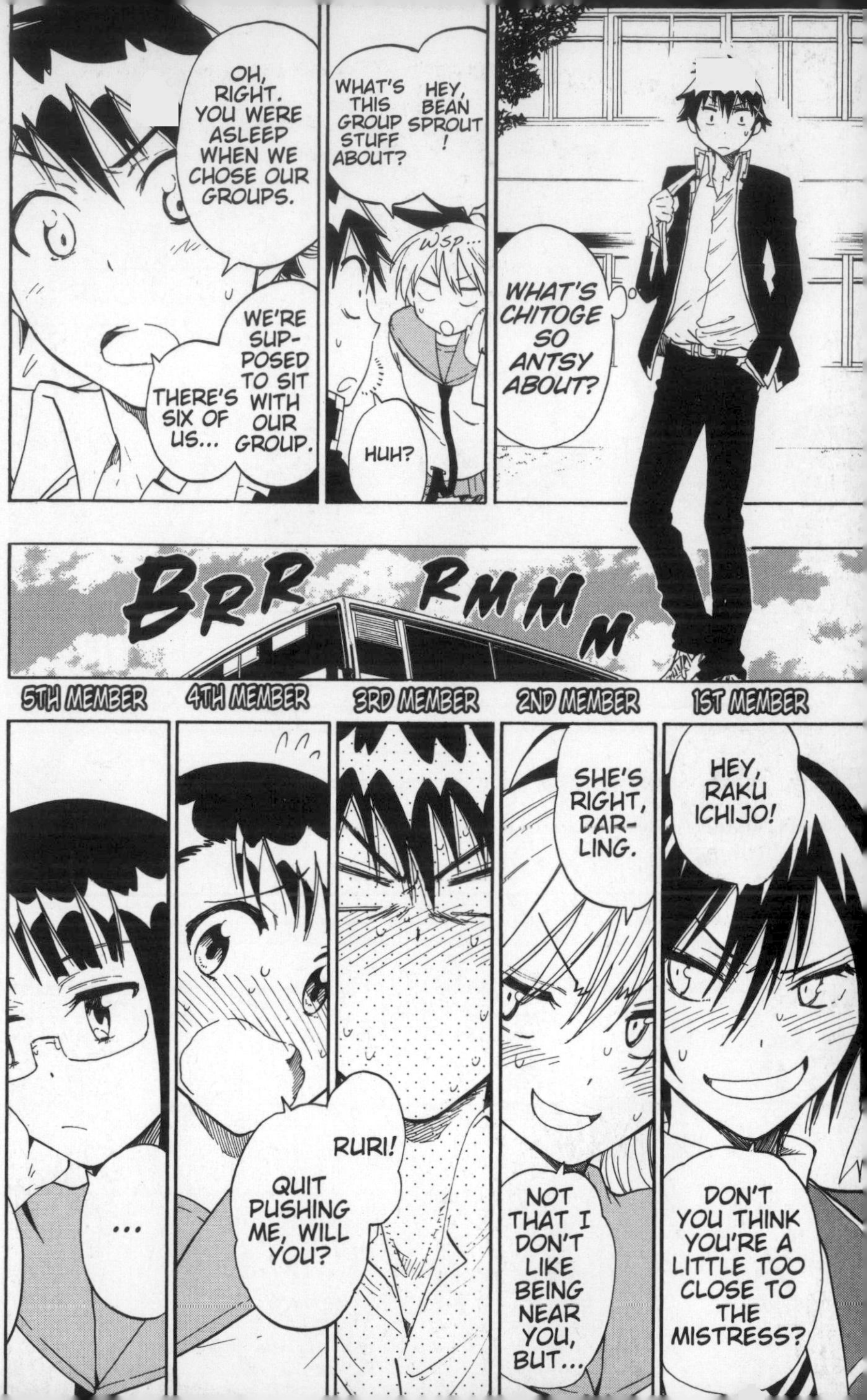
WHAT'S CHITOGE SO ANTSY ABOUT?
HEY, BEAN SPROUT!
WHAT'S THIS GROUP STUFF ABOUT?
WSP...
HUH?
OH, RIGHT. YOU WERE ASLEEP WHEN WE CHOSE OUR GROUPS.
WE'RE SUP-POSED TO SIT WITH OUR GROUP.
THERE'S SIX OF US...
BRR RMMMM
1ST MEMBER
HEY, RAKU ICHIJO!
DON'T YOU THINK YOU'RE A LITTLE TOO CLOSE TO THE MISTRESS?
2ND MEMBER
SHE'S RIGHT, DAR-LING.
NOT THAT I DON'T LIKE BEING NEAR YOU, BUT...
3RD MEMBER
RURI!
QUIT PUSHING ME, WILL YOU?
4TH MEMBER
5TH MEMBER
...

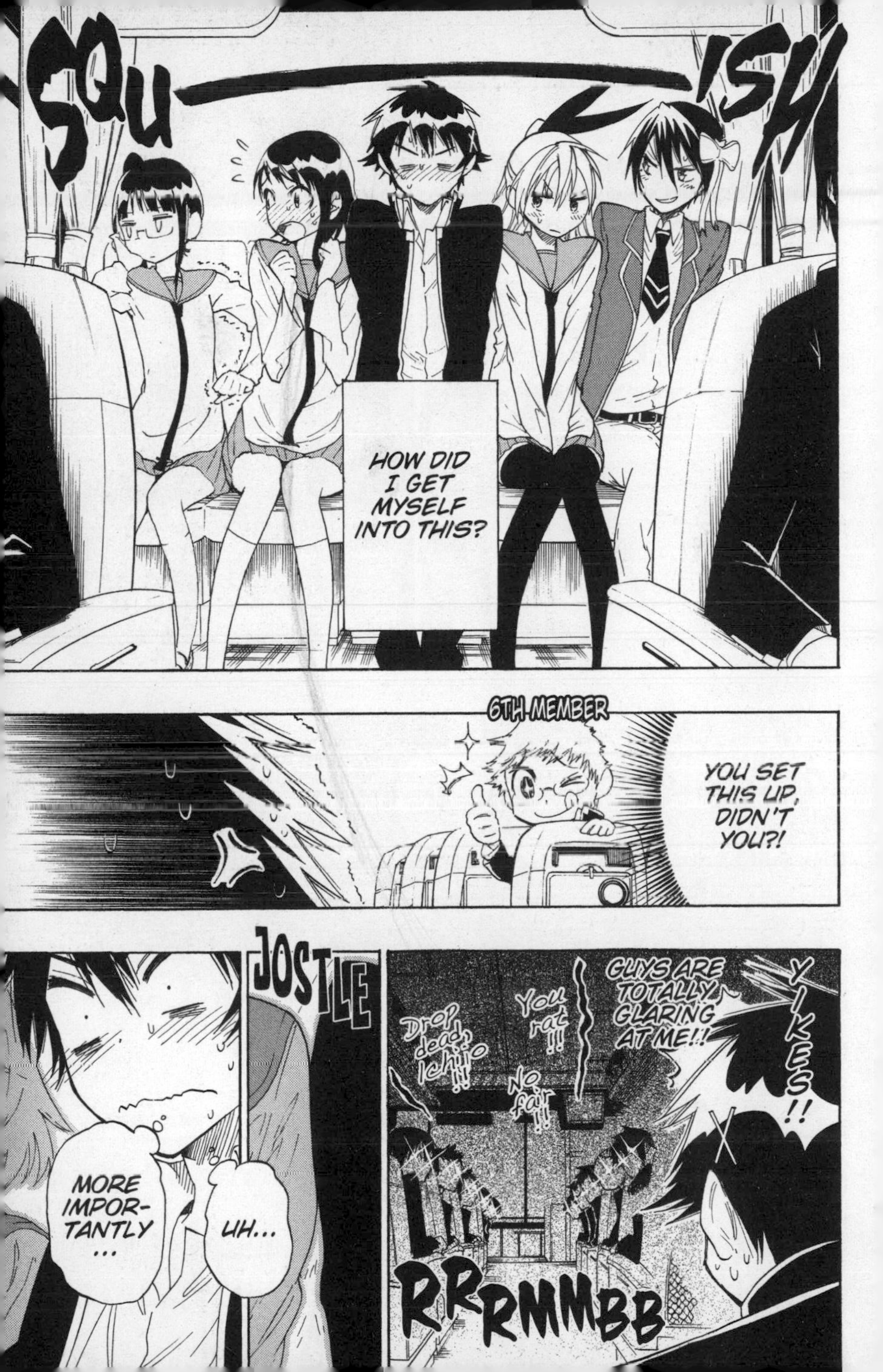
SQU—ISH
HOW DID I GET MYSELF INTO THIS?
6TH MEMBER
YOU SET THIS UP, DIDN'T YOU?!
YIKES!!
GUYS ARE TOTALLY GLARING AT ME!!
You rat!!
Drop dead, Ichijo!!
No fair!!
RRRMMBB
JOSTLE
UH...
MORE IMPORTANTLY...

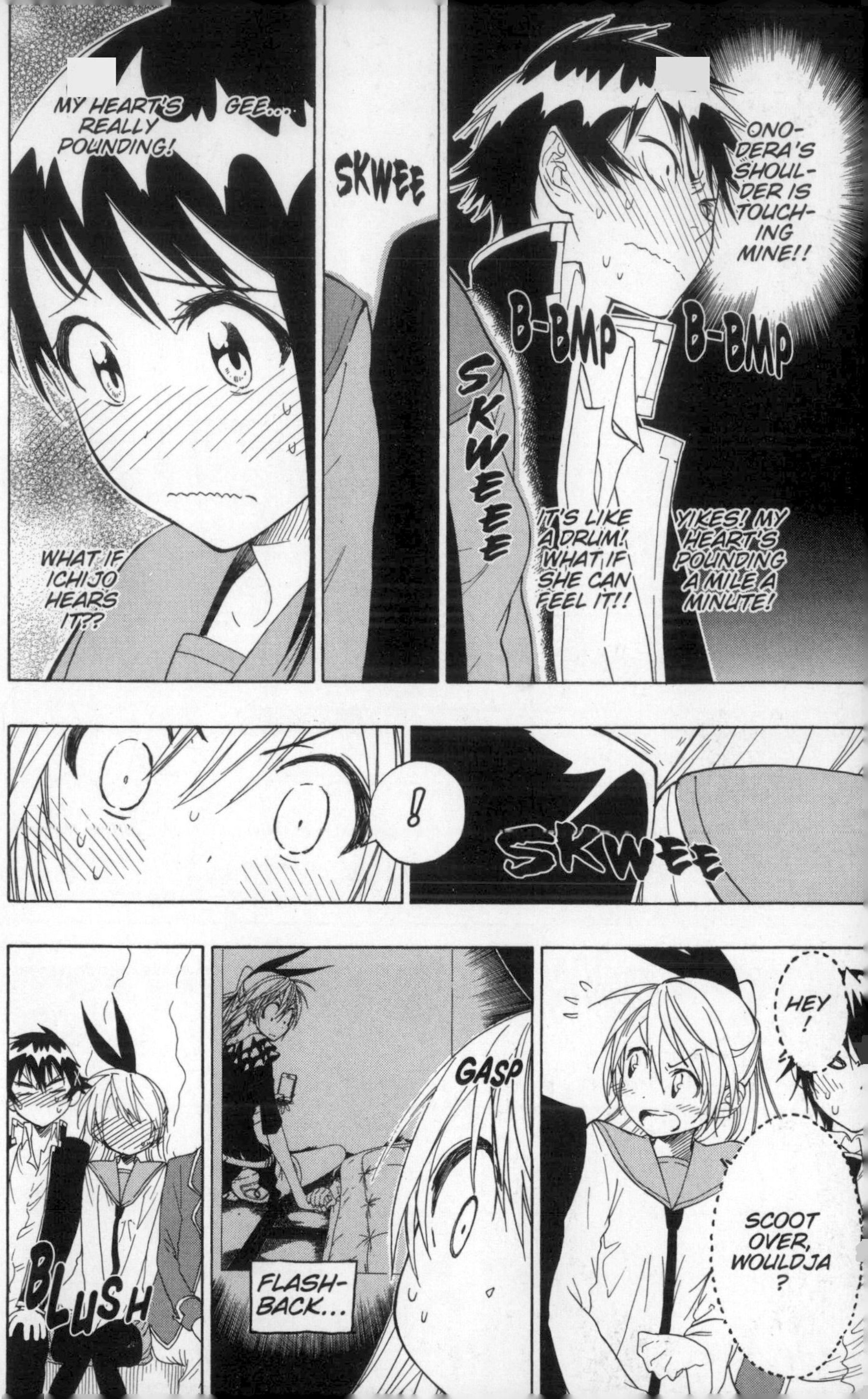
ONO-DERA'S SHOULDER IS TOUCHING MINE!!
B-BMP
B-BMP
YIKES! MY HEART'S POUNDING A MILE A MINUTE!
IT'S LIKE A DRUM! WHAT IF SHE CAN FEEL IT!!
SKWEEE
SKWEE
GEE...
MY HEART'S REALLY POUNDING!
WHAT IF ICHIJO HEARS IT??
SKWEE
!
HEY!
SCOOT OVER, WOULDJA?
GASP
FLASH-BACK...
BLUSH

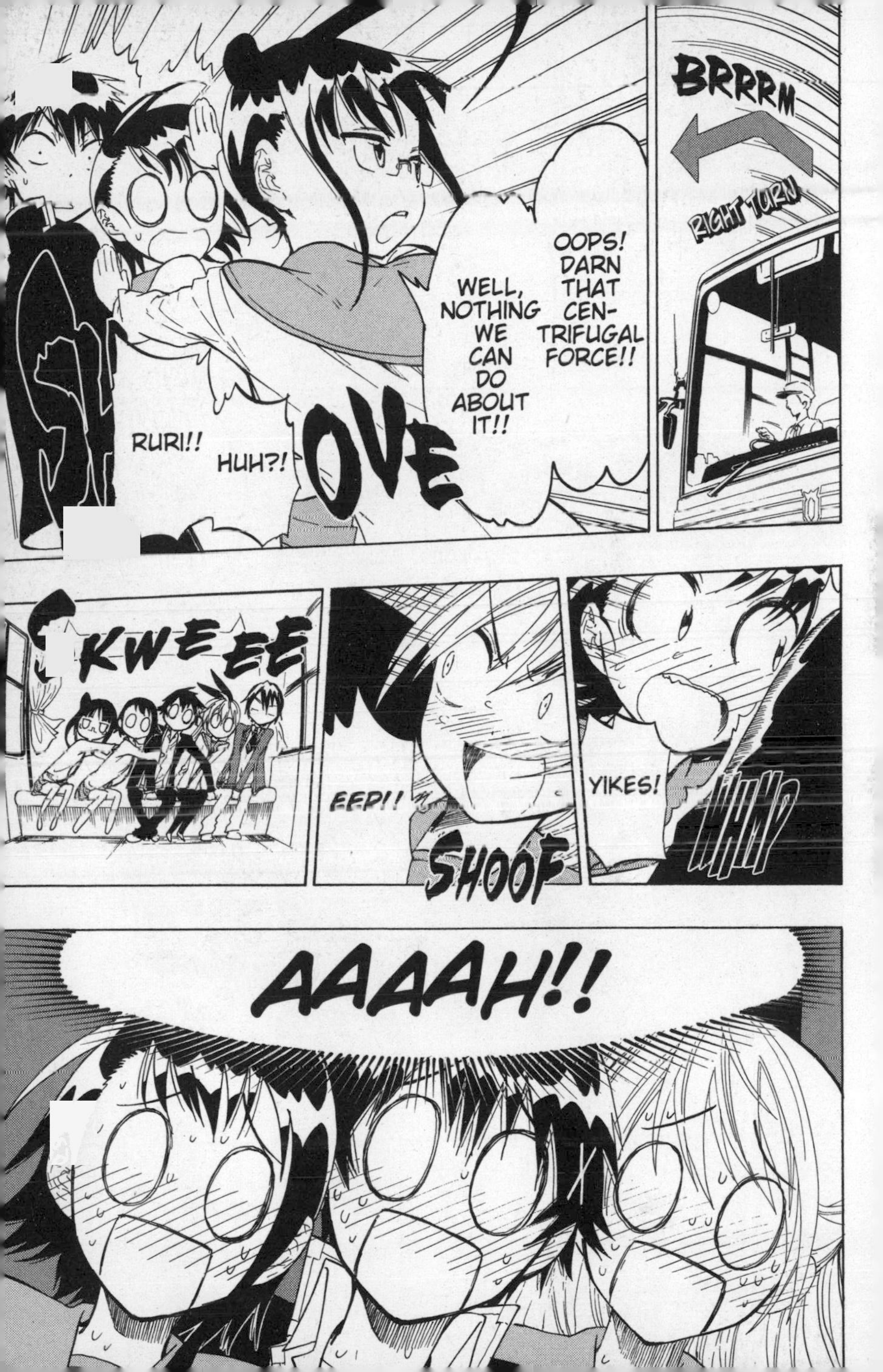
BRRRM
RIGHT TURN
OOPS! DARN THAT CEN-TRIFUGAL FORCE!!
WELL, NOTHING WE CAN DO ABOUT IT!!
OVE
HUH?!
RURI!!
YIKES!
SHOOF
EEP!!
KWEEEE
AAAAH!!

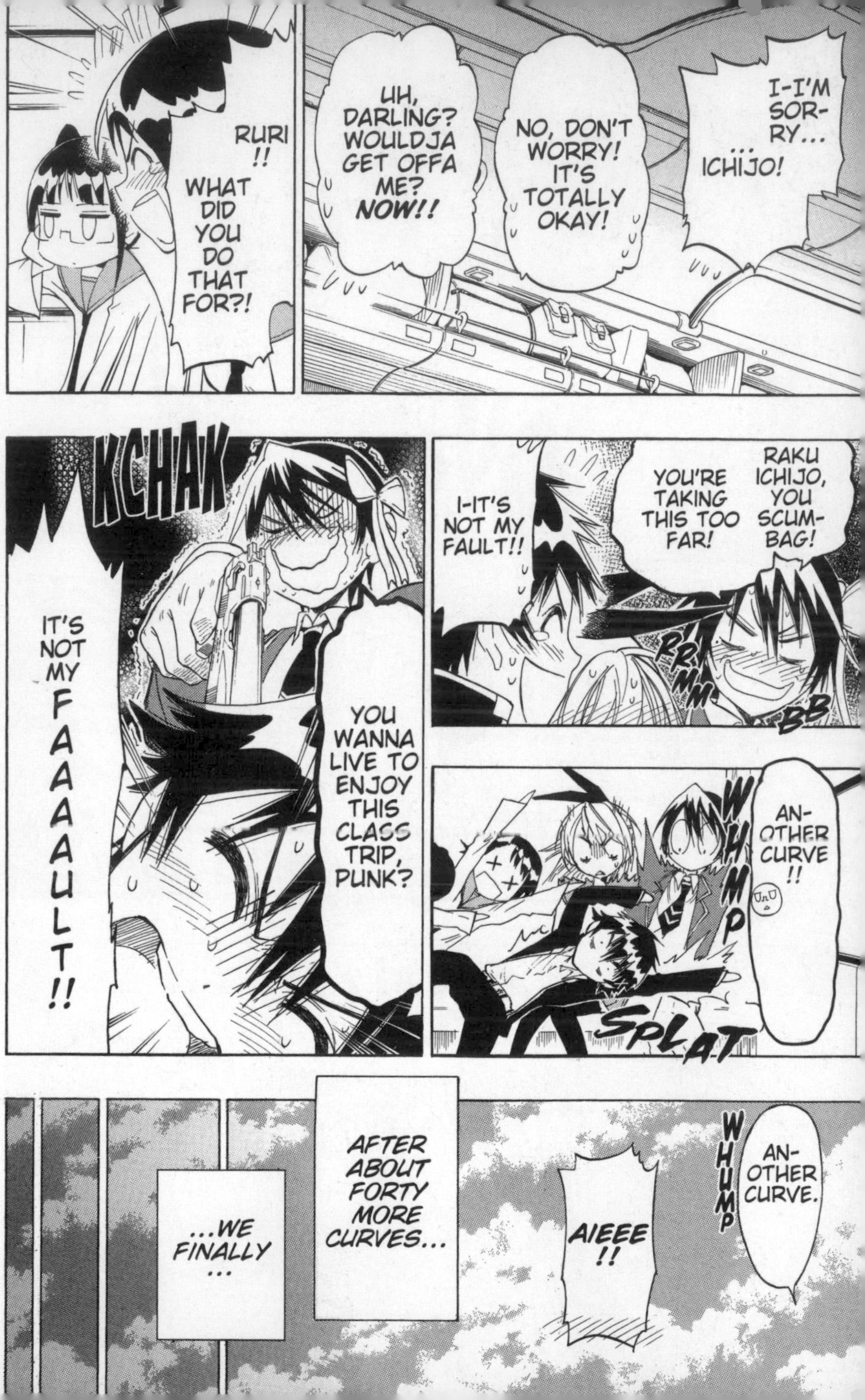
I-I'M SORRY... ICHIJO!
NO, DON'T WORRY! IT'S TOTALLY OKAY!
UH, DARLING? WOULDJA GET OFFA ME? NOW!!
RURI!! WHAT DID YOU DO THAT FOR?!
RAKU ICHIJO, YOU SCUM-BAG!
YOU'RE TAKING THIS TOO FAR!
I-IT'S NOT MY FAULT!!
RRRMM
BB
AN-OTHER CURVE!!
WHMP
SPLAT
KCHAK
YOU WANNA LIVE TO ENJOY THIS CLASS TRIP, PUNK?
IT'S NOT MY FAAAAAAULT!!
AN-OTHER CURVE.
WHUMP
AIEEE!!
AFTER ABOUT FORTY MORE CURVES...
...WE FINALLY ...

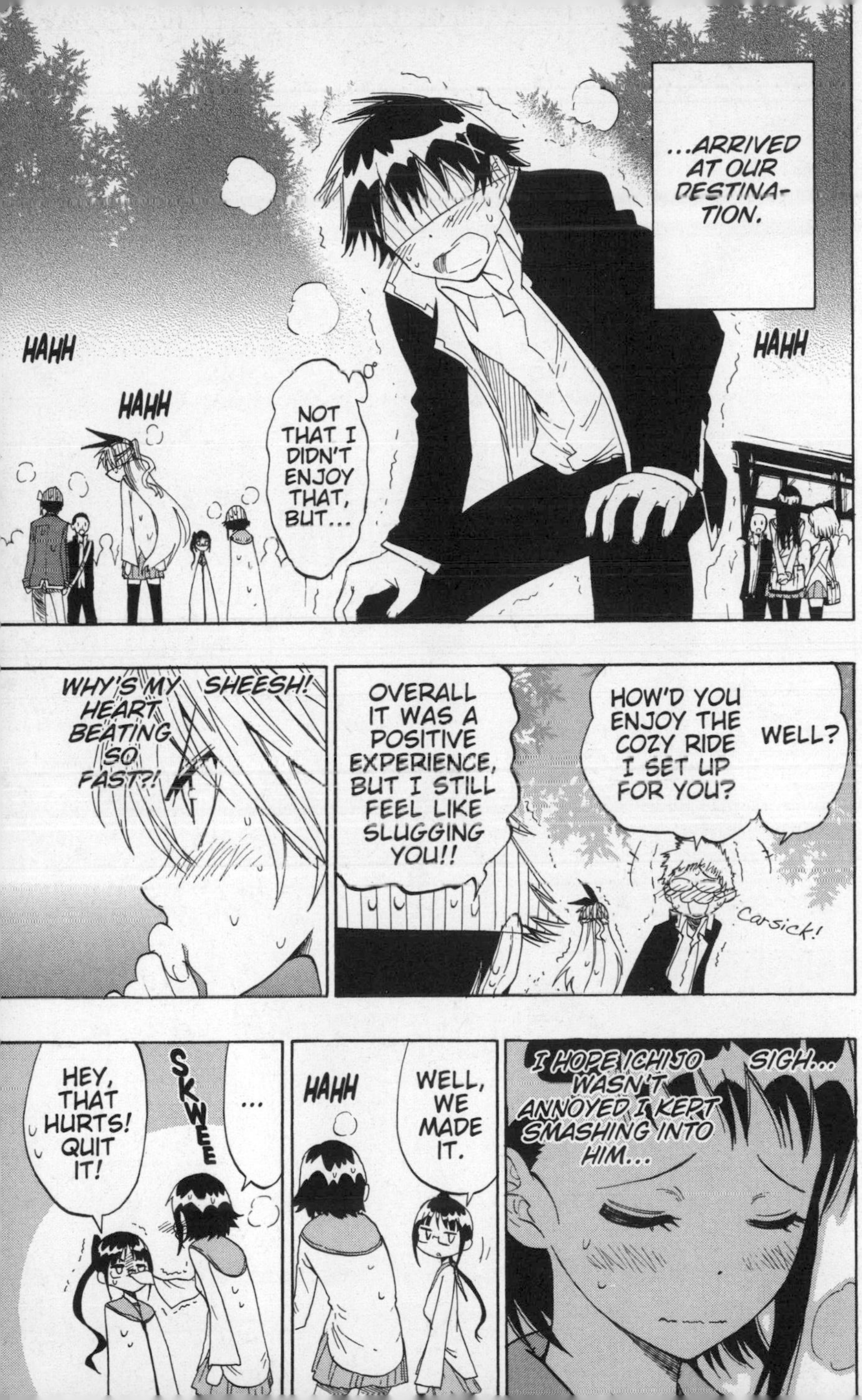
...ARRIVED AT OUR DESTINA-TION.
HAHH
NOT THAT I DIDN'T ENJOY THAT, BUT...
HAHH
HAHH
WELL?
HOW'D YOU ENJOY THE COZY RIDE I SET UP FOR YOU?
Carsick!
OVERALL IT WAS A POSITIVE EXPERIENCE, BUT I STILL FEEL LIKE SLUGGING YOU!!
SHEESH!
WHY'S MY HEART BEATING SO FAST?!
SIGH...
I HOPE ICHIJO WASN'T ANNOYED I KEPT SMASHING INTO HIM...
WELL, WE MADE IT.
HAHH
...
SKWEE
HEY, THAT HURTS! QUIT IT!

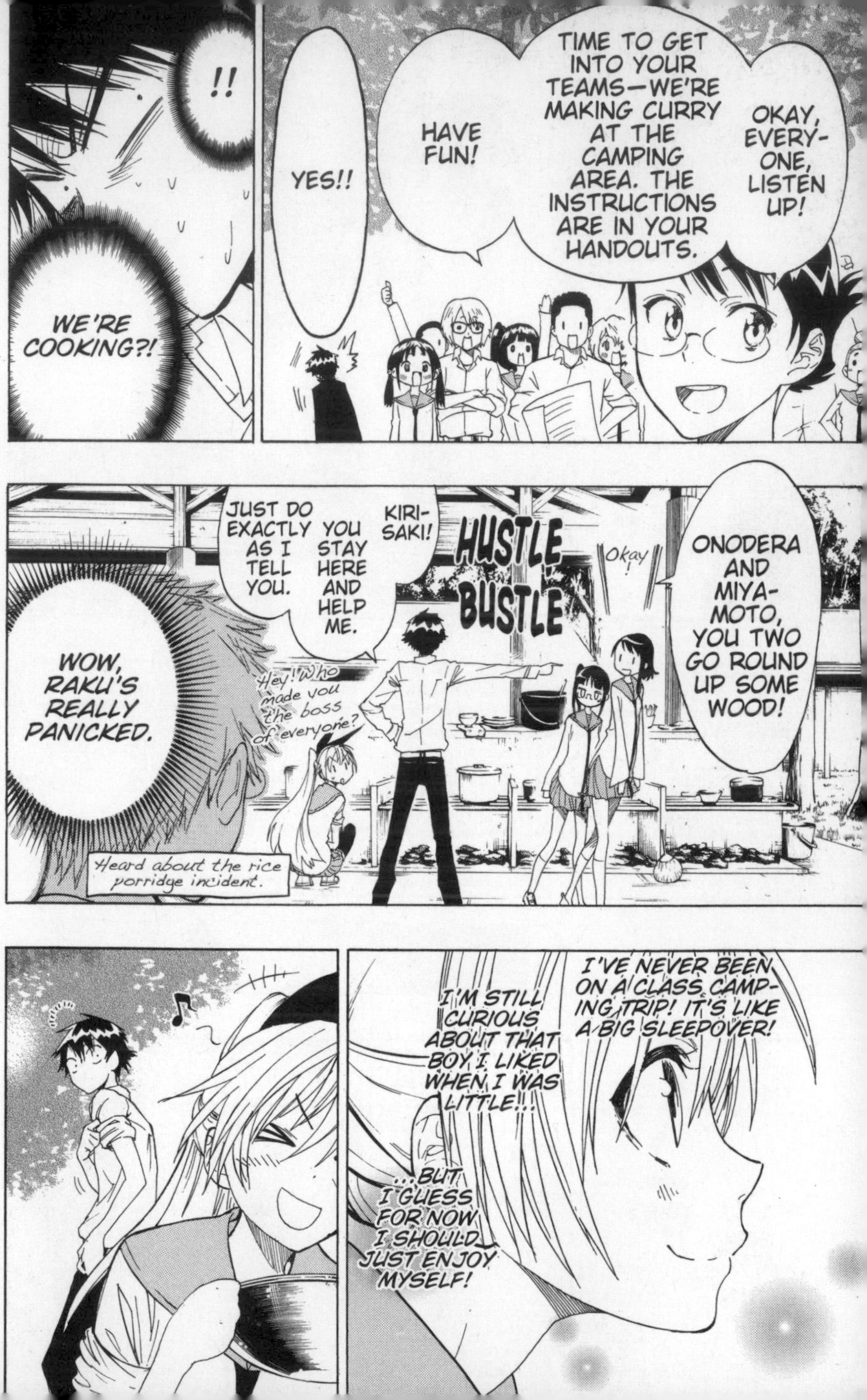
OKAY, EVERY-ONE, LISTEN UP!
TIME TO GET INTO YOUR TEAMS—WE'RE MAKING CURRY AT THE CAMPING AREA. THE INSTRUCTIONS ARE IN YOUR HANDOUTS.
HAVE FUN!
YES!!
!!
WE'RE COOKING?!
ONODERA AND MIYA-MOTO, YOU TWO GO ROUND UP SOME WOOD!
Okay!
HUSTLE BUSTLE
KIRI-SAKI!
YOU STAY HERE AND HELP ME.
JUST DO EXACTLY AS I TELL YOU.
Hey! Who made you the boss of everyone?
WOW, RAKU'S REALLY PANICKED.
Heard about the rice porridge incident.
I'VE NEVER BEEN ON A CLASS CAMP-ING TRIP! IT'S LIKE A BIG SLEEPOVER!
I'M STILL CURIOUS ABOUT THAT BOY I LIKED WHEN I WAS LITTLE...
...BUT I GUESS FOR NOW I SHOULD JUST ENJOY MYSELF!

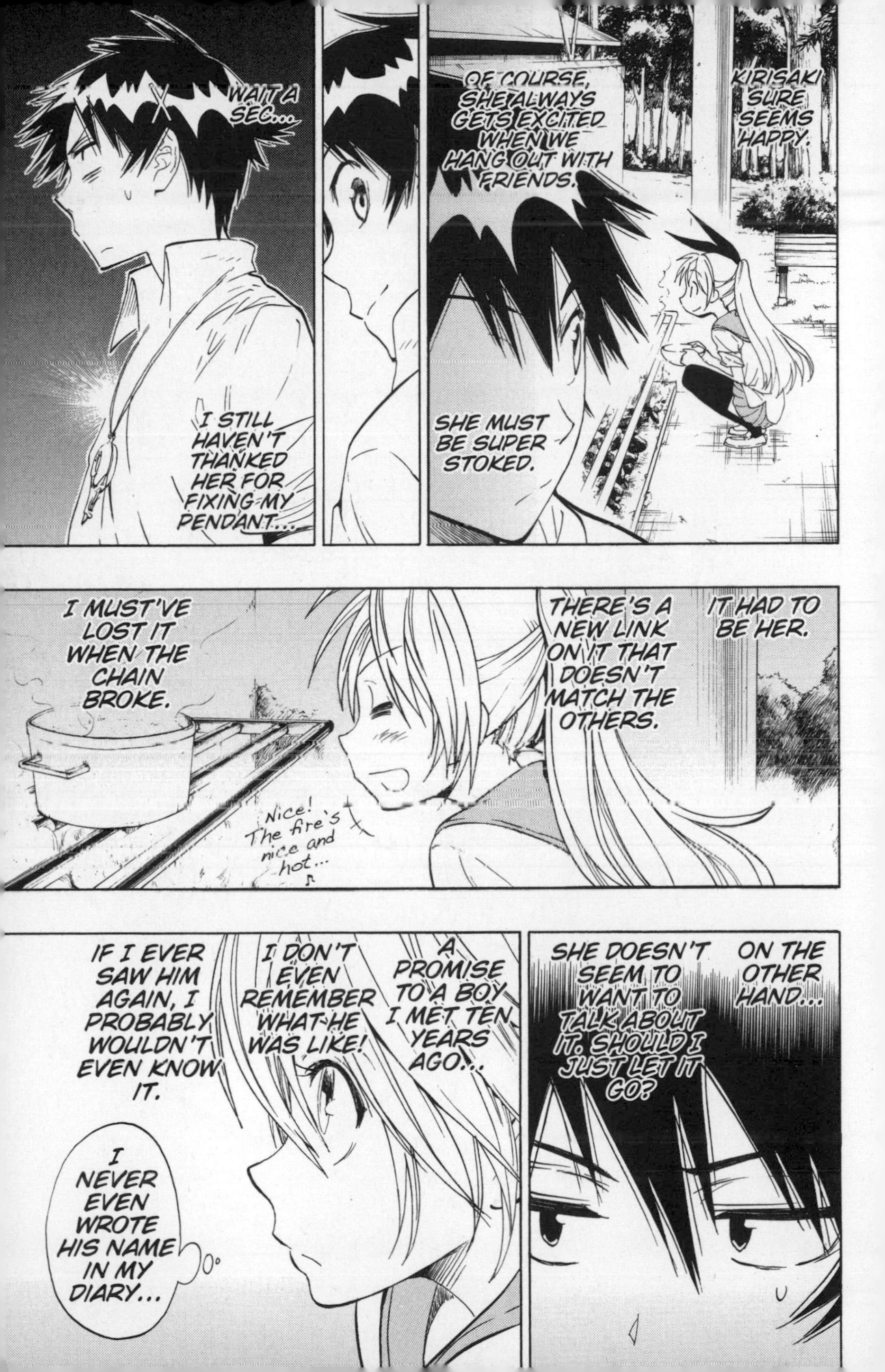
KIRISAKI SURE SEEMS HAPPY.
OF COURSE, SHE ALWAYS GETS EXCITED WHEN WE HANG OUT WITH FRIENDS.
SHE MUST BE SUPER STOKED.
WAIT A SEC...
I STILL HAVEN'T THANKED HER FOR FIXING MY PENDANT...
IT HAD TO BE HER.
THERE'S A NEW LINK ON IT THAT DOESN'T MATCH THE OTHERS.
I MUST'VE LOST IT WHEN THE CHAIN BROKE.
Nice! The fire's nice and hot... ♪
ON THE OTHER HAND...
SHE DOESN'T SEEM TO WANT TO TALK ABOUT IT. SHOULD I JUST LET IT GO?
A PROMISE TO A BOY I MET TEN YEARS AGO...
I DON'T EVEN REMEMBER WHAT HE WAS LIKE!
IF I EVER SAW HIM AGAIN, I PROBABLY WOULDN'T EVEN KNOW IT.
I NEVER EVEN WROTE HIS NAME IN MY DIARY...

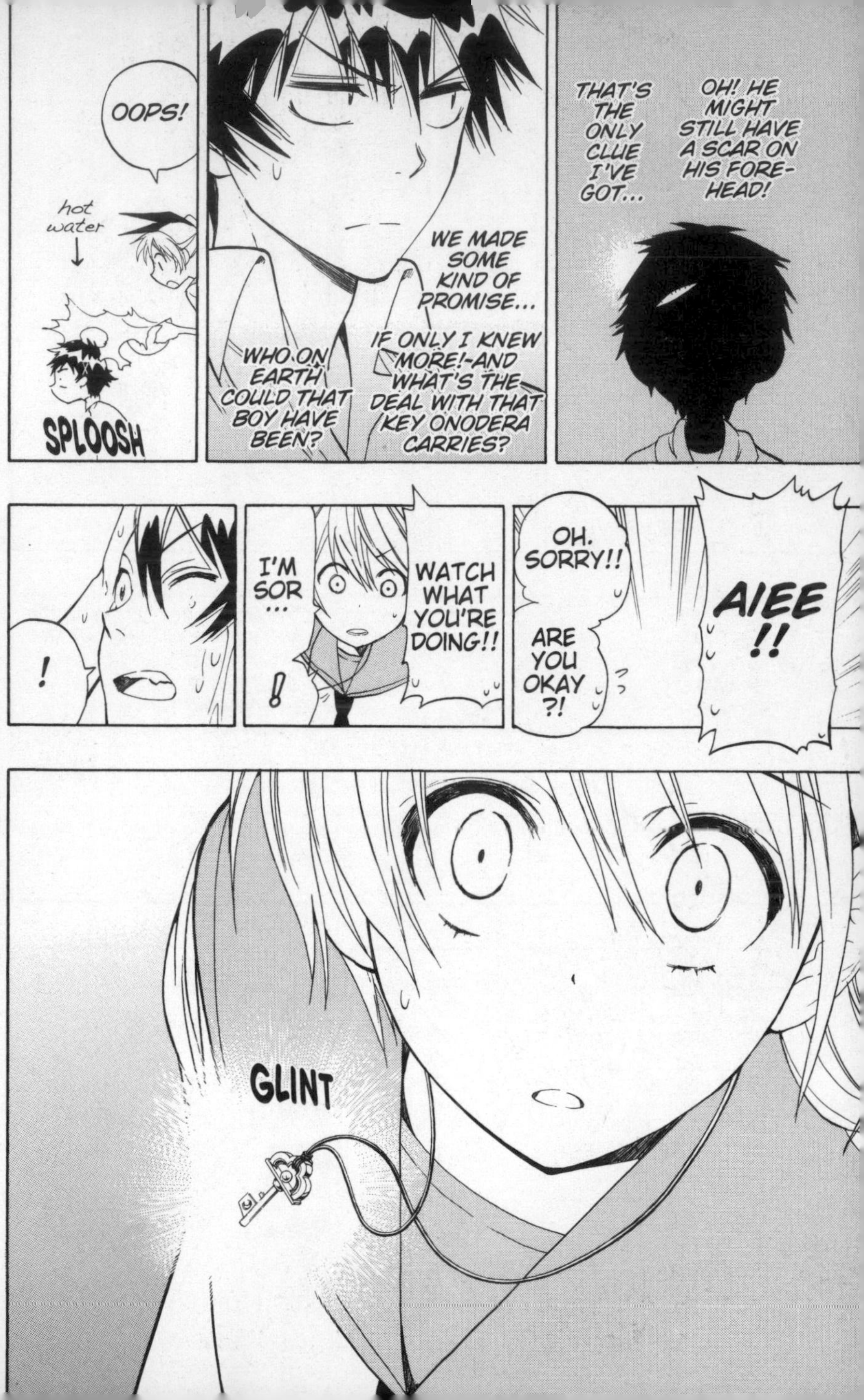
OH! HE MIGHT STILL HAVE A SCAR ON HIS FOREHEAD!
THAT'S THE ONLY CLUE I'VE GOT...
WE MADE SOME KIND OF PROMISE...
IF ONLY I KNEW MORE!-AND WHAT'S THE DEAL WITH THAT KEY ONODERA CARRIES?
WHO ON EARTH COULD THAT BOY HAVE BEEN?
OOPS!
hot water
SPLOOSH
AIEE !!
OH. SORRY!!
ARE YOU OKAY ?!
WATCH WHAT YOU'RE DOING!!
I'M SOR ...
!
!
GLINT

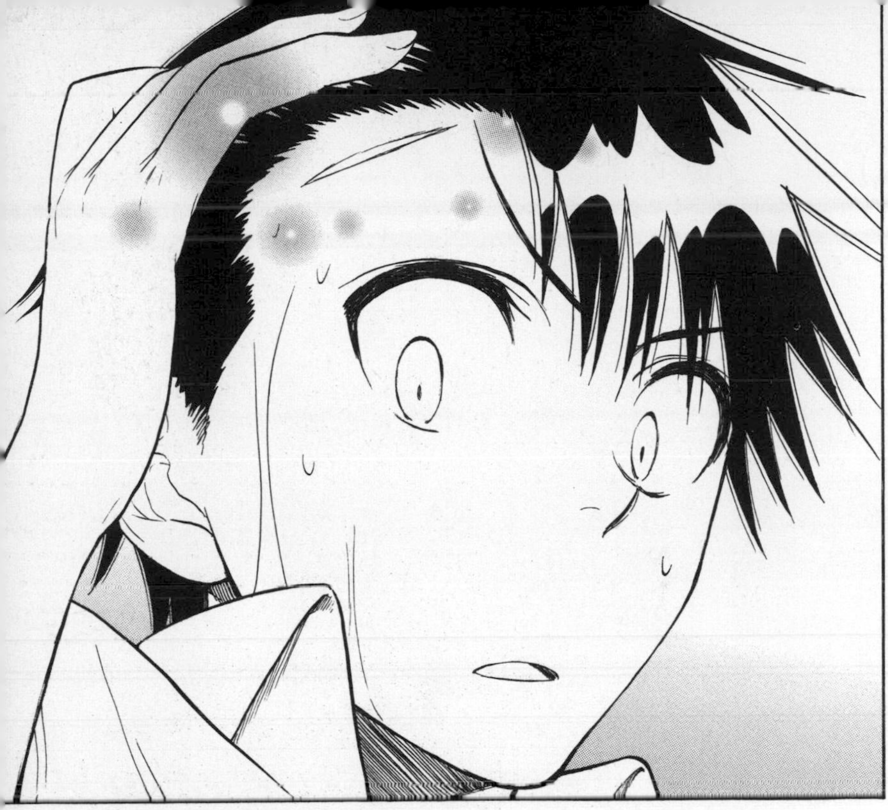
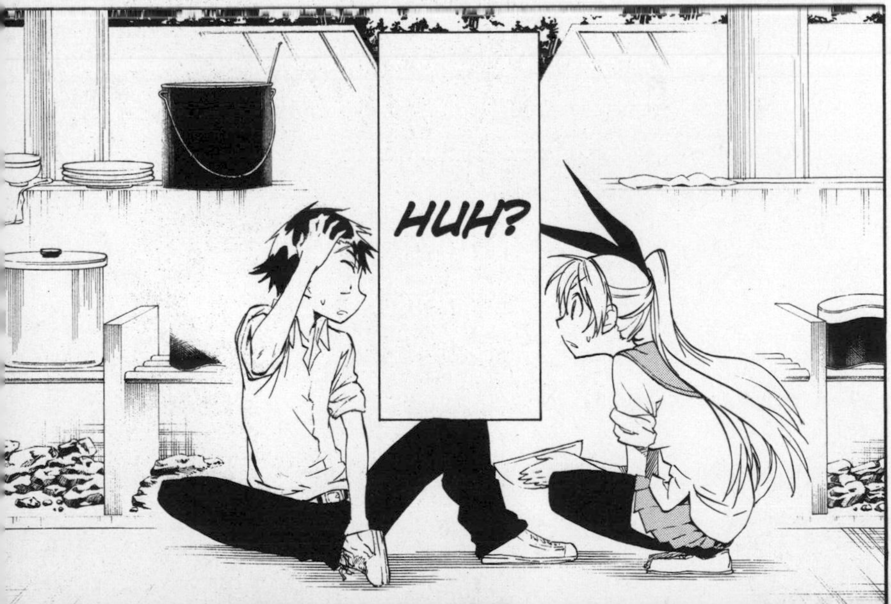
HUH?

By the way, how're you dangling out there?
Oh, I'm hooking my toes on the window ledge.
That's impressive.

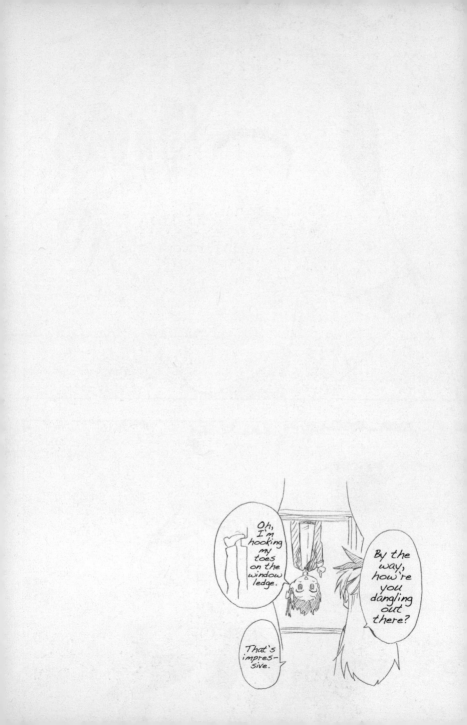

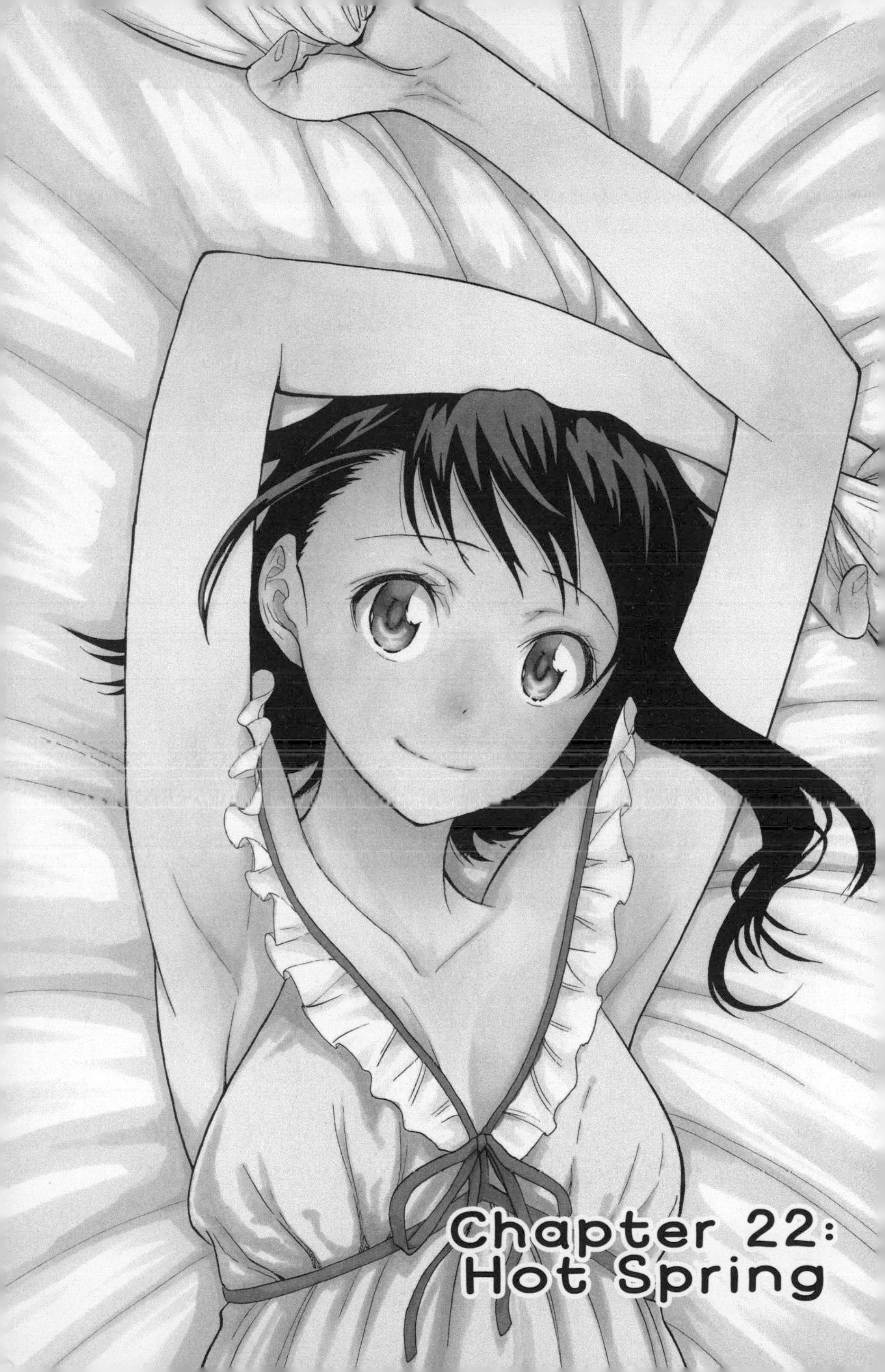
Chapter 22:
Hot Spring

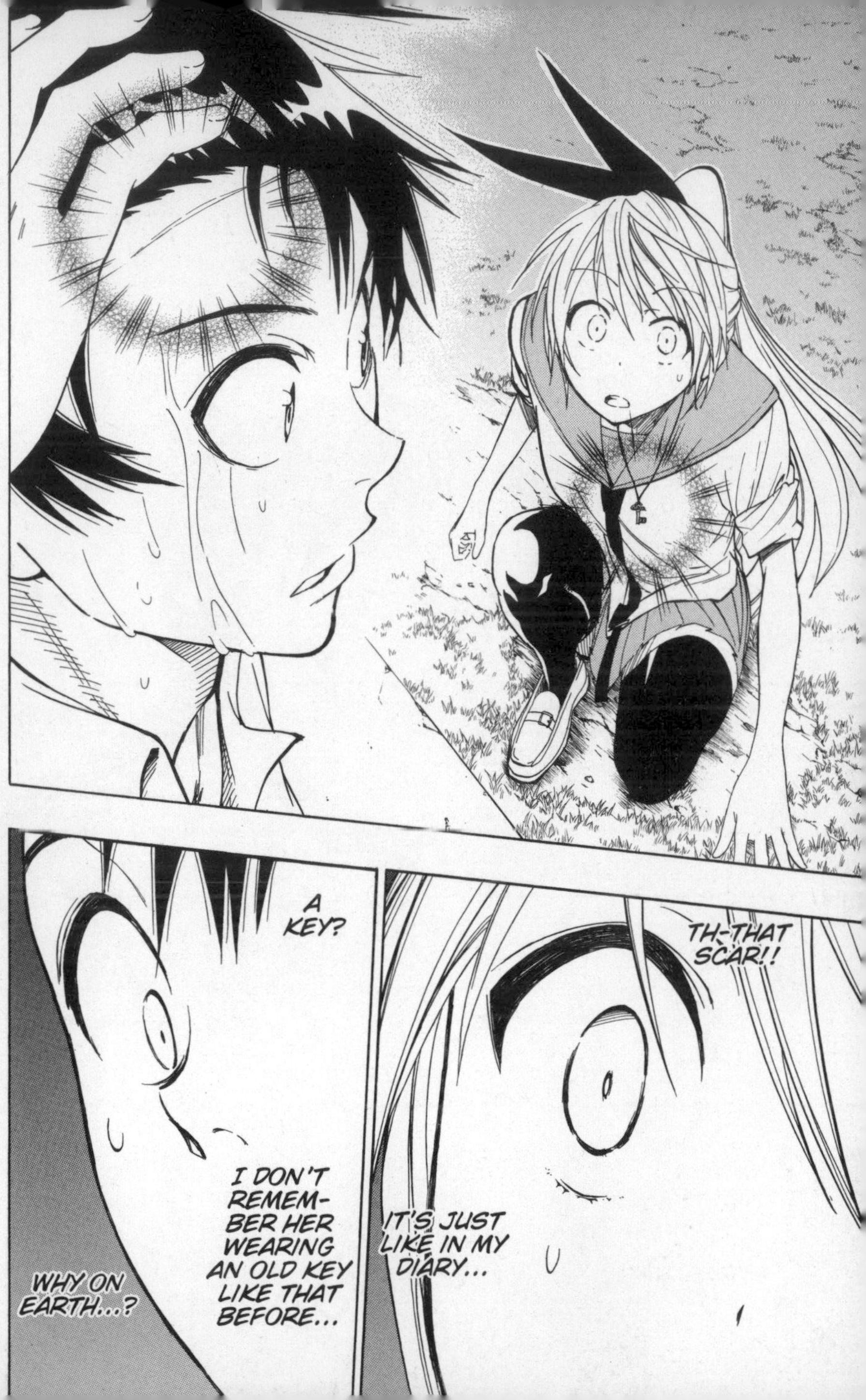
TH-THAT SCAR!!
IT'S JUST LIKE IN MY DIARY...
A KEY?
I DON'T REMEM-BER HER WEARING AN OLD KEY LIKE THAT BEFORE...
WHY ON EARTH...?

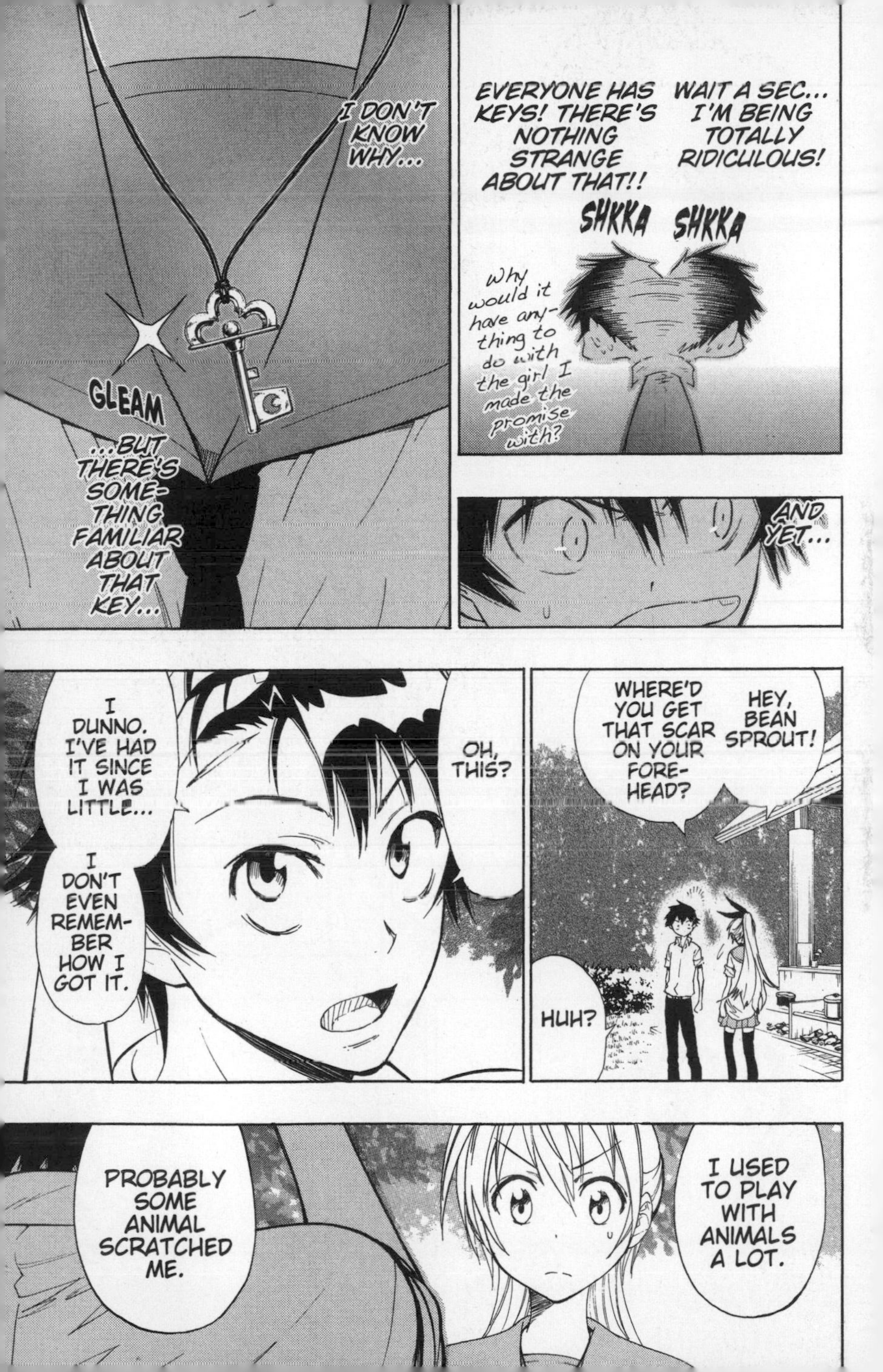
WAIT A SEC... I'M BEING TOTALLY RIDICULOUS!
EVERYONE HAS KEYS! THERE'S NOTHING STRANGE ABOUT THAT!!
SHKKA SHKKA
Why would it have anything to do with the girl I made the promise with?
AND YET...
I DON'T KNOW WHY...
GLEAM
...BUT THERE'S SOMETHING FAMILIAR ABOUT THAT KEY...
HEY, BEAN SPROUT!
WHERE'D YOU GET THAT SCAR ON YOUR FOREHEAD?
HUH?
OH, THIS?
I DUNNO. I'VE HAD IT SINCE I WAS LITTLE...
I DON'T EVEN REMEMBER HOW I GOT IT.
I USED TO PLAY WITH ANIMALS A LOT.
PROBABLY SOME ANIMAL SCRATCHED ME.

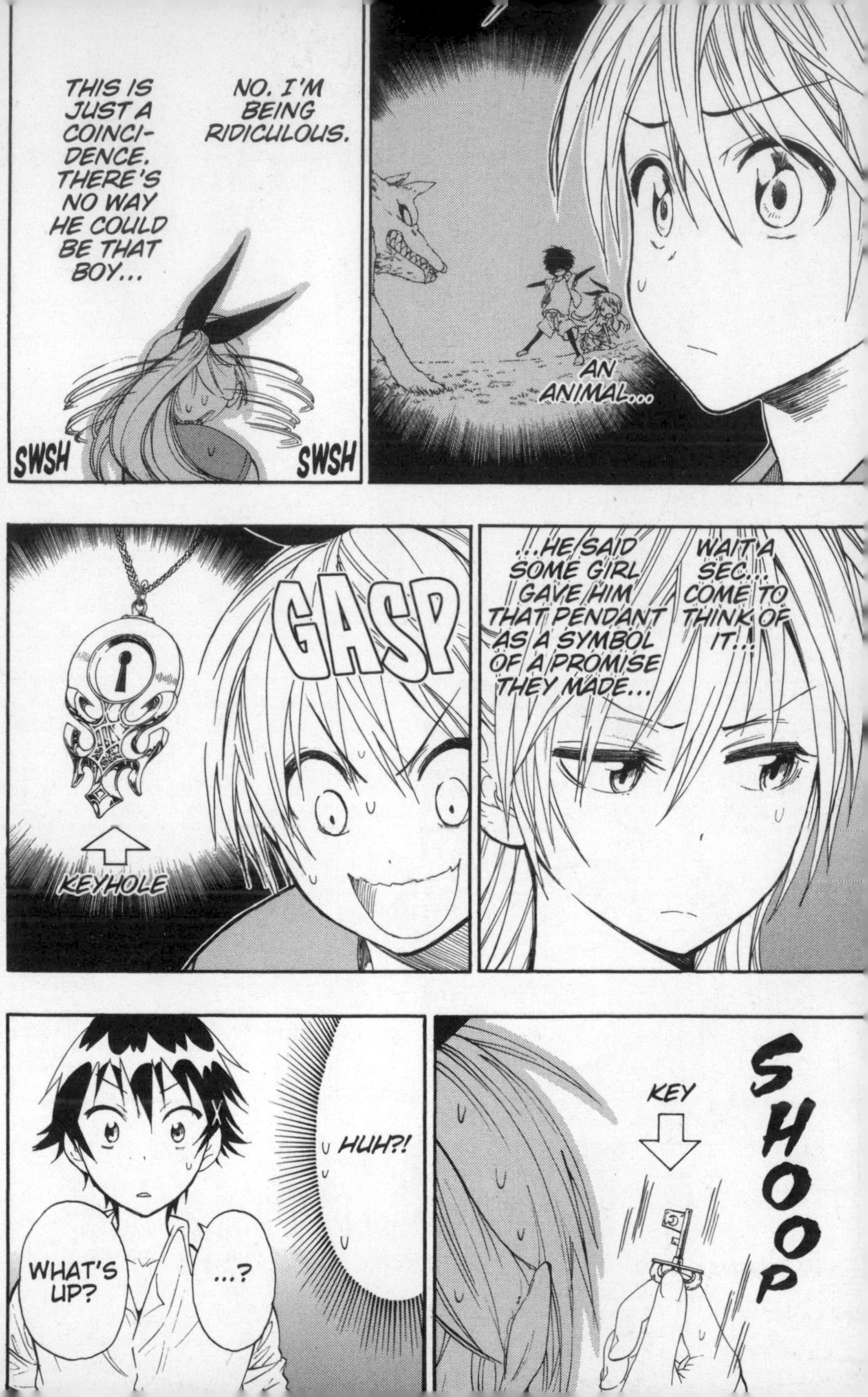
AN ANIMAL...
NO. I'M BEING RIDICULOUS.
THIS IS JUST A COINCIDENCE. THERE'S NO WAY HE COULD BE THAT BOY...
SWSH
SWSH
WAIT A SEC... COME TO THINK OF IT...
...HE SAID SOME GIRL GAVE HIM THAT PENDANT AS A SYMBOL OF A PROMISE THEY MADE...
GASP
KEYHOLE
SHOOP
KEY
HUH?!
...?
WHAT'S UP?

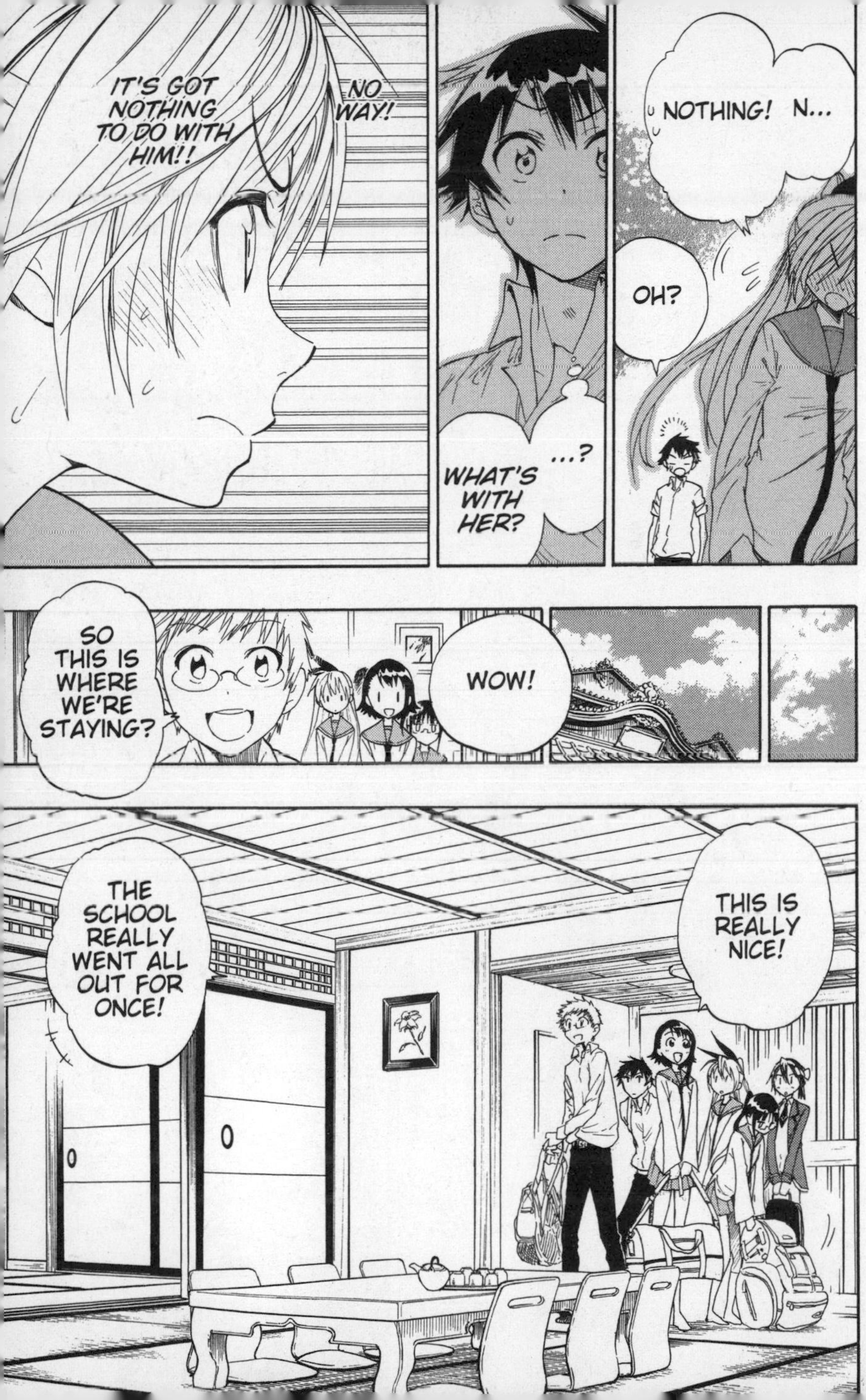
N...
NOTHING!
OH?
...?
WHAT'S WITH HER?
NO WAY!
IT'S GOT NOTHING TO DO WITH HIM!!
WOW!
SO THIS IS WHERE WE'RE STAYING?
THIS IS REALLY NICE!
THE SCHOOL REALLY WENT ALL OUT FOR ONCE!

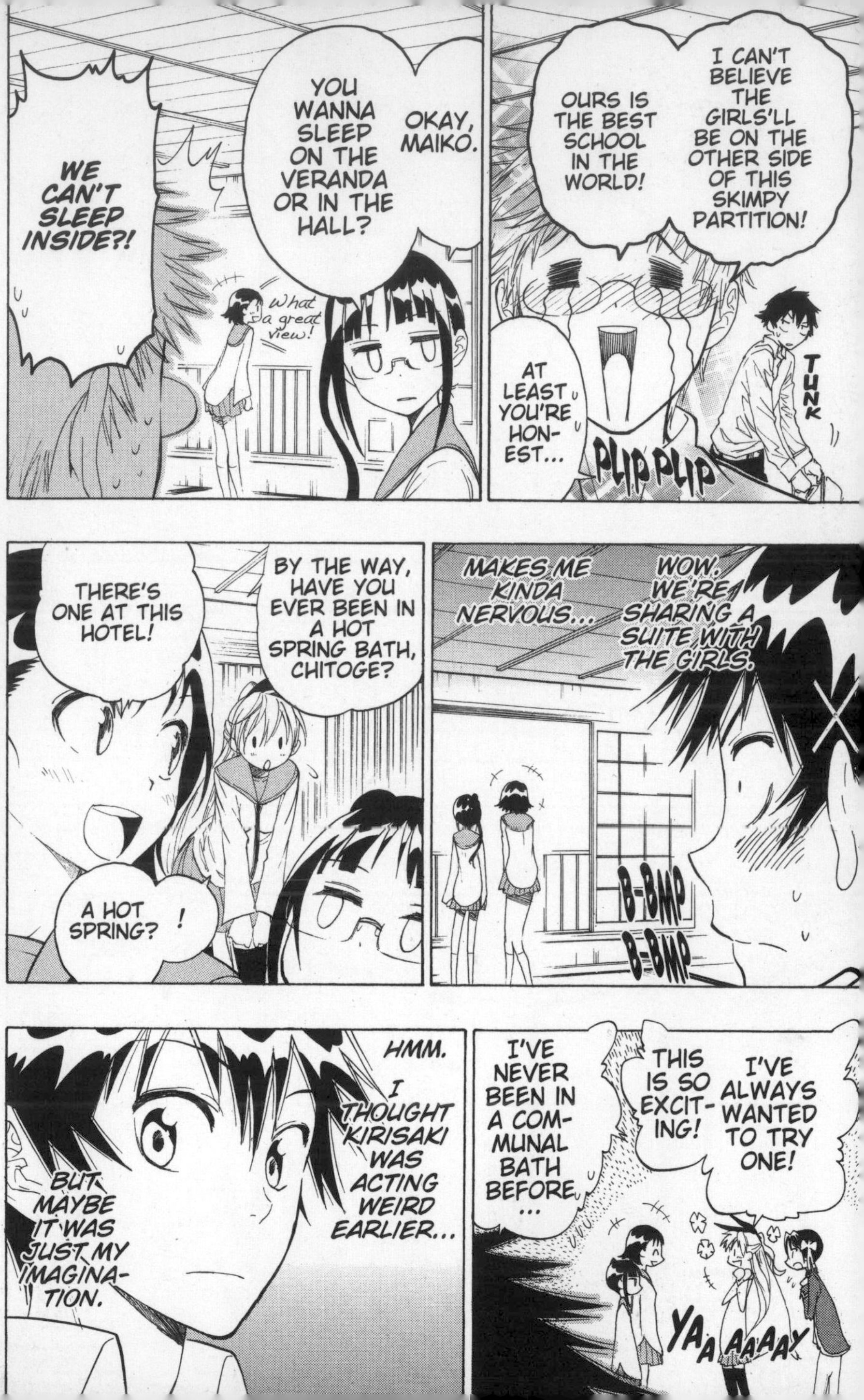
I CAN'T BELIEVE THE GIRLS'LL BE ON THE OTHER SIDE OF THIS SKIMPY PARTITION!
OURS IS THE BEST SCHOOL IN THE WORLD!
AT LEAST YOU'RE HON-EST...
TUNK
PLIP PLIP
OKAY, MAIKO.
YOU WANNA SLEEP ON THE VERANDA OR IN THE HALL?
WE CAN'T SLEEP INSIDE?!
What a great view!
WOW. WE'RE SHARING A SUITE WITH THE GIRLS.
MAKES ME KINDA NERVOUS...
B-BMP
B-BMP
BY THE WAY, HAVE YOU EVER BEEN IN A HOT SPRING BATH, CHITOGE?
THERE'S ONE AT THIS HOTEL!
A HOT SPRING? !
I'VE ALWAYS WANTED TO TRY ONE!
THIS IS SO EXCIT-ING!
I'VE NEVER BEEN IN A COM-MUNAL BATH BEFORE...
YAAAAAAY
HMM.
I THOUGHT KIRISAKI WAS ACTING WEIRD EARLIER...
BUT MAYBE IT WAS JUST MY IMAGINA-TION.

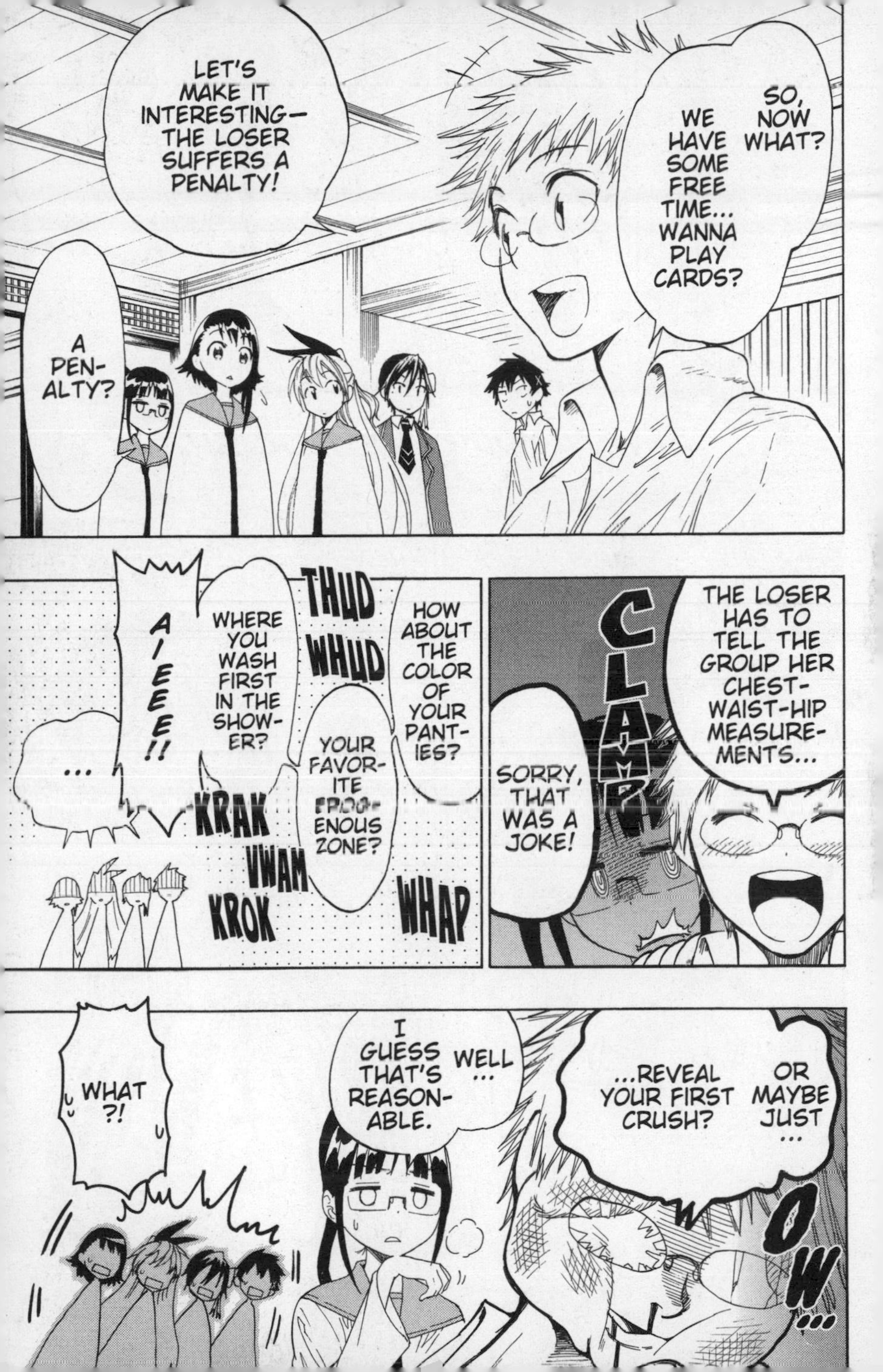
SO, NOW WHAT?
WE HAVE SOME FREE TIME... WANNA PLAY CARDS?
LET'S MAKE IT INTERESTING—THE LOSER SUFFERS A PENALTY!
A PEN-ALTY?
THE LOSER HAS TO TELL THE GROUP HER CHEST-WAIST-HIP MEASURE-MENTS...
CLAMP
SORRY, THAT WAS A JOKE!
HOW ABOUT THE COLOR OF YOUR PANT-IES?
THUD
WHUD
WHERE YOU WASH FIRST IN THE SHOW-ER?
YOUR FAVOR-ITE EROG-ENOUS ZONE?
A/EEEE!!
WHAP
KRAK
VWAM
KROK
...
OR MAYBE JUST ...
...REVEAL YOUR FIRST CRUSH?
OW...
WELL ...
I GUESS THAT'S REASON-ABLE.
WHAT ?!

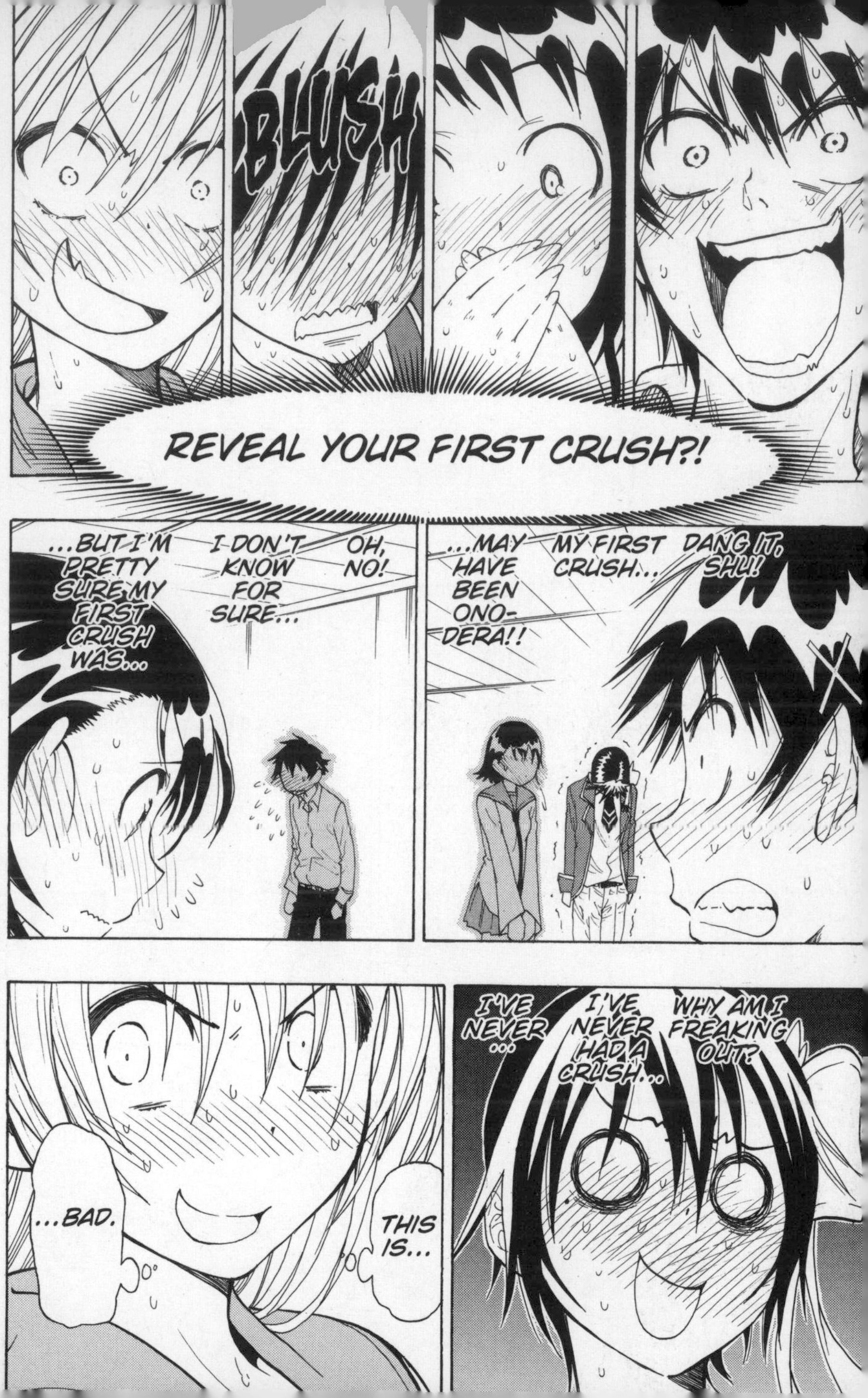
BLUSH
REVEAL YOUR FIRST CRUSH?!
DANG IT, SHU!
MY FIRST CRUSH...
...MAY HAVE BEEN ONO-DERA!!
OH, NO!
I DON'T KNOW FOR SURE...
...BUT I'M PRETTY SURE MY FIRST CRUSH WAS...
WHY AM I FREAKING OUT?
I'VE NEVER HAD A CRUSH...
I'VE NEVER...
THIS IS...
...BAD.

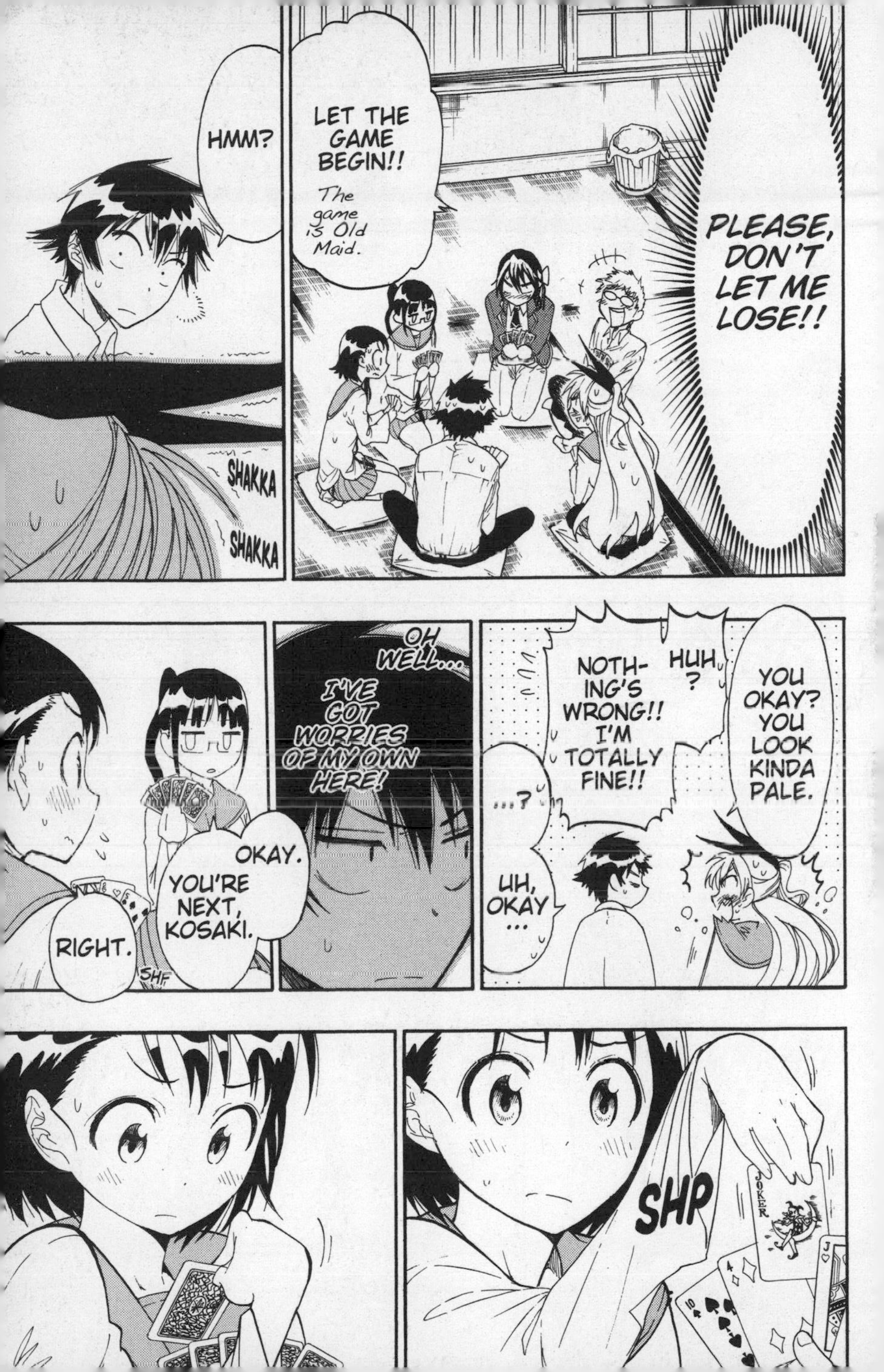
LET THE GAME BEGIN!!
The game is Old Maid.
PLEASE, DON'T LET ME LOSE!!
HMM?
SHAKKA
SHAKKA
YOU OKAY? YOU LOOK KINDA PALE.
HUH?
NOTH-ING'S WRONG!! I'M TOTALLY FINE!!
...?
UH, OKAY...
OH WELL...
I'VE GOT WORRIES OF MY OWN HERE!
OKAY.
YOU'RE NEXT, KOSAKI.
RIGHT.
SHF
SHP
JOKER

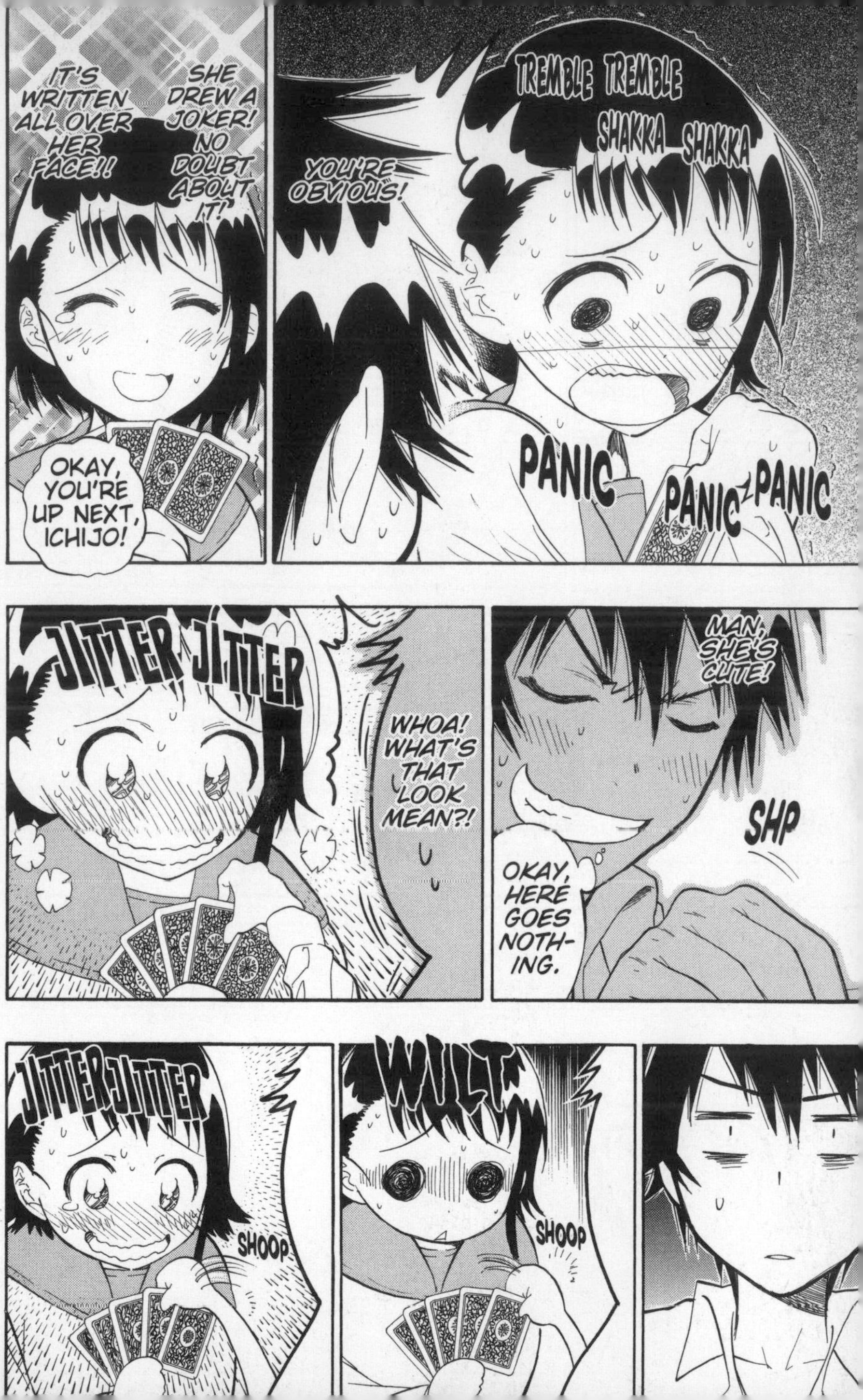
TREMBLE TREMBLE
SHAKKA SHAKKA
YOU'RE OBVIOUS!
PANIC
PANIC PANIC
SHE DREW A JOKER! NO DOUBT ABOUT IT!
IT'S WRITTEN ALL OVER HER FACE!!
OKAY, YOU'RE UP NEXT, ICHIJO!
MAN, SHE'S CUTE!
SHP
OKAY, HERE GOES NOTHING.
WHOA! WHAT'S THAT LOOK MEAN?!
JITTER JITTER
WILT
SHOOP
JITTER JITTER
SHOOP

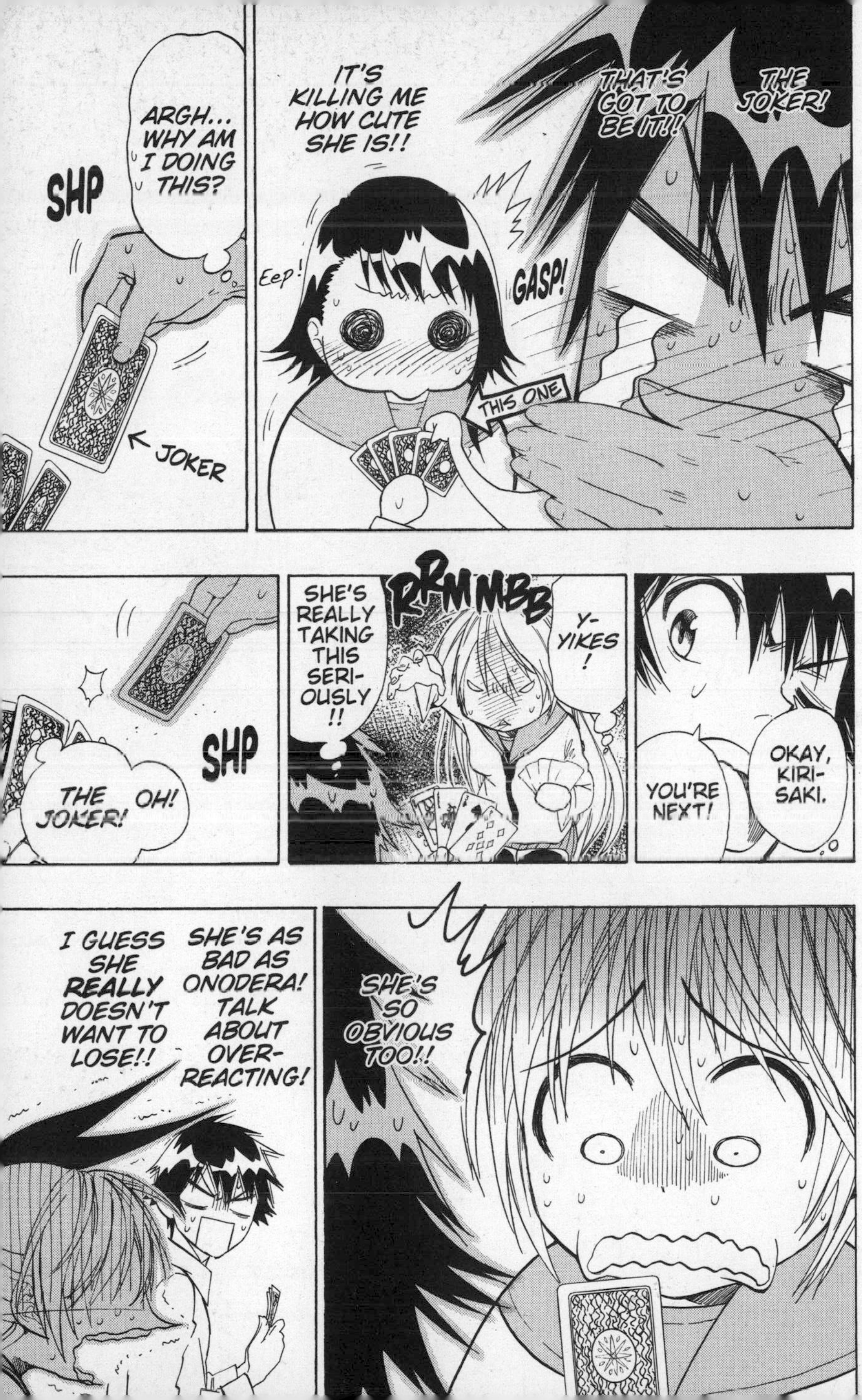
THE JOKER!
THAT'S GOT TO BE IT!!
IT'S KILLING ME HOW CUTE SHE IS!!
GASP!
Eep!
THIS ONE
ARGH... WHY AM I DOING THIS?
SHP
JOKER
OKAY, KIRI-SAKI.
YOU'RE NEXT!
Y-YIKES!
RRMMBB
SHE'S REALLY TAKING THIS SERI-OUSLY!!
SHP
OH!
THE JOKER!
SHE'S SO OBVIOUS TOO!!
SHE'S AS BAD AS ONODERA! TALK ABOUT OVER-REACTING!
I GUESS SHE REALLY DOESN'T WANT TO LOSE!!

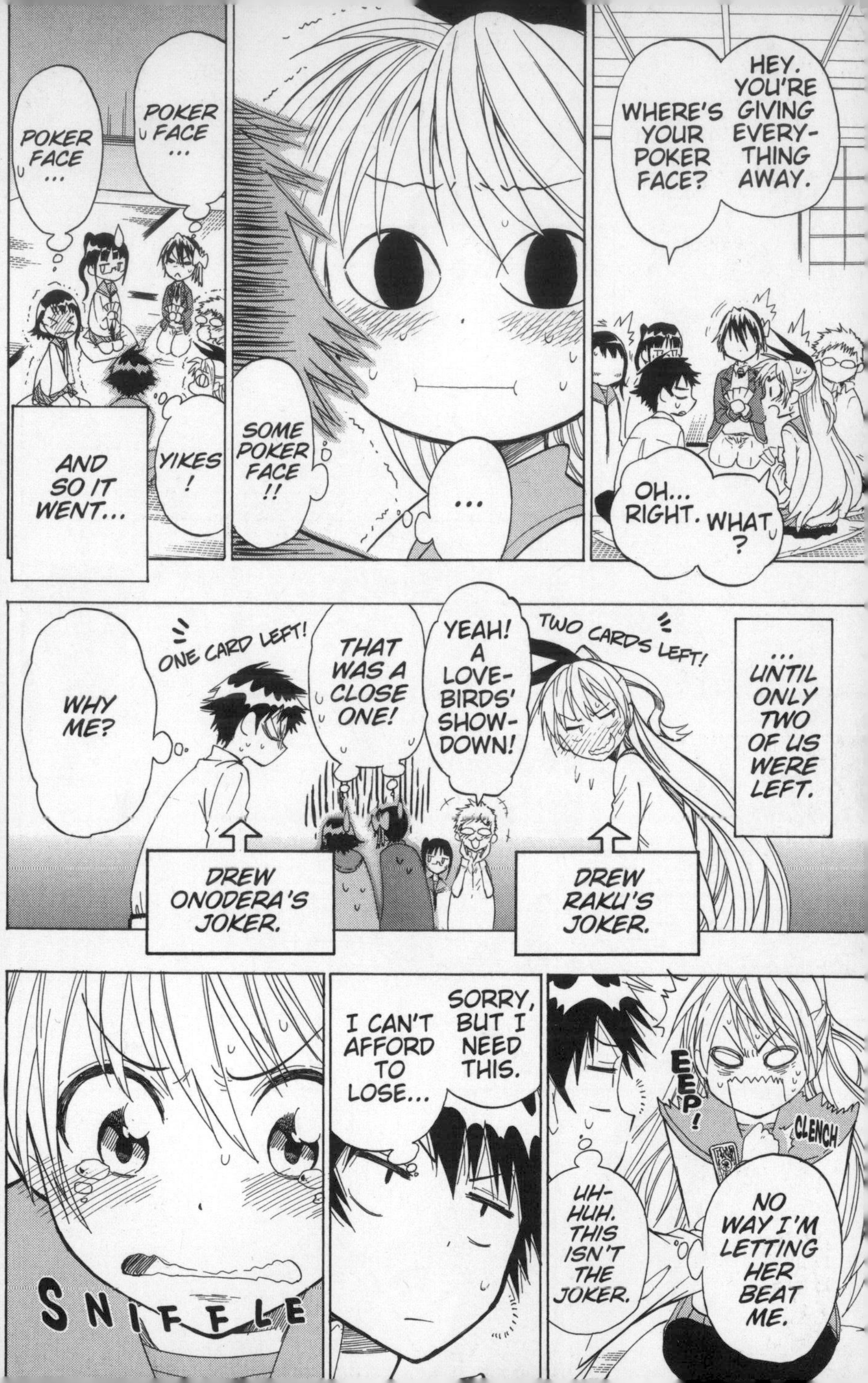
HEY. YOU'RE GIVING EVERYTHING AWAY.
WHERE'S YOUR POKER FACE?
WHAT?
OH... RIGHT.
...
SOME POKER FACE!!
POKER FACE...
POKER FACE...
YIKES!
AND SO IT WENT...
...UNTIL ONLY TWO OF US WERE LEFT.
TWO CARDS LEFT!
DREW RAKU'S JOKER.
YEAH! A LOVE-BIRDS' SHOW-DOWN!
THAT WAS A CLOSE ONE!
ONE CARD LEFT!
DREW ONODERA'S JOKER.
WHY ME?
EEP!
CLENCH
NO WAY I'M LETTING HER BEAT ME.
UH-HUH. THIS ISN'T THE JOKER.
SORRY, BUT I NEED THIS.
I CAN'T AFFORD TO LOSE...
SNIFFLE

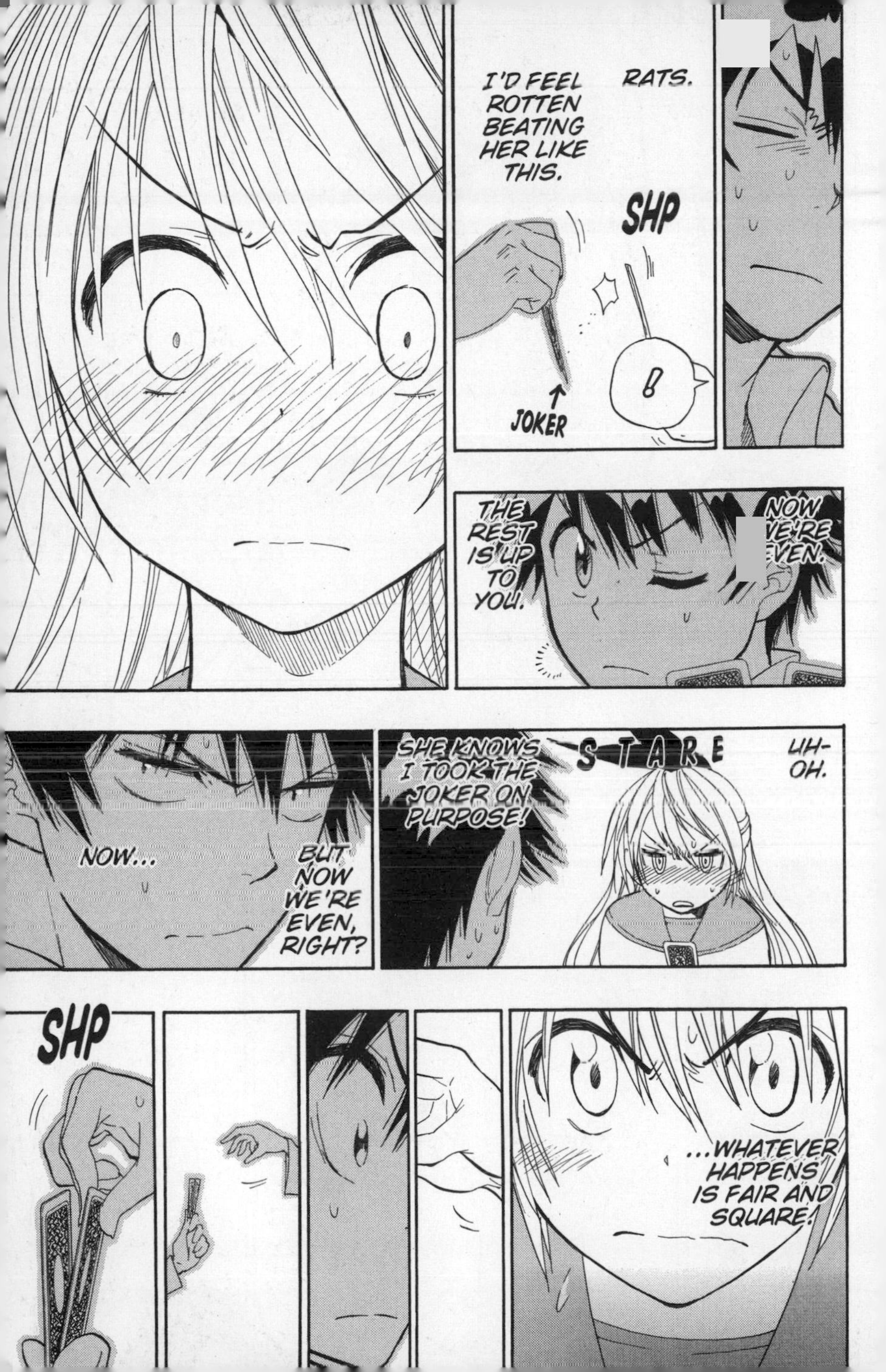
RATS.
I'D FEEL ROTTEN BEATING HER LIKE THIS.
SHP
!
JOKER
NOW WE'RE EVEN.
THE REST IS UP TO YOU.
UH-OH.
STARE
SHE KNOWS I TOOK THE JOKER ON PURPOSE!
BUT NOW WE'RE EVEN, RIGHT?
NOW...
...WHATEVER HAPPENS IS FAIR AND SQUARE!
SHP

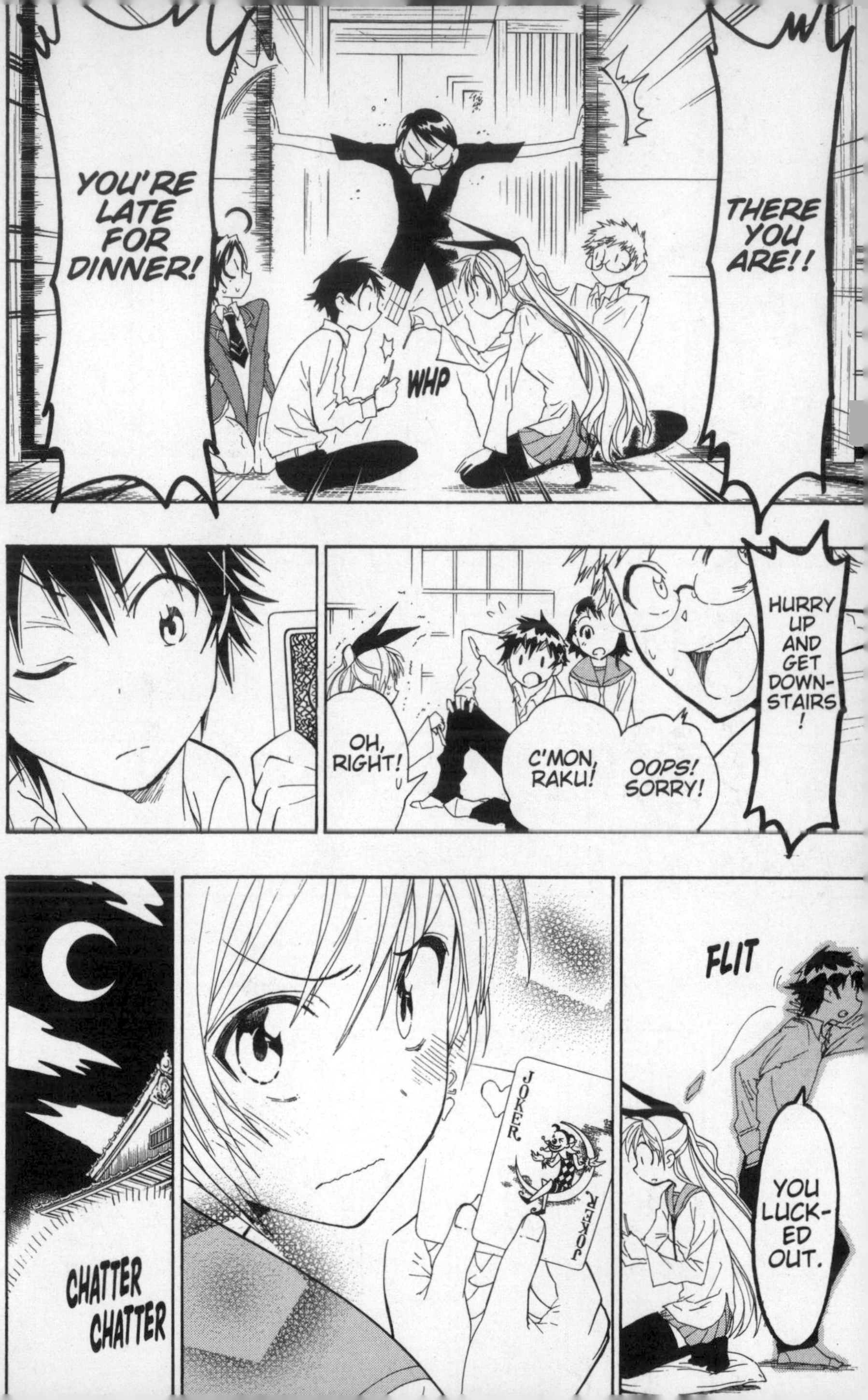
THERE YOU ARE!!
YOU'RE LATE FOR DINNER!
WHP
HURRY UP AND GET DOWN-STAIRS!
OOPS! SORRY!
C'MON, RAKU!
OH, RIGHT!
FLIT
YOU LUCK-ED OUT.
JOKER
CHATTER CHATTER

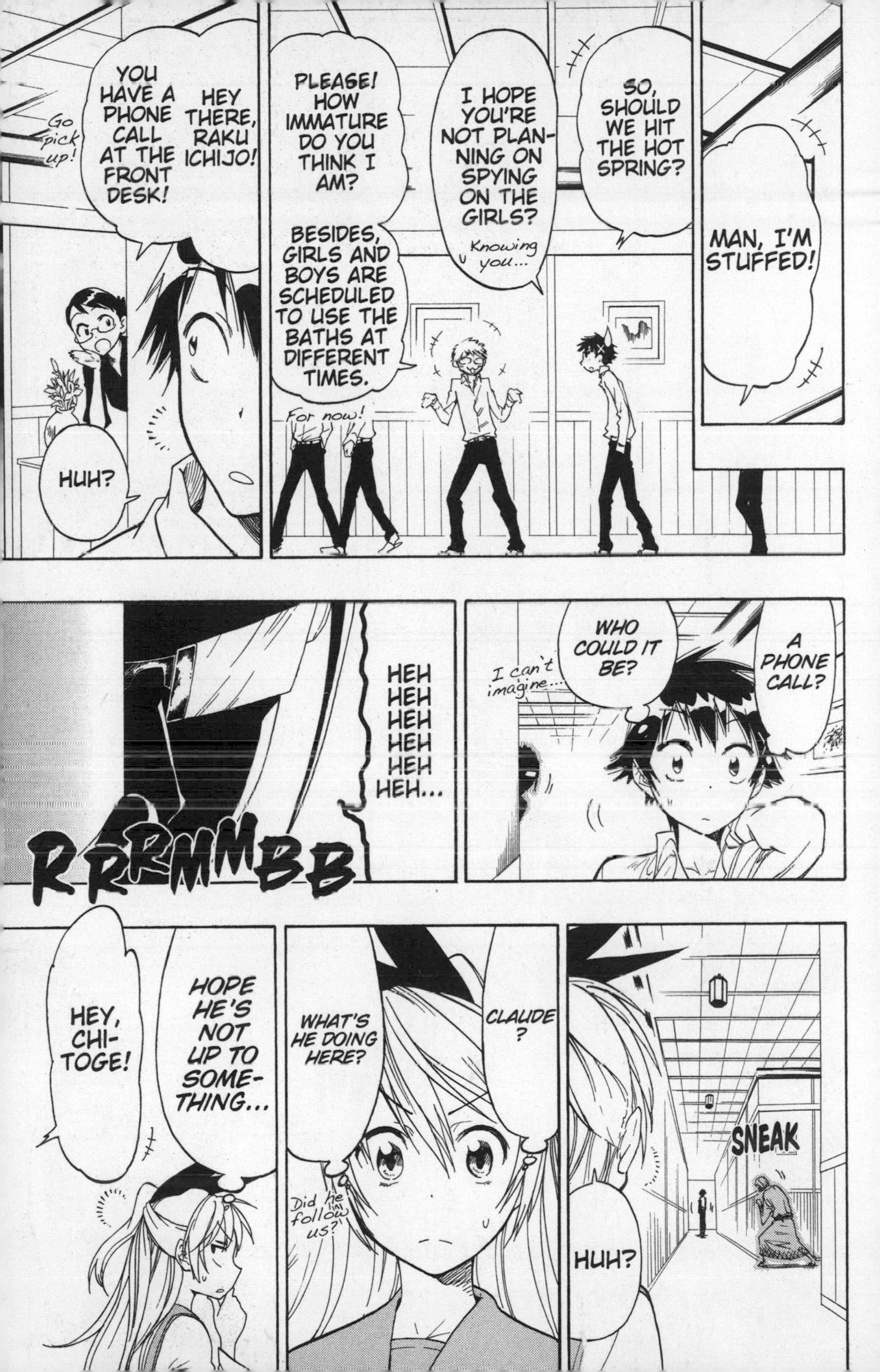
MAN, I'M STUFFED!
SO, SHOULD WE HIT THE HOT SPRING?
I HOPE YOU'RE NOT PLANNING ON SPYING ON THE GIRLS?
Knowing you...
PLEASE! HOW IMMATURE DO YOU THINK I AM?
BESIDES, GIRLS AND BOYS ARE SCHEDULED TO USE THE BATHS AT DIFFERENT TIMES.
For now!
HEY THERE, RAKU ICHIJO!
YOU HAVE A PHONE CALL AT THE FRONT DESK!
Go pick up!
HUH?
A PHONE CALL?
WHO COULD IT BE?
I can't imagine...
HEH HEH HEH HEH HEH HEH...
RRRMMBB
SNEAK
HUH?
CLAUDE?
WHAT'S HE DOING HERE?
Did he follow us?
HOPE HE'S NOT UP TO SOMETHING...
HEY, CHITOGE!

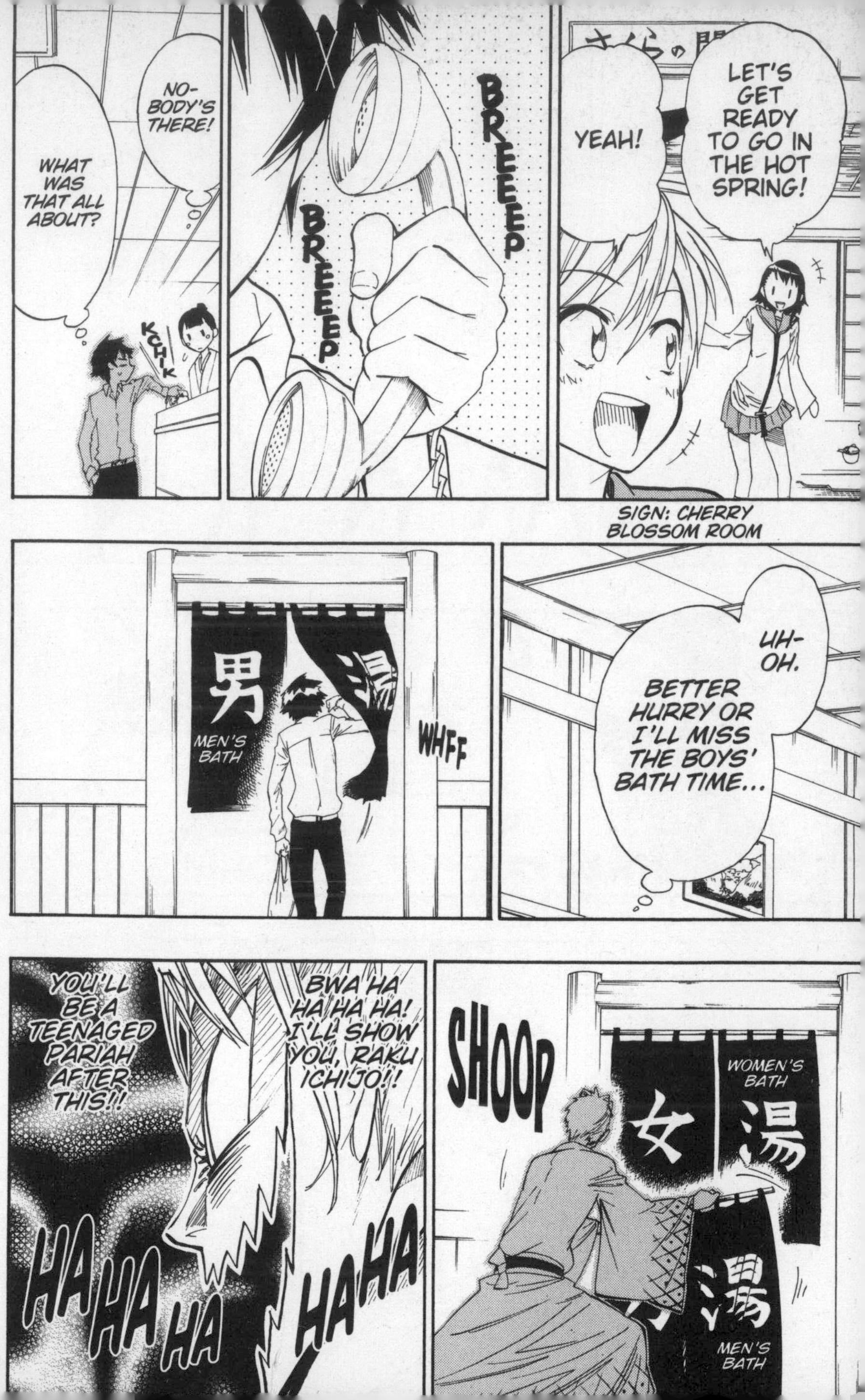
LET'S GET READY TO GO IN THE HOT SPRING!
YEAH!
SIGN: CHERRY BLOSSOM ROOM
BREEEEP
BREEEEP
NO-BODY'S THERE!
WHAT WAS THAT ALL ABOUT?
KCHIK
UH-OH. BETTER HURRY OR I'LL MISS THE BOYS' BATH TIME...
WHFF
MEN'S BATH
SHOOP
WOMEN'S BATH
MEN'S BATH
BWA HA HA HA HA! I'LL SHOW YOU, RAKU ICHIJO!!
YOU'LL BE A TEENAGED PARIAH AFTER THIS!!
HA HA HA HA
HA HA HA

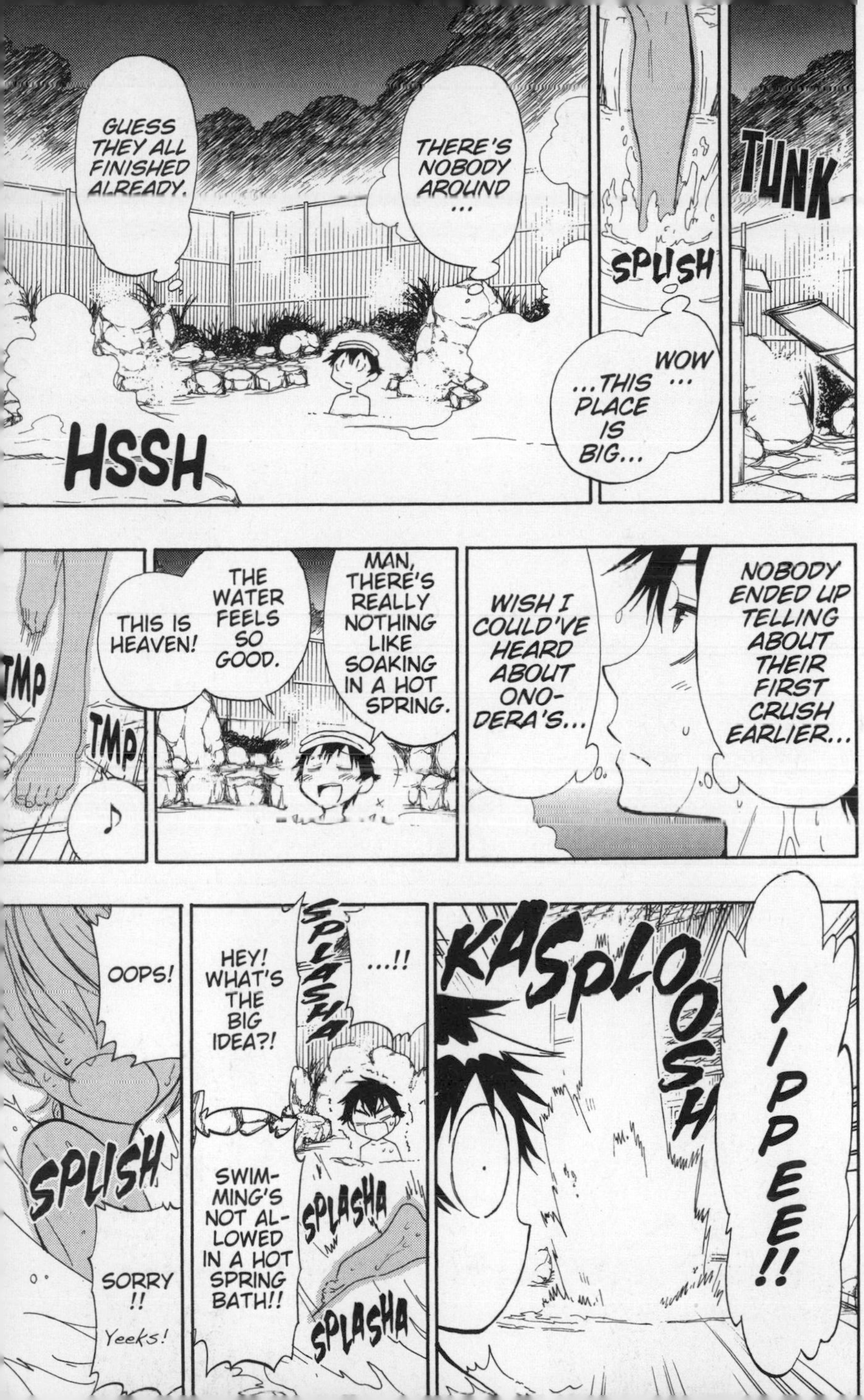
TUNK
SPLUSH
WOW...
...THIS PLACE IS BIG...
THERE'S NOBODY AROUND...
GUESS THEY ALL FINISHED ALREADY.
HSSH
NOBODY ENDED UP TELLING ABOUT THEIR FIRST CRUSH EARLIER...
WISH I COULD'VE HEARD ABOUT ONO-DERA'S...
MAN, THERE'S REALLY NOTHING LIKE SOAKING IN A HOT SPRING.
THE WATER FEELS SO GOOD.
THIS IS HEAVEN!
TMP
TMP
♪
YIPPEE!!
KASPLOOOSH
...!!
SPLASHA
HEY! WHAT'S THE BIG IDEA?!
SWIMMING'S NOT ALLOWED IN A HOT SPRING BATH!!
SPLASHA
SPLASHA
OOPS!
SPLISH
SORRY!!
Yeeks!

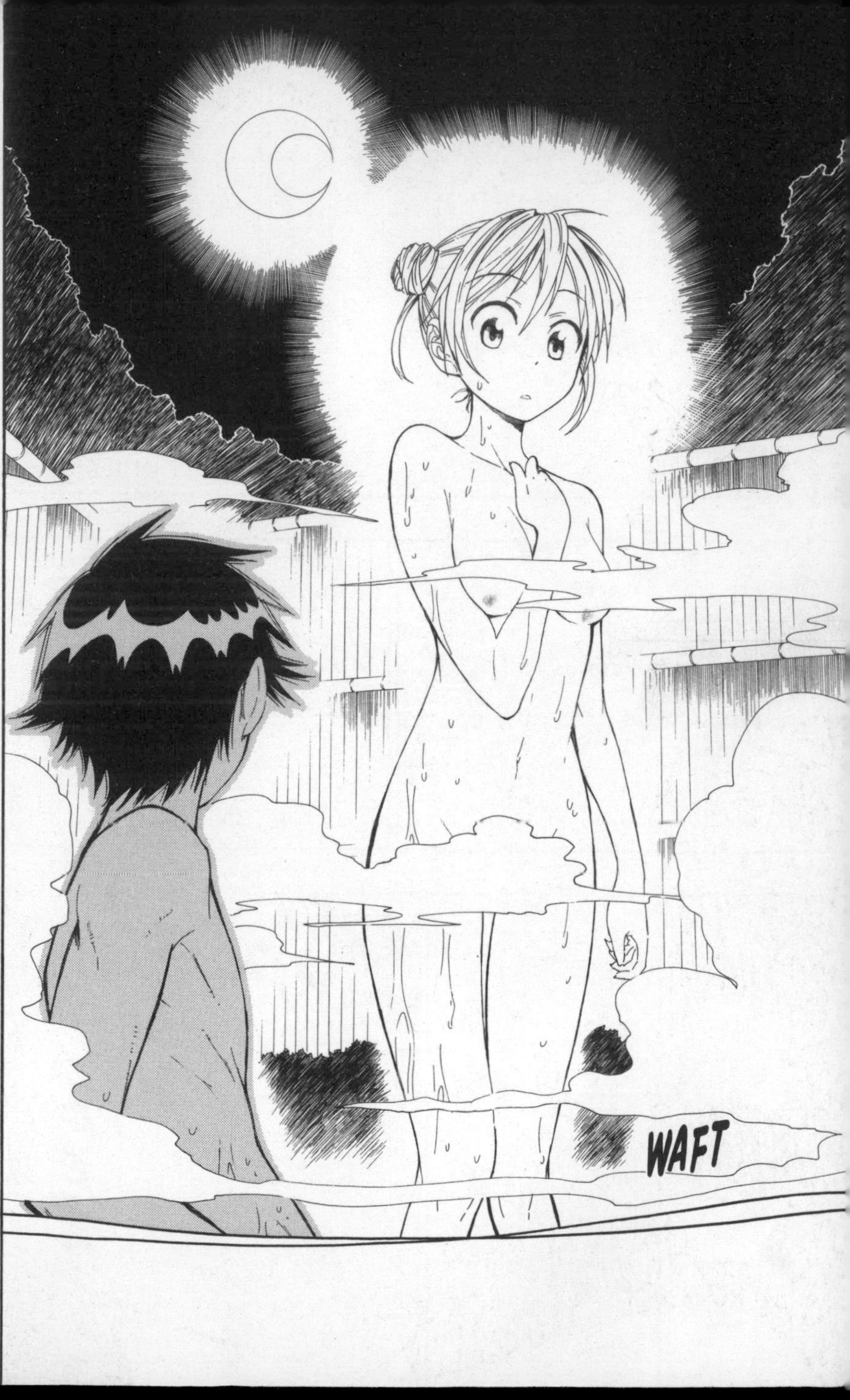
WAFT

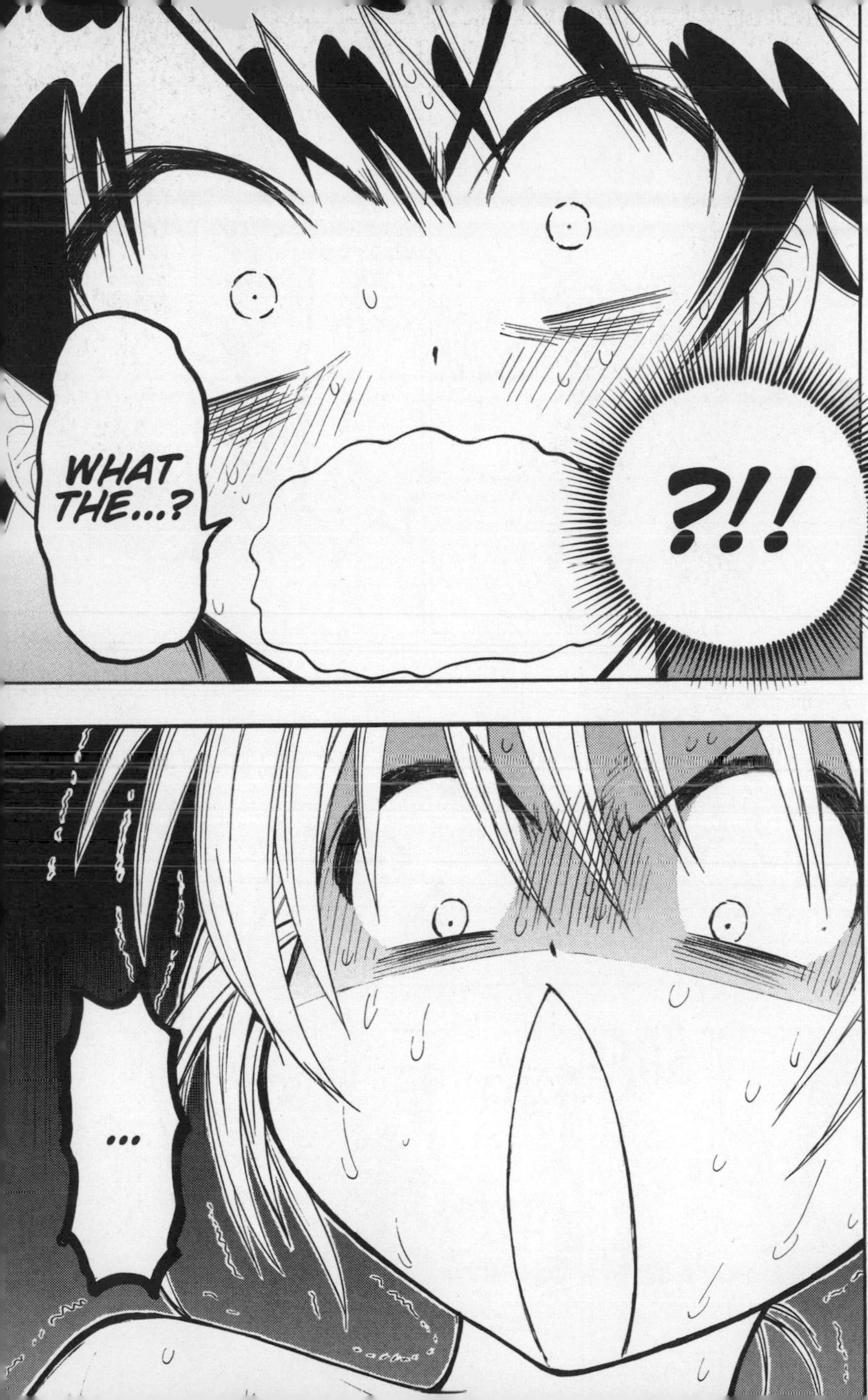
?!!
WHAT THE...?
...

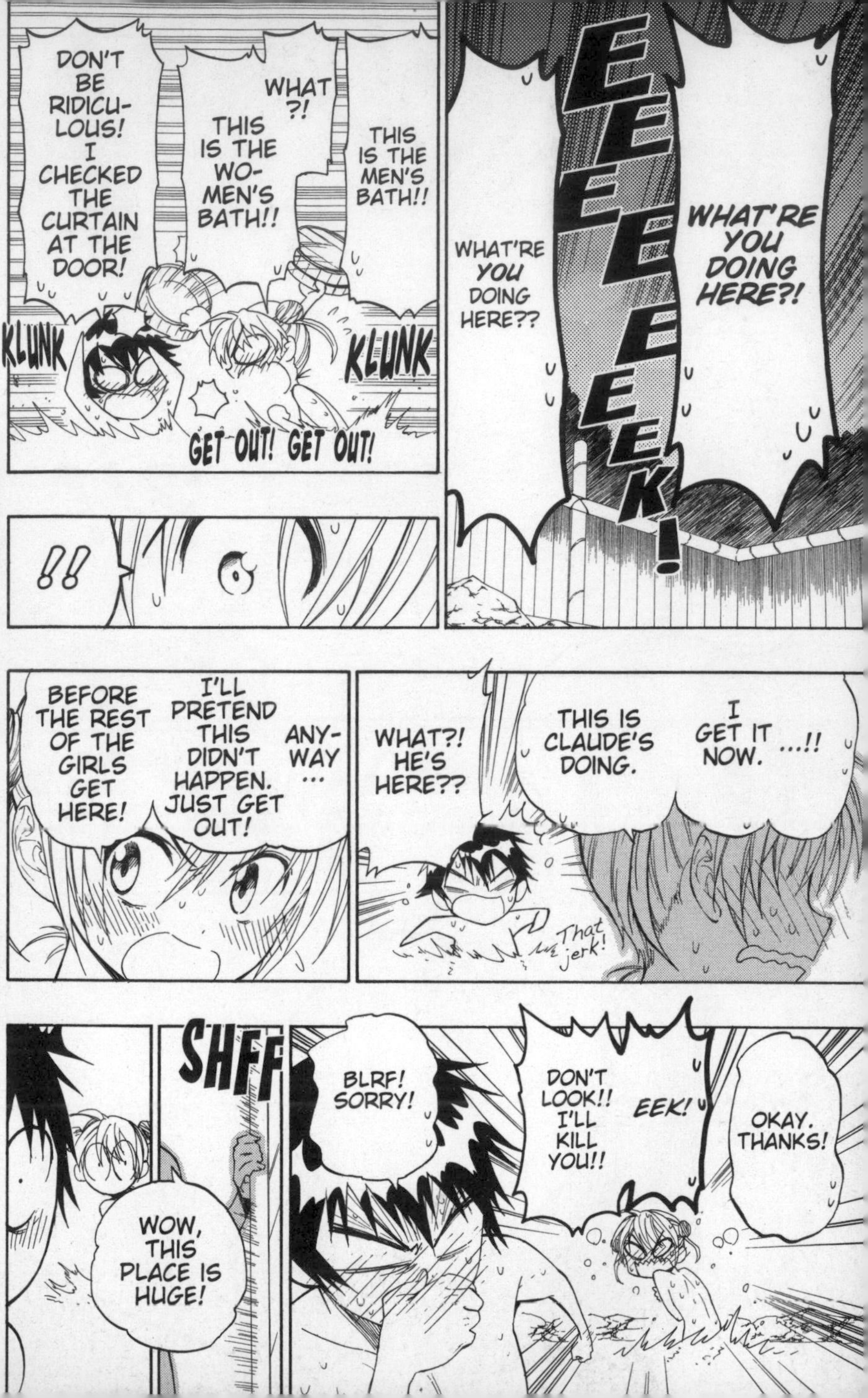
WHAT'RE YOU DOING HERE?!
EEEEEEK!
WHAT'RE YOU DOING HERE??
THIS IS THE MEN'S BATH!!
WHAT?!
THIS IS THE WOMEN'S BATH!!
DON'T BE RIDICULOUS! I CHECKED THE CURTAIN AT THE DOOR!
KLUNK
KLUNK
GET OUT! GET OUT!
!!
...!!
I GET IT NOW.
THIS IS CLAUDE'S DOING.
WHAT?! HE'S HERE??
That jerk!
ANYWAY...
I'LL PRETEND THIS DIDN'T HAPPEN. JUST GET OUT!
BEFORE THE REST OF THE GIRLS GET HERE!
OKAY. THANKS!
EEK!
DON'T LOOK!! I'LL KILL YOU!!
BLRF! SORRY!
SHFF
WOW, THIS PLACE IS HUGE!

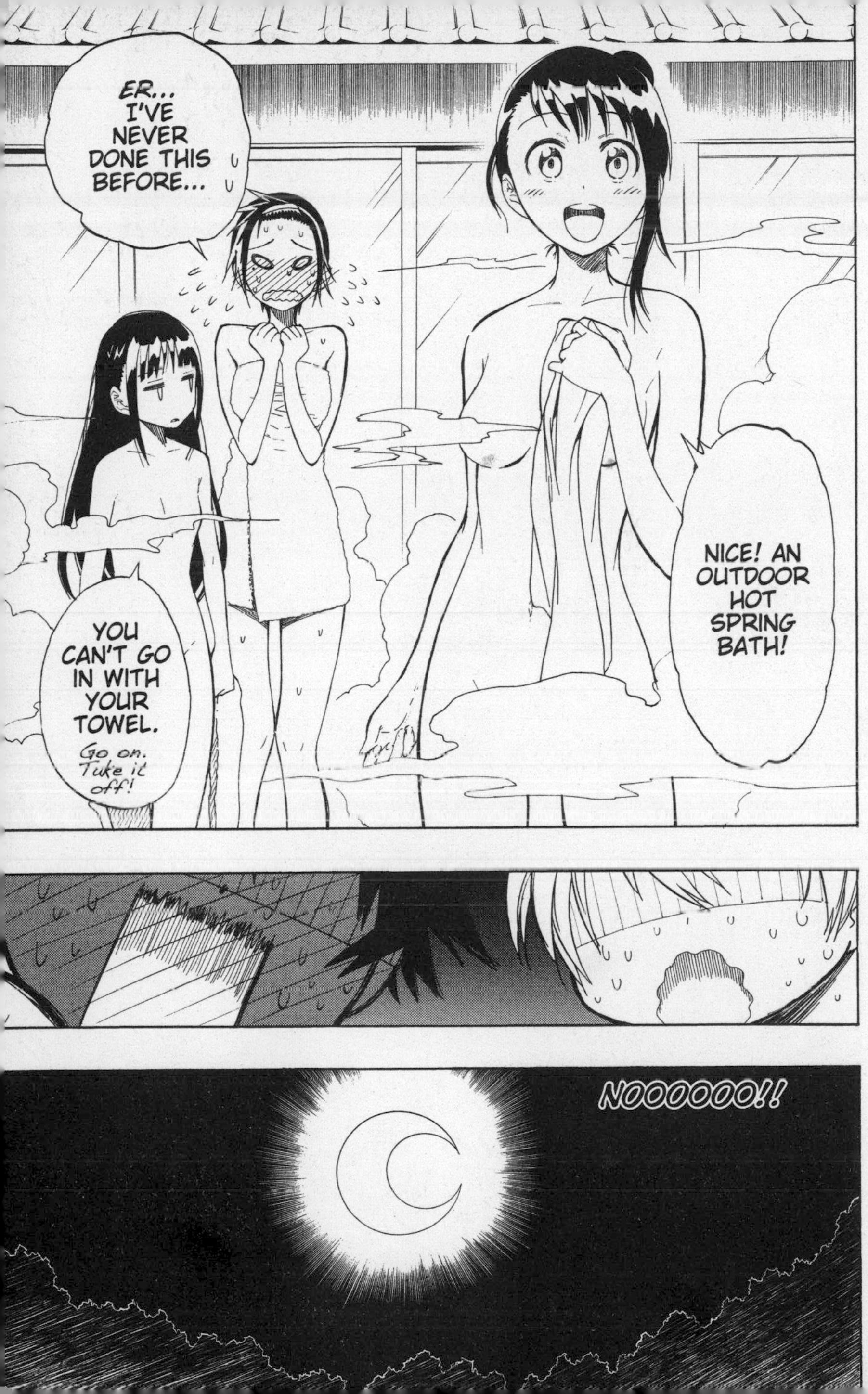
NICE! AN OUTDOOR HOT SPRING BATH!
ER... I'VE NEVER DONE THIS BEFORE...
YOU CAN'T GO IN WITH YOUR TOWEL.
Go on. Take it off!
NOOOOOO!!

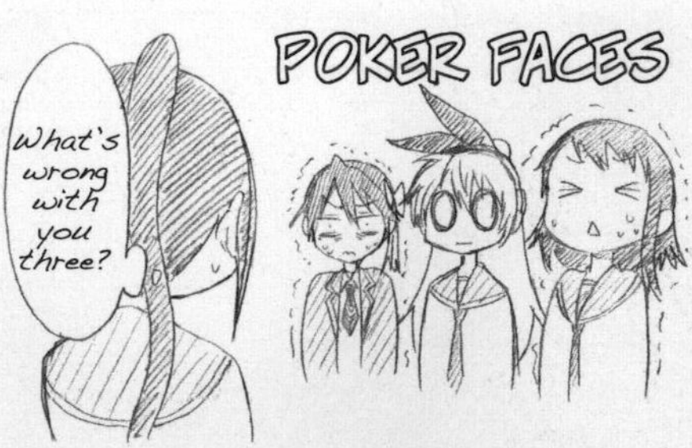
POKER FACES
What's wrong with you three?

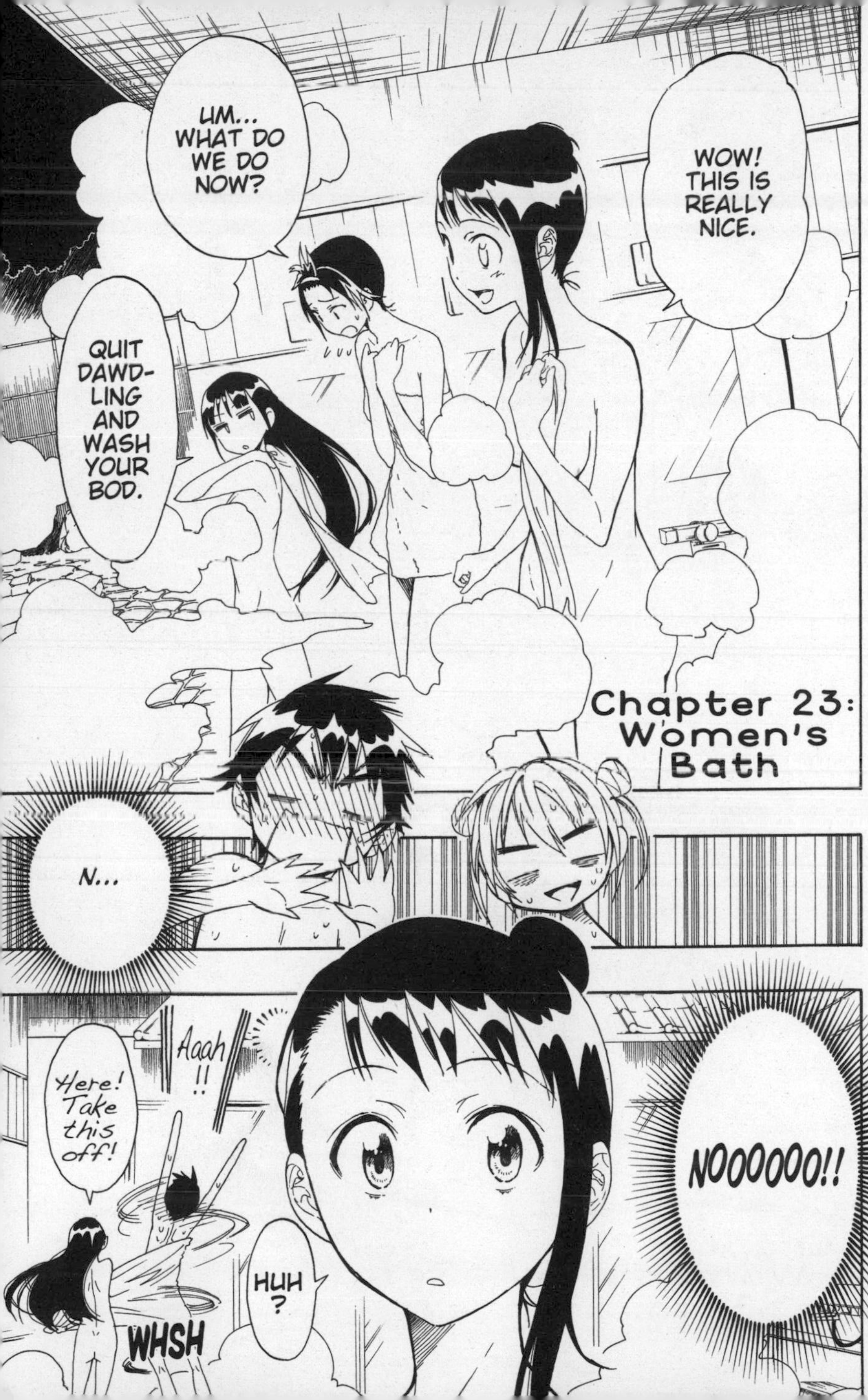
WOW! THIS IS REALLY NICE.
UM... WHAT DO WE DO NOW?
QUIT DAWDLING AND WASH YOUR BOD.
Chapter 23: Women's Bath
N...
NOOOOOO!!
Aaah!!
Here! Take this off!
HUH?
WHSH

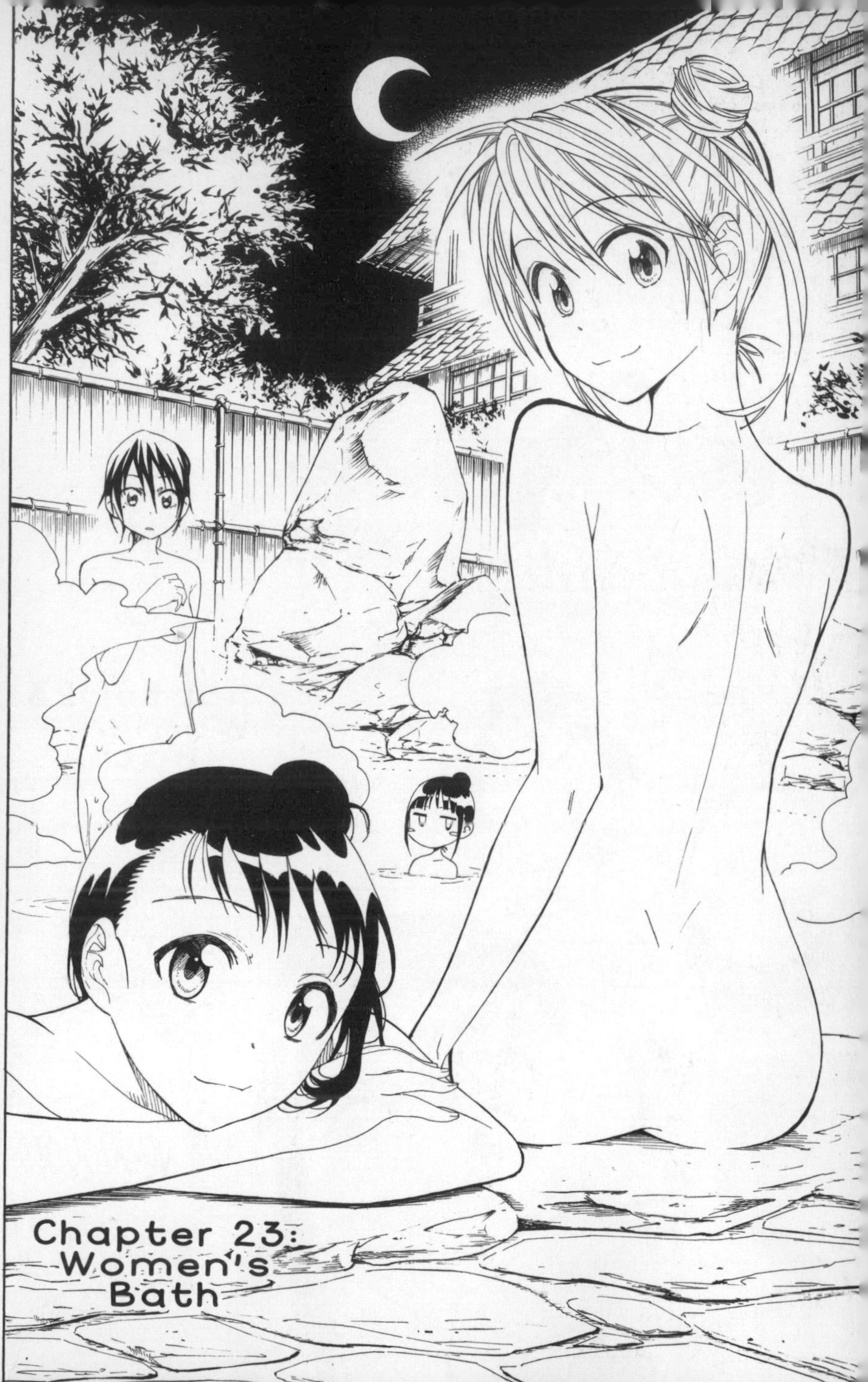
Chapter 23:
Women's
Bath

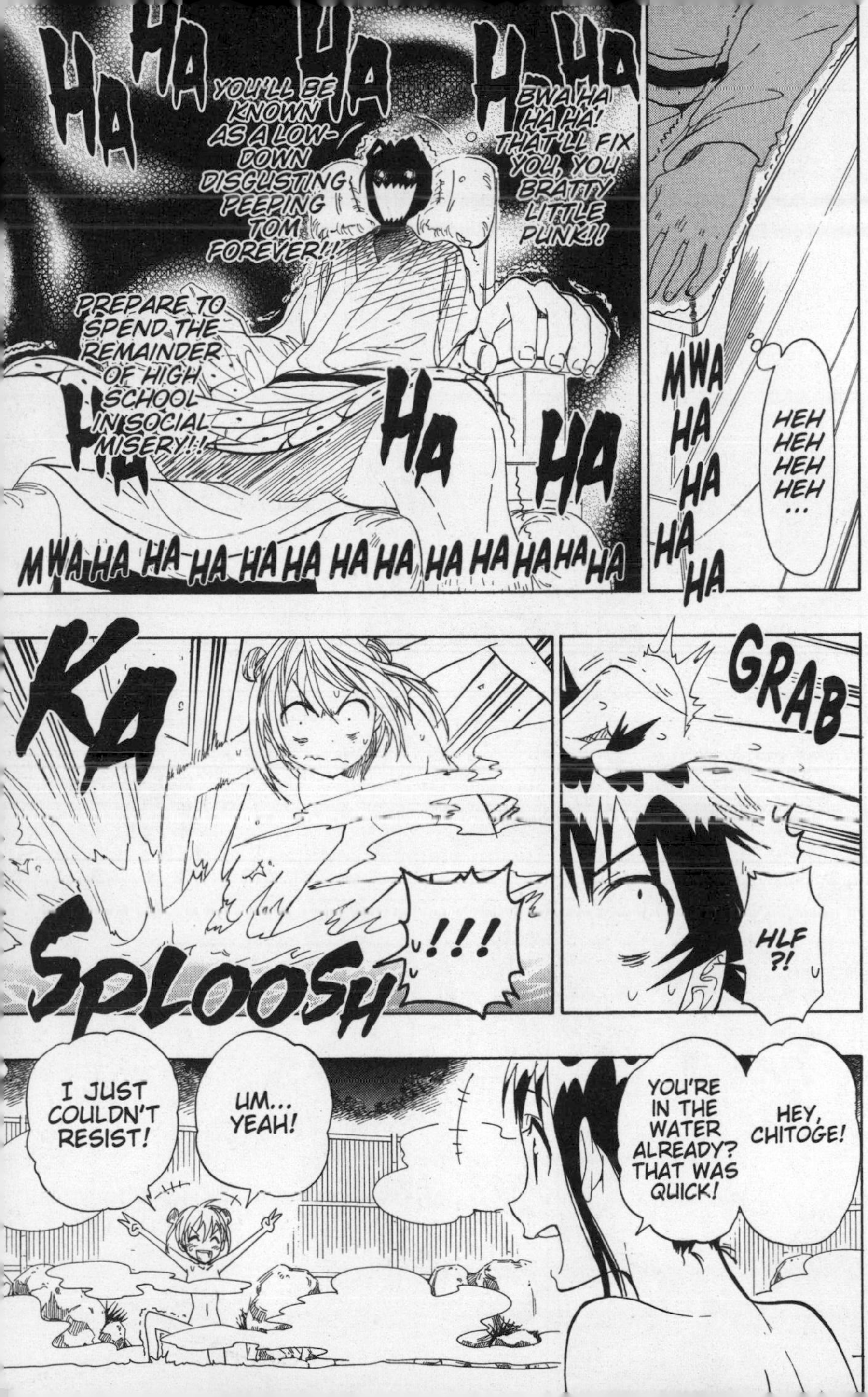
HEH HEH HEH HEH ...
MWA HA HA HA HA HA
HA HA HA HA H-HA
BWA HA HA HA! THAT'LL FIX YOU, YOU BRATTY LITTLE PUNK!!
YOU'LL BE KNOWN AS A LOW-DOWN DISGUSTING PEEPING TOM FOREVER!!
PREPARE TO SPEND THE REMAINDER OF HIGH SCHOOL IN SOCIAL MISERY!!
HA HA HA
MWA HA HA HA HA HA HA HA HA HA HA HA HA
GRAB
HLF ?!
KA
!!!
SPLOOSH
HEY, CHITOGE!
YOU'RE IN THE WATER ALREADY? THAT WAS QUICK!
UM... YEAH!
I JUST COULDN'T RESIST!

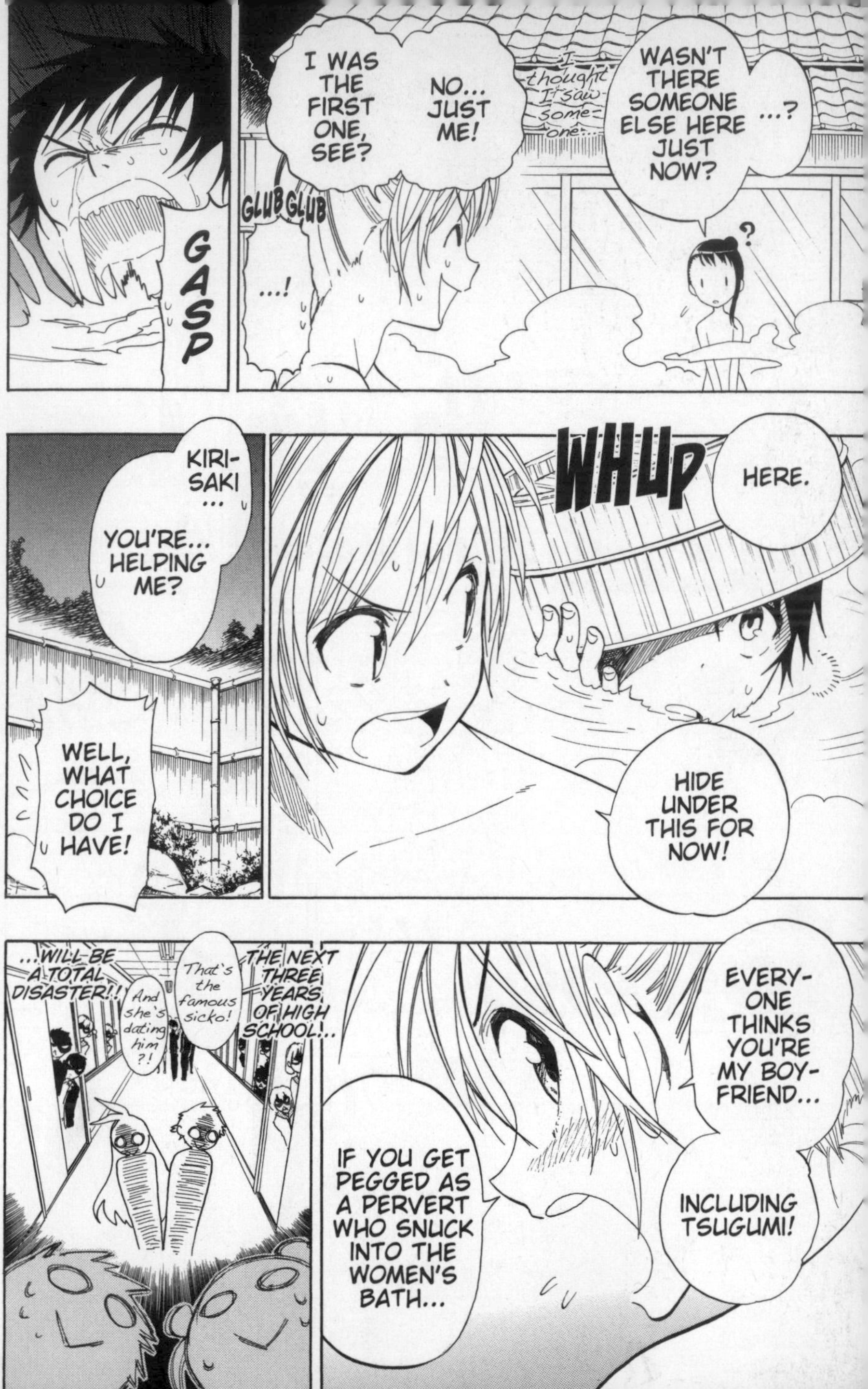
I thought I saw someone...
WASN'T THERE SOMEONE ELSE HERE JUST NOW?
...?
?
NO... JUST ME!
I WAS THE FIRST ONE, SEE?
GLUB GLUB
...!
GASP
WHUP
HERE.
HIDE UNDER THIS FOR NOW!
KIRI-SAKI...
YOU'RE... HELPING ME?
WELL, WHAT CHOICE DO I HAVE!
EVERY-ONE THINKS YOU'RE MY BOY-FRIEND...
INCLUDING TSUGUMI!
IF YOU GET PEGGED AS A PERVERT WHO SNUCK INTO THE WOMEN'S BATH...
THE NEXT THREE YEARS OF HIGH SCHOOL...
That's the famous sicko!
And she's dating him?!
...WILL BE A TOTAL DISASTER!!

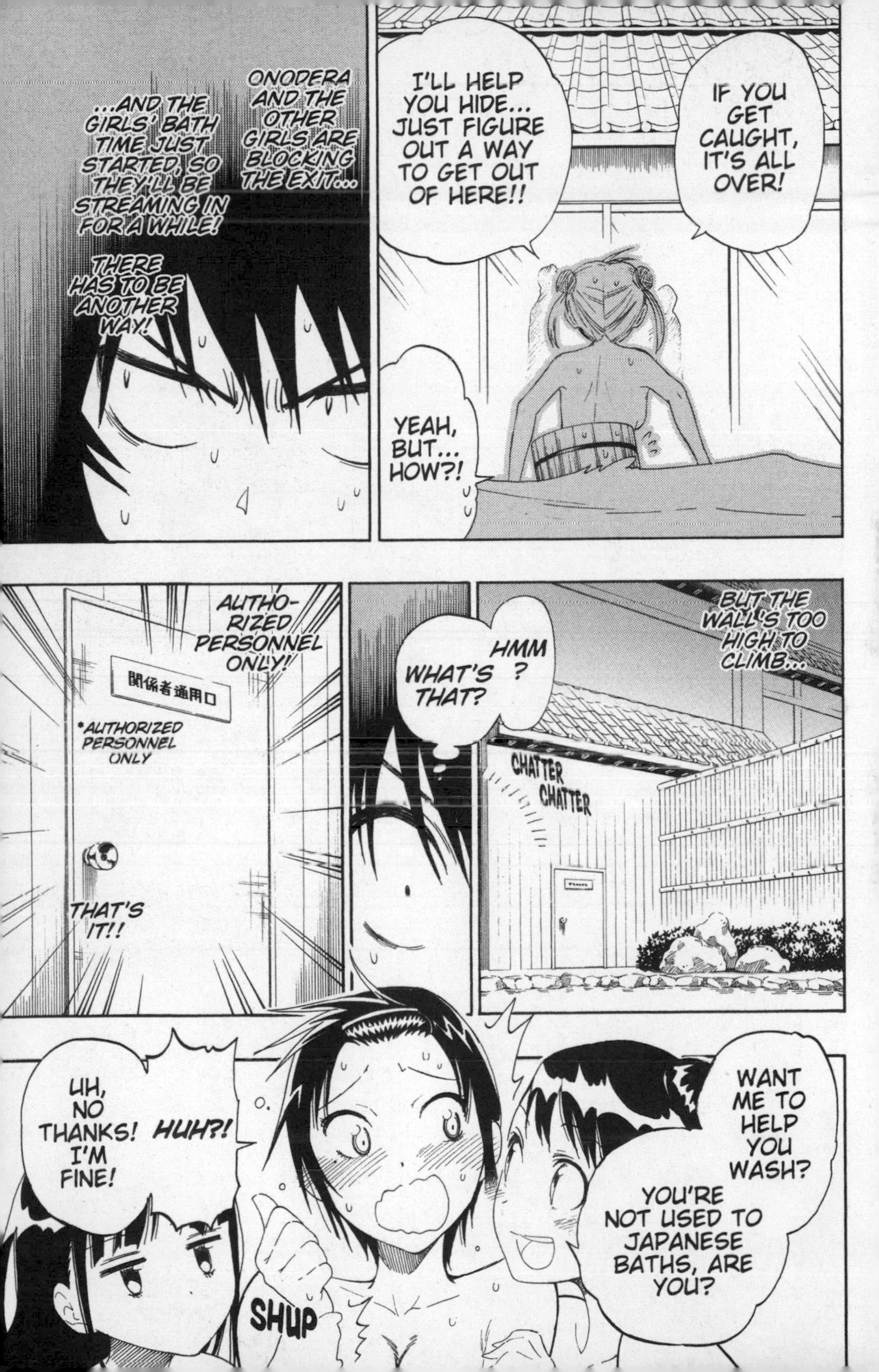
IF YOU GET CAUGHT, IT'S ALL OVER!
I'LL HELP YOU HIDE... JUST FIGURE OUT A WAY TO GET OUT OF HERE!!
YEAH, BUT... HOW?!
ONODERA AND THE OTHER GIRLS ARE BLOCKING THE EXIT...
...AND THE GIRLS' BATH TIME JUST STARTED, SO THEY'LL BE STREAMING IN FOR A WHILE!
THERE HAS TO BE ANOTHER WAY!
BUT THE WALL'S TOO HIGH TO CLIMB...
CHATTER CHATTER
HMM?
WHAT'S THAT?
AUTHO-RIZED PERSONNEL ONLY!
関係者通用口
*AUTHORIZED PERSONNEL ONLY
THAT'S IT!!
WANT ME TO HELP YOU WASH?
YOU'RE NOT USED TO JAPANESE BATHS, ARE YOU?
HUH?!
UH, NO THANKS! I'M FINE!
SHUP

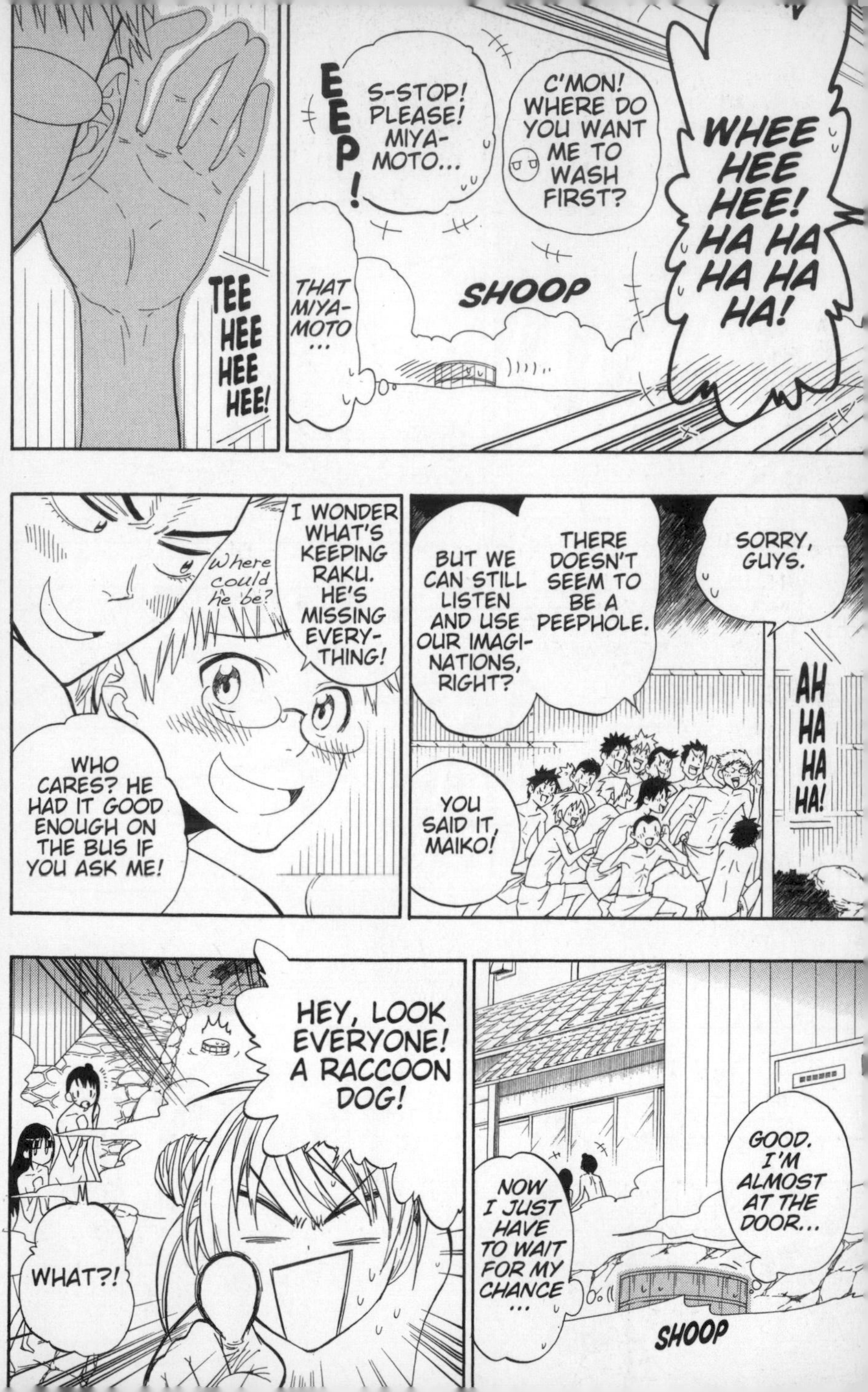
WHEE HEE HEE! HA HA HA HA HA!
C'MON! WHERE DO YOU WANT ME TO WASH FIRST?
S-STOP! PLEASE! MIYA-MOTO...
EEP!
SHOOP
THAT MIYA-MOTO ...
TEE HEE HEE HEE!
SORRY, GUYS.
AH HA HA HA!
THERE DOESN'T SEEM TO BE A PEEPHOLE.
BUT WE CAN STILL LISTEN AND USE OUR IMAGI-NATIONS, RIGHT?
YOU SAID IT, MAIKO!
I WONDER WHAT'S KEEPING RAKU. HE'S MISSING EVERY-THING!
Where could he be?
WHO CARES? HE HAD IT GOOD ENOUGH ON THE BUS IF YOU ASK ME!
GOOD. I'M ALMOST AT THE DOOR...
NOW I JUST HAVE TO WAIT FOR MY CHANCE ...
SHOOP
HEY, LOOK EVERYONE! A RACCOON DOG!
WHAT?!

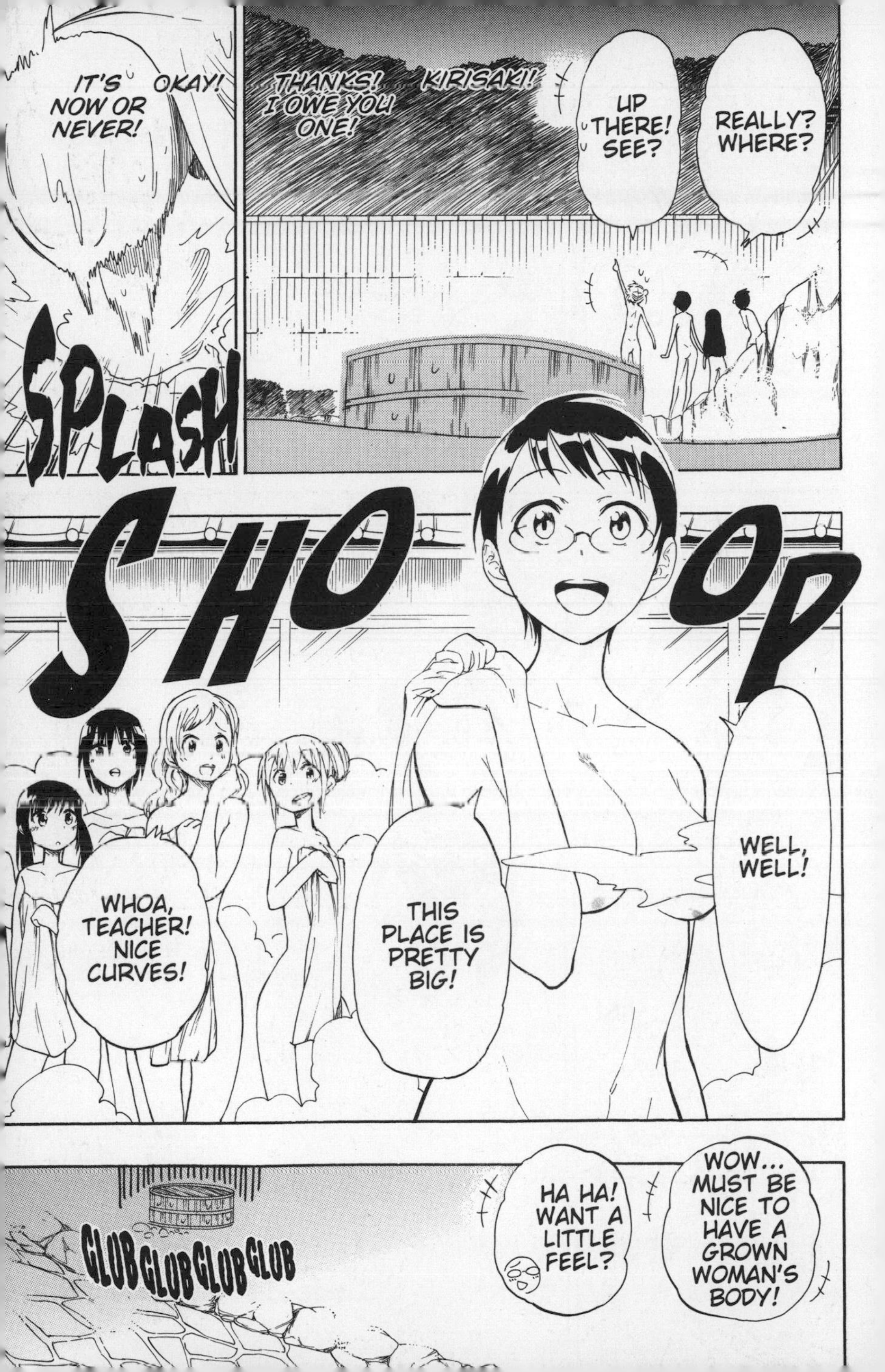
REALLY? WHERE?
UP THERE! SEE?
KIRISAKI!
THANKS! I OWE YOU ONE!
OKAY!
IT'S NOW OR NEVER!
SPLASH
SHOOP
WELL, WELL!
THIS PLACE IS PRETTY BIG!
WHOA, TEACHER! NICE CURVES!
WOW... MUST BE NICE TO HAVE A GROWN WOMAN'S BODY!
HA HA! WANT A LITTLE FEEL?
GLUB GLUB GLUB GLUB

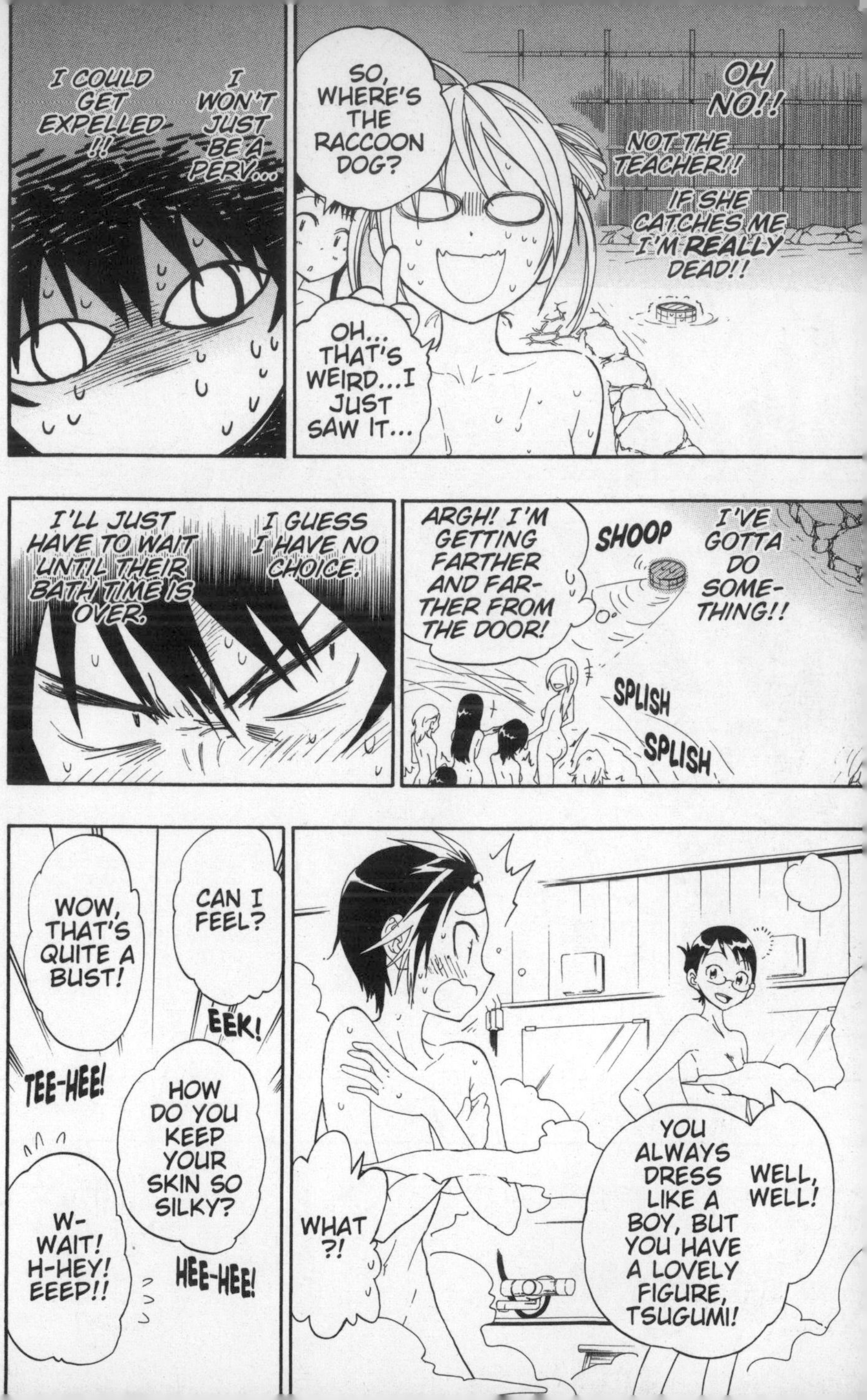
OH NO!!
NOT THE TEACHER!!
IF SHE CATCHES ME I'M REALLY DEAD!!
SO, WHERE'S THE RACCOON DOG?
OH... THAT'S WEIRD...I JUST SAW IT...
I WON'T JUST BE A PERV...
I COULD GET EXPELLED!!
I'VE GOTTA DO SOMETHING!!
SHOOP
ARGH! I'M GETTING FARTHER AND FARTHER FROM THE DOOR!
SPLISH
SPLISH
I GUESS I HAVE NO CHOICE.
I'LL JUST HAVE TO WAIT UNTIL THEIR BATH TIME IS OVER.
WELL, WELL!
YOU ALWAYS DRESS LIKE A BOY, BUT YOU HAVE A LOVELY FIGURE, TSUGUMI!
WHAT?!
CAN I FEEL?
EEK!
WOW, THAT'S QUITE A BUST!
TEE-HEE!
HOW DO YOU KEEP YOUR SKIN SO SILKY?
HEE-HEE!
W-WAIT! H-HEY! EEEP!!

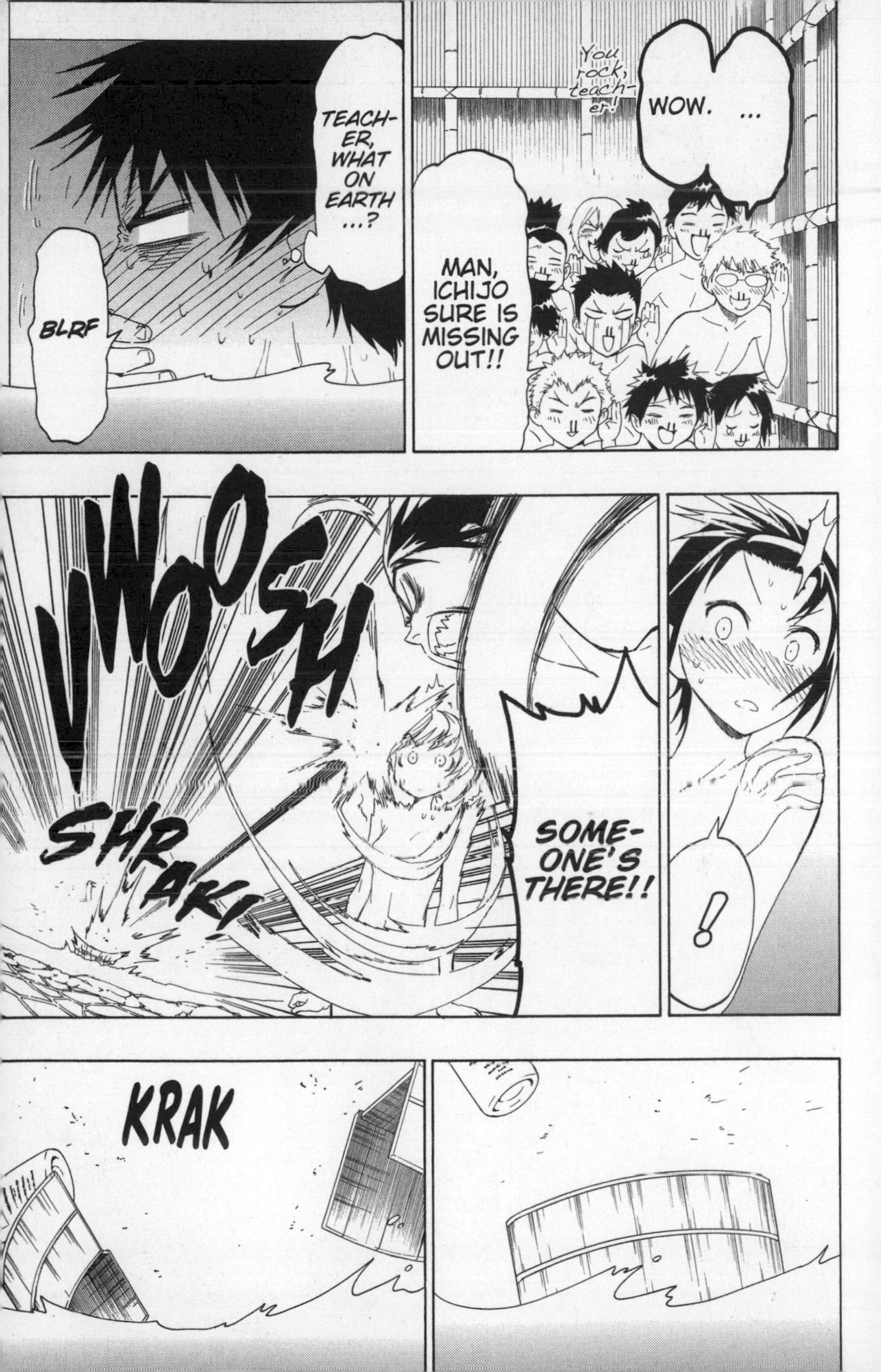
WOW. ...
You rock, teacher!
MAN, ICHIJO SURE IS MISSING OUT!!
TEACHER, WHAT ON EARTH ...?
BLRF
!
SOME-ONE'S THERE!!
WHOOSH
SHRAKI
KRAK

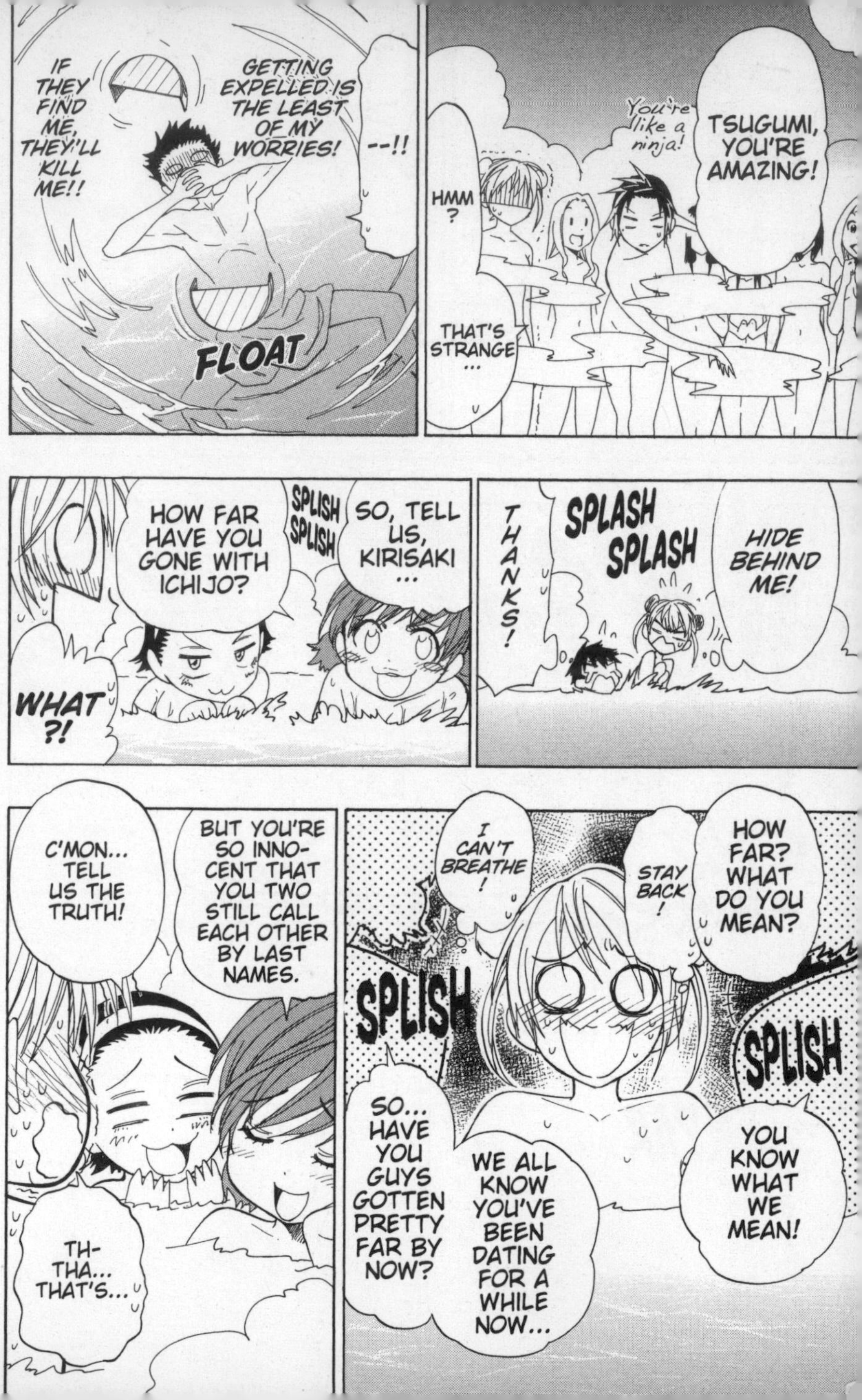
TSUGUMI, YOU'RE AMAZING!
You're like a ninja!
HMM?
THAT'S STRANGE...
--!!
GETTING EXPELLED IS THE LEAST OF MY WORRIES!
IF THEY FIND ME, THEY'LL KILL ME!!
FLOAT
HIDE BEHIND ME!
SPLASH SPLASH
THANKS!
SO, TELL US, KIRISAKI...
SPLISH SPLISH
HOW FAR HAVE YOU GONE WITH ICHIJO?
WHAT?!
HOW FAR? WHAT DO YOU MEAN?
STAY BACK!
I CAN'T BREATHE!
SPLISH
YOU KNOW WHAT WE MEAN!
SPLISH
WE ALL KNOW YOU'VE BEEN DATING FOR A WHILE NOW...
SO... HAVE YOU GUYS GOTTEN PRETTY FAR BY NOW?
BUT YOU'RE SO INNO-CENT THAT YOU TWO STILL CALL EACH OTHER BY LAST NAMES.
C'MON... TELL US THE TRUTH!
TH-THA... THAT'S...

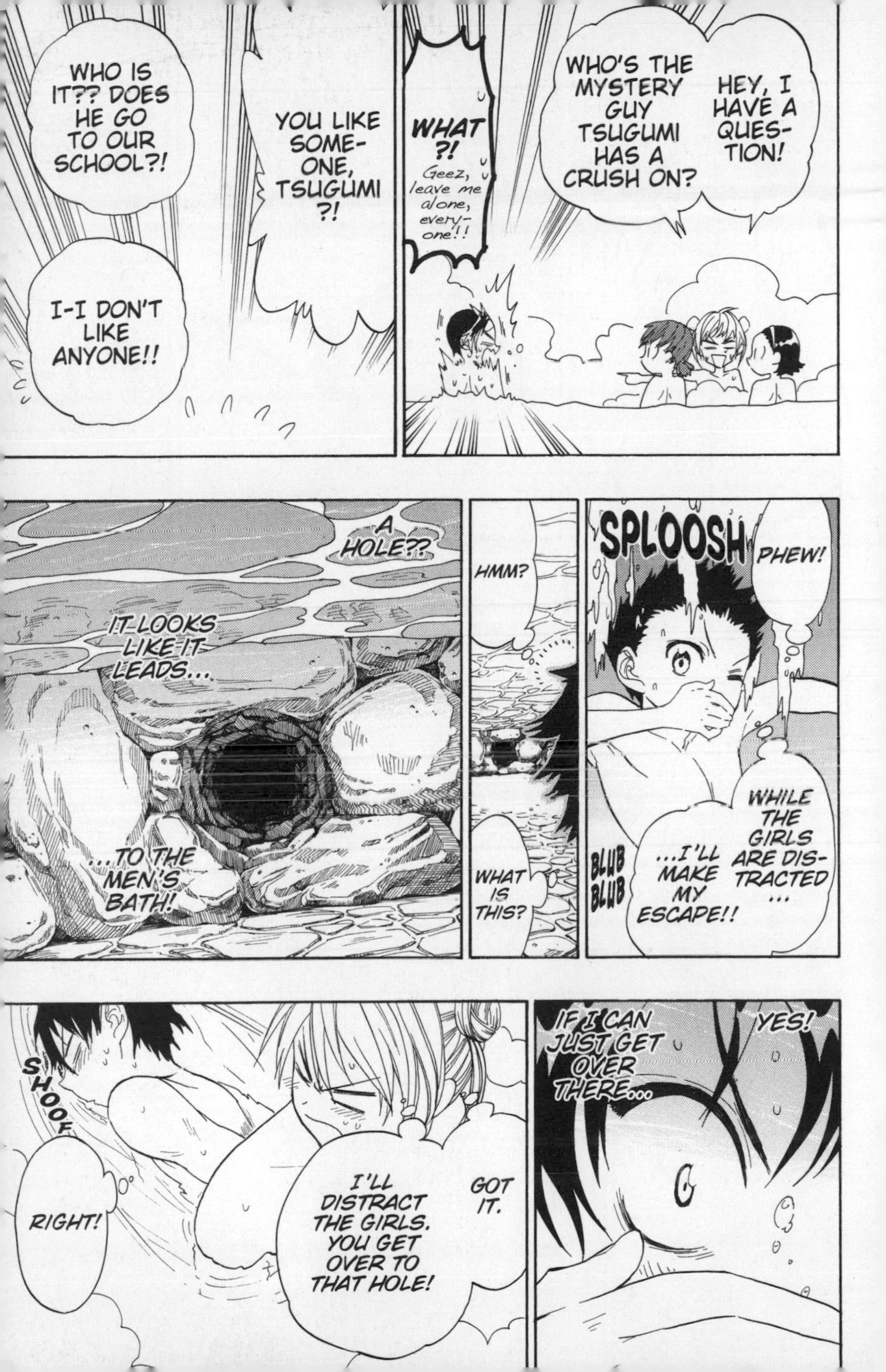
HEY, I HAVE A QUESTION!
WHO'S THE MYSTERY GUY TSUGUMI HAS A CRUSH ON?
WHAT?!
Geez, leave me alone, every-one!!
YOU LIKE SOME-ONE, TSUGUMI?!
WHO IS IT?? DOES HE GO TO OUR SCHOOL?!
I-I DON'T LIKE ANYONE!!
SPLOOSH
PHEW!
WHILE THE GIRLS ARE DIS-TRACTED...
...I'LL MAKE MY ESCAPE!!
BLUB BLUB
HMM?
WHAT IS THIS?
A HOLE??
IT LOOKS LIKE IT LEADS...
...TO THE MEN'S BATH!
YES!
IF I CAN JUST GET OVER THERE...
GOT IT.
I'LL DISTRACT THE GIRLS. YOU GET OVER TO THAT HOLE!
RIGHT!
SHOOF

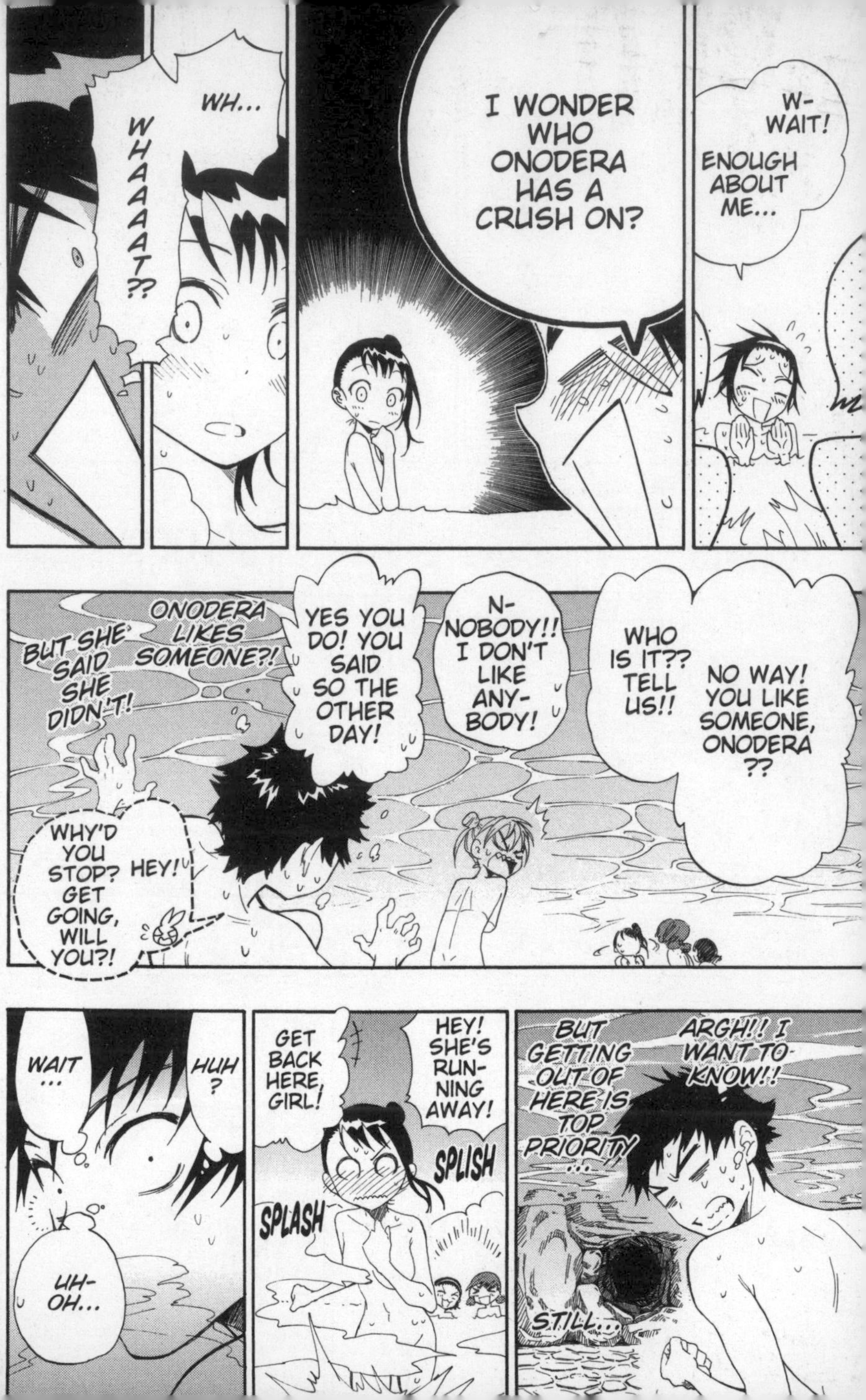
W-WAIT!
ENOUGH ABOUT ME...
I WONDER WHO ONODERA HAS A CRUSH ON?
WH...
WHAAAAAT??
NO WAY! YOU LIKE SOMEONE, ONODERA??
WHO IS IT?? TELL US!!
N-NOBODY!! I DON'T LIKE ANY-BODY!
YES YOU DO! YOU SAID SO THE OTHER DAY!
ONODERA LIKES SOMEONE?!
BUT SHE SAID SHE DIDN'T!
HEY!
WHY'D YOU STOP? GET GOING, WILL YOU?!
ARGH!! I WANT TO KNOW!!
BUT GETTING OUT OF HERE IS TOP PRIORITY...
STILL...
HEY! SHE'S RUN-NING AWAY!
GET BACK HERE, GIRL!
SPLISH
SPLASH
HUH?
WAIT...
UH-OH...

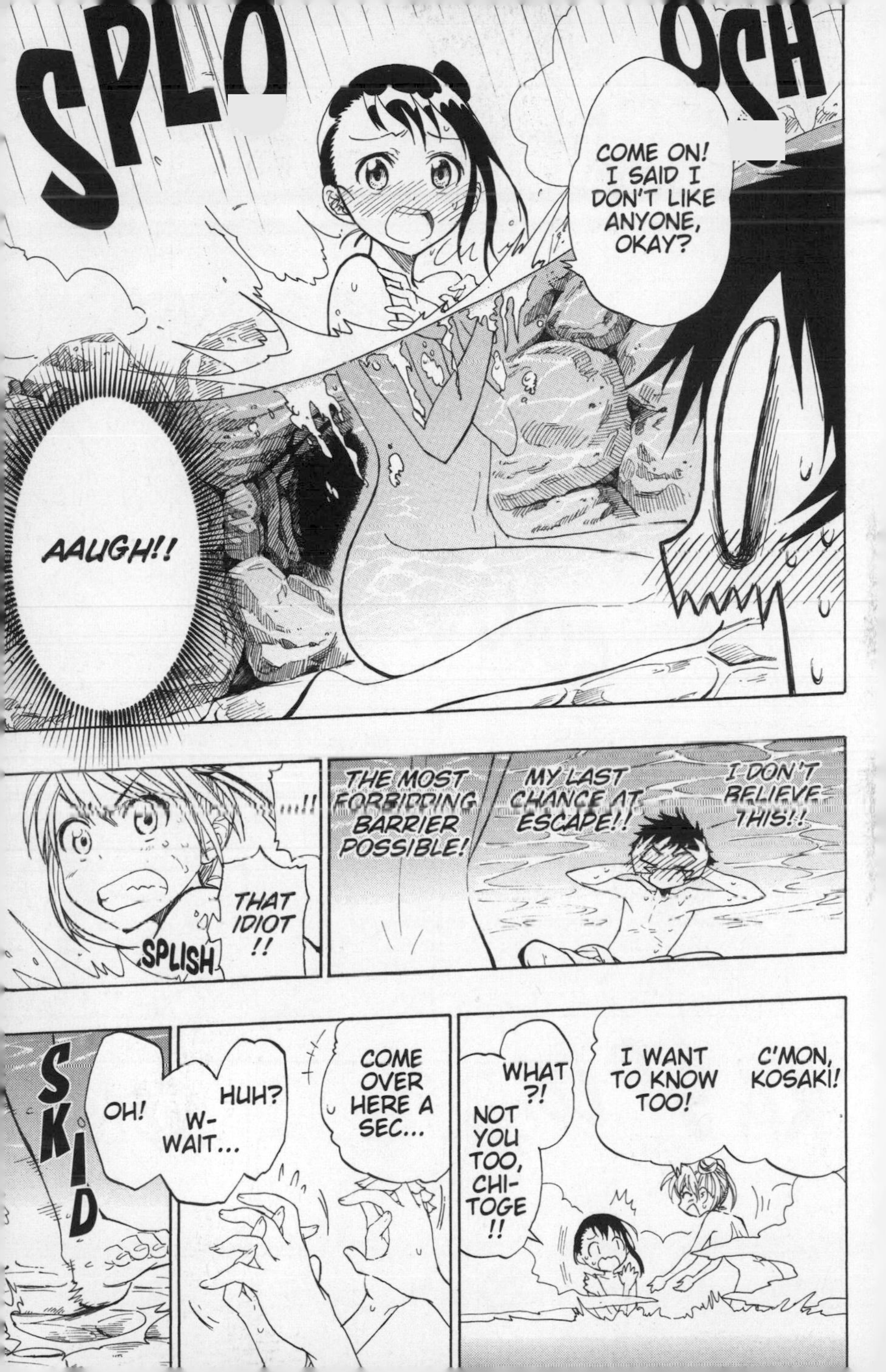
SPLO
OCH
COME ON! I SAID I DON'T LIKE ANYONE, OKAY?
AAUGH!!
I DON'T BELIEVE THIS!!
MY LAST CHANCE AT ESCAPE!!
THE MOST FORBIDDING BARRIER POSSIBLE!
...!!
THAT IDIOT!!
SPLISH
C'MON, KOSAKI!
I WANT TO KNOW TOO!
WHAT?!
NOT YOU TOO, CHITOGE!!
COME OVER HERE A SEC...
HUH?
W-WAIT...
OH!
SKID

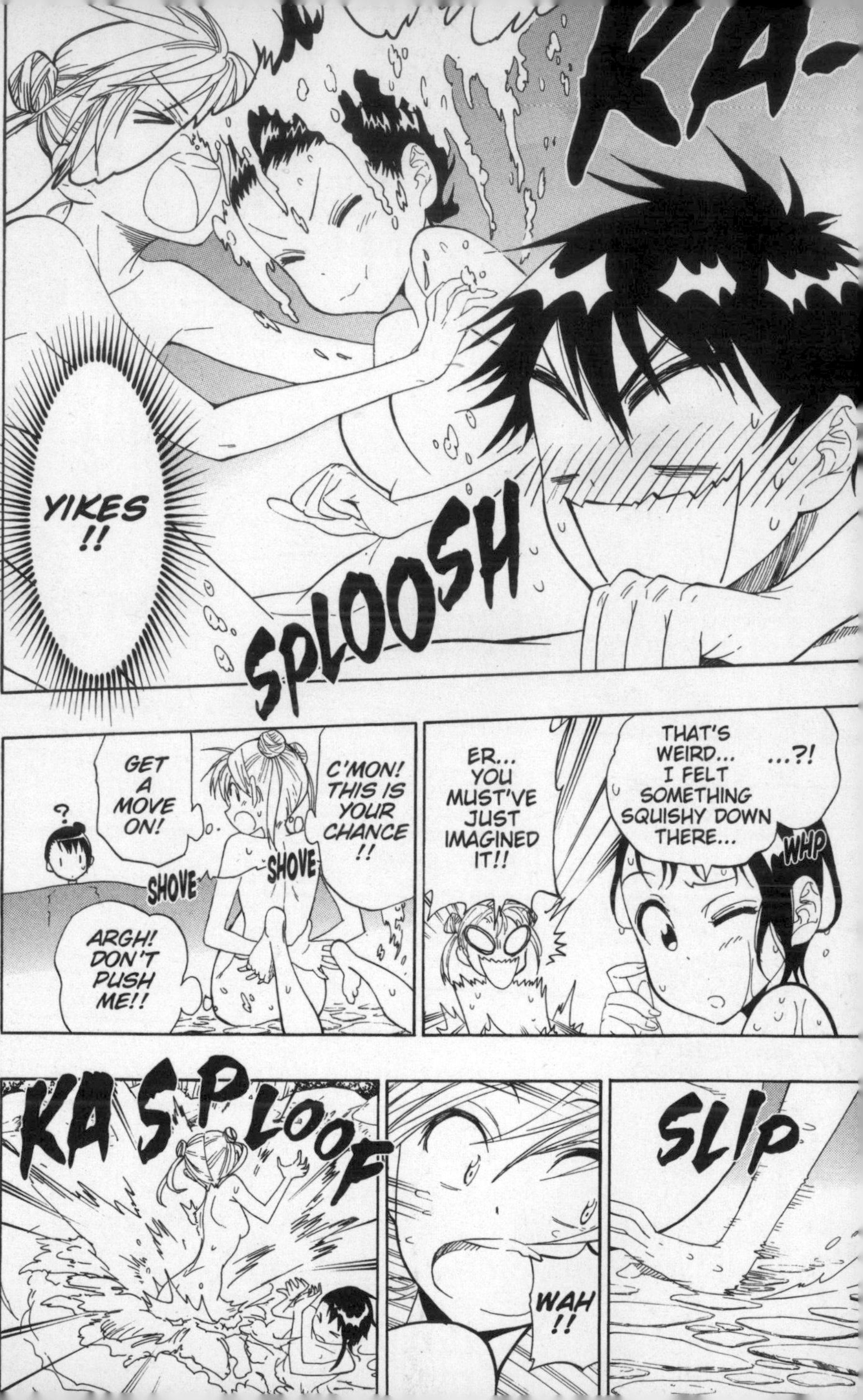
KA-
SPLOOSH
YIKES !!
THAT'S WEIRD... I FELT SOMETHING SQUISHY DOWN THERE...
...?!
WHP
ER... YOU MUST'VE JUST IMAGINED IT!!
C'MON! THIS IS YOUR CHANCE !!
GET A MOVE ON!
SHOVE
SHOVE
?
ARGH! DON'T PUSH ME!!
SLIP
WAH !!
KASPLOOF

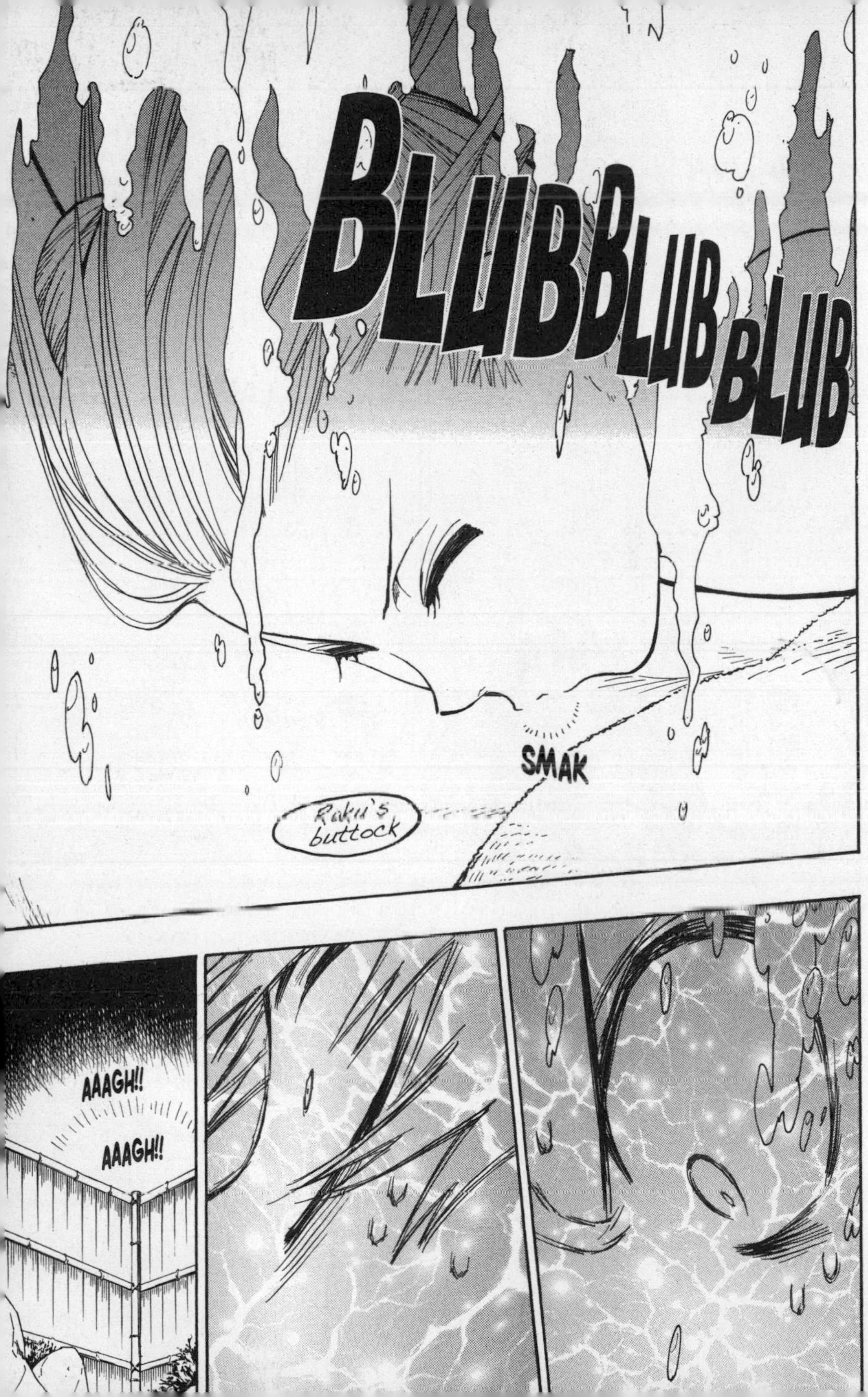
BLUBBLUB BLUB
SMAK
Raku's buttock
AAAGH!!
AAAGH!!

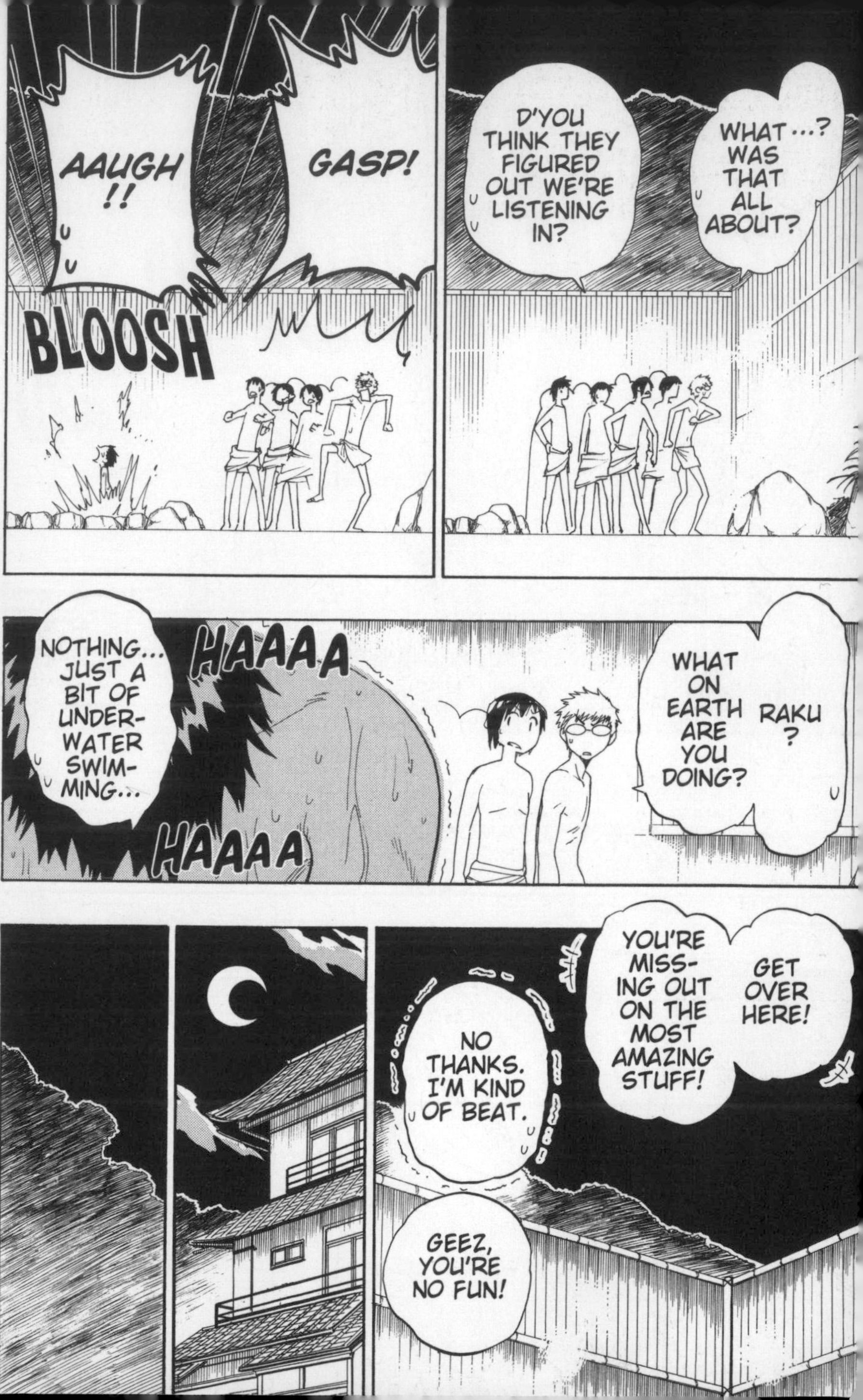
WHAT...? WAS THAT ALL ABOUT?
D'YOU THINK THEY FIGURED OUT WE'RE LISTENING IN?
GASP!
AAUGH!!
BLOOSH
RAKU?
WHAT ON EARTH ARE YOU DOING?
HAAAA
NOTHING... JUST A BIT OF UNDER-WATER SWIM-MING...
HAAAA
GET OVER HERE!
YOU'RE MISS-ING OUT ON THE MOST AMAZING STUFF!
NO THANKS. I'M KIND OF BEAT.
GEEZ, YOU'RE NO FUN!

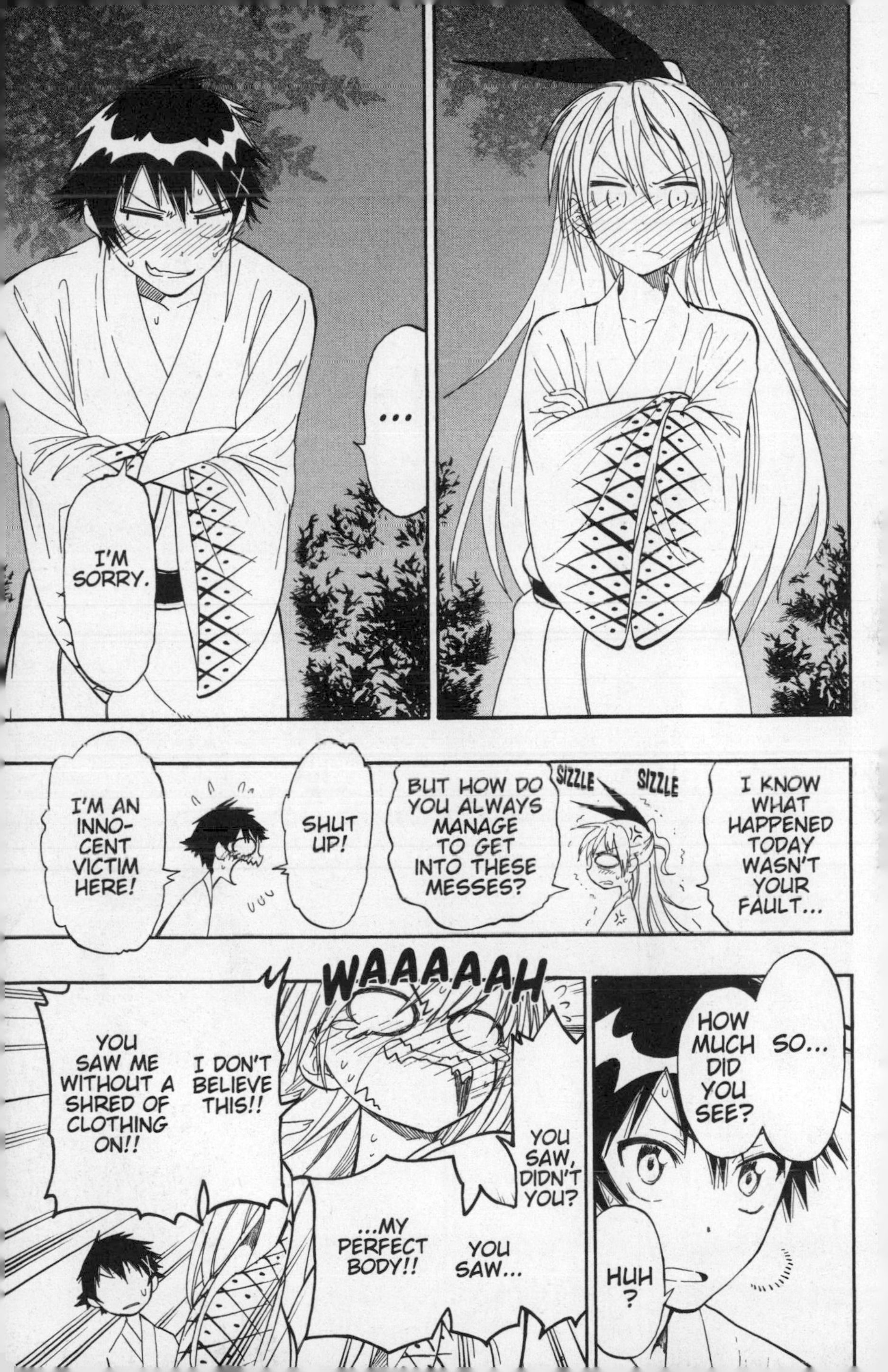
...
I'M SORRY.
I KNOW WHAT HAPPENED TODAY WASN'T YOUR FAULT...
SIZZLE
SIZZLE
BUT HOW DO YOU ALWAYS MANAGE TO GET INTO THESE MESSES?
SHUT UP!
I'M AN INNO-CENT VICTIM HERE!
SO...
HOW MUCH DID YOU SEE?
HUH?
WAAAAAH
YOU SAW, DIDN'T YOU?
YOU SAW...
...MY PERFECT BODY!!
I DON'T BELIEVE THIS!!
YOU SAW ME WITHOUT A SHRED OF CLOTHING ON!!

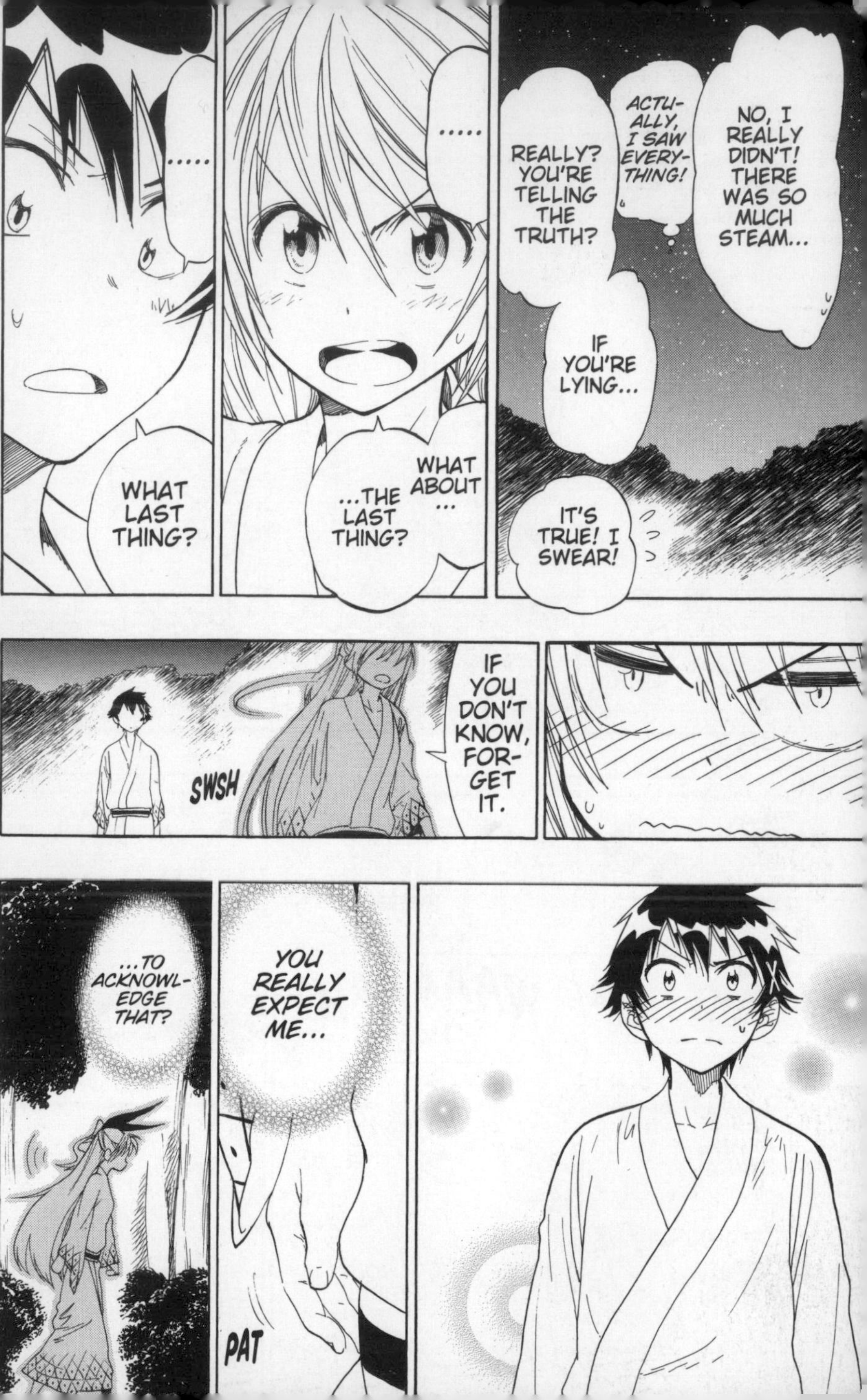
NO, I REALLY DIDN'T! THERE WAS SO MUCH STEAM...
ACTU-ALLY, I SAW EVERY-THING!
REALLY? YOU'RE TELLING THE TRUTH?
IF YOU'RE LYING...
IT'S TRUE! I SWEAR!
.....
WHAT ABOUT ...
...THE LAST THING?
.....
WHAT LAST THING?
IF YOU DON'T KNOW, FOR-GET IT.
SWSH
YOU REALLY EXPECT ME...
PAT
...TO ACKNOWL-EDGE THAT?

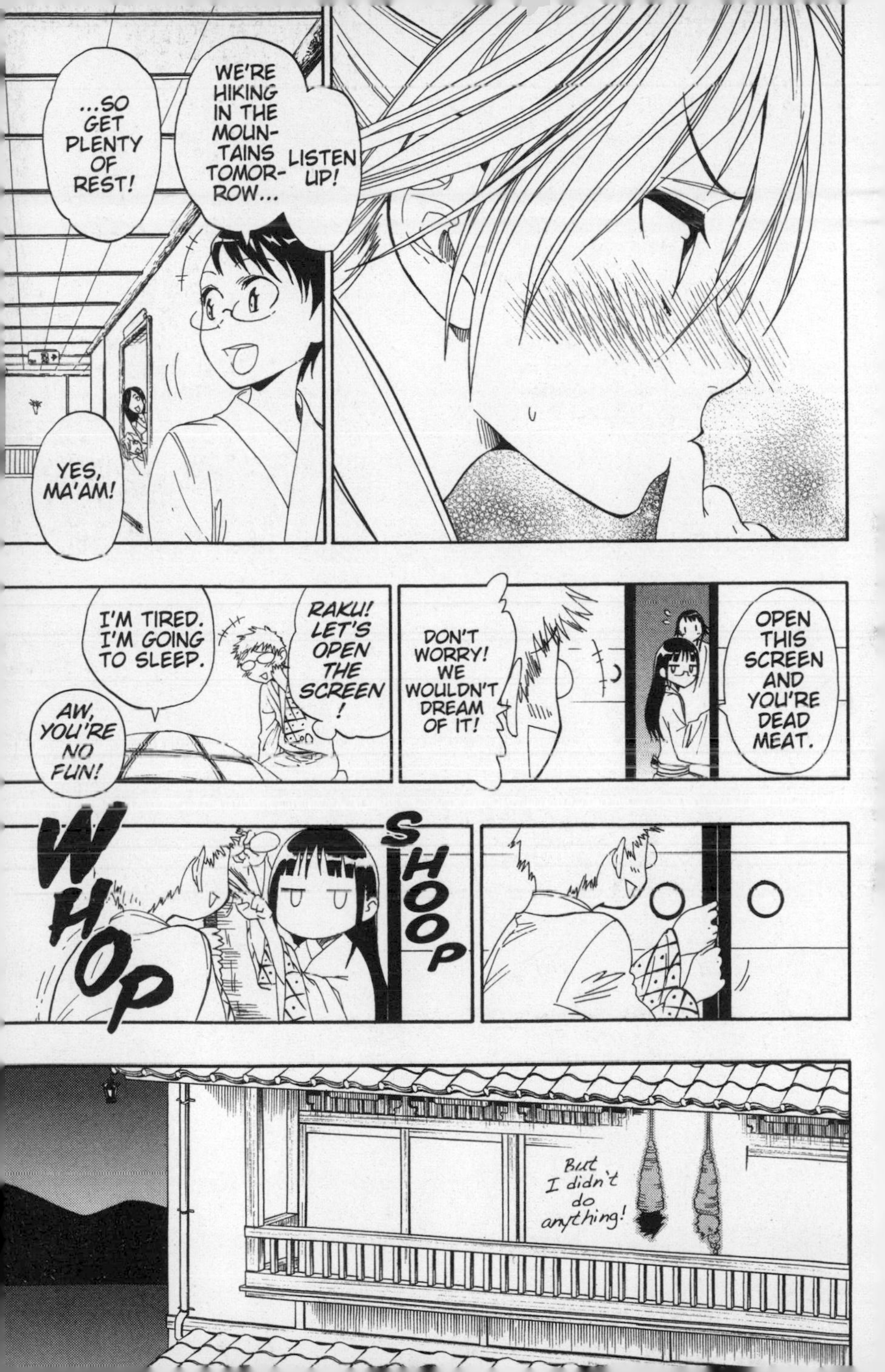
LISTEN UP!
WE'RE HIKING IN THE MOUN-TAINS TOMOR-ROW...
...SO GET PLENTY OF REST!
YES, MA'AM!
OPEN THIS SCREEN AND YOU'RE DEAD MEAT.
DON'T WORRY! WE WOULDN'T DREAM OF IT!
RAKU! LET'S OPEN THE SCREEN!
I'M TIRED. I'M GOING TO SLEEP.
AW, YOU'RE NO FUN!
SHOOP
WHOP
But I didn't do anything!

Inside Ruri's backpack☆
What's all this for?
Fighting off perverts.

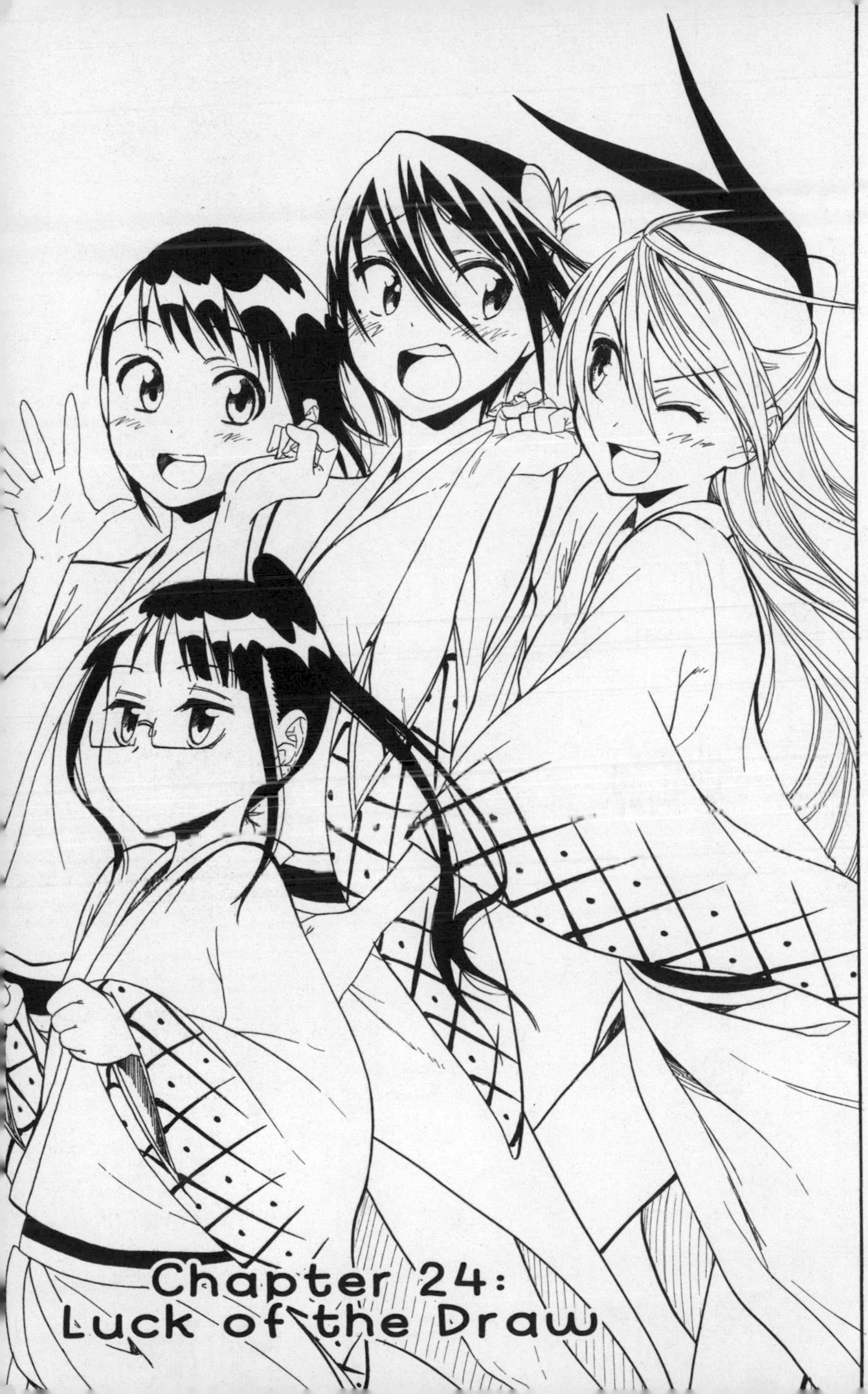
Chapter 24:
Luck of the Draw

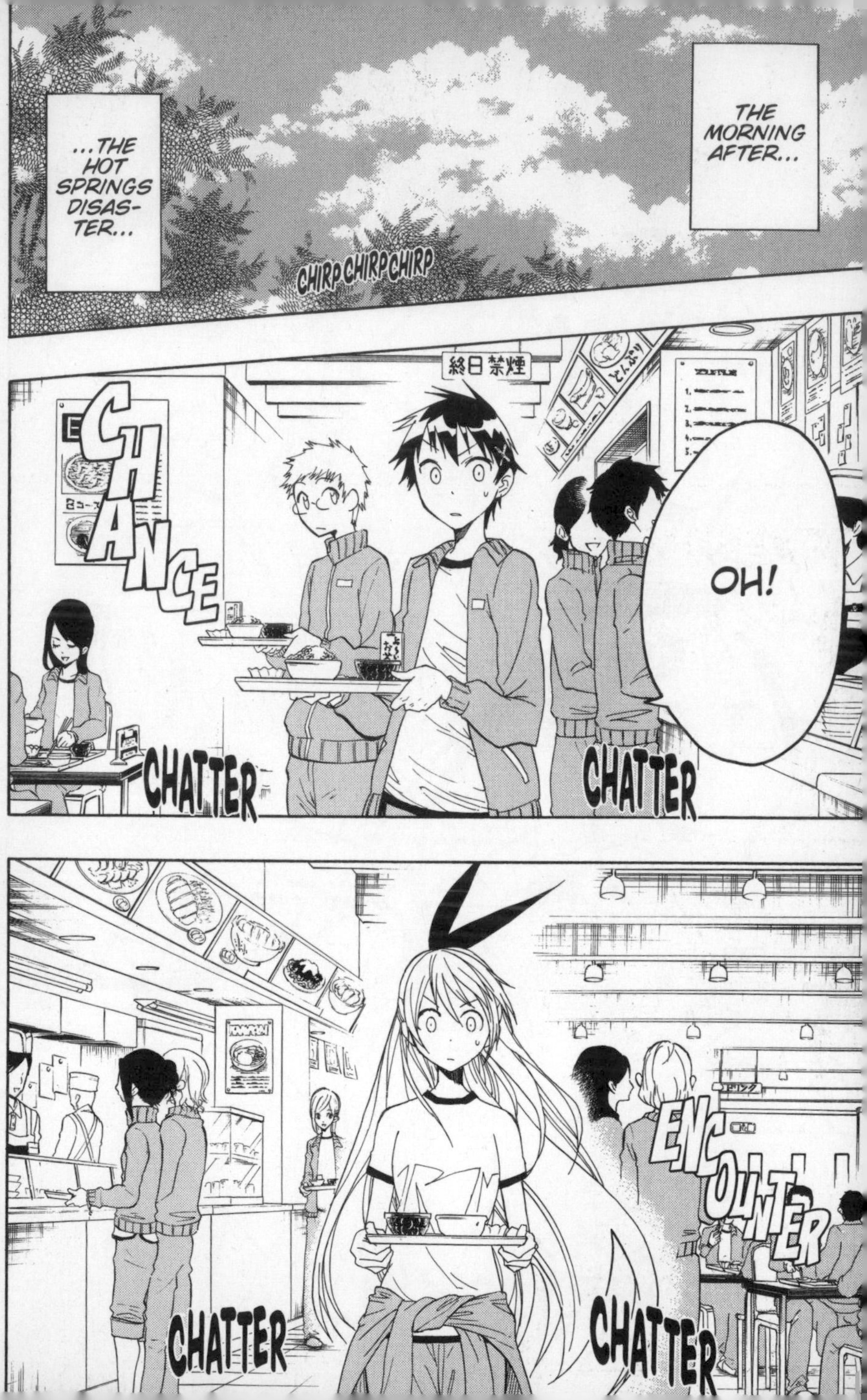
THE MORNING AFTER...
...THE HOT SPRINGS DISASTER...
CHIRP CHIRP CHIRP
終日禁煙
OH!
CHATTER
CHANCE
CHATTER
ENCOUNTER
CHATTER
CHATTER

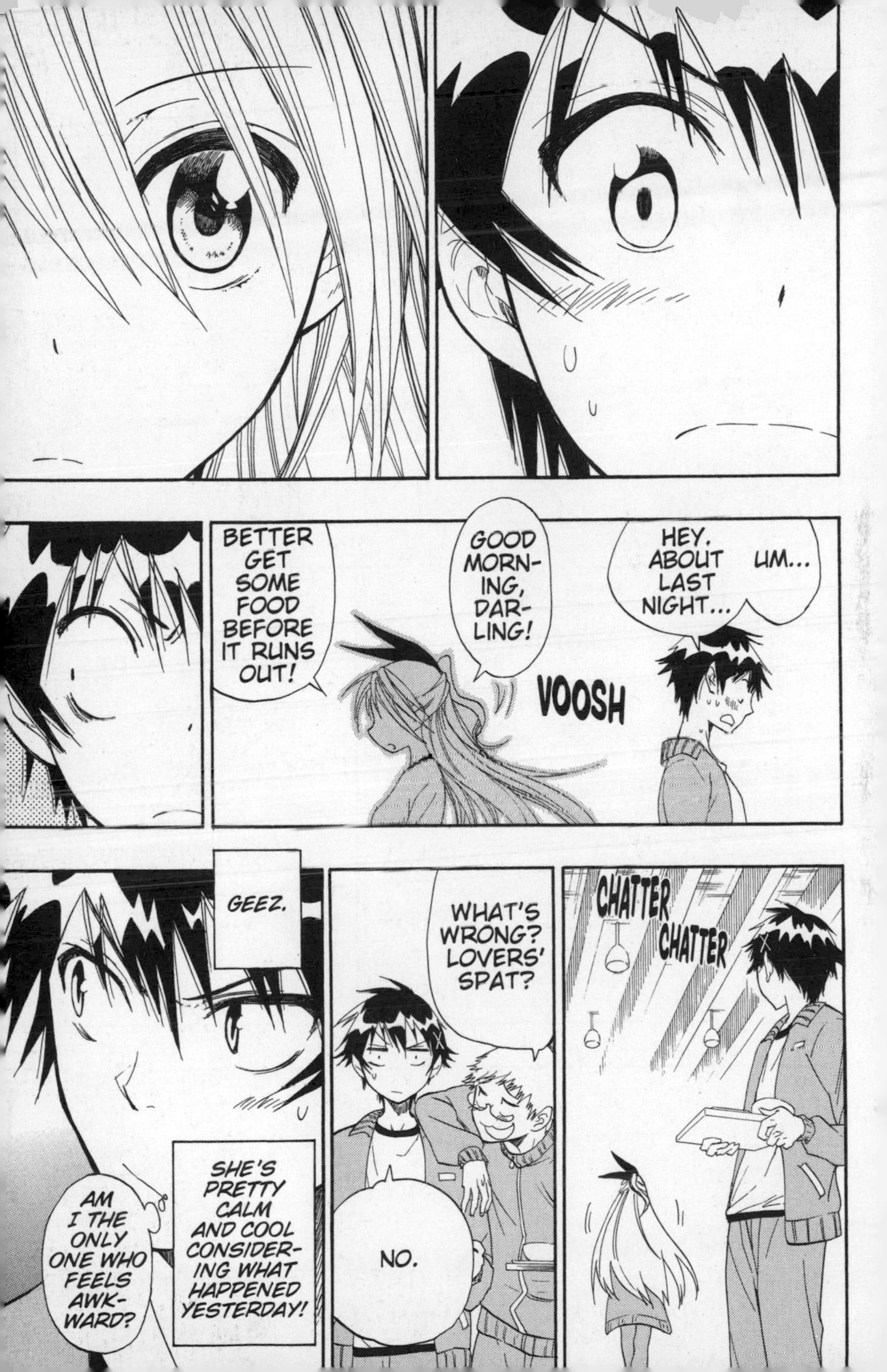
UM...
HEY. ABOUT LAST NIGHT...
GOOD MORNING, DARLING!
VOOSH
BETTER GET SOME FOOD BEFORE IT RUNS OUT!
CHATTER
CHATTER
WHAT'S WRONG? LOVERS' SPAT?
NO.
GEEZ.
SHE'S PRETTY CALM AND COOL CONSIDERING WHAT HAPPENED YESTERDAY!
AM I THE ONLY ONE WHO FEELS AWKWARD?

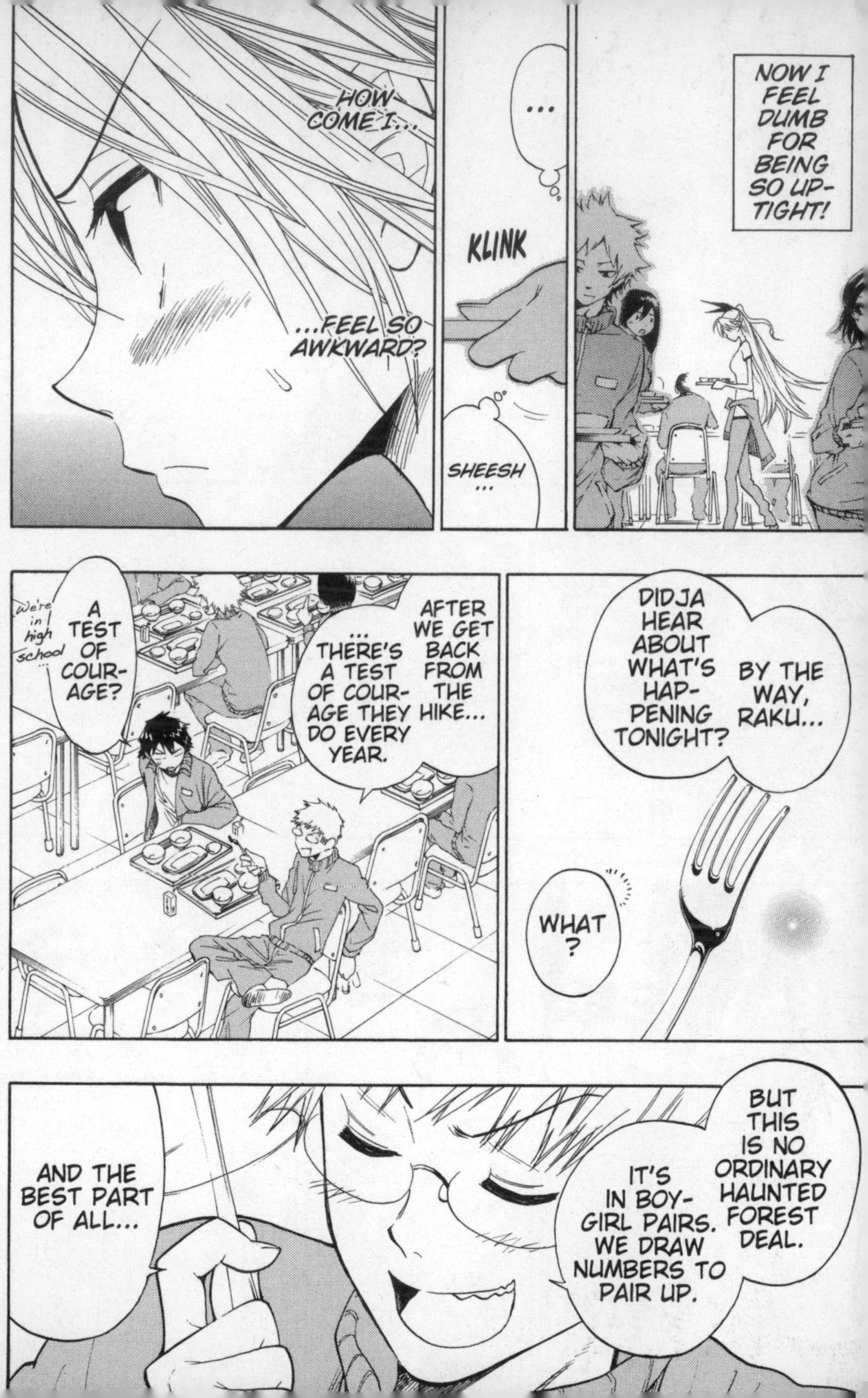
NOW I FEEL DUMB FOR BEING SO UP-TIGHT!
...
KLINK
SHEESH ...
HOW COME I...
...FEEL SO AWKWARD?
BY THE WAY, RAKU...
DIDJA HEAR ABOUT WHAT'S HAP-PENING TONIGHT?
WHAT?
AFTER WE GET BACK FROM THE HIKE...
... THERE'S A TEST OF COUR-AGE THEY DO EVERY YEAR.
A TEST OF COUR-AGE?
We're in high school...
BUT THIS IS NO ORDINARY HAUNTED FOREST DEAL.
IT'S IN BOY-GIRL PAIRS. WE DRAW NUMBERS TO PAIR UP.
AND THE BEST PART OF ALL...

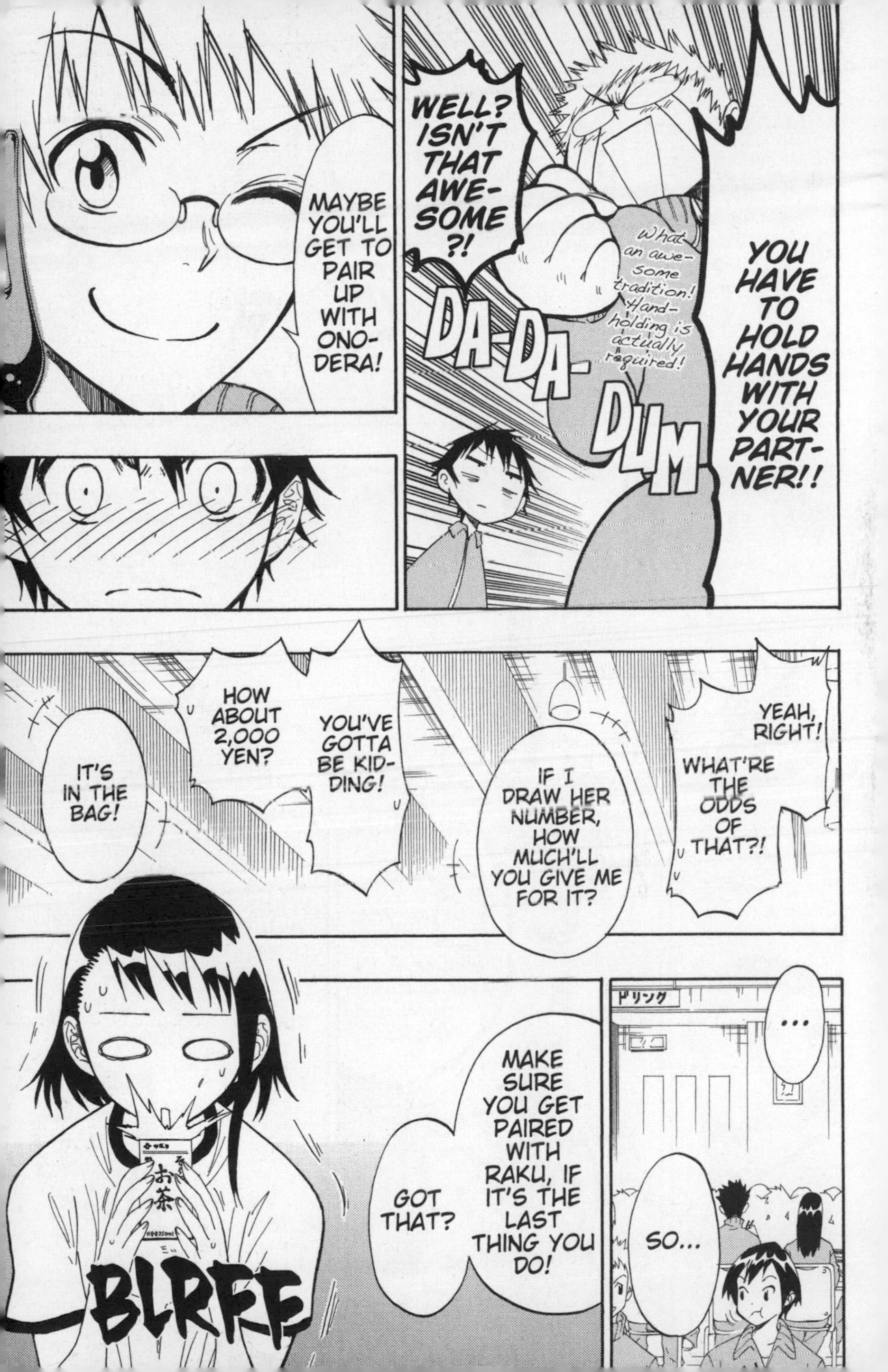
YOU HAVE TO HOLD HANDS WITH YOUR PARTNER!!
WELL? ISN'T THAT AWE-SOME?!
What an awe-some tradition! Hand-holding is actually required!
DA-DA-DUM
MAYBE YOU'LL GET TO PAIR UP WITH ONO-DERA!
YEAH, RIGHT!
WHAT'RE THE ODDS OF THAT?!
IF I DRAW HER NUMBER, HOW MUCH'LL YOU GIVE ME FOR IT?
YOU'VE GOTTA BE KID-DING!
HOW ABOUT 2,000 YEN?
IT'S IN THE BAG!
ドリンク
...
SO...
MAKE SURE YOU GET PAIRED WITH RAKU, IF IT'S THE LAST THING YOU DO!
GOT THAT?
お茶
BLRFF

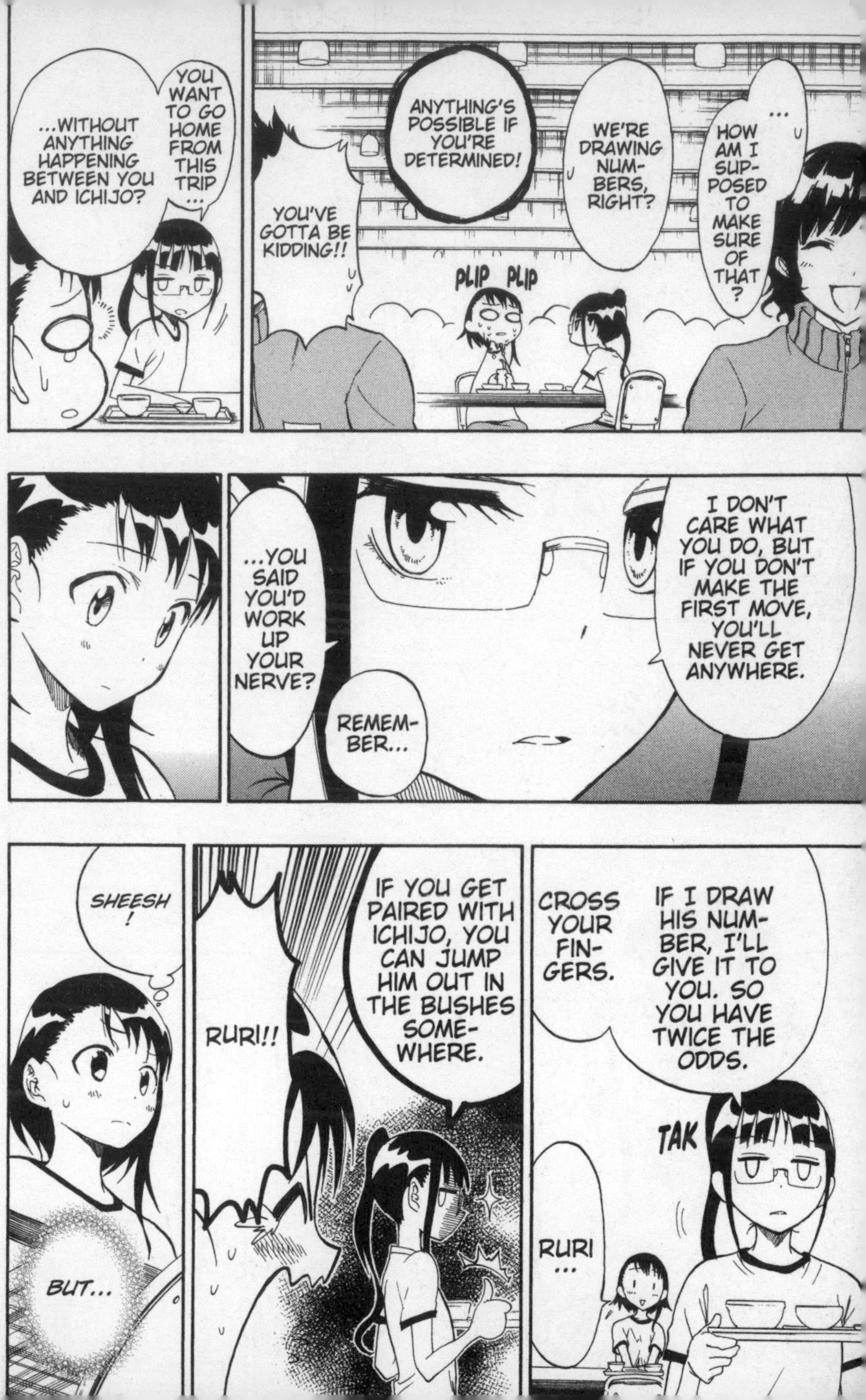
... HOW AM I SUPPOSED TO MAKE SURE OF THAT?
WE'RE DRAWING NUMBERS, RIGHT?
ANYTHING'S POSSIBLE IF YOU'RE DETERMINED!
YOU'VE GOTTA BE KIDDING!!
PLIP PLIP
YOU WANT TO GO HOME FROM THIS TRIP...
...WITHOUT ANYTHING HAPPENING BETWEEN YOU AND ICHIJO?
I DON'T CARE WHAT YOU DO, BUT IF YOU DON'T MAKE THE FIRST MOVE, YOU'LL NEVER GET ANYWHERE.
REMEMBER...
...YOU SAID YOU'D WORK UP YOUR NERVE?
IF I DRAW HIS NUMBER, I'LL GIVE IT TO YOU. SO YOU HAVE TWICE THE ODDS.
CROSS YOUR FINGERS.
TAK
RURI...
IF YOU GET PAIRED WITH ICHIJO, YOU CAN JUMP HIM OUT IN THE BUSHES SOMEWHERE.
RURI!!
SHEESH!
BUT...

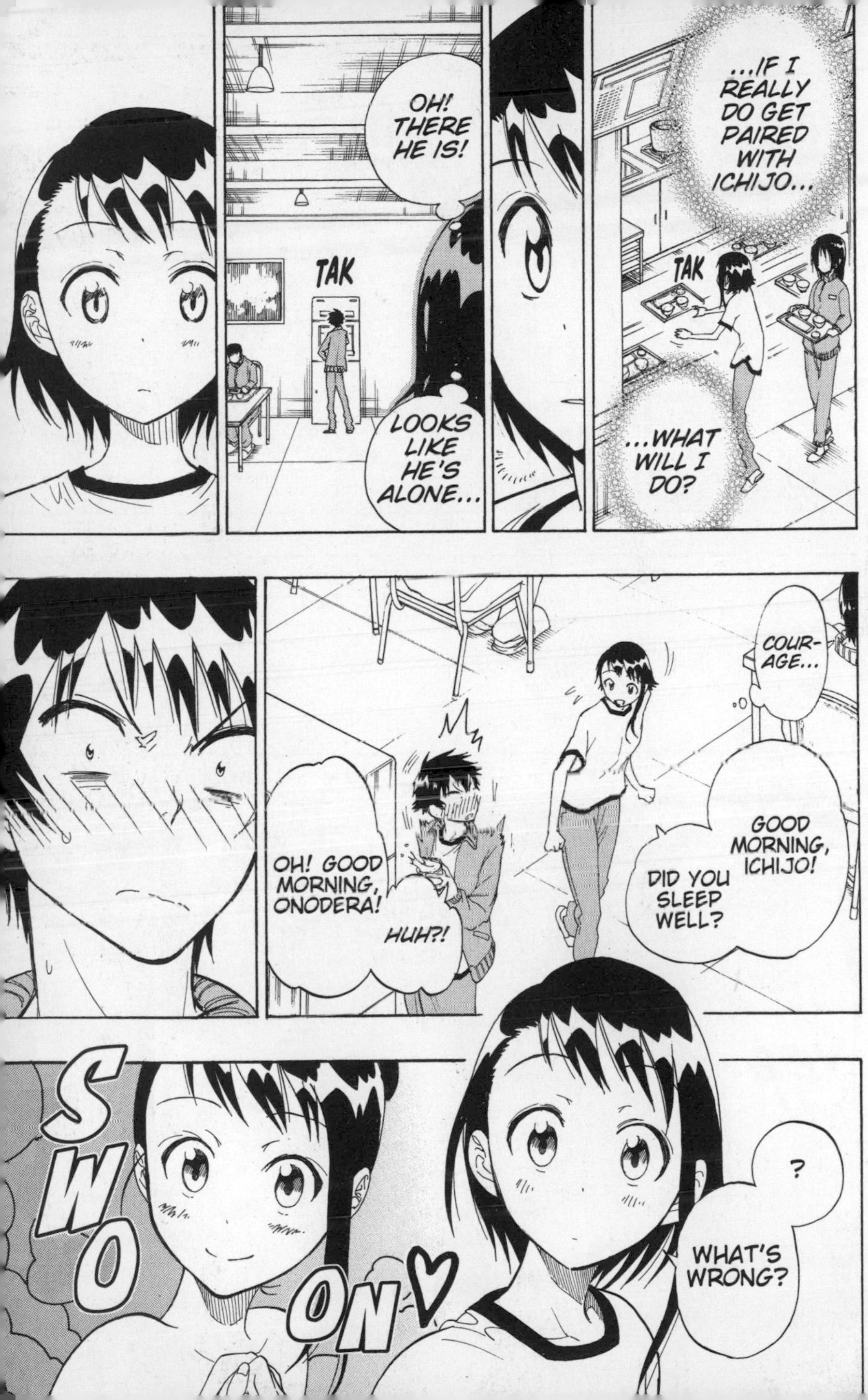
...IF I REALLY DO GET PAIRED WITH ICHIJO...
TAK
...WHAT WILL I DO?
OH! THERE HE IS!
TAK
LOOKS LIKE HE'S ALONE...
COUR-AGE...
GOOD MORNING, ICHIJO!
DID YOU SLEEP WELL?
HUH?!
OH! GOOD MORNING, ONODERA!
?
WHAT'S WRONG?
SWOON♥

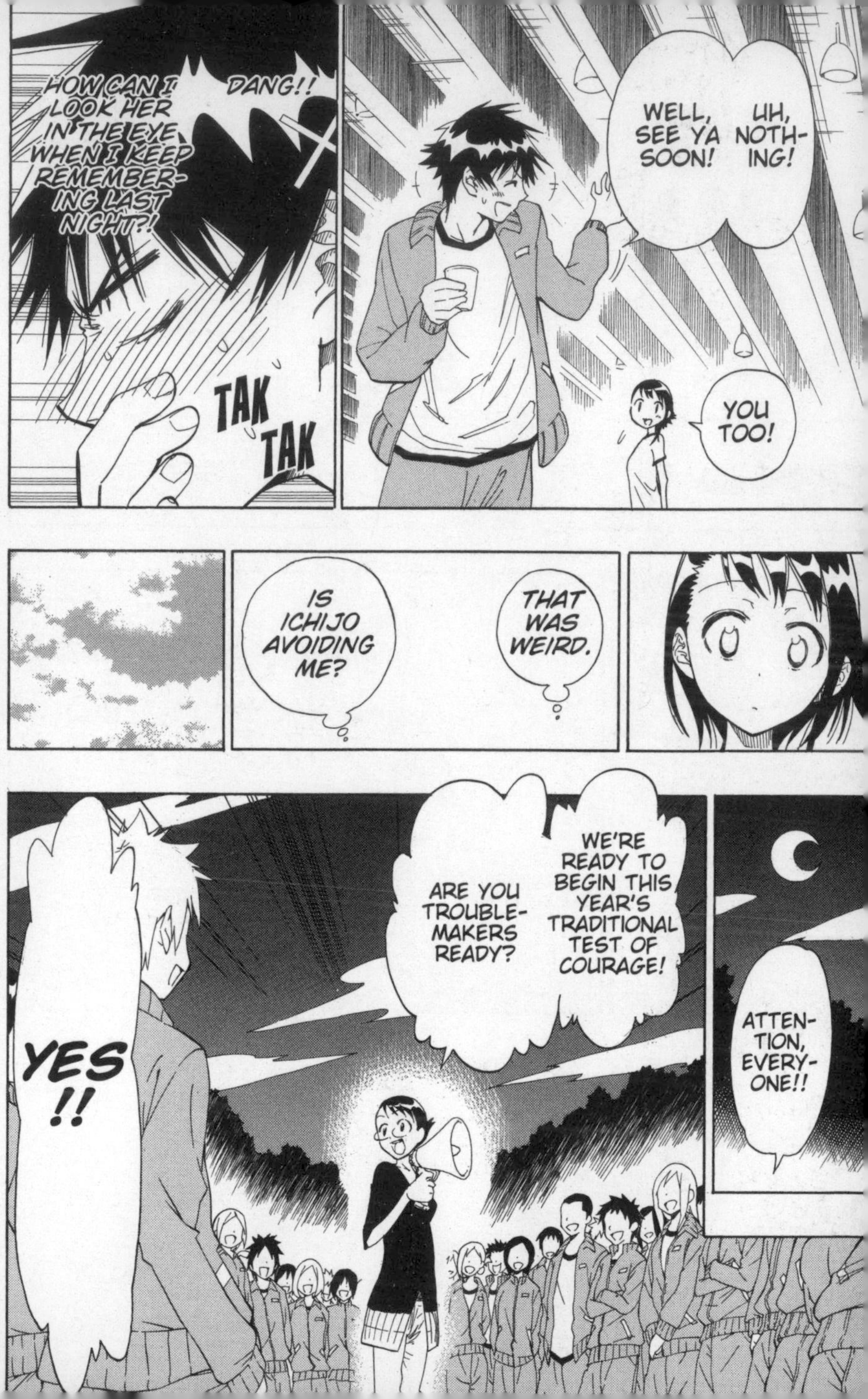
UH, NOTHING!
WELL, SEE YA SOON!
YOU TOO!
DANG!!
HOW CAN I LOOK HER IN THE EYE WHEN I KEEP REMEMBERING LAST NIGHT?!
TAK TAK
THAT WAS WEIRD.
IS ICHIJO AVOIDING ME?
ATTENTION, EVERYONE!!
WE'RE READY TO BEGIN THIS YEAR'S TRADITIONAL TEST OF COURAGE!
ARE YOU TROUBLEMAKERS READY?
YES!!

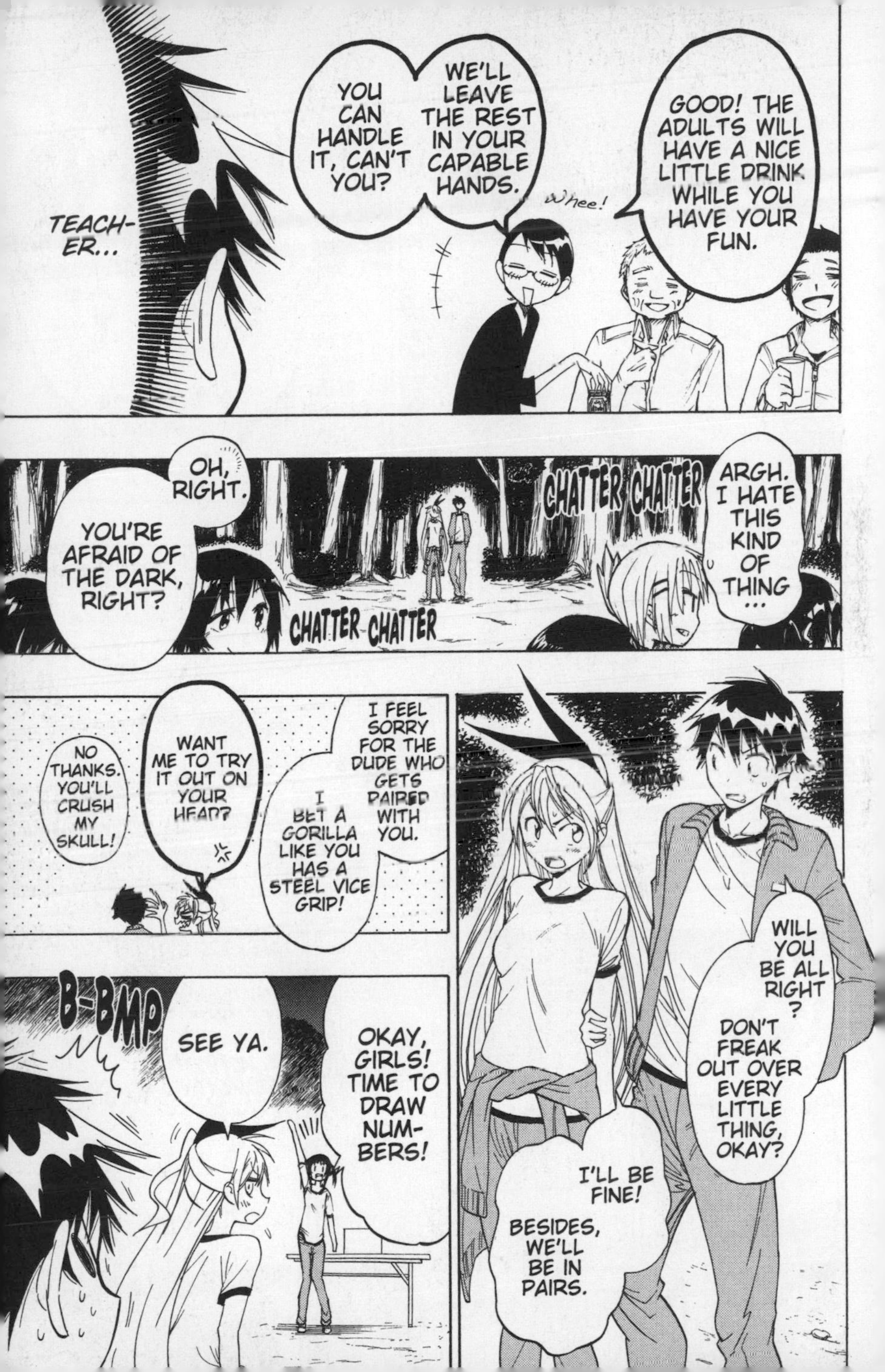
GOOD! THE ADULTS WILL HAVE A NICE LITTLE DRINK WHILE YOU HAVE YOUR FUN.
Whee!
WE'LL LEAVE THE REST IN YOUR CAPABLE HANDS.
YOU CAN HANDLE IT, CAN'T YOU?
TEACHER...
ARGH. I HATE THIS KIND OF THING...
CHATTER CHATTER
OH, RIGHT.
YOU'RE AFRAID OF THE DARK, RIGHT?
CHATTER CHATTER
WILL YOU BE ALL RIGHT?
DON'T FREAK OUT OVER EVERY LITTLE THING, OKAY?
I'LL BE FINE!
BESIDES, WE'LL BE IN PAIRS.
I FEEL SORRY FOR THE DUDE WHO GETS PAIRED WITH YOU.
I BET A GORILLA LIKE YOU HAS A STEEL VICE GRIP!
WANT ME TO TRY IT OUT ON YOUR HEAD?
NO THANKS. YOU'LL CRUSH MY SKULL!
OKAY, GIRLS! TIME TO DRAW NUMBERS!
SEE YA.
B-BMP

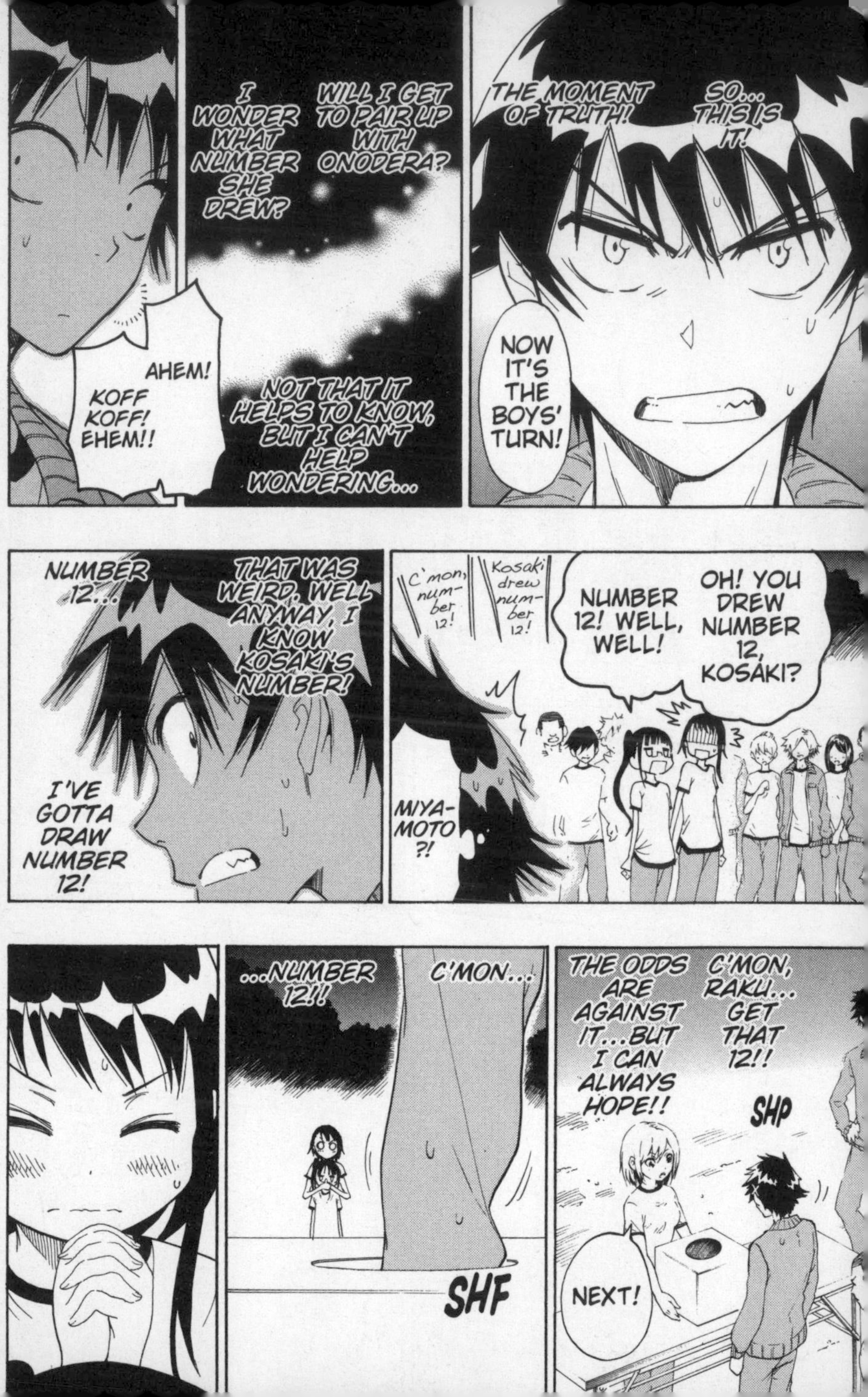
SO... THIS IS IT!
THE MOMENT OF TRUTH!
NOW IT'S THE BOYS' TURN!
WILL I GET TO PAIR UP WITH ONODERA?
I WONDER WHAT NUMBER SHE DREW?
NOT THAT IT HELPS TO KNOW, BUT I CAN'T HELP WONDERING...
AHEM!
KOFF KOFF! EHEM!!
OH! YOU DREW NUMBER 12, KOSAKI?
NUMBER 12! WELL, WELL!
Kosaki drew number 12!
C'mon, number 12!
MIYAMOTO?!
THAT WAS WEIRD. WELL ANYWAY, I KNOW KOSAKI'S NUMBER!
NUMBER 12...
I'VE GOTTA DRAW NUMBER 12!
C'MON, RAKU... GET THAT 12!!
THE ODDS ARE AGAINST IT...BUT I CAN ALWAYS HOPE!!
SHP
NEXT!
C'MON...
...NUMBER 12!!
SHF

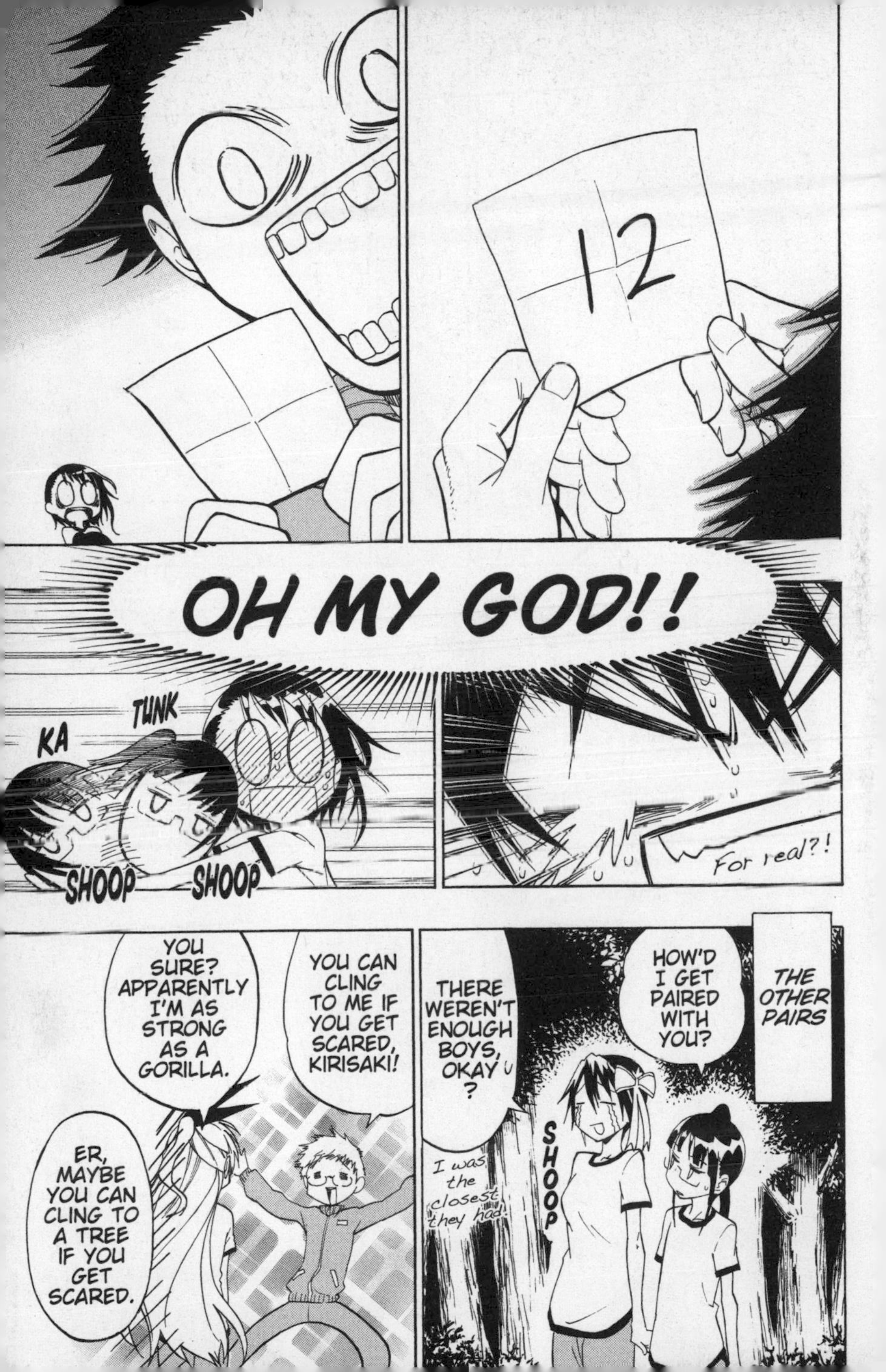
OH MY GOD!!
For real?!
KA
TUNK
SHOOP
SHOOP
THE OTHER PAIRS
HOW'D I GET PAIRED WITH YOU?
THERE WEREN'T ENOUGH BOYS, OKAY?
SHOOP
I was the closest they had!
YOU CAN CLING TO ME IF YOU GET SCARED, KIRISAKI!
YOU SURE? APPARENTLY I'M AS STRONG AS A GORILLA.
ER, MAYBE YOU CAN CLING TO A TREE IF YOU GET SCARED.

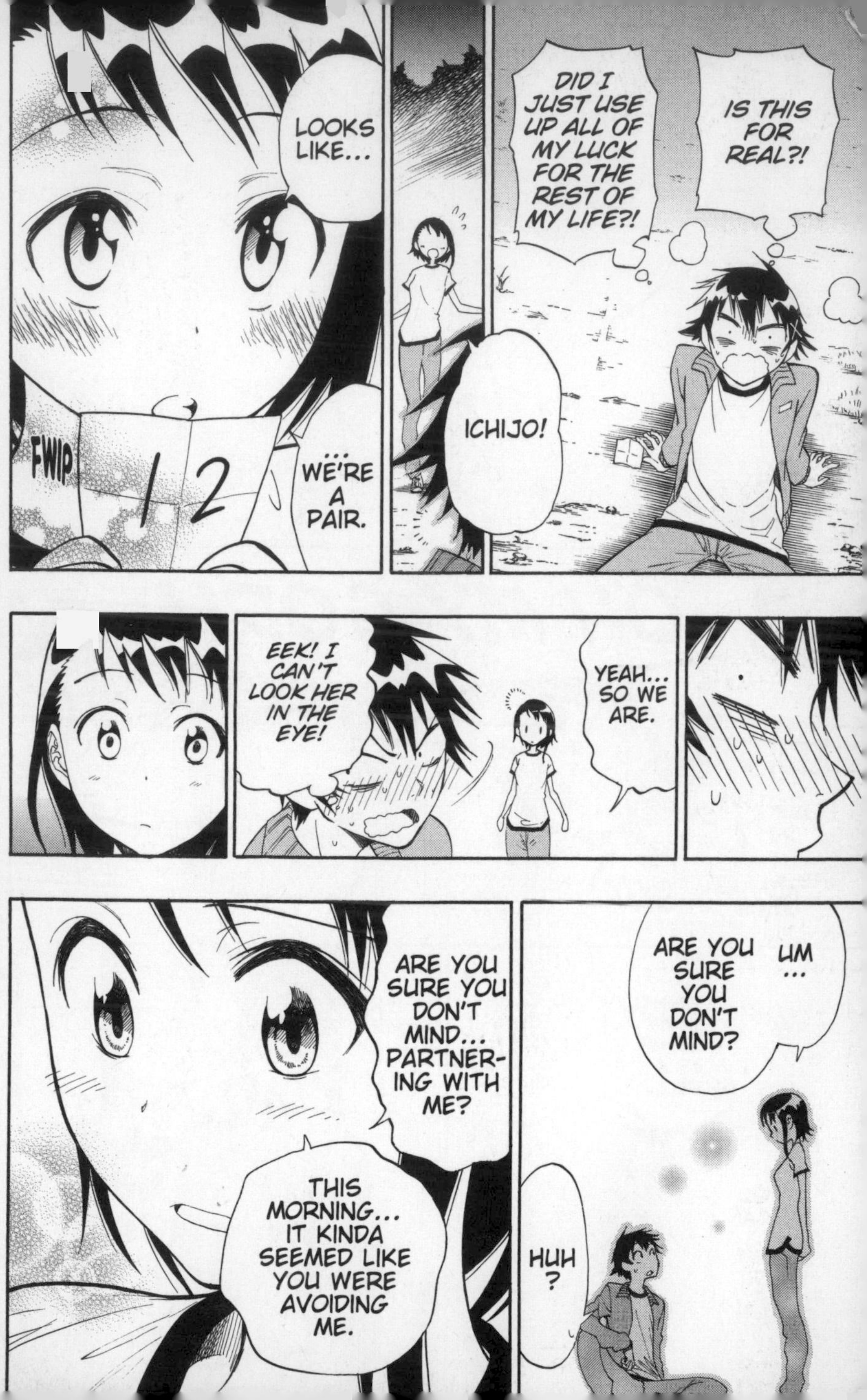
IS THIS FOR REAL?!
DID I JUST USE UP ALL OF MY LUCK FOR THE REST OF MY LIFE?!
ICHIJO!
LOOKS LIKE...
...WE'RE A PAIR.
FWIP
YEAH... SO WE ARE.
EEK! I CAN'T LOOK HER IN THE EYE!
UM...
ARE YOU SURE YOU DON'T MIND?
HUH?
ARE YOU SURE YOU DON'T MIND... PARTNERING WITH ME?
THIS MORNING... IT KINDA SEEMED LIKE YOU WERE AVOIDING ME.

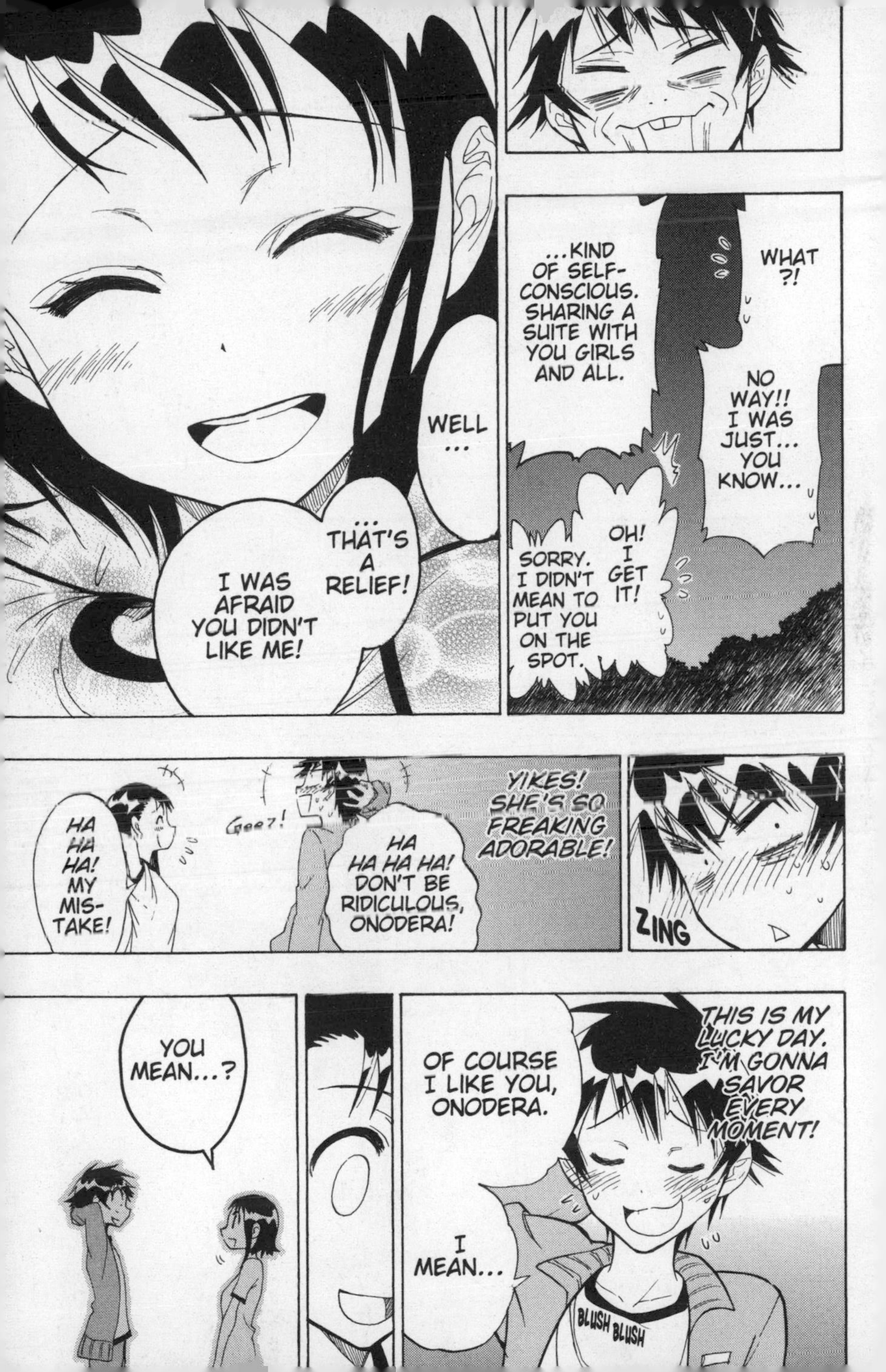
WHAT ?!
...KIND OF SELF-CONSCIOUS. SHARING A SUITE WITH YOU GIRLS AND ALL.
NO WAY!! I WAS JUST... YOU KNOW...
OH! I GET IT!
SORRY. I DIDN'T MEAN TO PUT YOU ON THE SPOT.
WELL ...
...THAT'S A RELIEF!
I WAS AFRAID YOU DIDN'T LIKE ME!
ZING
YIKES! SHE'S SO FREAKING ADORABLE!
HA HA HA HA! DON'T BE RIDICULOUS, ONODERA!
Geez!
HA HA HA! MY MIS-TAKE!
THIS IS MY LUCKY DAY. I'M GONNA SAVOR EVERY MOMENT!
OF COURSE I LIKE YOU, ONODERA.
I MEAN...
BLUSH BLUSH
YOU MEAN...?

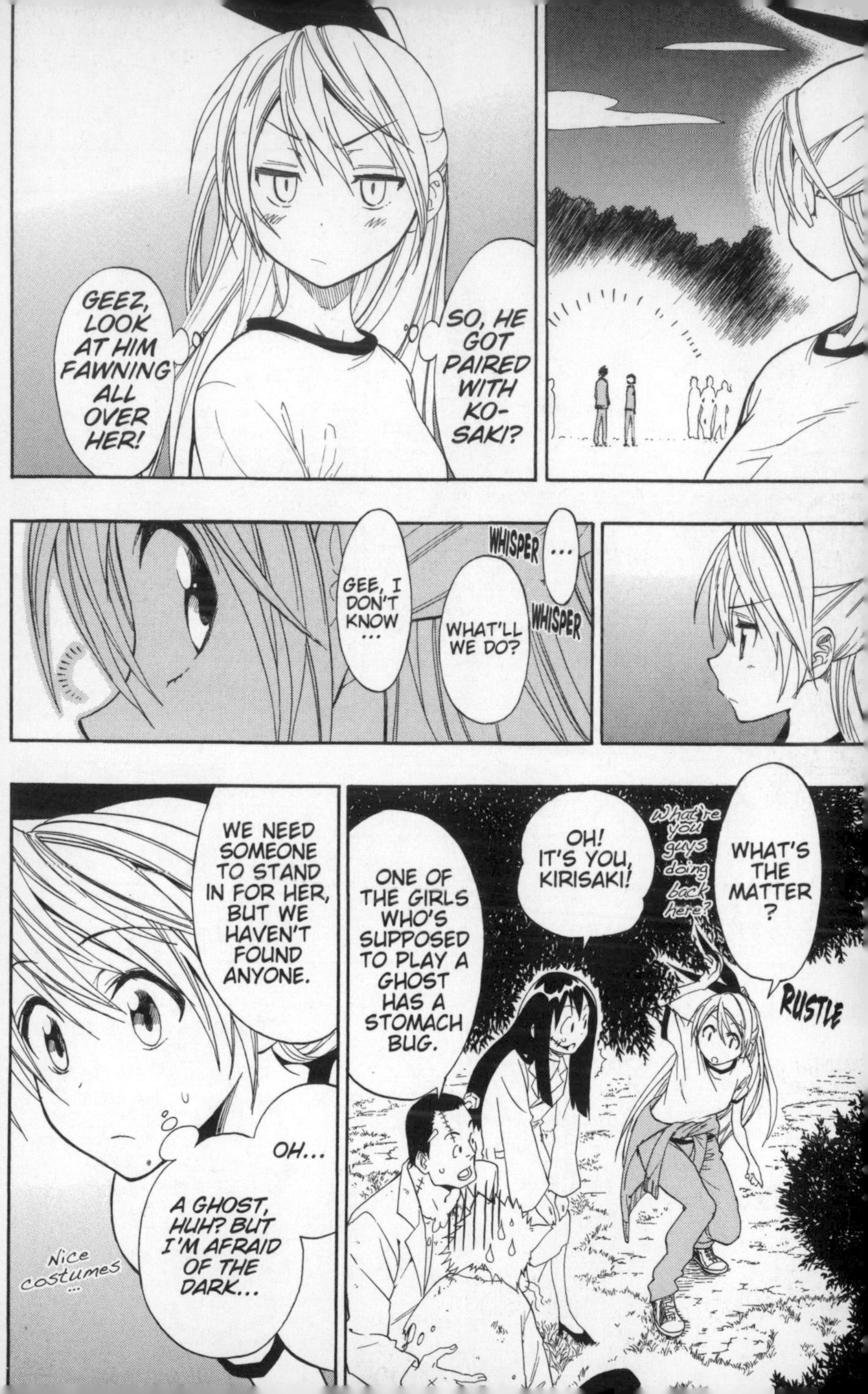
SO, HE GOT PAIRED WITH KO-SAKI?
GEEZ, LOOK AT HIM FAWNING ALL OVER HER!
WHISPER
...
WHAT'LL WE DO?
WHISPER
GEE, I DON'T KNOW ...
WHAT'S THE MATTER?
RUSTLE
What're you guys doing back here?
OH! IT'S YOU, KIRISAKI!
ONE OF THE GIRLS WHO'S SUPPOSED TO PLAY A GHOST HAS A STOMACH BUG.
WE NEED SOMEONE TO STAND IN FOR HER, BUT WE HAVEN'T FOUND ANYONE.
OH...
A GHOST, HUH? BUT I'M AFRAID OF THE DARK...
Nice costumes ...

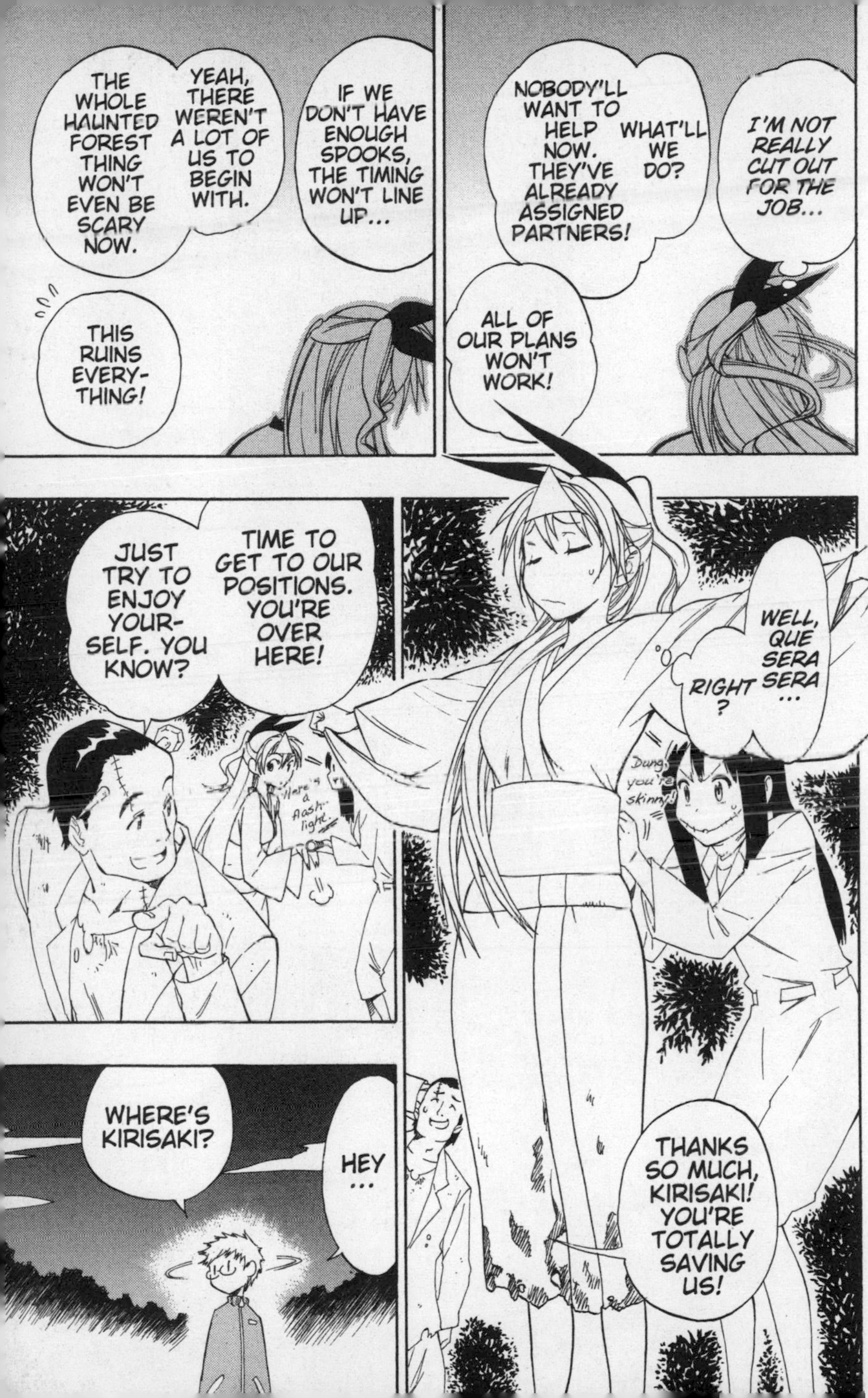
I'M NOT REALLY CUT OUT FOR THE JOB...
WHAT'LL WE DO?
NOBODY'LL WANT TO HELP NOW. THEY'VE ALREADY ASSIGNED PARTNERS!
ALL OF OUR PLANS WON'T WORK!
IF WE DON'T HAVE ENOUGH SPOOKS, THE TIMING WON'T LINE UP...
YEAH, THERE WEREN'T A LOT OF US TO BEGIN WITH.
THE WHOLE HAUNTED FOREST THING WON'T EVEN BE SCARY NOW.
THIS RUINS EVERY-THING!
WELL, QUE SERA SERA...
RIGHT?
Dung, you're skinny!
THANKS SO MUCH, KIRISAKI! YOU'RE TOTALLY SAVING US!
TIME TO GET TO OUR POSITIONS. YOU'RE OVER HERE!
JUST TRY TO ENJOY YOUR-SELF. YOU KNOW?
Here's a flash-light.
HEY...
WHERE'S KIRISAKI?

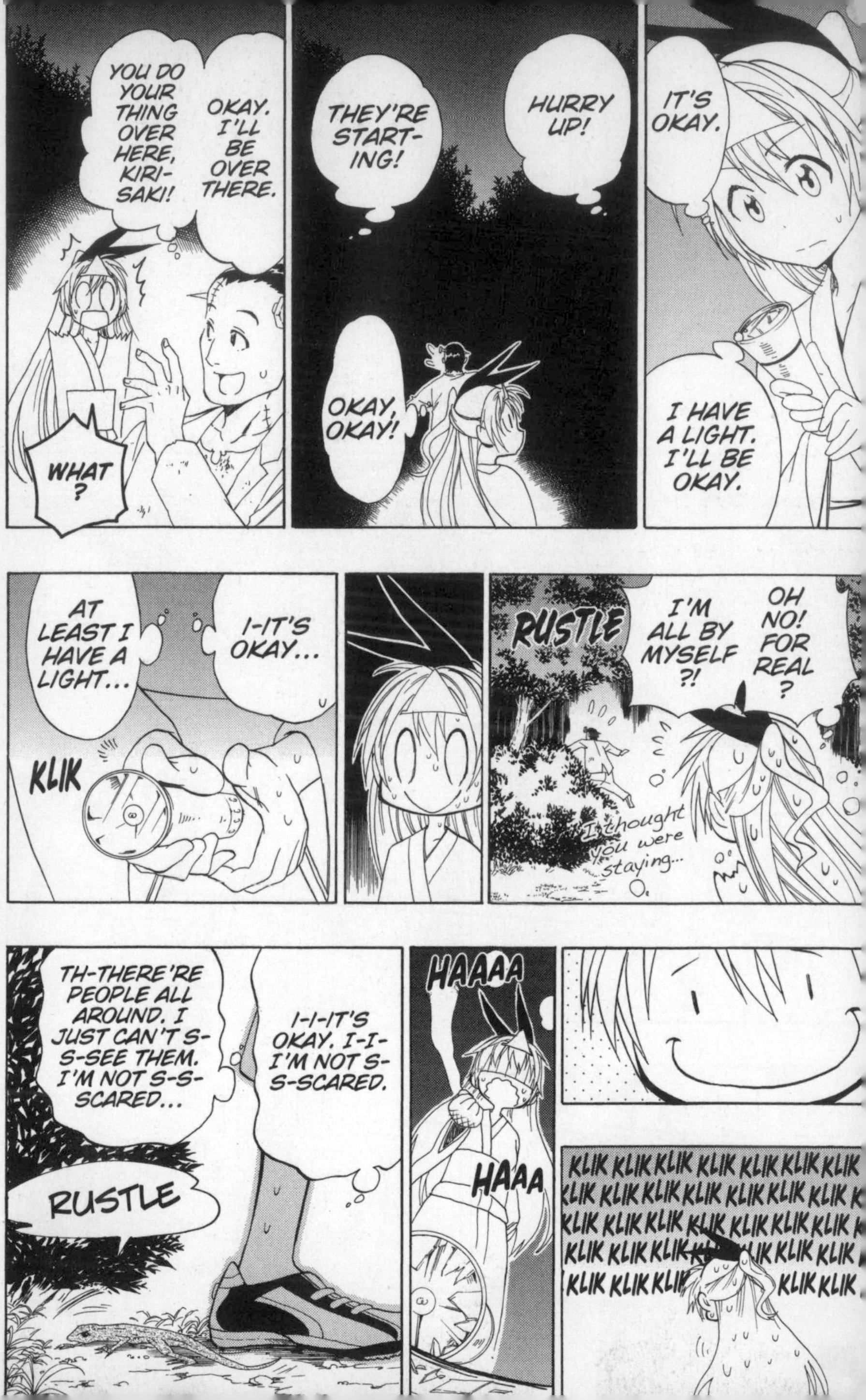
IT'S OKAY.
I HAVE A LIGHT. I'LL BE OKAY.
HURRY UP!
THEY'RE STARTING!
OKAY, OKAY!
OKAY. I'LL BE OVER THERE.
YOU DO YOUR THING OVER HERE, KIRISAKI!
WHAT?
OH NO! FOR REAL?
I'M ALL BY MYSELF?!
RUSTLE
I thought you were staying...
I-IT'S OKAY...
AT LEAST I HAVE A LIGHT...
KLIK
KLIK KLIK KLIK KLIK KLIK KLIK KLIK
KLIK KLIK KLIK KLIK KLIK KLIK KLIK
KLIK KLIK KLIK KLIK KLIK KLIK KLIK
KLIK KLIK KLIK KLIK KLIK
KLIK KLIK KLIK KLIK
HAAAA
HAAA
I-I-IT'S OKAY. I-I-I'M NOT S-S-SCARED.
TH-THERE'RE PEOPLE ALL AROUND. I JUST CAN'T S-SEE THEM. I'M NOT S-S-SCARED...
RUSTLE

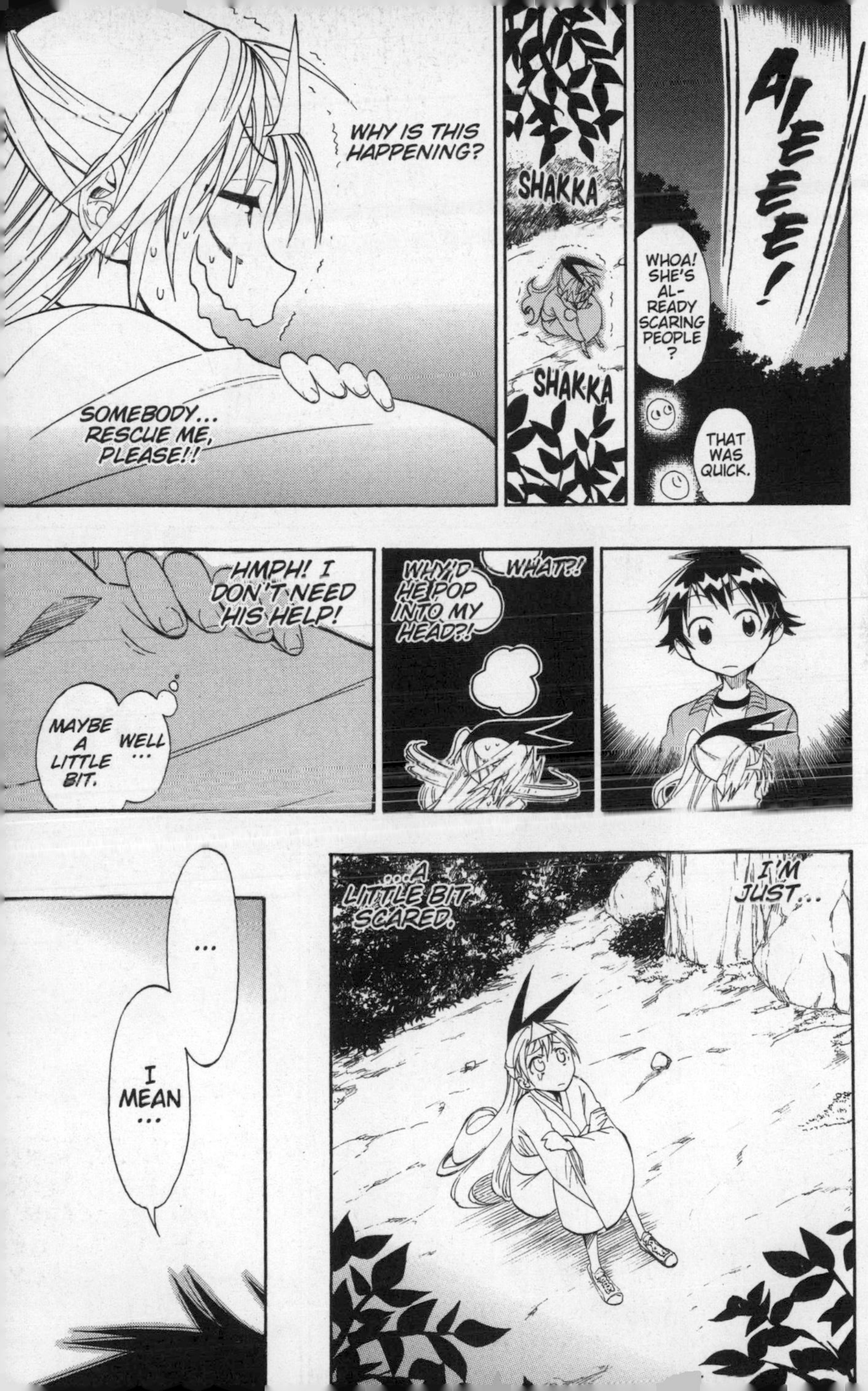
AIEEEE!
WHOA! SHE'S AL-READY SCARING PEOPLE?
THAT WAS QUICK.
SHAKKA
SHAKKA
WHY IS THIS HAPPENING?
SOMEBODY... RESCUE ME, PLEASE!!
WHAT?!
WHY'D HE POP INTO MY HEAD?!
HMPH! I DON'T NEED HIS HELP!
WELL...
MAYBE A LITTLE BIT.
I'M JUST...
...A LITTLE BIT SCARED.
...
I MEAN...

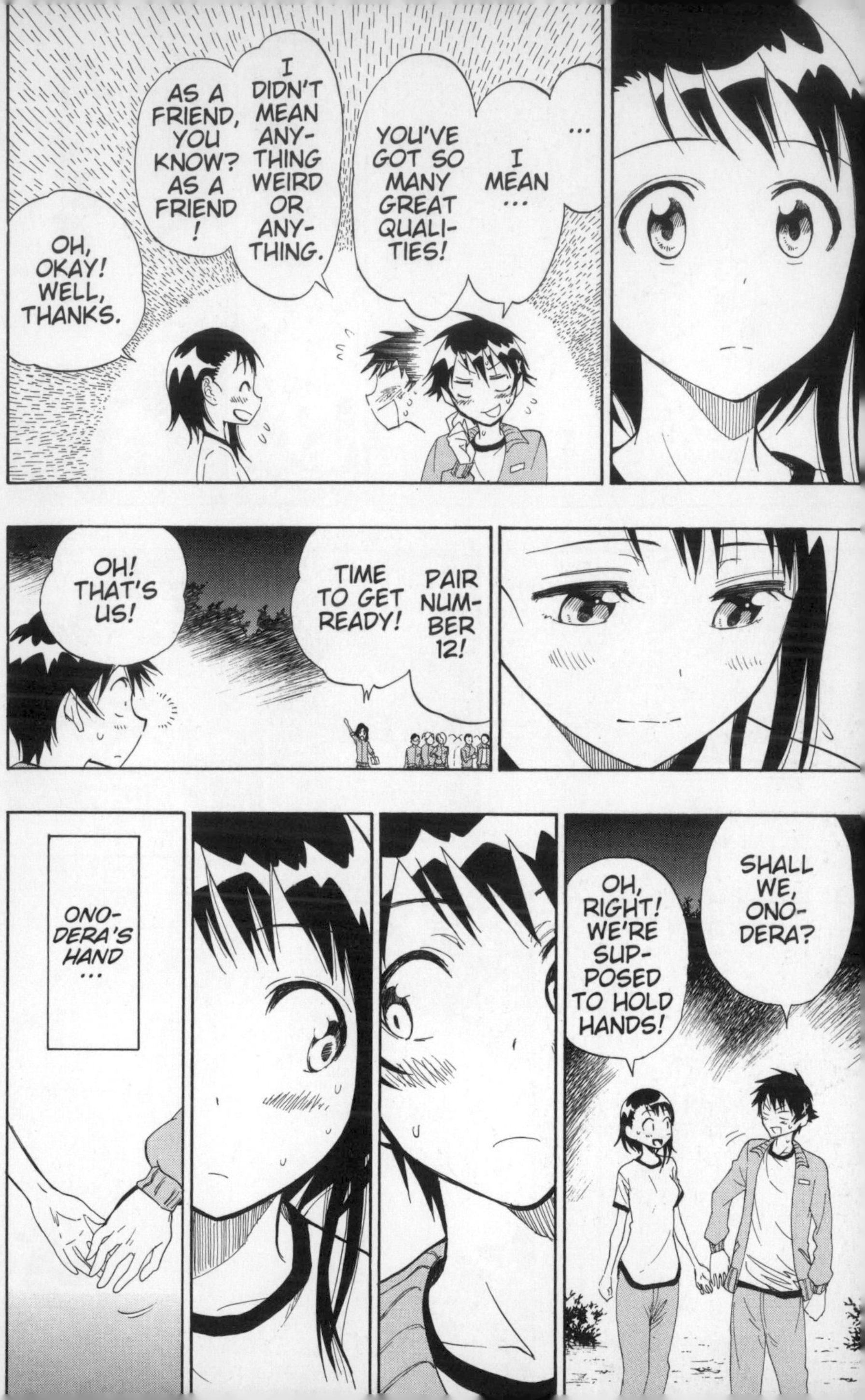
... I MEAN ...
YOU'VE GOT SO MANY GREAT QUALITIES!
I DIDN'T MEAN ANYTHING WEIRD OR ANYTHING.
AS A FRIEND, YOU KNOW? AS A FRIEND!
OH, OKAY! WELL, THANKS.
PAIR NUMBER 12!
TIME TO GET READY!
OH! THAT'S US!
SHALL WE, ONODERA?
OH, RIGHT! WE'RE SUPPOSED TO HOLD HANDS!
ONODERA'S HAND ...

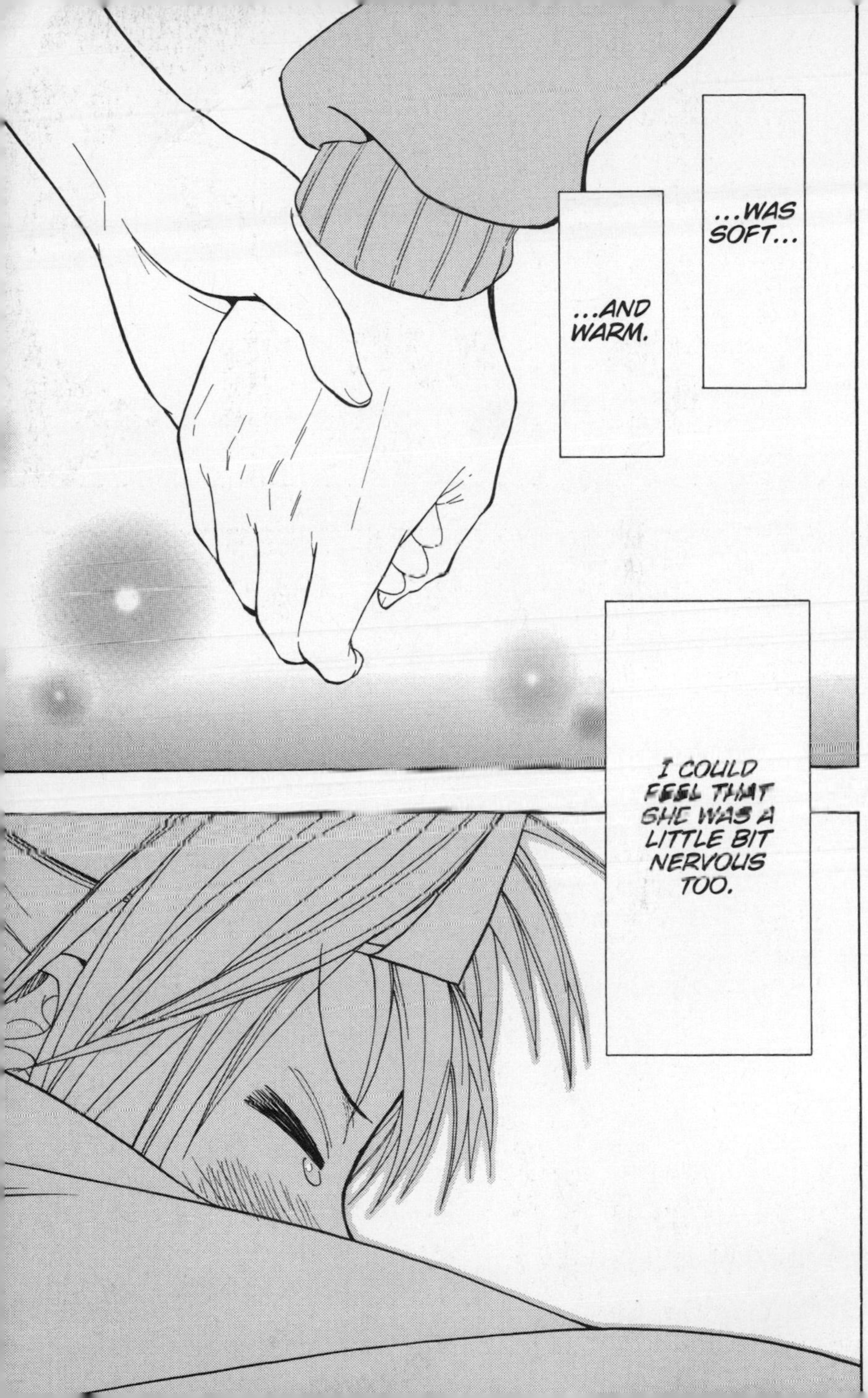
...WAS SOFT...
...AND WARM.
I COULD FEEL THAT SHE WAS A LITTLE BIT NERVOUS TOO.

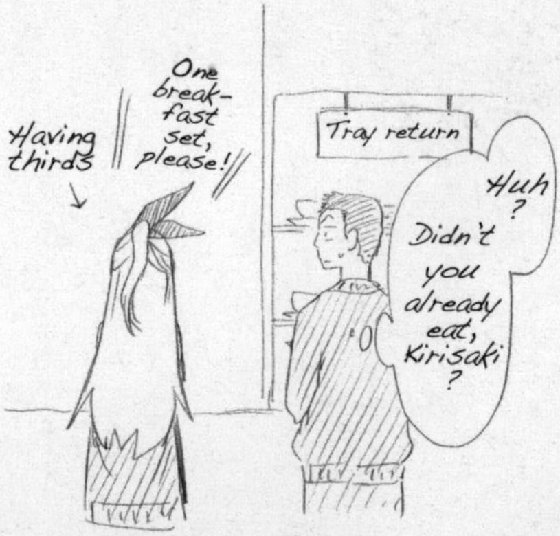
One breakfast set, please!
Having thirds
Tray return
Huh? Didn't you already eat, Kirisaki?

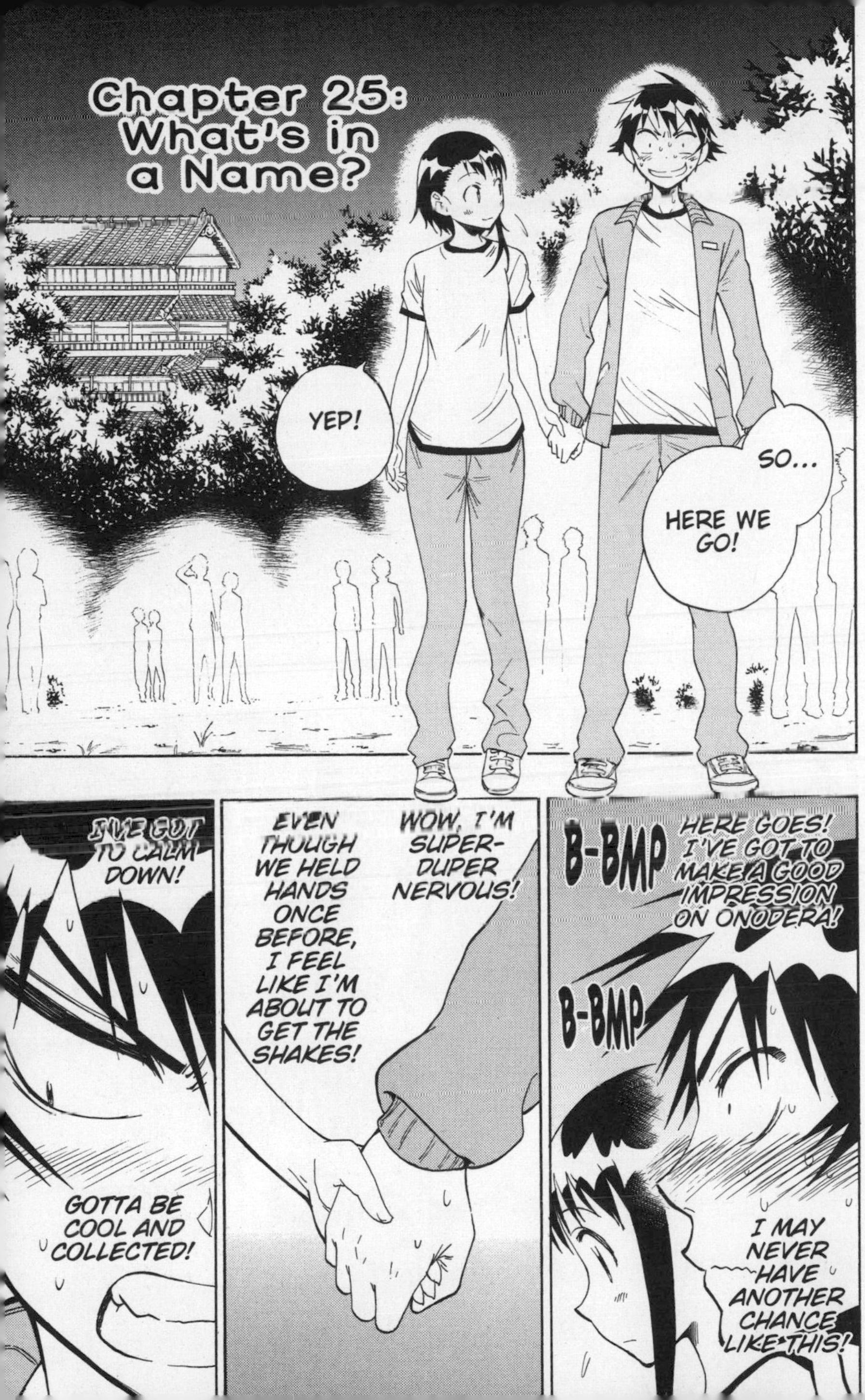
Chapter 25: What's in a Name?
SO... HERE WE GO!
YEP!
B-BMP
HERE GOES! I'VE GOT TO MAKE A GOOD IMPRESSION ON ONODERA!
B-BMP
I MAY NEVER HAVE ANOTHER CHANCE LIKE THIS!
WOW, I'M SUPER-DUPER NERVOUS!
EVEN THOUGH WE HELD HANDS ONCE BEFORE, I FEEL LIKE I'M ABOUT TO GET THE SHAKES!
I'VE GOT TO CALM DOWN!
GOTTA BE COOL AND COLLECTED!

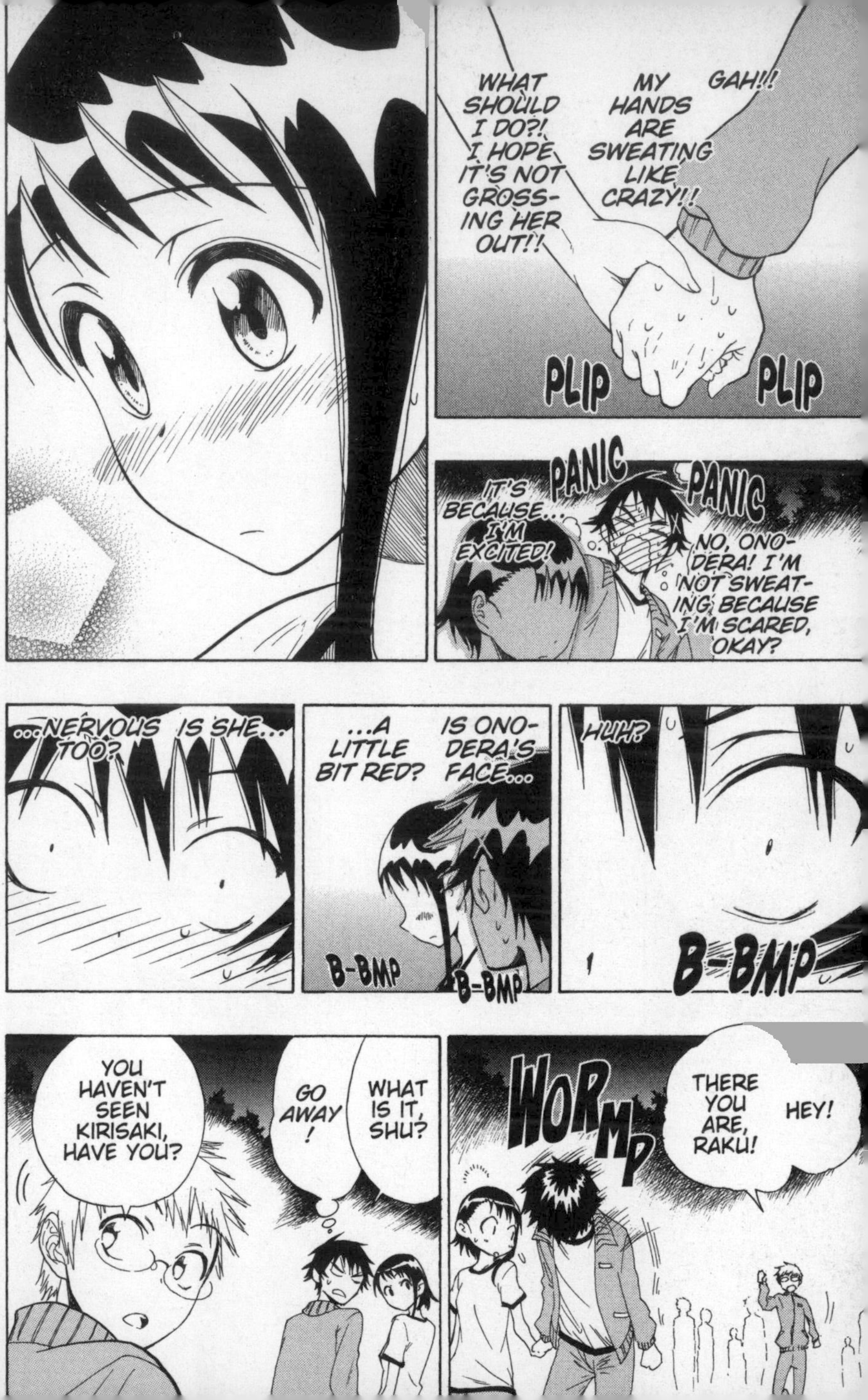
GAH!!
MY HANDS ARE SWEATING LIKE CRAZY!!
WHAT SHOULD I DO?! I HOPE IT'S NOT GROSSING HER OUT!!
PLIP
PLIP
PANIC
PANIC
NO, ONODERA! I'M NOT SWEATING BECAUSE I'M SCARED, OKAY?
IT'S BECAUSE... I'M EXCITED!
HUH?
B-BMP
IS ONODERA'S FACE...
...A LITTLE BIT RED?
B-BMP
B-BMP
IS SHE...
...NERVOUS TOO?
HEY!
THERE YOU ARE, RAKU!
WORMP
WHAT IS IT, SHU?
GO AWAY!
YOU HAVEN'T SEEN KIRISAKI, HAVE YOU?

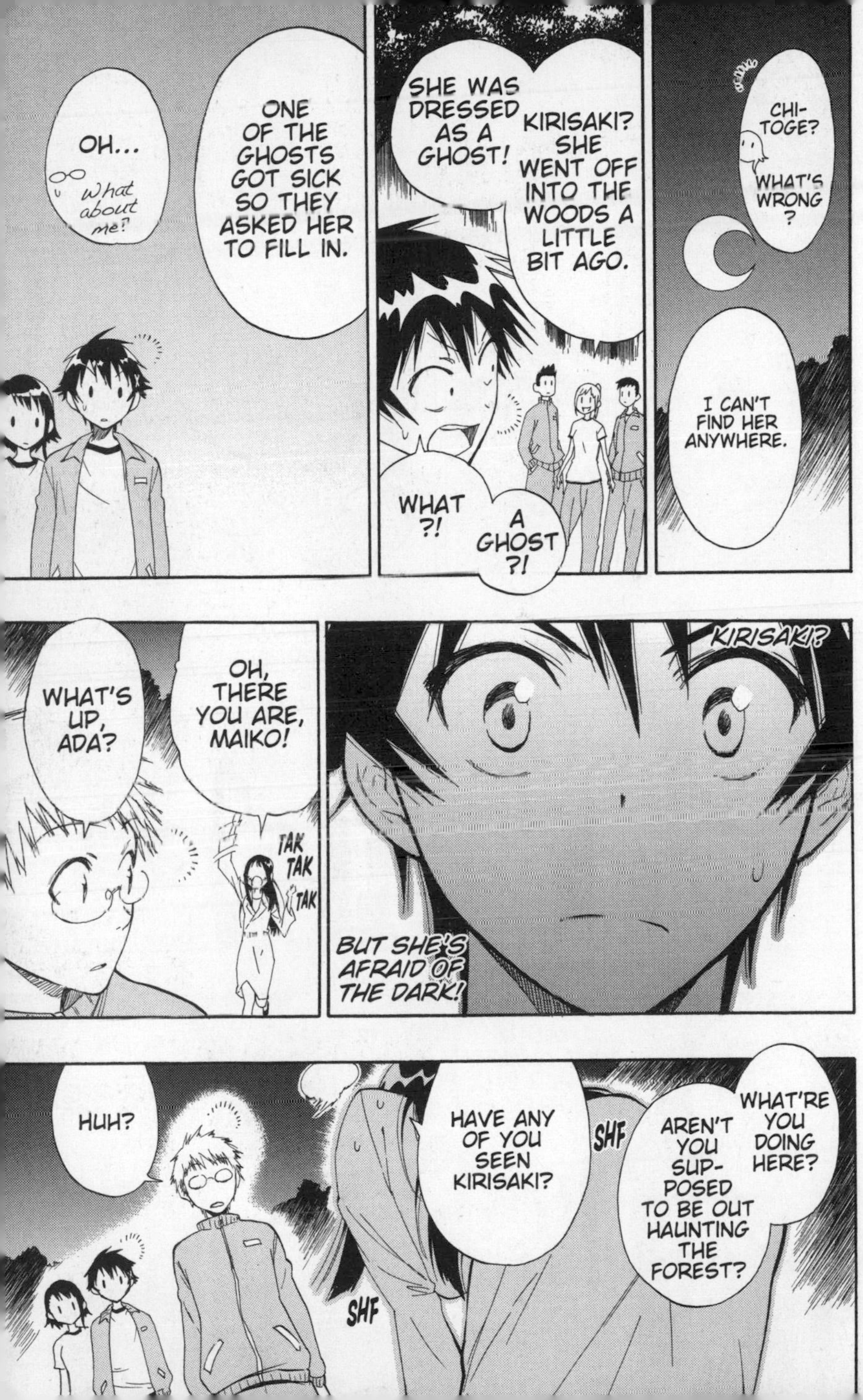
CHI-TOGE?
WHAT'S WRONG?
I CAN'T FIND HER ANYWHERE.
KIRISAKI? SHE WENT OFF INTO THE WOODS A LITTLE BIT AGO.
SHE WAS DRESSED AS A GHOST!
WHAT?!
A GHOST?!
ONE OF THE GHOSTS GOT SICK SO THEY ASKED HER TO FILL IN.
OH...
What about me?
KIRISAKI?
BUT SHE'S AFRAID OF THE DARK!
OH, THERE YOU ARE, MAIKO!
TAK TAK TAK
WHAT'S UP, ADA?
WHAT'RE YOU DOING HERE?
AREN'T YOU SUPPOSED TO BE OUT HAUNTING THE FOREST?
SHF
HAVE ANY OF YOU SEEN KIRISAKI?
SHF
HUH?

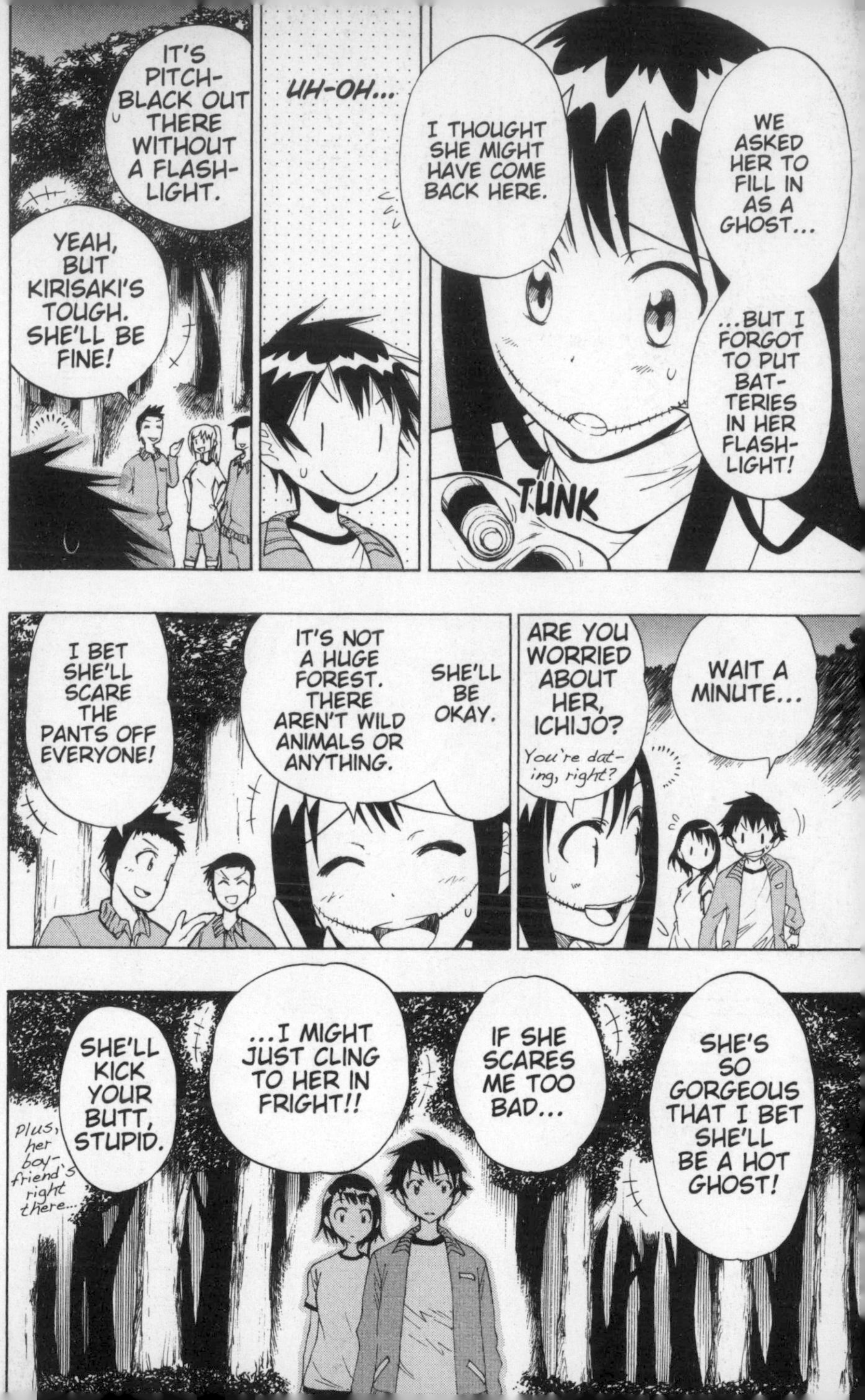
WE ASKED HER TO FILL IN AS A GHOST...
I THOUGHT SHE MIGHT HAVE COME BACK HERE.
...BUT I FORGOT TO PUT BATTERIES IN HER FLASHLIGHT!
TUNK
UH-OH...
IT'S PITCH-BLACK OUT THERE WITHOUT A FLASHLIGHT.
YEAH, BUT KIRISAKI'S TOUGH. SHE'LL BE FINE!
WAIT A MINUTE...
ARE YOU WORRIED ABOUT HER, ICHIJO?
You're dating, right?
SHE'LL BE OKAY.
IT'S NOT A HUGE FOREST. THERE AREN'T WILD ANIMALS OR ANYTHING.
I BET SHE'LL SCARE THE PANTS OFF EVERYONE!
SHE'S SO GORGEOUS THAT I BET SHE'LL BE A HOT GHOST!
IF SHE SCARES ME TOO BAD...
...I MIGHT JUST CLING TO HER IN FRIGHT!!
SHE'LL KICK YOUR BUTT, STUPID.
Plus, her boyfriend's right there...

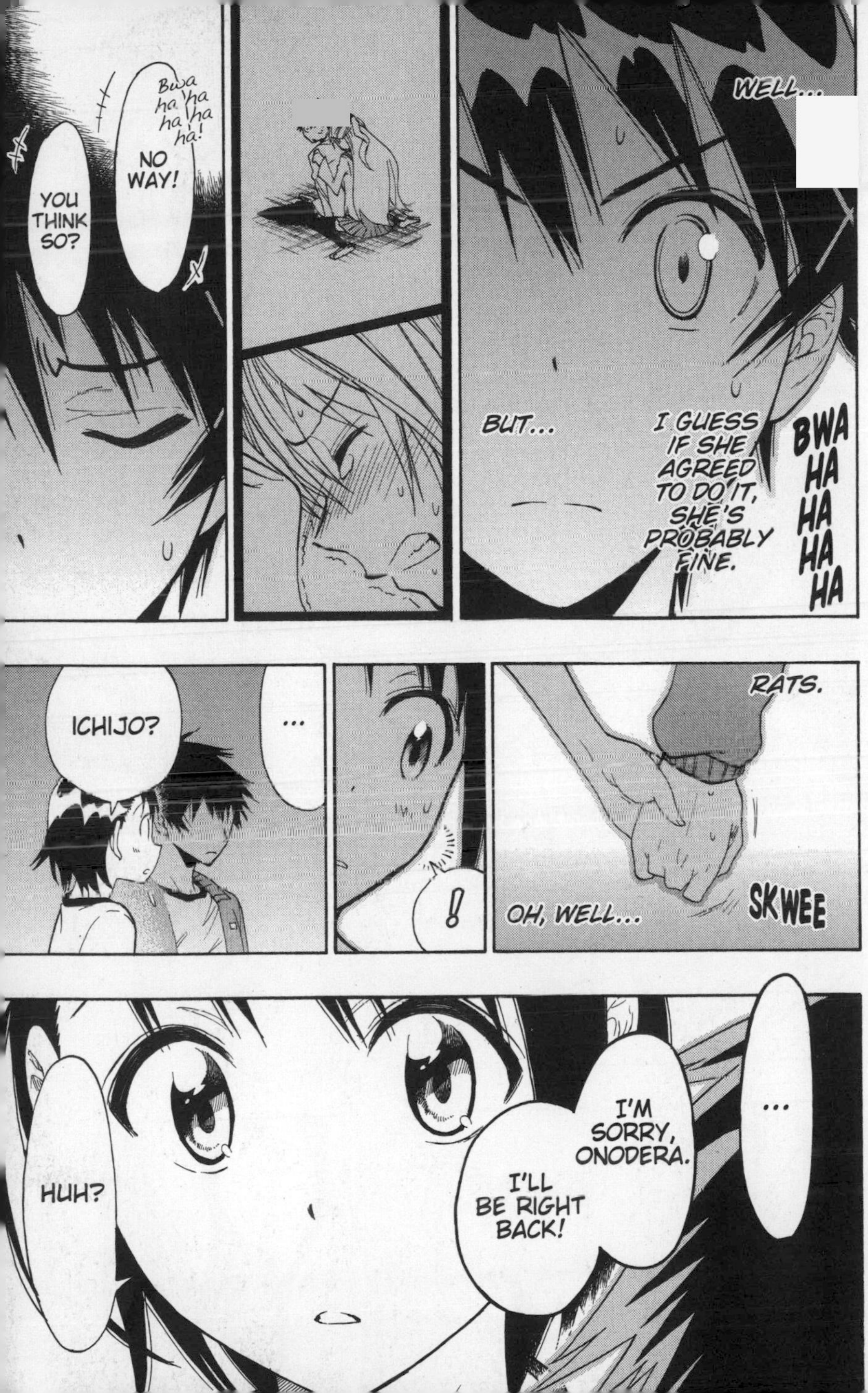
WELL...
I GUESS IF SHE AGREED TO DO IT, SHE'S PROBABLY FINE.
BWA HA HA HA HA HA
BUT...
Bwa ha ha ha ha ha!
NO WAY!
YOU THINK SO?
RATS.
SKWEE
OH, WELL...
!
...
ICHIJO?
...
I'M SORRY, ONODERA.
I'LL BE RIGHT BACK!
HUH?

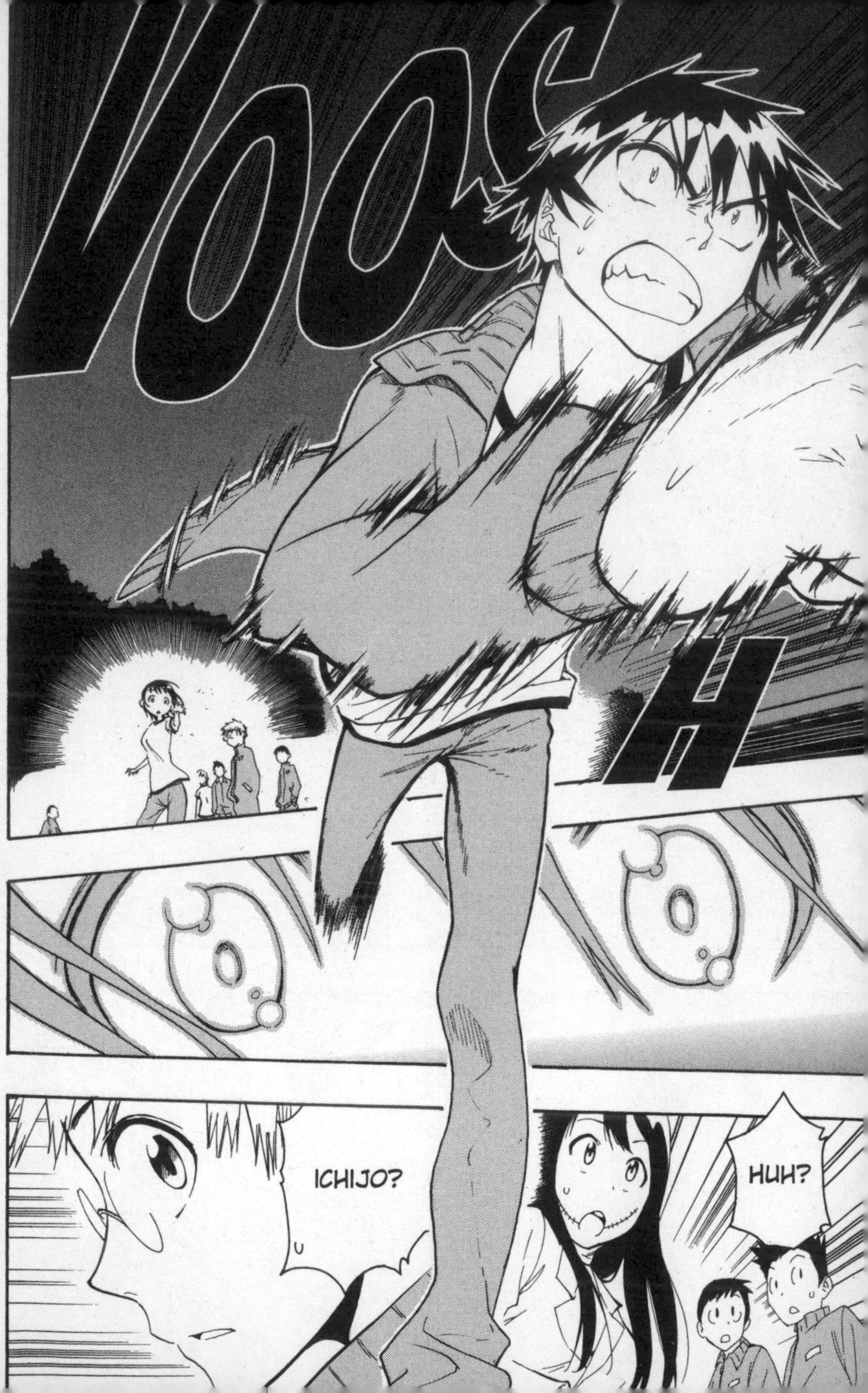
HUH?
ICHIJO?

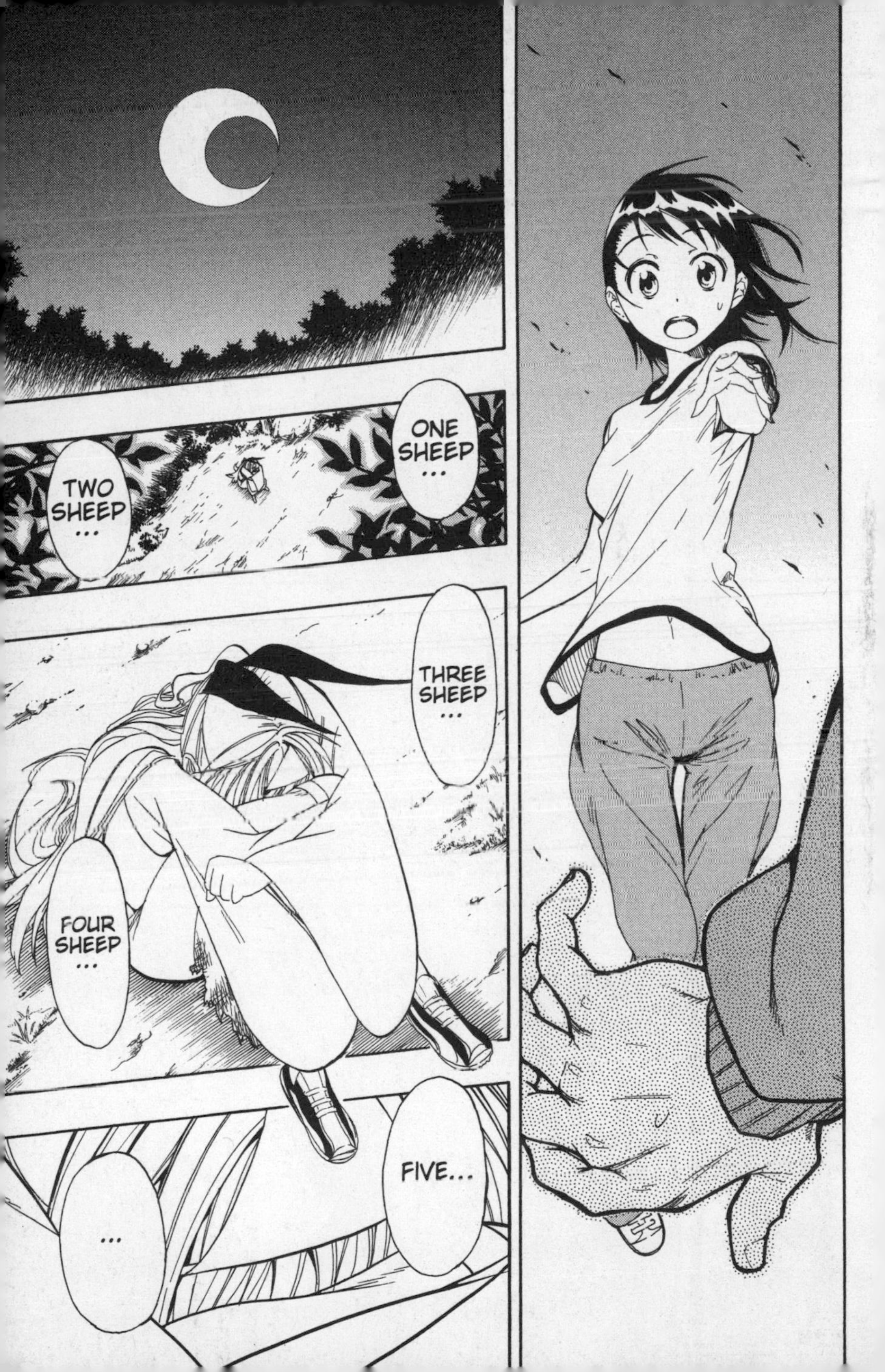
ONE SHEEP ...
TWO SHEEP ...
THREE SHEEP ...
FOUR SHEEP ...
FIVE...
...

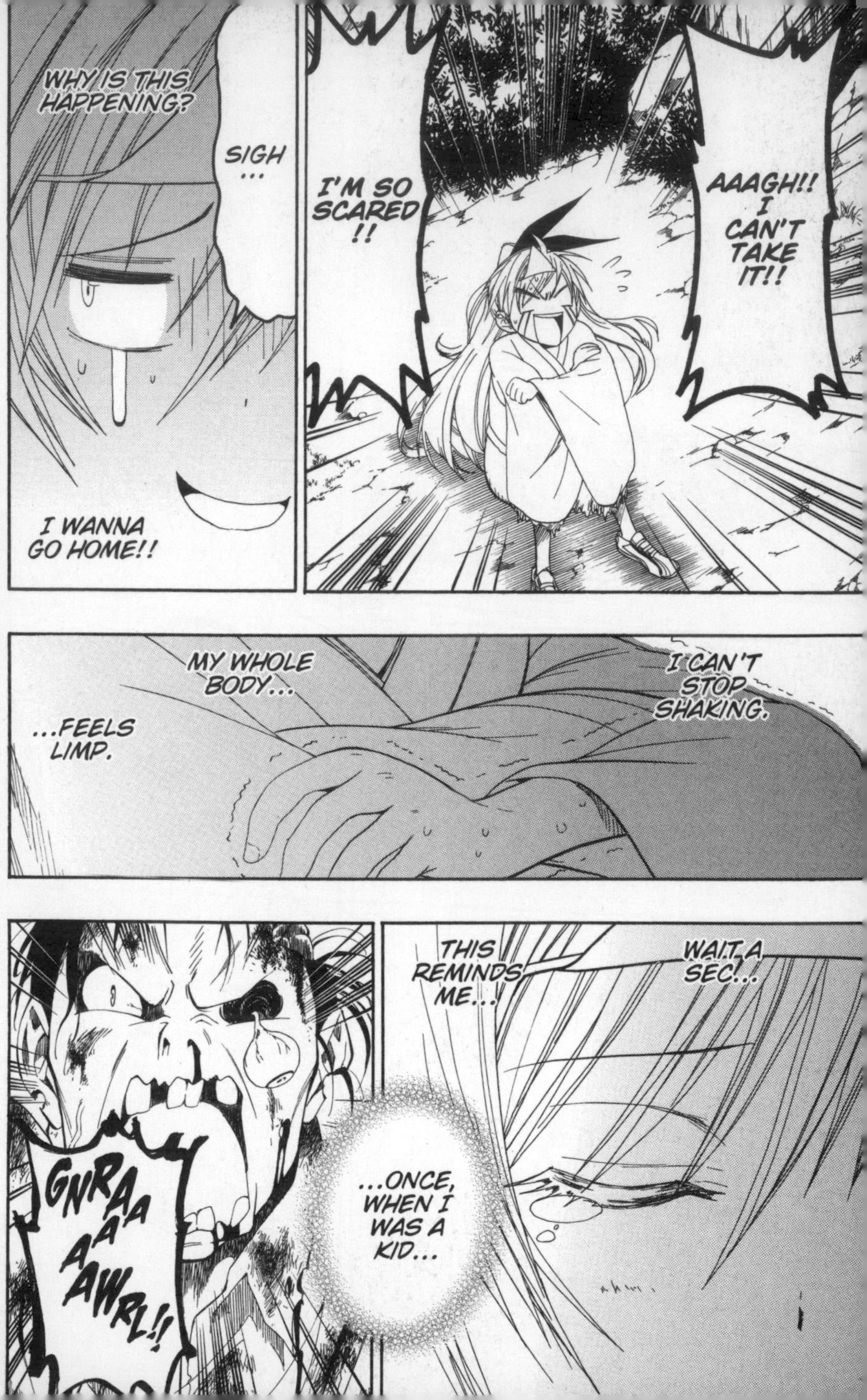
AAAGH!! I CAN'T TAKE IT!!
I'M SO SCARED!!
WHY IS THIS HAPPENING?
SIGH...
I WANNA GO HOME!!
I CAN'T STOP SHAKING.
MY WHOLE BODY...
...FEELS LIMP.
WAIT A SEC...
THIS REMINDS ME...
...ONCE, WHEN I WAS A KID...
GNRAAAAAWRL!!

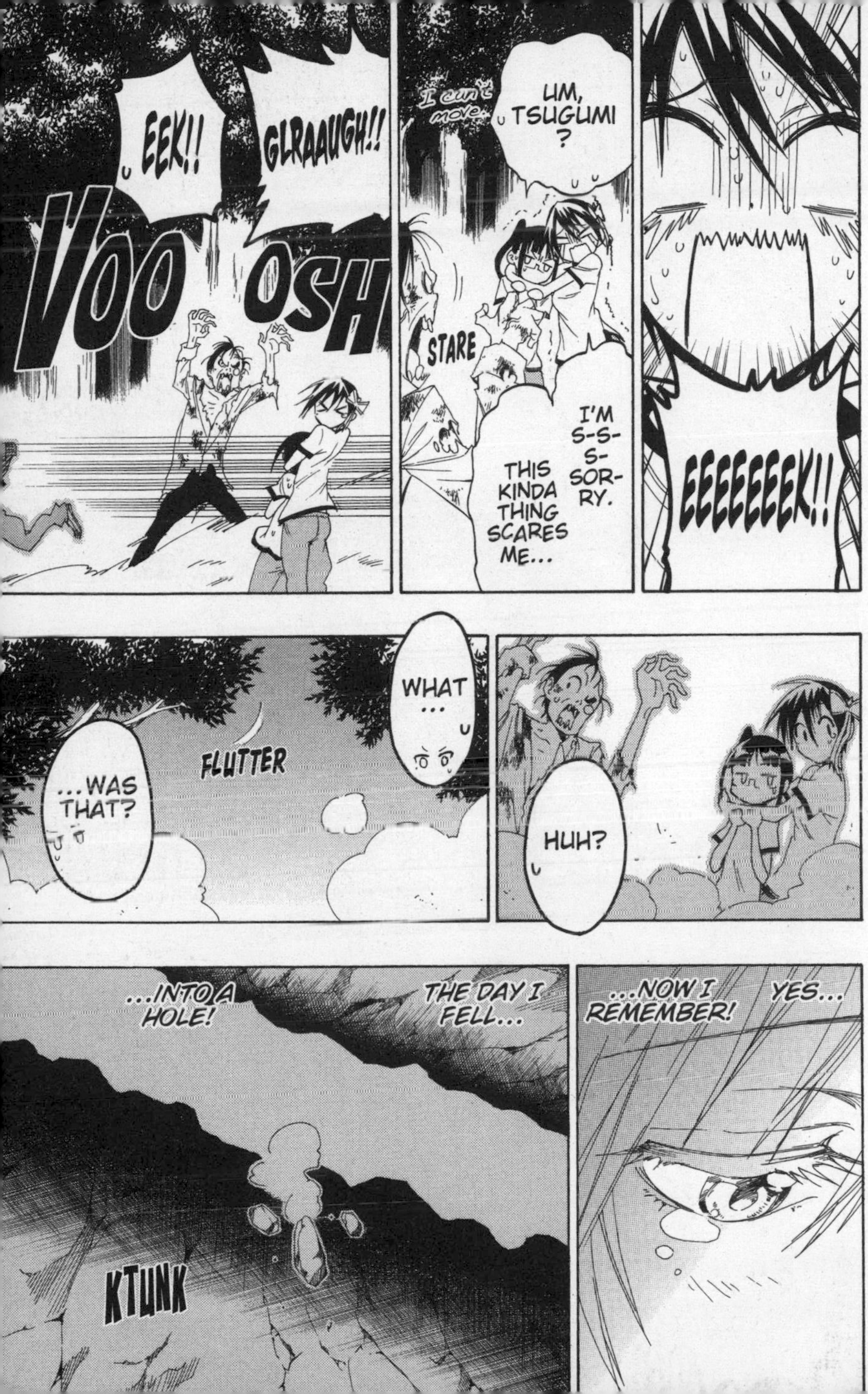
EEEEEEEK!!
UM, TSUGUMI?
I can't move.
STARE
I'M S-S-S-SORRY.
THIS KINDA THING SCARES ME...
GLRAAUGH!!
EEK!!
VOOSH
HUH?
WHAT...
FLUTTER
...WAS THAT?
YES...
...NOW I REMEMBER!
THE DAY I FELL...
...INTO A HOLE!
KTUNK

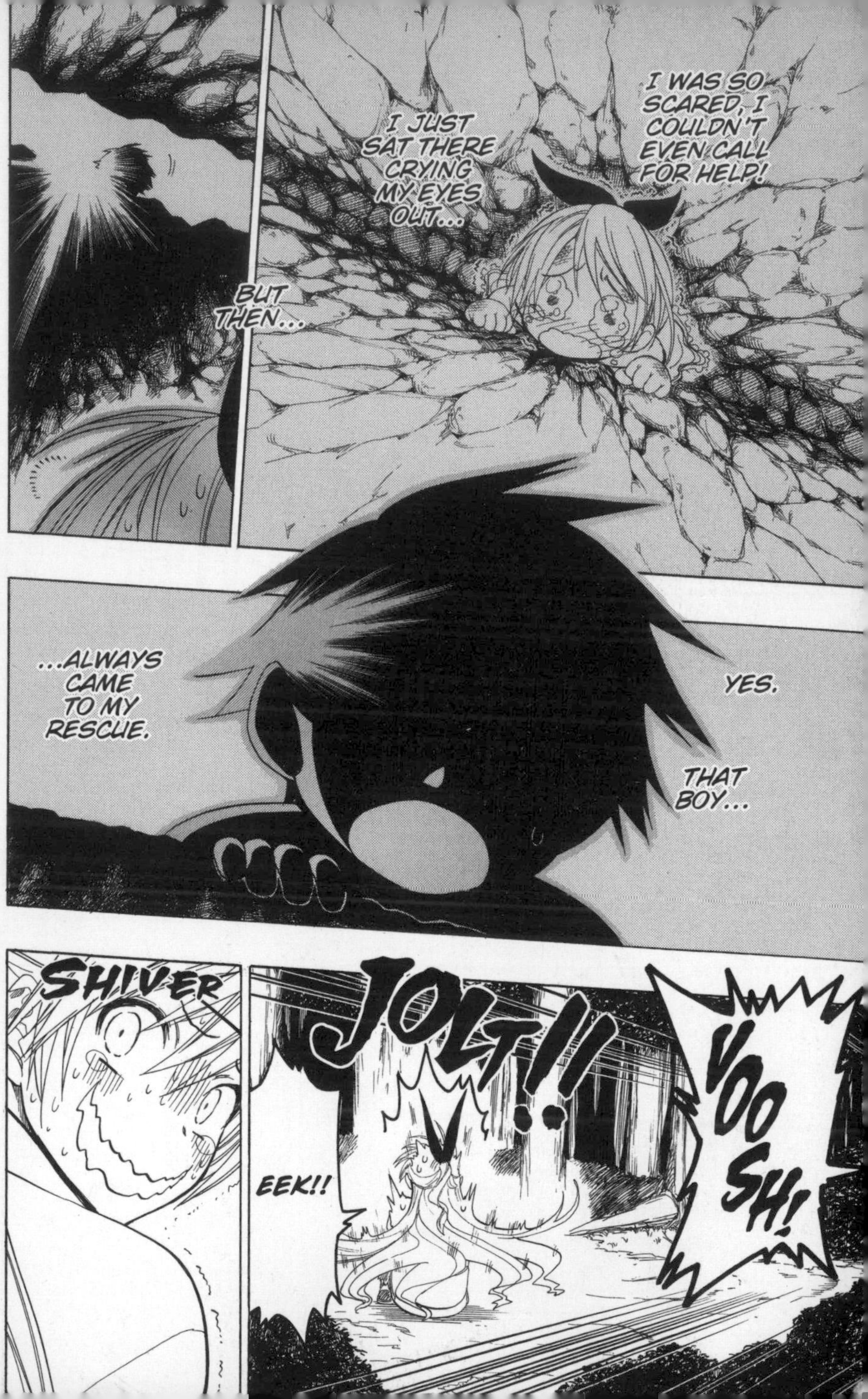
I WAS SO SCARED, I COULDN'T EVEN CALL FOR HELP!
I JUST SAT THERE CRYING MY EYES OUT...
BUT THEN...
YES.
THAT BOY...
...ALWAYS CAME TO MY RESCUE.
VOOSH!
JOLT!!
EEK!!
SHIVER

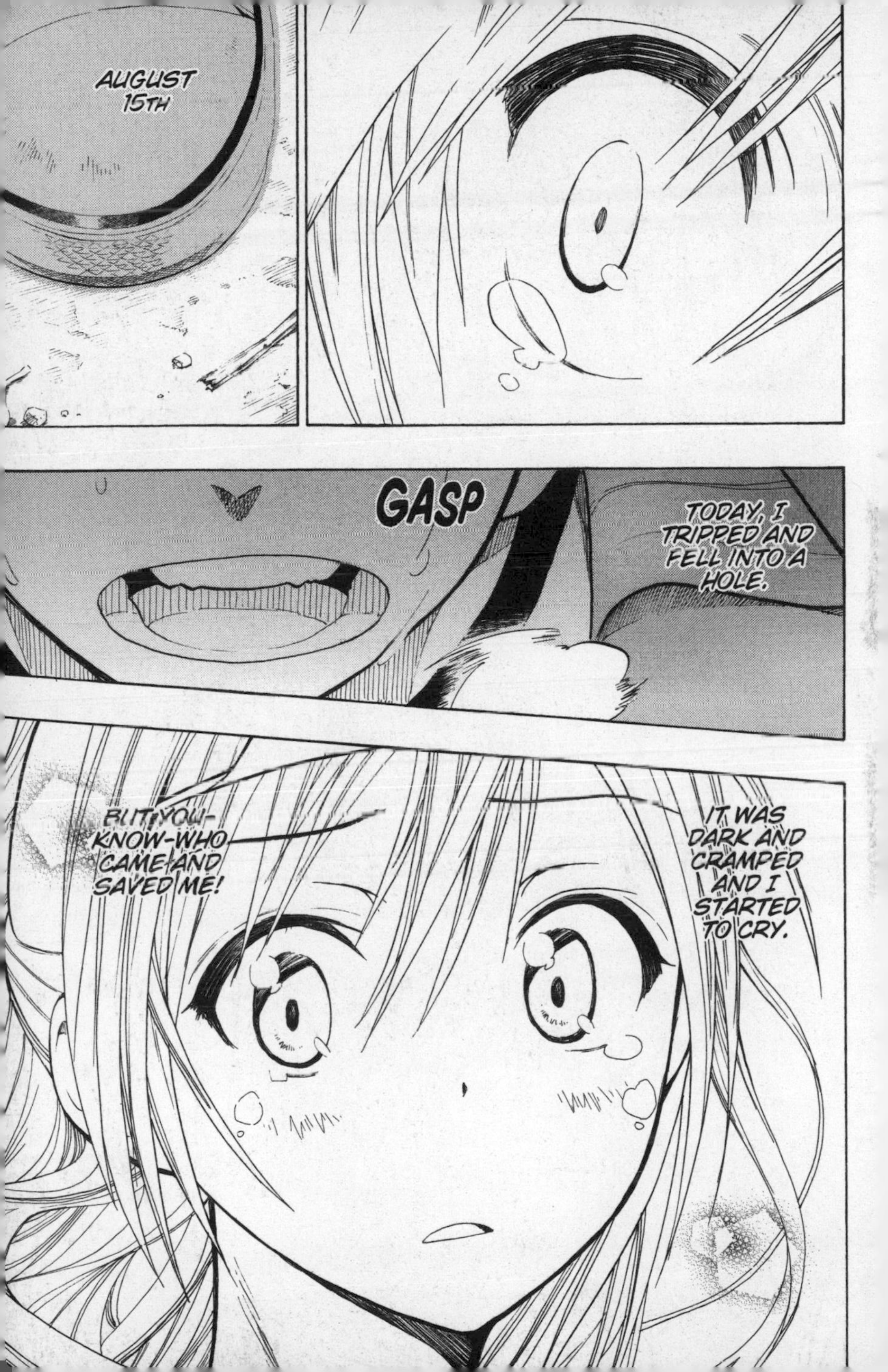
AUGUST 15TH
TODAY, I TRIPPED AND FELL INTO A HOLE.
GASP
IT WAS DARK AND CRAMPED AND I STARTED TO CRY.
BUT YOU-KNOW-WHO CAME AND SAVED ME!

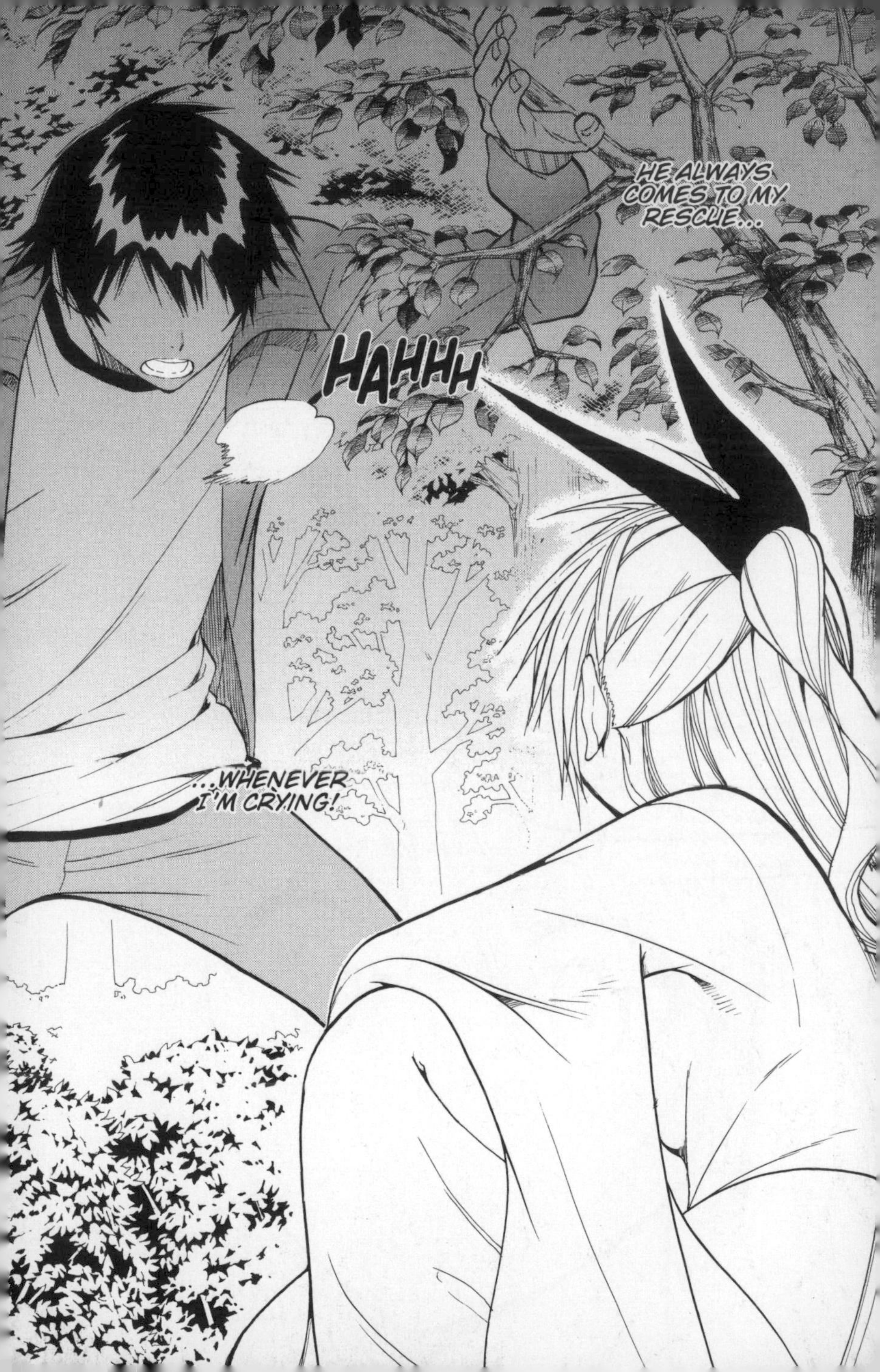
HE ALWAYS COMES TO MY RESCUE...
HAHHH
...WHENEVER I'M CRYING!

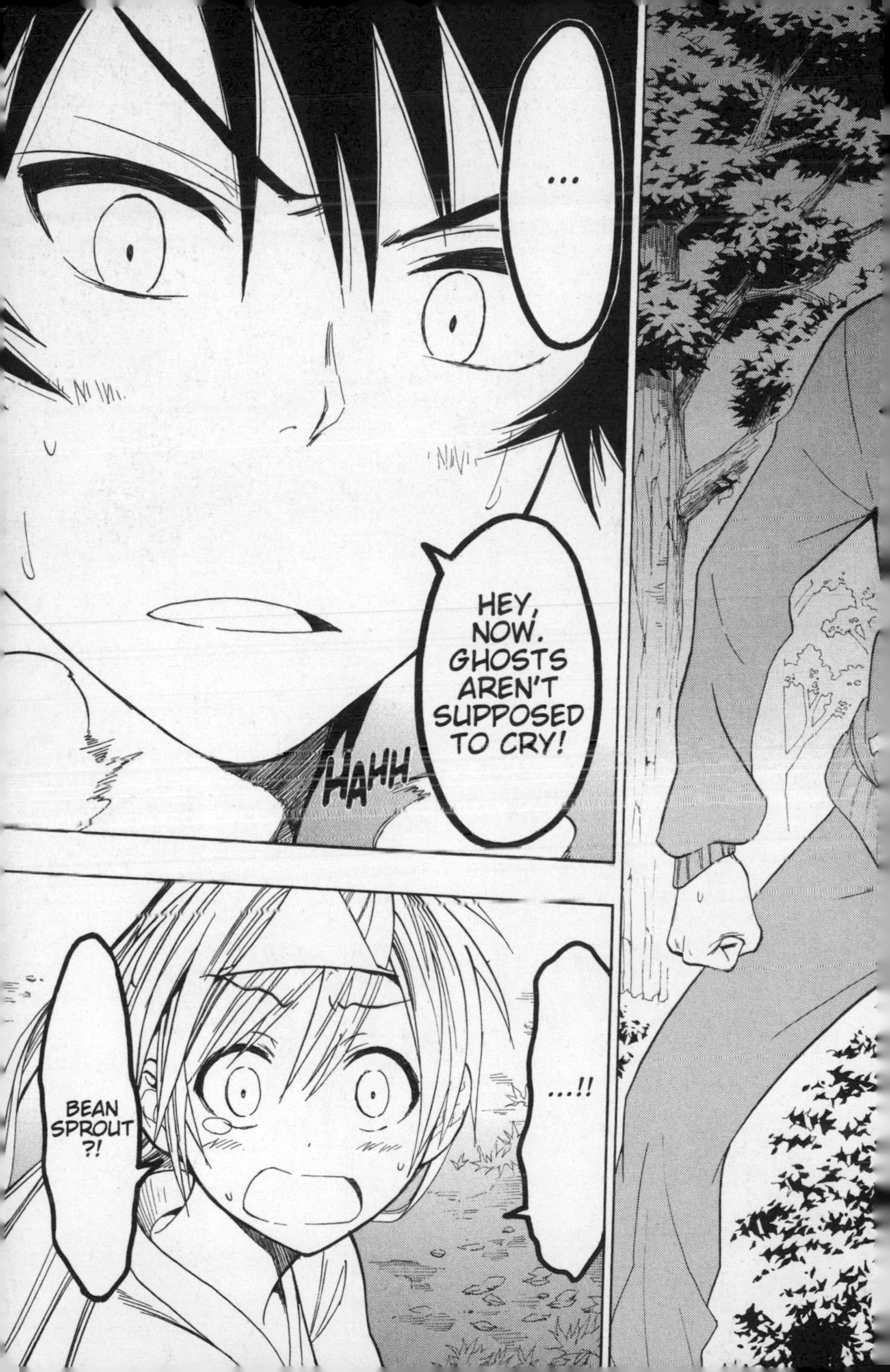
...
HEY, NOW. GHOSTS AREN'T SUPPOSED TO CRY!
HAHH
...!!
BEAN SPROUT ?!

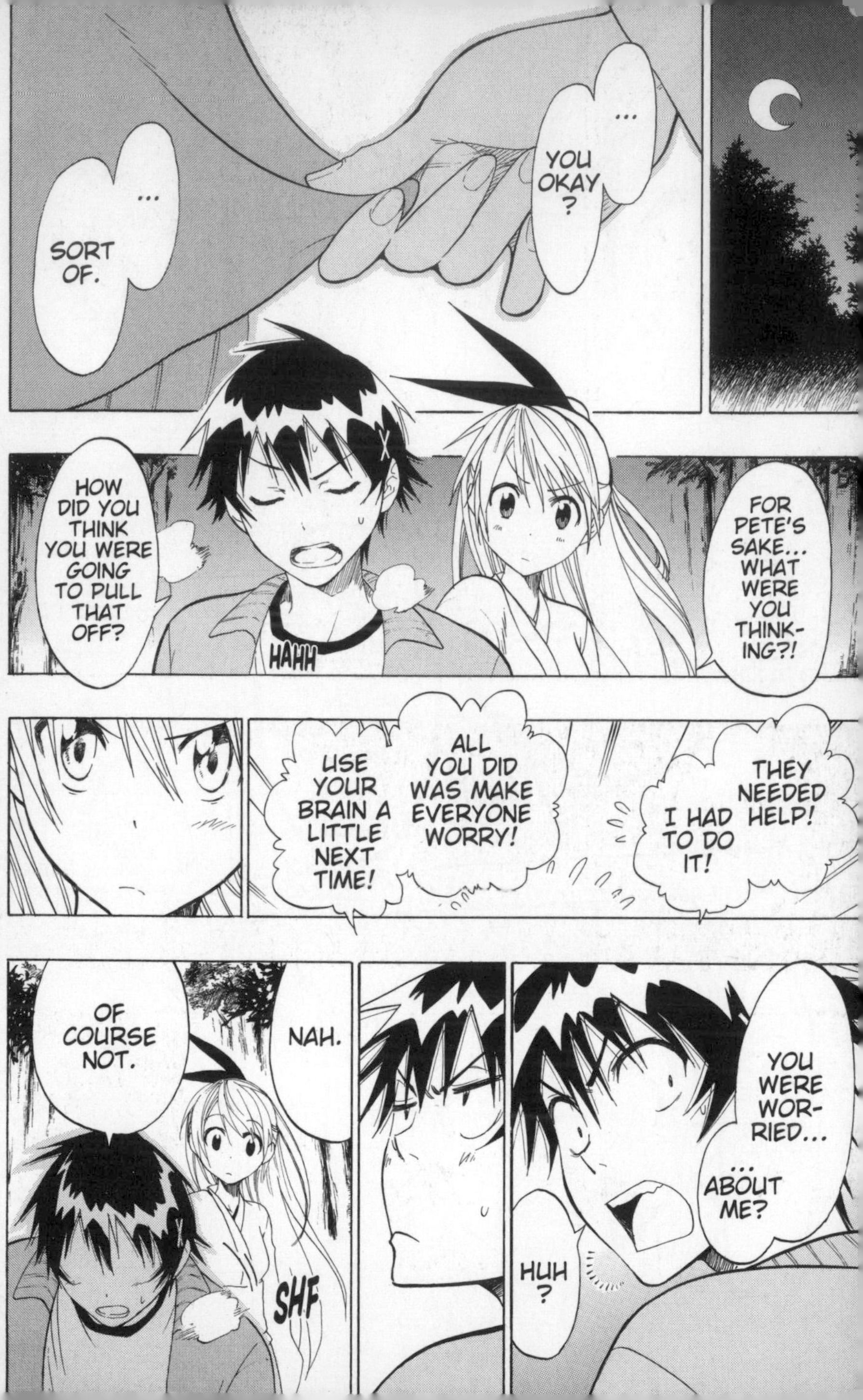
... YOU OKAY ?
... SORT OF.
FOR PETE'S SAKE... WHAT WERE YOU THINK-ING?!
HOW DID YOU THINK YOU WERE GOING TO PULL THAT OFF?
HAHH
THEY NEEDED HELP! I HAD TO DO IT!
ALL YOU DID WAS MAKE EVERYONE WORRY!
USE YOUR BRAIN A LITTLE NEXT TIME!
YOU WERE WOR-RIED...
... ABOUT ME?
HUH ?
NAH.
OF COURSE NOT.
SHF

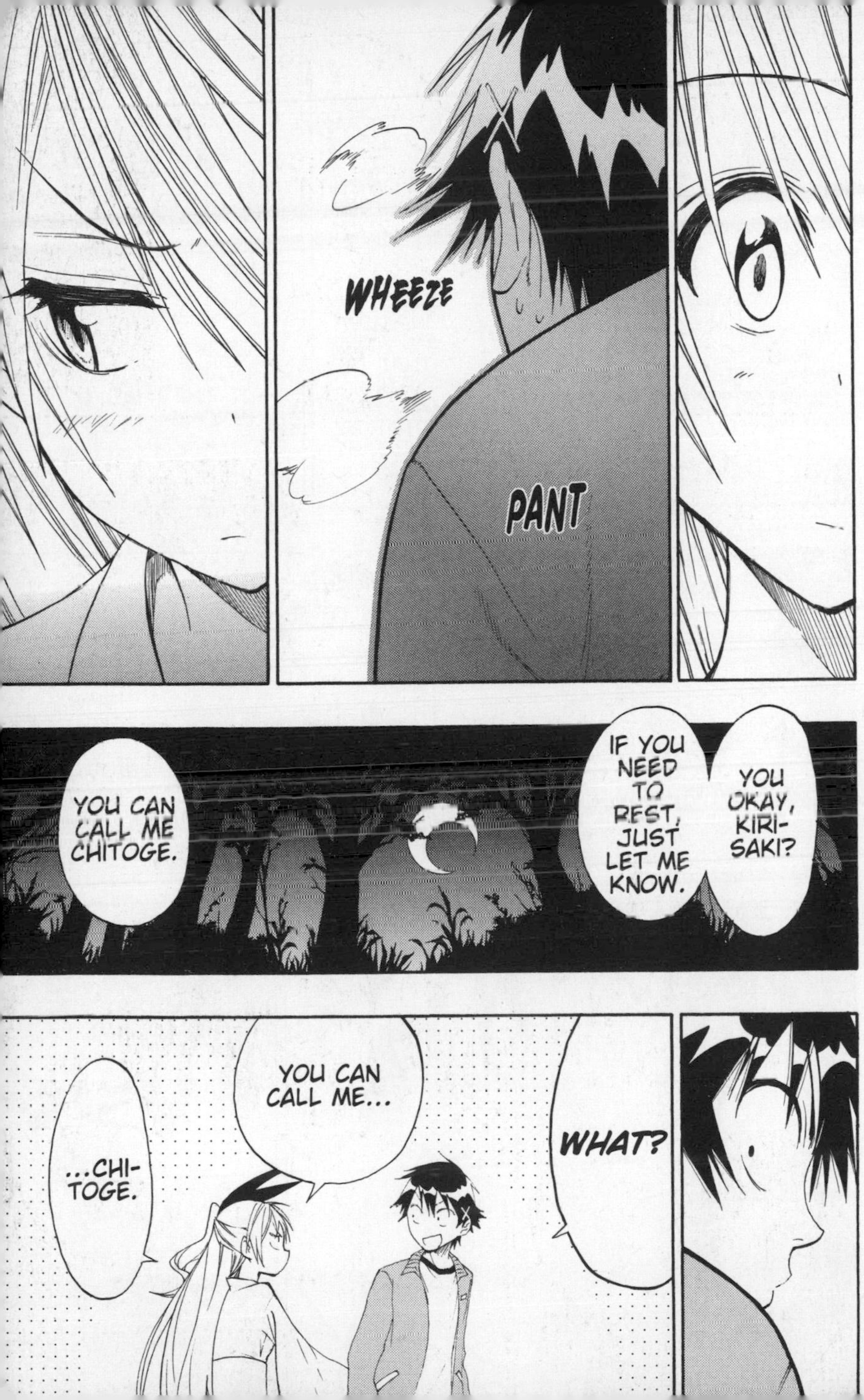
WHEEZE
PANT
YOU OKAY, KIRI-SAKI?
IF YOU NEED TO REST, JUST LET ME KNOW.
YOU CAN CALL ME CHITOGE.
WHAT?
YOU CAN CALL ME...
...CHI-TOGE.

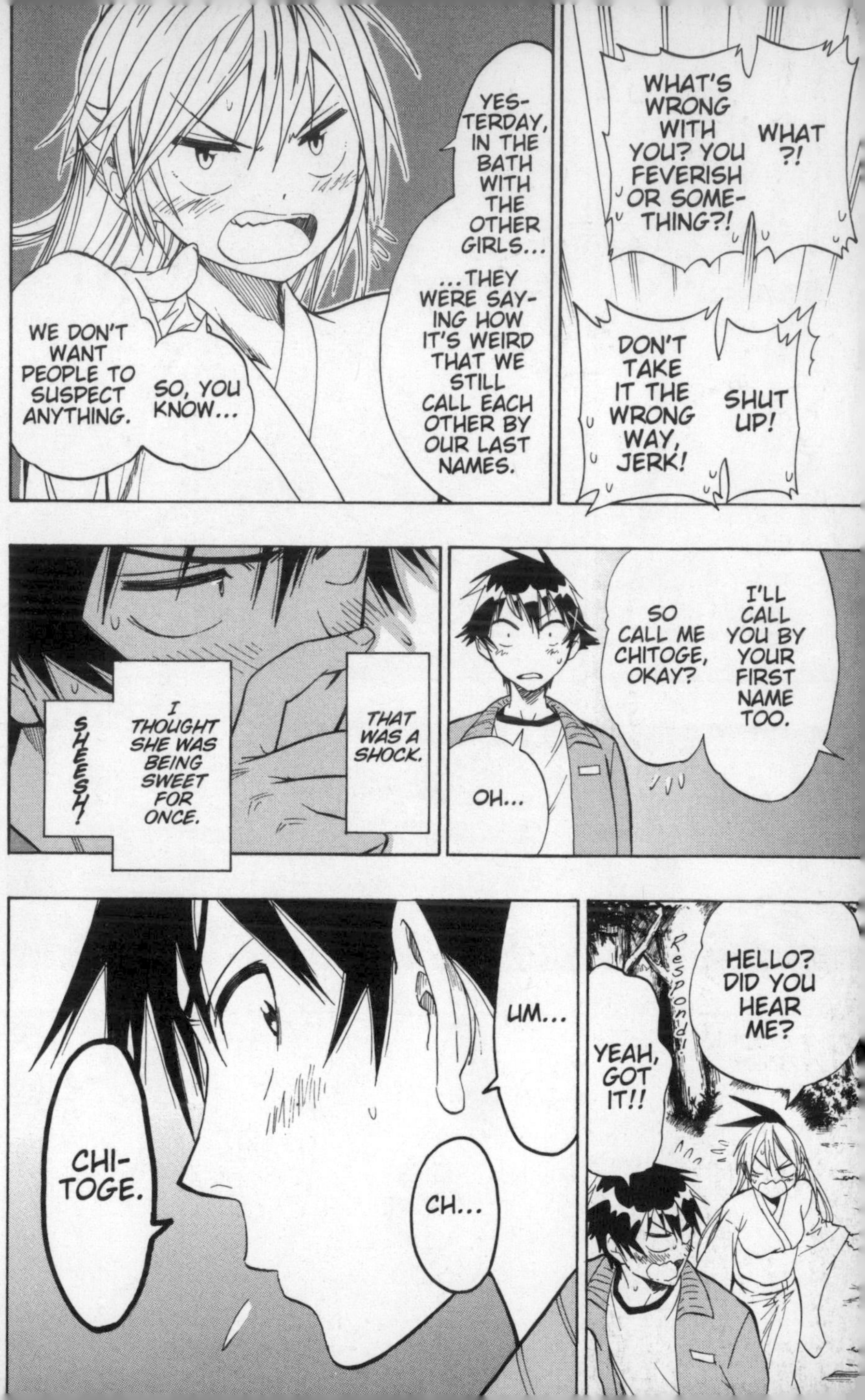
WHAT?!
WHAT'S WRONG WITH YOU? YOU FEVERISH OR SOME-THING?!
SHUT UP!
DON'T TAKE IT THE WRONG WAY, JERK!
YES-TERDAY, IN THE BATH WITH THE OTHER GIRLS...
...THEY WERE SAY-ING HOW IT'S WEIRD THAT WE STILL CALL EACH OTHER BY OUR LAST NAMES.
SO, YOU KNOW...
WE DON'T WANT PEOPLE TO SUSPECT ANYTHING.
I'LL CALL YOU BY YOUR FIRST NAME TOO.
SO CALL ME CHITOGE, OKAY?
OH...
THAT WAS A SHOCK.
I THOUGHT SHE WAS BEING SWEET FOR ONCE.
SHEESH!
HELLO? DID YOU HEAR ME?
Respond!
YEAH, GOT IT!!
UM...
CH...
CHI-TOGE.

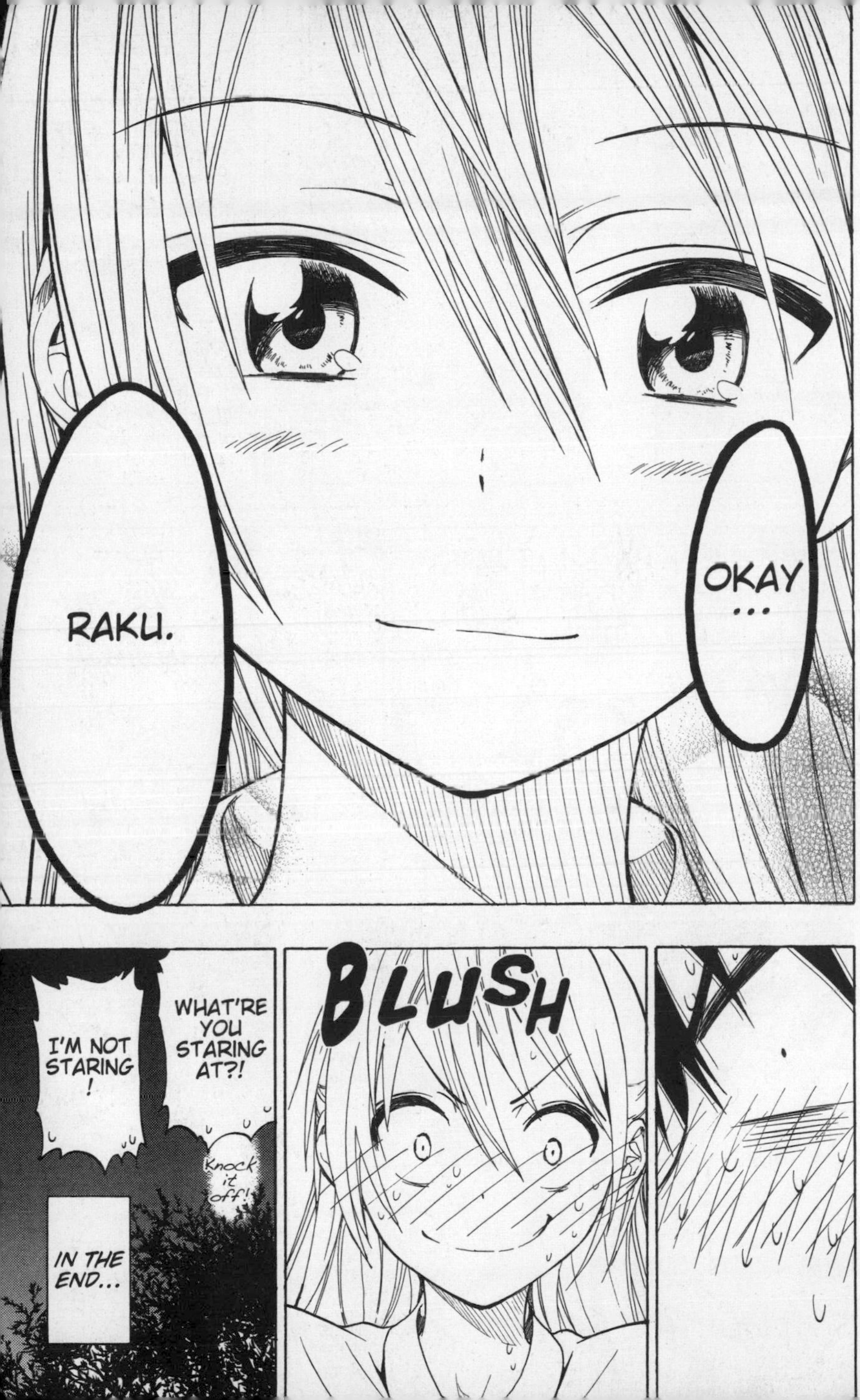
OKAY ...
RAKU.
BLUSH
WHAT'RE YOU STARING AT?!
I'M NOT STARING!
Knock it off!
IN THE END...

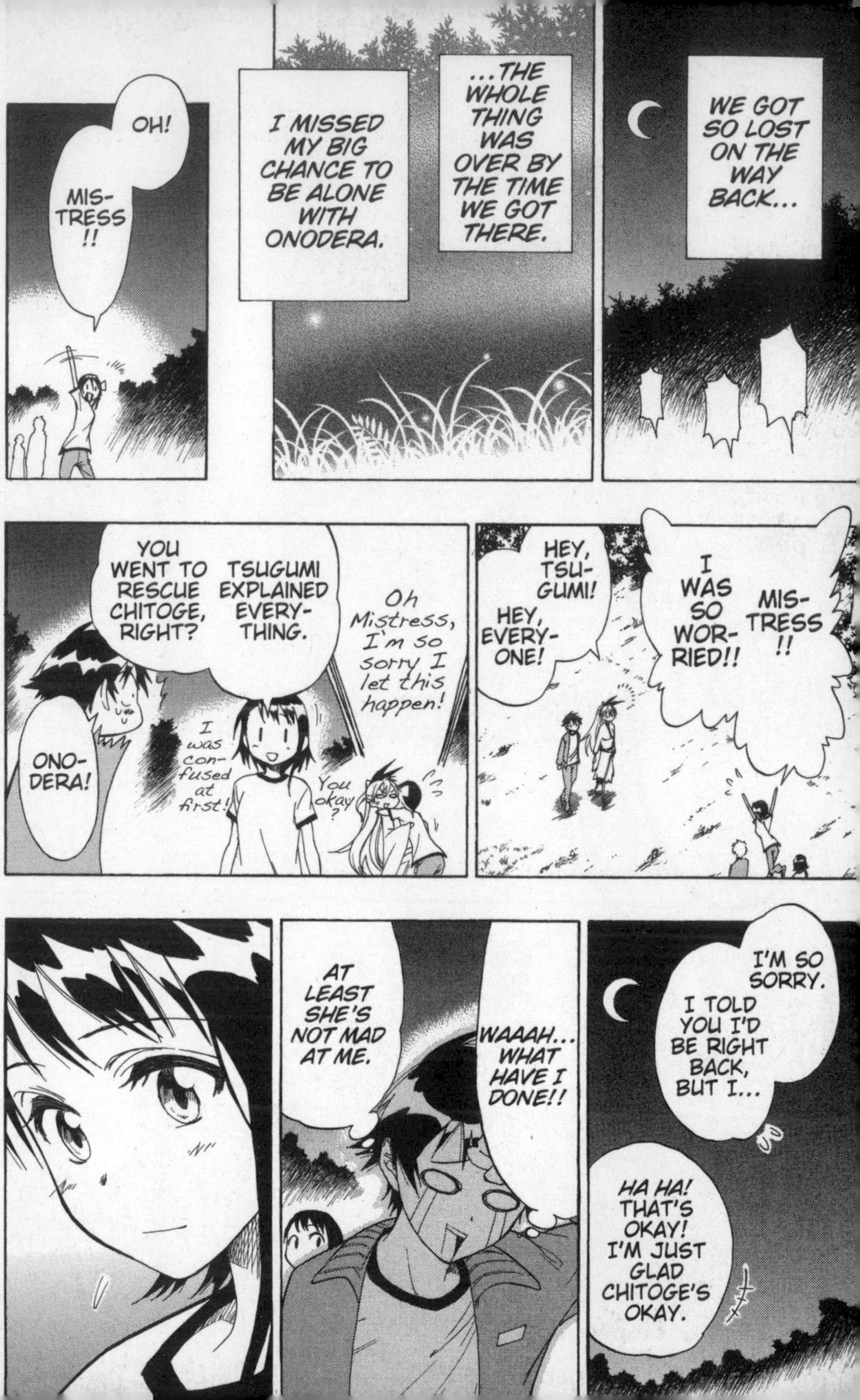
WE GOT SO LOST ON THE WAY BACK...
...THE WHOLE THING WAS OVER BY THE TIME WE GOT THERE.
I MISSED MY BIG CHANCE TO BE ALONE WITH ONODERA.
OH!
MIS-TRESS!!
MIS-TRESS!!
I WAS SO WOR-RIED!!
HEY, TSU-GUMI!
HEY, EVERY-ONE!
Oh Mistress, I'm so sorry I let this happen!
You okay?
TSUGUMI EXPLAINED EVERYTHING.
I was con-fused at first!
YOU WENT TO RESCUE CHITOGE, RIGHT?
ONO-DERA!
I'M SO SORRY.
I TOLD YOU I'D BE RIGHT BACK, BUT I...
HA HA! THAT'S OKAY! I'M JUST GLAD CHITOGE'S OKAY.
WAAAH... WHAT HAVE I DONE!!
AT LEAST SHE'S NOT MAD AT ME.

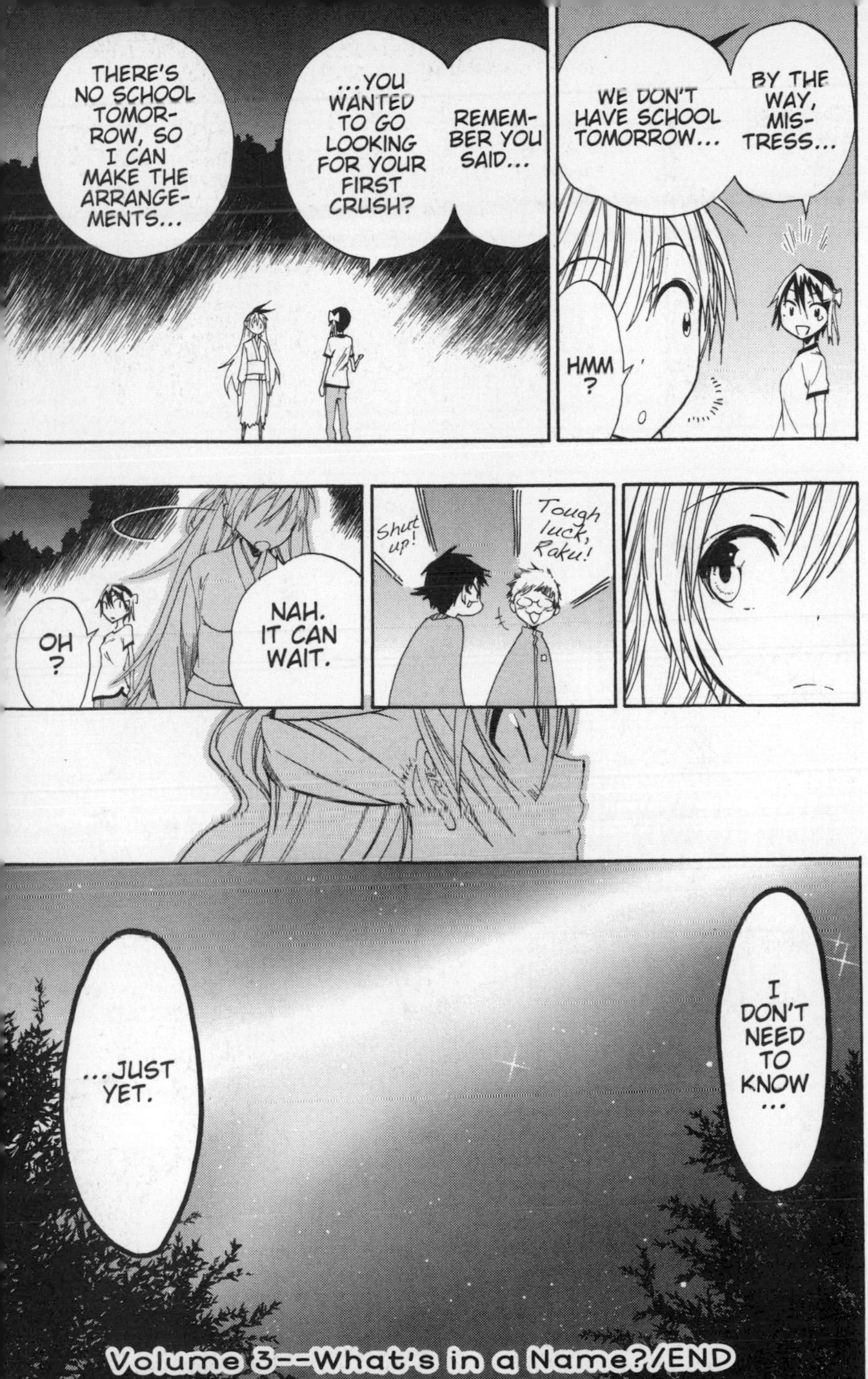
BY THE WAY, MIS-TRESS...
WE DON'T HAVE SCHOOL TOMORROW...
HMM?
REMEMBER YOU SAID...
...YOU WANTED TO GO LOOKING FOR YOUR FIRST CRUSH?
THERE'S NO SCHOOL TOMORROW, SO I CAN MAKE THE ARRANGEMENTS...
Tough luck, Raku!
Shut up!
NAH. IT CAN WAIT.
OH?
I DON'T NEED TO KNOW...
...JUST YET.
Volume 3--What's in a Name?/END

Bonus Comic

☆ A Day in the Life of Tsugumi ☆

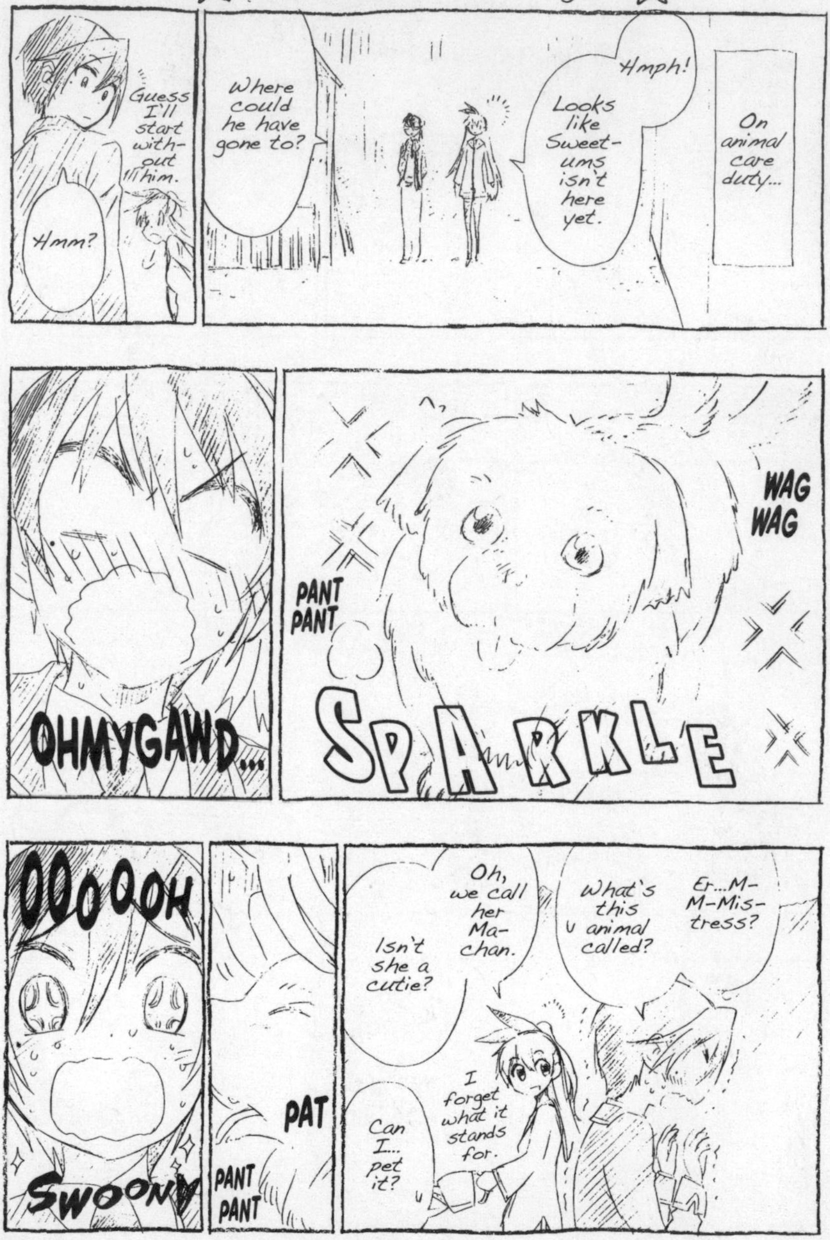

On animal care duty...
Hmph!
Looks like Sweetums isn't here yet.
Where could he have gone to?
Guess I'll start without him.
Hmm?
WAG WAG
PANT PANT
SPARKLE
OHMYGAWD...
Er...M-M-Mistress?
What's this animal called?
Oh, we call her Ma-chan.
Isn't she a cutie?
I forget what it stands for.
Can I... pet it?
PAT
PANT PANT
OOOOOH
SWOON

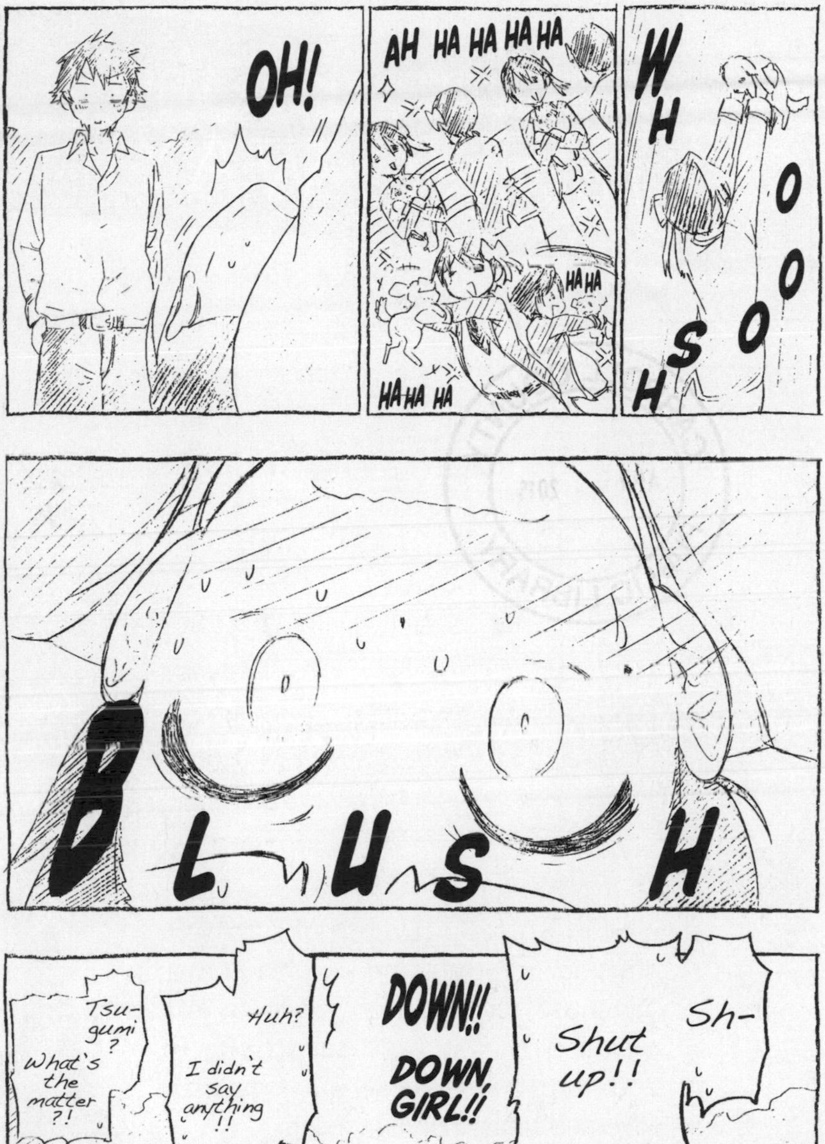
WHOOOOSH
AH HA HA HA HA
HA HA
HA HA HA
OH!
BLUSH
Sh-
Shut up!!
DOWN!!
DOWN, GIRL!!
Huh?
I didn't say anything!!
Tsu-gumi?
What's the matter?!

THE END

You're Reading the WRONG WAY!

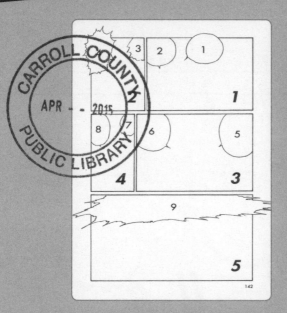

NISEKOI reads from right to left, starting in the upper-right corner. Japanese is read from right to left, meaning that action, sound effects, and word-balloon order are completely reversed from English order.